COMPUTER SCIENCES

COMPUTER SCIENCES

Second Edition
Volume 3
Social Applications

K. Lee Lerner
Editor-in-Chief

Brenda Wilmoth Lerner
Managing Editor

MACMILLAN REFERENCE USA
A part of Gale, Cengage Learning

GALE
CENGAGE Learning·

Detroit • New York • San Francisco • New Haven, Conn • Waterville, Maine • London

GALE
CENGAGE Learning·

Computer Sciences
2ⁿᵈ Edition

Editor-in-Chief: K. Lee Lerner

Managing Editor: Brenda Wilmoth Lerner

Product Manager: Douglas A. Dentino

Project Editor: Kimberley A. McGrath

Rights Acquisition and Management: Margaret Chamberlain-Gaston

Composition: Evi Abou-El-Seoud

Manufacturing: Wendy Blurton; Dorothy Maki

Imaging: John Watkins

Product Design: Kristine Julien

For product information and technology assistance, contact us at
Gale Customer Support, 1-800-877-4253.
For permission to use material from this text or product,
submit all requests online at **www.cengage.com/permissions.**
Further permissions questions can be emailed to
permissionrequest@cengage.com

Cover photographs courtesy of the following: Technician working on server rack; © Yurchyks/ShutterStock.com. Screens with program web code; © Taiga/ShutterStock.com. Three business people working at meeting; © Dmitriy Shironosov/ShutterStock.com. Hands holding a tablet or a Pad; © Luis Louro/ShutterStock.com. Computer classroom; © sixninepixels/ShutterStock.com. Wireless computer mouse; © AlexGul/ShutterStock.com.

While every effort has been made to ensure the reliability of the information presented in this publication, Gale, a part of Cengage Learning, does not guarantee the accuracy of the data contained herein. Gale accepts no payment for listing; and inclusion in the publication of any organization, agency, institution, publication, service, or individual does not imply endorsement of the editors or publisher. Errors brought to the attention of the publisher and verified to the satisfaction of the publisher will be corrected in future editions.

LIBRARY OF CONGRESS CATALOGING-IN-PUBLICATION DATA

Computer sciences / K. Lee Lerner, editor-in-Chief, Brenda Wilmoth Lerner, managing editor. -- Second edition.
  v. cm
Summary: "Computer Sciences, 2nd Edition reviews the history of the discipline and concepts, as well as profiles contributors in the field. The impact of computers on the economy and society is explored, with examples in literature, film, and science provided to illustrate and support trends. These illustrated volumes also include sidebars, bibliographies, a timeline, charts, and a glossary. This title is organized in four separate topical volumes, although articles in each volume will be in an A-Z arrangement; the set's comprehensive cumulative index is found in each volume"-- Provided by publisher.
  Includes bibliographical references and index.
  Contents: v. 1. Foundations : ideas and people
  ISBN-13: 978-0-02-866220-6 (set : hardback)
  ISBN-10: 0-02-866220-2 (set : hardback)
  ISBN-13: 978-0-02-866221-3 (v. 1 : hardback)
  ISBN-10: 0-02-866221-0 (v. 1 : hardback)
[etc.]
  1. Computer science. I. Lerner, K. Lee. II. Lerner, Brenda Wilmoth.
QA76.C572 2013
004--dc23
                                                        2012037340

Gale
27500 Drake Rd.
Farmington Hills, MI, 48331-3535

ISBN-13: 978-0-02-866220-6 (set)   ISBN-10: 0-02-866220-2 (set)
ISBN-13: 978-0-02-866221-3 (vol. 1)   ISBN-10: 0-02-866221-0 (vol. 1)
ISBN-13: 978-0-02-866222-0 (vol. 2)   ISBN-10: 0-02-866222-9 (vol. 2)
ISBN-13: 978-0-02-866223-7 (vol. 3)   ISBN-10: 0-02-866223-7 (vol. 3)
ISBN-13: 978-0-02-866224-4 (vol. 4)   ISBN-10: 0-02-866224-5 (vol. 4)

This title is also available as an e-book.
ISBN-13: 978-0-02-866225-1 ISBN-10: 0-02-866225-3
Contact your Gale, a part of Cengage Learning, sales representative for ordering information.

Printed in China
1 2 3 4 5 6 7 17 16 15 14 13

Table of Contents

Table of Contents

Volume 2: Software And Hardware

Volume 3: Social Applications

Table of Contents

Volume 4: Electronic Universe

Preface

. . . .

omputer Sciences, 2nd *Edition* is devoted to providing younger students and general readers with a foundation upon which to build an understanding of modern computer science. Because applications of technology now invigorate almost all fields of study, topics in *Computer Sciences* are carefully selected to present insightful information related to topics in the news. Both updated and new entries, for example, help explain both technical and ethical dimensions of issues related to social media and online privacy. Special entries on digital photography and digital filmmaking highlight applications of computer science that enhance how we view and understand our world.

The articles in *Computer Sciences* are meant to be understandable by anyone with a curiosity about basic computer science. When topics move into highly technical research and development areas, every effort has been taken to explain concepts clearly and simply, without sacrifice of fundamental accuracy. Accordingly, entries in *Computer Sciences* include treatments of topics designed to excite less-experienced students while simultaneously providing a solid reference for students preparing for more specialized studies. The editors have taken special care to provide treatment of topics that foster essential critical thinking skills that will enable students and readers to tackle emerging issues.

We live in an increasingly digital world where an understanding of basic computer science principles and applications is essential. The Internet, for example, is now a global network connecting, with more than a billion computers used by billions of people. Personal information, medical records, opinions, industrial secrets, military communications, financial transactions, messages between conspirators, orders for goods and services, and many other types of communications travel over the Internet. *Computer Sciences* enables students and readers to understand how the digital world works.

Equally as important, however, for citizens of the digital age, *Computer Sciences* enables students and readers to understand how increases in computing capacity relate to the capacity to wage cyberwarfare; how viruses transform from annoyances to instruments of covert operations and computer crime; and how breakthroughs in technology enable online activism that contributes to social and political change.

Contributors and Advisors

In addition to engineers specializing in computer science, *Computer Sciences* contributors include scientists, journalists, artists, teachers, and writers who explain the practical applications of computer science.

In this and the previous edition of *Computer Sciences*, a number of experts have written and advised on topics related to their expertise. We would like to express our sincere appreciation to:

Tom Abel: Penn State University, University Park, PA.

Martyn Amos: University of Liverpool, United Kingdom.

Richard Archer: Pittsburgh, PA.

Pamela Willwerth Aue: Royal Oak, MI.

William Atkins: Independent research consultant, Normal, IL.

Nancy J. Becker: St. John's University, New York.

Mark Bedau: Reed College, Portland, OR.

John Micheal Bell: LMG research associate. Harvard DCE Graduate Professional Program in Journalism. Harvard University, Cambridge MA.

Mercy Bell: LMG research associate. Nashville, TN.

Pierfrancesco Bellini: University of Florence, Italy.

Gary H. Bernstein: University of Notre Dame, Noire Dame, IN.

Anne Bissonnette: Kent State University Museum, Kent, OH.

Kevin W. Bowyer: University of Notre Dame, Notre Dame, IN.

Stefan Brass: University of Giessen, Germany.

Barbara Britton: Windsor Puttie Library, Windsor, Ontario, Canada.

Kimberly Mann Bruch: San Diego Supercomputer Center, University of California, San Diego.

Ivan Bruno: University of Florence, Italy.

Dennis R. Buckmaster: Pennsylvania State University, University Park, PA.

Dan Burk: University of Minnesota, Minneapolis, MN.

Guoray Cai: Pennsylvania State University, University Park, PA.

Shirley Campbell: University of Pittsburgh, Pittsburgh, PA.

Sara V. Castillo: Independent media consultant. Dubai, United Arab Emirates.

Siddharth Chandra: University of Pittsburgh, Pittsburgh, PA.

J. Alex Chediak: University of California, Berkeley, CA.

Kara K. Choquette: Xerox Corporation.

John Cosgrove: Cosgrove Communications, Pittsburgh, PA.

Cheryl L. Cramer: Digimarc Corporation, Tualatin, OR.

Anthony Debons: University of Pittsburgh, Pittsburgh, PA.

Salvatore Domenick Desiano: NASA Ames Research Center (QSS Group, Inc.).

Ken Doerbecker: Perfection Services, Inc.; WeirNet LLC; and FreeAir Networks, Inc.

Judi Effis: KPMG, LLP, Pittsburgh, PA.

Karen E. Esch: Karen Esch Associates, Pittsburgh, PA.

Ming Fan: University of Notre Dame, Notre Dame, IN.

Jim Fike: Ohio University, Athens, OH.

Ida M. Flynn: University of Pittsburgh, Pittsburgh, PA.

Roger R. Flynn: University of Pittsburgh, Pittsburgh, PA.

H. Bruce Franklin: Rutgers University, Newark, NJ.

Thomas J. Froehlich: Kent State University, Kent, OH.

Chuck Gaidica: WDW-TV, Detroit, MI.

G. Christopher Hall: PricewaterhouseCoopers.

Gary Hanson: Kent State University, Kent, OH.

Shaquilla T. Harrigan, Production intern at LernerMedia Global, Summer 2012. Harvard College (Class of 2016), Cambridge, MA.

Karen Hartman: James Monroe Center Library, Mary Washington College, Fredericksburg, VA.

Melissa J. Harvey: Carnegie Mellon University, Pittsburgh, PA.

Albert D. Helfnck: Embry-Riddle Aeronautical University, Daytona Beach, PL.

Angelia Herrin: Harvard Business Publishing, Cambridge, MA.

Stephen Hughes: University of Pittsburgh, Pittsburgh, PA.

Joseph Patterson Hyder: Hyder Law Group, Jacksonville, FL.

Bruce Jacob: University of Maryland, College Park, MD.

Radhika Jain: Georgia State University, Atlanta, GA.

Wesley Jamison: University of Pittsburgh at Greensburg.

Sid Karin: San Diego Supercomputer Center, University of California, San Diego.

Declan P. Kelly: Philips Research, The Netherlands.

Betty Kirke: New York, NY.

Mikko Kovalainen: University of Jyväskylä, Finland.

Paul R. Kraus: Pittsburgh, PA.

Prashant Krishnamurthy: University of Pittsburgh, Pittsburgh, PA.

Marina Krol: Mount Sinai School of Medicine, New York, NY.

Susan Landau: Sun Microsystems Inc., Mountain View, CA.

Nicholas C. Laudato: University of Pittsburgh, Pittsburgh, Pennsylvania.

George Lawton: Eutopian Enterprises.

Cynthia Tumilry Lazzaro: Pinnacle Training Corp., Stonebam, MA.

Joseph J. Lazzaro: Massachusetts Commission for the Blind, Boston, MA.

John Leaney: University of Technology, Sydney, Australia.

Robert Lembersky: Ann Taylor, Inc., New York, NY.

Adrienne Wilmoth Lerner: Hyder Law Group, Jacksonville, FL.

Terri L. Lenox: Westminster College, New Wilmington, PA.

Joyce H-S Li: University of Pittsburgh, Pittsburgh, PA.

Michael R. Macedonia: USA STPJCOM, Orlando,.

Dirk E. Mahling: University of Pittsburgh, Pittsburgh, PA.

Cynthia J. Martincic: St. Vincent College, Latrobe, PA.

Michael J. McCarthy: Carnegie Mellon University, Pittsburgh, PA.

Ann Mclver McHoes: Carlow College, Pittsburgh PA.

Genevieve McHoes: University of Maryland, College Park, MD.

John McHugh: CERTTM Coordination Center, Software Engineering Institute, Carnegie Mellon Pittsburgh, PA.

Donald M. Mclver: Northrop Grumman Corporation, Baltimore, MD.

Maurice Mclver: Integrated Databases, Inc., Honolulu, HI.

William J. Mclver, Jr.: University at Albany, State University of New York.

Trevor T. Moores: University of Nevada, Las Vegas.

Christopher Morgan: Association for Computing Machinery, Nero York, NY.

Bertha Kugelman Morimoto: University of Pittsburgh, Pittsburgh, PA.

Tracy Mullen: NEC Research Inc., Princeton, NJ.

Paul Munro: University of Pittsburgh, Pittsburgh, PA.

Stephen Murray: University of Technology, Sydney, Australia.

Carey Nachenberg: Symantec Corporation.

John Nau: Frank R. Rusch.

Paolo Nesi: University of Florence, Italy.

Kai A. Olsen: Molde College and University of Bergen, Norway.

Evan Austin Ott: University of Texas, Austin, TX.

Ipek Ozkaya: Carnegie Mellon University, Pittsburgh, PA.

Bob Patterson: Perfection Services, Inc.

Robert R. Perkoski: University of Pittsburgh, Pittsburgh, PA.

Thomas A. Pollack: Duquesne University, Pittsburgh, PA.

Guylaine M. Pollock: IEEE Computer Society; Sandia National Laboratories, Albuquerque, NM.

Wolfgang Porod: University of Notre Dame, Notre Dame, IN.

Anwer H. Puthawala: Park Avenue Associates in Radiology, P.C., Binghamton, NY.

Mary Mclver Puthawala: Binghamton, NY.

Sudha Ram: University of Arizona, Tucson, AZ.

Edie M. Rasmussen: University of Pittsburgh, Pittsburgh, PA.

Robert D. Regan: Consultant, Pittsburgh, PA.

Allen Renear: University of Illinois, Urbana-Champaign.

Sarah K. Rich: Pennsylvania State University, University Park, PA.

Mike Robinson: Sageforce Ltd., Kingston on Thames, Surrey, United Kingdom.

Elke A. Rudensteiner: Worcester Polytechnic Institute, Worcester, MA.

Frank R. Rusch: University of Illinois at Urbana-Champaign.

William Sherman: National Center for Supercomputing Applications, University of Illinois at Urbana-Champaign.

Marc Silverman: University of Pittsburgh, Pittsburgh, PA.

Munindar P. Singh: North Carolina State University, Raleigh, NC.

Cindy Smith: PricewaterhouseCoopers, Pittsburgh, PA.

Barry Smyth: Smart Media Institute, University College, Dublin, Ireland.

Amanda Spink: Pennsylvania State University, University Park, PA.

Michael B. Spring: University of Pittsburgh, Pittsburgh, PA.

Savitha Srinivasan: IBM Almaden Research Center, San Jose, CA.

Maria Stenzel: Photojournalist. *National Geographic*, Washington, D.C.

Igor Tarnopolsky: Westchester County Department of Laboratories and Research, Valhalla, NY.

George A. Tarnow: Georgetown University, Washington, DC.

Lucy A. Tedd: University of Wales, Aberystwyth, Wales, United Kingdom.

Umesh Thakkar: National Center for Supercomputing Applications, University of Illinois at Urbana-Champaign.

Richard A- Thompson: University of Pittsburgh, Pittsburgh, PA.

James E. Tomayko: Carnegie Mellon University, Pittsburgh, PA.

Christinger Tomer: University of Pittsburgh, Pittsburgh, PA.

Upkar Varshney: Georgia State University, Atlanta, GA.

Jonathan Vos Post: Magic Dragon Multimedia, http://magicdragon.com.

Tom Wall: Duke University, Durham, N.

Brett A. Warneke: University of California, Berkeley, CA.

Patricia S. Wehman: University of Pittsburgh, Pittsburgh, PA.

Isaac Weiss: University of Maryland, College Park, MD.

Martin B. Weiss: University of Pittsburgh, Pittsburgh, PA.

Jeffrey C. Wingard: Leesburg, VA.

Victor L. Winter: University of Nebraska, Omaha.

Charles R. Woratschek: Robert Morris University, Moon Township, PA.

Peter Y. Wu: University of Pittsburgh, Pittsburgh, PA.

William J. Yurcik: Illinois State University, Normal, IL.

Gregg R. Zegarelli: Zegarelli Law Group, P.C.

Acknowledgments

The editors offer special thanks to: Angelia Herrin and Maria Stenzel for bringing their expertise in modern practice of journalism and photojournalism to, respectively, the *Computer Sciences*. Herrin, a former Knight Fellow in Journalism at Stanford University reporter for Knight-Ridder newspapers, served as Washington, D.C., editor of *USA Today*. Herrin is now an editor at Harvard Business School

Publishing. Stenzel, a frequent and long-time contributor to *National Geographic* served as a Knight Fellow in Science Journalism at MIT.

Writing on tight deadlines from Dubai in the United Arab Emirates, Sara V. Castillo contributed the article on digital filmmaking.

Evan Ott at the University of Texas offered invaluable assistance in advising and updating topics related to on emerging applications of computer science.

The editors thank Shaquilla T. Harrigan, our summer 2012 production intern at LernerMedia Global. Ms. Harrigan, a member of the class of 2016 at Harvard College in Cambridge, Massachusetts, assisted in photo selection and captioning.

This book would not have been possible without the efforts of project manager Kim McGrath. Her perspectives, patience, and penchant for asking good questions across a broad spectrum of topics added significantly to the quality of all aspects of *Computer Sciences*.

K. Lee Lerner and Brenda Wilmoth Lerner, editors
Cambridge, MA

December, 2012

How To Use This Book

. . . .

Computer Sciences, 2nd Edition provides an overview of the history and current status of the computer science industry, as well as its economic and cultural impact. This is a broad scope, and for ease of use, entries have been grouped into four subject-based volumes.

Volume 1: Foundations: Ideas and People   This volume discusses the foundation of computer science, including computing history and important innovators. Ranging from Charles Babbage, binary numbers, and slide rule to Steve Jobs, World Wide Web, and windows interfaces, the entries in this volume provide a solid background on the development of the field of computer sciences.

Volume 2: Software and Hardware   Articles in this volume cover topics from system analysis and design (the cornerstone of building a system) to operating systems, compilers, and parallel processing (which discuss some of the technical aspects of computing). Here, too, users will find valuable information on the growing field of telecommunications, including cellular and wireless technologies.

Volume 3: Social Applications   From ATM machines to social media and weather forecasting, the use of computers impacts our everyday lives. For example, computer technology has greatly influence the study of biology, molecular biology, physics, and mathematics, not to mention the large role it plays in air traffic management and aircraft flight control, navigation and geographic information systems. Businesses—large and small—have significantly benefited from applications that track product growth, costs, and the way products are managed. Other articles in this volume include economic modeling, hacking, and home system software.

Volume 4: Electronic Universe   Volume 4 delves into our vastly interconnected, networked society. The Internet is explored in detail, including its history, applications, and backbone. Molecular computing and artificial life are discussed as are mobile computing and encryption technology. The reader will find articles on censorship (national and international), online privacy, digital filmmaking, E-commerce, and search engines. Ethical matters pertaining to the electronic universe are also addressed.

All entries include a bibliography to assist in conducting additional research. Where appropriate, technical terms are defined in the margins of the entries, and photos and charts are used to illustrate most entries.

Entries are arranged in alphabetical order within each volume, with biographies listed by their last names. All four volumes include a comprehensive table of contents and cumulative index that can further assist the reader in locating the information they need. Other features found in every volume are:

- ■ **Preface** — An essay by editors K. Lee Lerner and Brenda Wilmoth Lerner discussing the importance of computer sciences as it relates to critical thinking and living in the digital age.

- ■ **For Your Reference** — This section defines scientific units of measurement and supplies conversion charts to customary units of measurement. It also provides examples from various base numbering systems and their equivalents, as well as the relative sizes of objects.

- ■ **Timeline: Significant Events in the History of Computing** — This chronology lists major events and milestones in the field of computer sciences.

- **Timeline: The History of Programming, Markup, and Scripting Languages** — This chronology is focused on achievements and milestones as related to computer programming and languages.

- **Glossary** — The glossary defines over 580 technical terms used throughout the set.

- **Directory of Computer Sciences Organizations** — This directory provides contact information for over 50 computer sciences-related organizations.

For Your Reference

This section provides information that may be of assistance in understanding the entries that make up this book: definitions for SI terms and symbols, and; conversion tables for SI measurements to other measurement systems. Also included are examples from various base numbering systems and their equivalents, as well as the relative sizes of objects.

SI BASE AND SUPPLEMENTARY UNIT NAMES AND SYMBOLS

Physical Quality	Name	Symbol
Length	meter	m
Mass	kilogram	kg
Time	second	s
Electric current	ampere	A
Thermodynamic temperature	kelvin	K
Amount of substance	mole	mol
Luminous intensity	candela	cd
Plane angle	radian	rad
Solid angle	steradian	sr

Temperature

Scientists commonly use the Celsius system. Although not recommended for scientific and technical use, earth scientists also use the familiar Fahrenheit temperature scale (°F). 1°F = 1.8°C or K. The triple point of H_2O, where gas, liquid, and solid water coexist, is 32°F.

- To change from Fahrenheit (F) to Celsius (C): °C = (°F-32)/(1.8)
- To change from Celsius (C) to Fahrenheit (F): °F = (°C x 1.8) + 32
- To change from Celsius (C) to Kelvin (K): K = °C + 273.15
- To change from Fahrenheit (F) to Kelvin (K): K = (°F-32)/(1.8) + 273.15

UNITS DERIVED FROM SI, WITH SPECIAL NAMES AND SYMBOLS

Derived Quantity	Name of SI Unit	Symbol for SI Unit	Expression in Terms of SI Base Units
Frequency	hertz	Hz	s^{-1}
Force	newton	N	$m \cdot kg \cdot s^{-2}$
Pressure, stress	pascal	Pa	$m^{-1} \cdot kg \cdot s^{-2}$
Energy, work, heat	joule	J	$m^2 \cdot kg \cdot s^{-2}$
Power, radiant flux	watt	W	$m^2 \cdot kg \cdot s^{-3}$
Electric charge	coulomb	C	$s \cdot A$
Electric potential, electromotive force	volt	V	$m^2 \cdot kg \cdot s^{-3} \cdot A^{-1}$
Electric resistance	ohm	Ω	$m^2 \cdot kg \cdot s^{-3} \cdot A^{-2}$
Celsius temperature	degree Celsius	°C	K
Luminous flux	lumen	lm	Cd
Illuminance	lux	lx	$m^{-2} \cdot cd$

UNITS USED WITH SI, WITH NAME, SYMBOL, AND VALUES IN SI UNITS

The following units, not part of the SI, will continue to be used in appropriate contexts (e.g., angtsrom):

Physical Quantity	Name of Unit	Symbol for Unit	Value in SI Units
Time	minute	min	60 s
	hour	h	3,600 s
	day	d	86,400 s
Plane angle	degree	°	$(\pi/180)$ rad
	minute	'	$(\pi/10,800)$ rad
	second	"	$(\pi/648,000)$ rad
Length	angstrom	Å	10^{-10} m
Volume	liter	l, L	$1 \, dm^3 = 10^{-3} \, m^3$
Mass	ton	t	$1 \, Mg = 10^3$ kg
	unified atomic mass unit	u	$\approx 1.66054 \times 10^{-27}$ kg
Pressure	bar	bar	$10^5 \, Pa = 10^5 \, N \, m^{-2}$
Energy	electronvolt	eV (= e X V)	$\approx 1.60218 \times 10^{-19}$ J

CONVERSIONS FOR STANDARD, DERIVED, AND CUSTOMARY MEASUREMENTS

Length

1 angstrom (Å)	0.1 nanometer (exactly)
	0.000000004 inch
1 centimeter (cm)	0.3937 inches
1 foot (ft)	0.3048 meter (exactly)
1 inch (in)	2.54 centimeters (exactly)
1 kilometer (km)	0.621 mile
1 meter (m)	39.37 inches
	1.094 yards
1 mile (mi)	5,280 feet (exactly)
	1.609 kilometers
1 astronomical unit (AU)	1.495979×10^{13} cm
1 parsec (pc)	206,264.806 AU
	3.085678×10^{18} cm
	3.261633 light-years
1 light-year	9.460530×10^{17} cm

Area

1 acre	43,560 square feet (exactly)
	0.405 hectare
1 hectare	2.471 acres
1 square centimeter (cm²)	0.155 square inch
1 square foot (ft²)	929.030 square centimeters
1 square inch (in²)	6.4516 square centimeters (exactly)
1 square kilometer (km²)	247.104 acres
	0.386 square mile
1 square meter (m²)	1.196 square yards
	10.764 square feet
1 square mile (mi²)	258.999 hectares

MEASUREMENTS AND ABBREVIATIONS

Volume

1 barrel (bbl)*, liquid	31 to 42 gallons
1 cubic centimeter (cm³)	0.061 cubic inch
1 cubic foot (ft³)	7.481 gallons
	28.316 cubic decimeters
1 cubic inch (in³)	0.554 fluid ounce
1 dram, fluid (or liquid)	$\frac{1}{8}$ fluid ounce (exactly)
	0.226 cubic inch
	3.697 milliliters
1 gallon (gal) (U.S.)	231 cubic inches (exactly)
	3.785 liters
	128 U.S. fluid ounces (exactly)
1 gallon (gal) (British Imperial)	277.42 cubic inches
	1.201 U.S. gallons
	4.546 liters
1 liter	1 cubic decimeter (exactly)
	1.057 liquid quarts
	0.908 dry quart
	61.025 cubic inches
1 ounce, fluid (or liquid)	1.805 cubic inches
	29.573 mililiters
1 ounce, fluid (fl oz) (British)	0.961 U.S. fluid ounce
	1.734 cubic inches
	28.412 milliliters
1 quart (qt), dry (U.S.)	67.201 cubic inches
	1.101 liters
1 quart (qt), liquid (U.S.)	57.75 cubic inches (exactly)
	0.946 liter

Units of mass

1 carat (ct)	200 milligrams (exactly)
	3.086 grains
1 grain	64.79891 milligrams (exactly)
1 gram (g)	15.432 grains
	0.035 ounce
1 kilogram (kg)	2.205 pounds
1 microgram (µg)	0.000001 gram (exactly)
1 milligram (mg)	0.015 grain
1 ounce (oz)	437.5 grains (exactly)
	28.350 grams
1 pound (lb)	7,000 grains (exactly)
	453.59237 grams (exactly)
1 ton, gross or long	2,240 pounds
	1.12 net tons (exactly)
	1.016 metric tons
1 ton, metric (t)	2,204.623 pounds
	0.984 gross ton
	1.102 net tons
1 ton, net or short	2,000 pounds (exactly)
	0.893 gross ton
	0.907 metric ton

Pressure

1 kilogram/square centimeter (kg/cm²)	0.96784 atmosphere (atm)
	14.2233 pounds/square inch (lb/in²)
	0.98067 bar
1 bar	0.98692 atmosphere (atm)
	1.02 kilograms/square centimeter (kg/cm²)

---

* There are a variety of "barrels" established by law or usage. For example, U.S. federal taxes on fermented liquors are based on a barrel of 31 gallons (141 liters); many state laws fix the "barrel for liquids" as 31$\frac{1}{2}$ gallons (119.2 liters); one state fixes a 36-gallon (160.5 liters) barrel for cistern measurment; federal law recognizes a 40-gallon (178 liters) barrel for "proof spirts"; by custom, 42 gallons (159 liters) comprise a barrel of crude oil or petroleum products for statistical purposes, and this equivalent is recognized "for liquids" by four states.

For Your Reference

· ·

Base 2 (Binary)	Decimal (Base 10) Equivalent	Approximations to Powers of Ten
2^0	1	
2^1	2	
2^2	4	
2^3	8	
2^4	16	
2^5	32	
2^6	64	
2^7	128	10^2; 100; one hundred; 1 followed by 2 zeros
2^8	256	
2^9	512	
2^{10}	1,024	10^3; 1,000; one thousand; 1 followed by 3 zeros
2^{11}	2,048	
2^{12}	4,096	
2^{13}	8,192	
2^{14}	16,384	
2^{15}	32,768	
2^{16}	65,536	
2^{17}	131,072	
2^{18}	262,144	
2^{19}	524,288	
2^{20}	1,048,576	10^6; 1,000,000; one million; 1 followed by 6 zeros
2^{21}	2,097,152	
2^{22}	4,194,304	
2^{23}	8,388,608	
2^{24}	16,777,216	
2^{25}	33,554,432	
2^{26}	67,108,864	
2^{27}	134,217,728	
2^{28}	268,435,456	
2^{29}	536,870,912	
2^{30}	1,073,741,824	10^9; 1,000,000,000; one billion; 1 followed by 9 zeros
2^{31}	2,147,483,648	
2^{32}	4,294,967,296	
2^{33}	8,589,934,592	
2^{34}	17,179,869,184	
2^{35}	34,359,738,368	
2^{36}	68,719,476,736	
2^{37}	137,438,953,472	
2^{38}	274,877,906,944	
2^{39}	549,755,813,888	
2^{40}	1,099,511,627,776	10^{12}; 1,000,000,000,000; one trillion; 1 followed by 12 zeros
2^{50}	1,125,899,906,842,624	10^{15}; 1,000,000,000,000,000; one quadrillion; 1 followed by 15 zeros
2^{100}	1,267,650,600,228,229,401,496,703,205,376	10^{30}; 1 followed by 30 zeros
2^{-1}	1/2	
2^{-2}	1/4	
2^{-3}	1/8	
2^{-4}	1/16	
2^{-5}	1/32	
2^{-6}	1/64	
2^{-7}	1/128	1/100; 10^{-2}; 0.01; 1 hundredth
2^{-8}	1/256	
2^{-9}	1/512	
2^{-10}	1/1,024	1/1000; 10^{-3}; 0.001; 1 thousandth

Base 16 (Hexadecimal)	Binary (Base 2) Equivalent	Decimal (Base 10) Equivalent	Approximations to Powers of Ten
16^0	2^0	1	
16^1	2^4	16	
16^2	2^8	256	2×10^2; 2 hundred
16^3	2^{12}	4,096	4×10^3; 4 thousand
16^4	2^{16}	65,536	65×10^3; 65 thousand
16^5	2^{20}	1,048,576	1×10^6; 1 million
16^6	2^{24}	16,777,216	
16^7	2^{28}	268,435,456	
16^8	2^{32}	4,294,967,296	4×10^9; 4 billion
16^9	2^{36}	68,719,476,736	68×10^9; 68 billion
16^{10}	2^{40}	1,099,511,627,776	1×10^{12}; 1 trillion
16^{-1}	2^{-4}	1/16	
16^{-2}	2^{-8}	1/256	
16^{-3}	2^{-12}	1/4,096	$1/4 \times 10^{-3}$; 1/4-thousandth
16^{-4}	2^{-16}	1/65,536	
16^{-5}	2^{-20}	1/1,048,576	10^{-6}; 1 millionth
16^{-8}	2^{-32}	1/4,294,967,296	$1/4 \times 10^{-9}$; 1/4-billionth
16^{-10}	2^{-40}	1/1,099,511,627,776	10^{-12}; 1 trillionth

Base 10 (Decimal)	Equivalent	Verbal Equivalent
10^0	1	
10^1	10	
10^2	100	1 hundred
10^3	1,000	1 thousand
10^4	10,000	
10^5	100,000	
10^6	1,000,000	1 million
10^7	10,000,000	
10^8	100,000,000	
10^9	1,000,000,000	1 billion
10^{10}	10,000,000,000	
10^{11}	100,000,000,000	
10^{12}	1,000,000,000,000	1 trillion
10^{15}	1,000,000,000,000,000	1 quadrillion
10^{-1}	1/10	1 tenth
10^{-2}	1/100	1 hundredth
10^{-3}	1/1,000	1 thousandth
10^{-6}	1/1,000,000	1 millionth
10^{-9}	1/1,000,000,000	1 billionth
10^{-12}	1/1,000,000,000,000	1 trillionth
10^{-15}	1/1,000,000,000,000,000	1 quadrillionth

Sizes of and Distance to Objects	Equivalent	Additional Information
Diameter of Electron (classical)	5.6×10^{-13} centimeters	5.6×10^{-13} centimeters; roughly 10^{-12} centimeters
Mass of Electron	9.109×10^{-28} grams	roughly 10^{-27} grams (1 gram = 0.0353 ounce)
Diameter of Proton	10^{-15} meters	10^{-13} centimeters
Mass of Proton	1.67×10^{-24} grams	roughly 10^{-24} grams (about 1,836 times the mass of electron)
Diameter of Neutron	10^{-15} meters	10^{-13} centimeters
Mass of Neutron	1.673×10^{-24} grams	roughly 10^{-24} grams (about 1,838 times the mass of electron)
Diameter of Atomic Nucleus	10^{-14} meters	$\sim 10^{-12}$ centimeters (10,000 times smaller than an atom)
Atomic Mass (Atomic Mass Unit)	1.66×10^{-27} kilograms	one atomic mass unit (amu) is equal to 1.66×10^{-24} grams
Diameter of Atom (Electron Cloud)	ranges from 1×10^{-10} to 5×10^{-10} meters	$\sim 10^{-10}$ meters; $\sim 10^{-8}$ centimeters; $\sim 3.94 \times 10^{-9}$ inches (roughly 4 billionth of an inch across or 1/250 millionth of an inch across)
Diameter of (standard) Pencil	6 millimeters (0.236 inches)	roughly 10^{-2} meters
Height (average) of Man and Woman	man: 1.75 meters (5 feet, 8 inches) woman: 1.63 meters (5 feet, 4 inches)	human height roughly 2×10^{0} meters; 1/804.66 miles; 10^{-3} miles
Height of Mount Everest	8,850 meters (29,035 feet)	~ 5.5 miles; roughly 10^{4} meters
Radius (mean equatorial) of Earth	6,378.1 kilometers (3,960.8 miles)	$\sim 6,400$ kilometers (4,000 miles); roughly 6.4×10^{6} meters
Diameter (polar) of Earth	12,713.6 kilometers (7,895.1 miles)	$\sim 12,800$ kilometers (8,000 miles); roughly 1.28×10^{7} meters (Earth's diameter is twice the Earth's radius)
Circumference (based on mean equatorial radius) of Earth	40,075 kilometers (24,887 miles)	$\sim 40,000$ kilometers (25,000 miles) (about 8 times the width of the United States) (Circumference = $2 \times \pi \times$ Earth's radius)
Distance from Earth to Sun	149,600,000 kilometers (92,900,000 miles)	$\sim 93,000,000$ miles; ~ 8.3 light-minutes; roughly 10^{11} meters; roughly 10^{8} miles
Distance to Great Nebula in Andromeda Galaxy	2.7×10^{19} kilometers (1.7×10^{19} miles)	~ 2.9 million light-years; roughly 10^{22} meters; roughly 10^{19} miles

Timeline: Significant Events in the History of Computing

The history of computer sciences has been filled with many creative inventions and intriguing people. Here are some of the milestones and achievements in the field.

c. 300-500 BCE	The counting board, known as the ancient abacus, is used. (Babylonia)
1200 CE	The modern abacus is used. (China)
1500	Leonardo da Vinci drafts a design for a calculator. (Italy)
1614	John Napier suggests the use of logarithms. (Scotland)
1617	John Napier produces calculating rods, called "Napier's Bones." (Scotland)
	Henry Briggs formulates the common logarithm, Base 10. (England)
1620	Edmund Gunter devises the "Line of Numbers," the precursor to slide rule. (England)
1623	Wilhelm Schickard conceives a design of a mechanical calculator. (Germany)
1632	William Oughtred originates the slide rule. (England)
1642	Blaise Pascal makes a mechanical calculator which can add and subtract. (France)
1666	Sir Samuel Morland develops a multiplying calculator. (England)
1673	Gottfried von Leibniz proposes a general purpose calculating machine. (Germany)
1777	Charles Stanhope, 3rd Earl of Stanhope, Lord Mahon, invents a logic machine. (England)
1804	Joseph-Marie Jacquard mechanizes weaving with Jacquard's Loom, featuring punched cards. (France)
1820	Charles Xavier Thomas (Tomas de Colmar) creates a calculating machine, a prototype for the first commercially successful calculator. (France)
1822	Charles Babbage designs the Difference Engine. (England)
1834	Charles Babbage proposes the Analytical Engine. (England)
1838	Samuel Morse formulates the Morse Code. (United States)
1842	L. F. Menabrea publishes a description of Charles Babbage's Analytical Engine. (Published, Italy)
1843	Ada Byron King, Countess of Lovelace, writes a program for Babbage's Analytical Engine. (England)
1854	George Boole envisions the Laws of Thought. (Ireland)

1870	William Stanley Jevons produces a logic machine. (England)
1873	William Thomson, Lord Kelvin, devises the analog tide predictor. (Scotland)
	Christopher Sholes, Carlos Glidden, and Samuel W. Soule invent the Sholes and Glidden Typewriter; produced by E. Remington & Sons. (United States)
1875	Frank Stephen Baldwin constructs a pin wheel calculator. (United States)
1876	Alexander Graham Bell develops the telephone. (United States)
	Bell's rival, Elisha Gray, also produces the telephone. (United States)
1878	Swedish inventor Willgodt T. Odhner makes a pin wheel calculator. (Russia)
1884	Dorr Eugene Felt creates the key-driven calculator, the Comptometer. (United States)
1884	Paul Gotlieb Nipkow produces the Nipkow Disk, a mechanical television device. (Germany)
1886	Herman Hollerith develops his punched card machine, called the Tabulating Machine. (United States)
1892	William Seward Burroughs invents his Adding and Listing (printing) Machine. (United States)
1896	Herman-Hollerith forms the Tabulating Machine Company. (United States)
1901	Guglielmo Marconi develops wireless telegraphy. (Italy)
1904	John Ambrose Fleming constructs the diodevalve (vacuum tube). (England)
	Elmore Ambrose Sperry develops the circular slide rule. (United States)
1906	Lee De Forest invents the triode vacuum tube (audion). (United States)
1908	Elmore Ambrose Sperry produces the gyrocompass. (United States)
1910	Sperry Gyroscope Company is established. (United States)
1912	Frank Baldwin and Jay Monroe found Monroe Calculating Machine Company. (United States)
1914	Leonardo Torres Quevado devises an electromechanical calculator, an electromechanical chess machine (End Move). (Spain)
	Thomas J. Watson Sr. joins the Computing Tabulating Recording Company (CTR) as General Manager. (United States)
1919	W. H. Eccles and F. W. Jordan develop the flip-flop (memory device). (England)
1922	Russian-born Vladimir Kosma Zworykin develops the iconoscope and kinescope (cathode ray tube), both used in electronic television for Westinghouse. (United States)
1924	The Computing Tabulating Recording Company (CTR), formed in 1911 by the merger of Herman Hollerith's Tabulating Machine Company with Computing

	Scale Company and the International Time Recording Company, becomes the IBM (International Business Machines).
1927	The Remington Rand Corporation forms from the merger of Remington Typewriter Company, Rand Kardex Bureau, and others. (United States)
1929	Vladimir Kosma Zworykin develops color television for RCA. (United States)
1931	Vannevar Bush develops the Differential Analyzer (an analog machine). (United States)
1933	Wallace J. Eckert applies punched card machines to astronomical data. (United States)
1937	Alan M. Turing proposes a Theoretical Model of Computation. (England)
	George R. Stibitz crafts the Binary Adder. (United States)
1939	John V. Atanasoff devises the prototype of an electronic digital computer. (United States)
	William R. Hewlett and David Packard establish the Hewlett-Packard Company. (United States)
1940	Claude E. Shannon applies Boolean algebra to switching circuits. (United States)
	George R. Stibitz uses the complex number calculator to perform Remote Job Entry (RJE), Dartmouth to New York. (United States)
1941	Konrad Zuse formulates a general-purpose, program-controlled computer. (Germany)
1942	John V. Atanasoff and Clifford Berry unveil the Atanasoff-Berry Computer (ABC). (United States)
1944	The Colossus, an English calculating machine, is put into use at Bletchley Park. (England)
	Howard Aiken develops, the Automatic Sequence Controlled Calculator (ASCC), the Harvard Mark I, which is the first American program-controlled computer. (United States)
	Grace Hopper allegedly coins the term "computer bug" while working on the Mark I. (United States)
1946	J. Presper Eckert Jr. and John W. Mauchly construct the ENIAC (Electronic Numerical Integrator and Computer), the first American general-purpose electronic computer, at the Moore School, University of Pennsylvania. (United States)
	J. Presper Eckert Jr. and John W. Mauchly form the Electronic Control Company, which later becomes the Eckert-Mauchly Computer Corporation. (United States)
1947	John Bardeen, Walter H. Brattain, and William B. Shockley invent the transistor at Bell Laboratories. (United States)
1948	F. C. Williams, Tom Kilburn, and G. C. (Geoff) Tootill create a small scale, experimental, stored-program computer (nicknamed "Baby") at the University of Manchester; it serves as the prototype of Manchester Mark I. (England)

1949	F. C. Williams, Tom Kilburn, and G. C. (Geoff) Tootill design the Manchester Mark I at the University of Manchester. (England)
	Maurice V. Wilkes develops the ED SAC (Electronic Delay Storage Automatic Calculator) at Cambridge University. (England)
	Jay Wright Forrester invents three-dimensional core memory at the Massachusetts Institute of Technology. (United States)
	Jay Wright Forrester and Robert Everett construct the Whirlwind I, a digital, real-time computer at Massachusetts Institute of Technology. (United States)
1950	J. H. Wilkinson and Edward A. Newman design the Pilot ACE (Automatic Computing Engine) implementing the Turing proposal for a computing machine at the National Physical Laboratory (NPL). (England)
	Remington Rand acquires the Eckert-Mauchly Computer Corporation. (United States)
1951	Engineering Research Associates develops the ERA 1101, an American commercial computer, for the U.S. Navy and National Security Agency (NSA). (United States)
	The UNIVAC I (Universal Automatic Computer), an American commercial computer, is created by Remington Rand for the U.S. Census Bureau. (United States)
	Ferranti Mark I, a British commercial computer, is unveiled. (England)
	Lyons Tea Co. announces Lyons Electronic Office, a British commercial computer. (England)
1952	UNIVAC I predicts election results as Dwight D. Eisenhower sweeps the U.S. presidential race. (United States)
	Remington Rand Model 409, an American commercial computer, is originated by Remington Rand for the Internal Revenue Service. (United States)
	Remington Rand acquires Engineering Research Associates. (United States)
1953	The IBM 701, a scientific computer, is constructed. (United States)
1954	The IBM 650 EDPM, electronic data processing machine, a stored-program computer in a punched-card environment, is produced. (United States)
1955	Sperry Corp. and Remington Rand merge to form the Sperry Rand Corporation. (United States)
1957	Robert N. Noyce, Gordon E. Moore, and others found Fairchild Semiconductor Corporation. (United States)
1957	Seymour Cray, William Norris, and others establish Control Data Corporation. (United States)
	Kenneth Olsen and Harlan Anderson launch Digital Equipment Corporation (DEC). (United States)

1958	Jack Kilby at Texas Instruments invents the integrated circuit. (United States)
1959	Robert N. Noyce at Fairchild Semiconductor invents the integrated circuit. Distinct patents are awarded to both Texas Instruments and Fairchild Semiconductor, as both efforts are recognized. (United States)
1960	The first PDP-1 is sold by Digital Equipment Corporation, which uses some technology from the Whirlwind Project. (United States)
	The UNIVAC 1100 series of computers is announced by Sperry Rand Corporation. (United States)
1961	The Burroughs B5000 series dual-processor, with virtual memory, is unveiled. (United States)
1964	The IBM/360 family of computers begins production. (United States)
	The CDC 6600 is created by Control Data Corporation. (United States)
1965	The UNIVAC 1108 from Sperry Rand Corporation is constructed. (United States)
1965	The PDP-8, the first minicomputer, is released by Digital Equipment Corporation. (United States)
	Robert N. Noyce and Gordon E. Moore found Intel Corporation. (United States)
1969	The U.S. Department of Defense (DoD) launches ARPANET, the beginning of the Internet. (United States)
1970	The PDP–11 series of computers from Digital Equipment Corporation is put into use. (United States)
	The Xerox Corporation's Palo Alto Research Center (PARC) begins to study the architecture of information. (United States)
1971	Ken Thompson devises the UNIX Operating System at Bell Laboratories. (United States)
	Marcian E. (Ted) Hoff, Federico Faggin, and Stanley Mazor at Intel create the first microprocessor, a 4-bit processor, 4004. (United States)
1972	Seymour Cray founds Cray Research Inc. (United States)
	Intel releases the 8008 microprocessor, an 8-bit processor. (United States)
1974	Intel announces the 8080 microprocessor, an 8-bit processor. (United States)
	Motorola Inc. unveils the Motorola 6800, its 8-bit microprocessor. (United States)
	Federico Faggin and Ralph Ungerman co-found Zilog, Inc., a manufacturer of microprocessors. (United States)
1975	Bill Gates and Paul Allen establish the Microsoft Corporation. (United States)

The kit-based Altair 8800 computer, using an 8080 microprocessor, is released by Ed Roberts with MITS (Model Instrumentation Telemetry Systems) in Albuquerque, New Mexico. (United States)

MITS purchases a version of the BASIC computer language from Microsoft. (United States)

The MOS 6502 microprocessor, an 8-bit microprocessor, is developed by MOS Technologies, Chuck Peddle, and others, who had left Motorola, (United States)

1976   Gary Kildall creates the CP/M (Control Program/Monitor or Control Program for Microprocessors) Operating System of Digital Research; this operating system for 8-bit micro-computers is the forerunner of DOS 1.0. (United States)

Steven Jobs and Stephen Wozniak found Apple Computer, Inc. and create the Apple I. (United States)

Seymour Cray devises the Cray-1 supercomputer. (United States)

Commodore Business Machines acquires MOS Technologies. (Canada)

1977   The Commodore PET (Personal Electronic Transactor) personal computer, developed by Jack Tramiel and Chuck Peddle for Commodore Business Machines, features the 6502 8-bit Microprocessor. (Canada)

The Apple II personal computer from Apple Computer, Inc., is released featuring a 6502 microprocessor. (United States)

The TRS-80 personal computer from Tandy Radio Shack, equipped with the Zilog Z80 8-bit microprocessor from Zilog, is unveiled. (United States)

Intel announces the 8086 16-bit microprocessor. (United States)

1978   Digital Equipment Corporation launches the VAX 11/780, a 4.3 billion byte computer with virtual memory. (United States)

1979   Intel presents the 8088 16-bit microprocessor. (United States)

Motorola Inc. crafts the MC 68000, Motorola 16-bit processor. (United States)

1980   Tim Patterson sells the rights to QDOS, an upgrade operating system of CP/M for 8088 and 8086 Intel microprocessors, 16-bit microprocessor, to Microsoft. (United States)

1981   The IBM Corporation announces the IBM Personal Computer featuring an 8088 microprocessor. (United States)

The Microsoft Operating System (MS-DOS) is put into use. (United States)

The Osborne I, developed by Adam Osborne and Lee Felsenstein with Osborne Computer Corporation, invent the first portable computer. (United States)

1982   Scott McNealy, Bill Joy, Andy Bechtolsheim, and Vinod Khosla found Sun Microsystems, Inc. (United States)

1984	The Macintosh PC from Apple Computer Inc., running with a Motorola 68000 microprocessor, revolutionizes the personal computer industry. (United States)
	Richard Stallman begins the GNU Project, advocating the free use and distribution of software. (United States)
1985	The Free Software Foundation is formed to seek freedom of use and distribution of software. (United States)
	Microsoft releases Windows 1.01. (United States)
1986	Sperry Rand and the Burroughs Corporation merge to form Unisys Corporation. (United States)
1989	SPARCstation I from Sun Microsystems is produced. (United States)
1991	Tim Berners-Lee begins the World Wide Web at CERN. (Switzerland)
	Linus Torvalds builds the Linux Operating System. (Finland)
	Paul Kunz develops the first Web server outside of Europe, at the Stanford Linear Accelerator Center (SLAG). (United States)
1993	Marc Andreesen and Eric Bina create Mosaic, a Web browser, at the National Center for Supercomputing Applications (NCSA), University of Illinois-Urbana Champaign. (United States)
1994	Marc Andreesen and James H. Clark form Mosaic Communications Corporation, later Netscape Communications Corporation. (United States)
	Netscape Navigator is launched by Netscape Communications Corporation. (United States)
1995	Java technology is announced by Sun Microsystems. (United States)
1996	World chess champion Garry Kasparov of Russia defeats Deep Blue, an IBM computer, in a man vs. computer chess matchup, four to two. (United States)
1997	IBM's Deep Blue defeats world chess champion Garry Kasparov in a rematch, 3.5 to 2.5. (United States)
	An injunction is filed against Microsoft to prohibit the company from requiring customers to accept Internet Explorer as their browser as a condition of using the Microsoft operating system Windows 95. (United States)
1998	America OnLine (AOL) acquires Netscape. (United States)
	Compaq Computer Corporation, a major producer of IBM compatible personal computers, buys Digital Equipment Corporation. (United States)
	America OnLine (AOL) and Sun form an alliance to produce Internet technology. (United States)

1999	Shawn Fanning writes code for Napster, a music file-sharing program. (United States)
1998	The Recording Industry Association of America (RIAA) files a lawsuit against Napster for facilitating copyright infringement. (United States)
2000	Zhores I. Alferov, Herbert Kroemer, and Jack Kilby share the Nobel Prize in Physics for contributions to information technology. Alferov, a Russian, and Kroemer, a German-born American, share half the prize for their contributions to semiconductor-based technology used in high speed circuits. Kilby is awarded the other half of the prize for invention of the integrated circuit.
	Google becomes the first search engine to index one billion pages. (United States)
2001	Wikipedia, a free online user originated encyclopedia, comes online. (United States)
	Windows XP is introduced. (United States)
	Dell becomes the world's top computer systems provider. (United States)
2002	Hewlett Packard purchases Compaq. (United States)
2003	Apple creates and opens iTunes, an online music-buying application. (United States)
2004	Mark Zuckerberg creates and launches the online social network, Facebook. (United States)
	Google introduces Gmail, an Internet service. (United States)
2005	Video-sharing Web site, YouTube, comes online. (United States)
	Chinese company, Lenovo, acquires IBM's Personal Computing Division, making it the world's third-largest PC purveyor. (China)
2006	Apple switches all computers to Intel core processors. (United States)
	The first Twitter post is posted by co-founder Jack Dorsey at Twitter.com. (United States)
2007	Steve Jobs and Apple release the iPhone.
	Microsoft releases Windows Vista to the public. (United States)
	Apple announces that it will discontinue the use of the word "computer" in its title as it was working with products other than computers. It is now known as Apple, Inc. (United States)
2008	Bill Gates steps down as chairman of Microsoft to focus on philanthropic work. (United States)
2009	Intel unveils the "iA32 processor single-chip cloud computer," a CPU with 48 processing cores on a single chip. (United States)
2010	2010 Cyber-warfare and cyber-counterterrorism goes public: Stuxnet worm disrupts Iran's centrifuges dedicated to uranium enrichment.

2011   Social media, especially Facebook and Twitter, are credited with helping organizers form Arab Spring protests across Middle East. Revolution in Egypt results in resignation of President Hosni Mubarak and first free elections in Egypt's history.

              IBM's Watson supercomputer defeats human champions on the game show "Jeopardy."

2012   Facebook begins trading on NASDAQ as a private company (IPO).

              Facebook Facebook announces 'Graph Search' tool.

Timeline: The History of Programming, Markup, and Scripting Languages

. . . .

The history of computer sciences has been filed with many creative inventions and innovations. Here are some of the milestones and achievements in the field of computer programming and languages.

c. 800	al-Khowarizmi, Mohammed ibn-Musa develops a treatise on algebra, his name allegedly giving rise to the term, algorithm.
1843	Ada Byron King, Countess of Lovelace, programs Charles Babbage's design of the Analytical Engine.
1945	Plankalkul is developed by Konrad Zuse.
1953	Sort-Merge Generator is created by Betty Holberton.
1957	FORTRAN is devised for IBM by John Backus and team of programmers.
	FLOW-MATIC is crafted for Remington-Rand's UNIVAC by Grace Hopper.
1958	LISP is produced by John McCarthy at Massachusetts Institute of Technology.
1959	COBOL is formulated by the CODASYL Committee, initiated by the U.S. Department of Defense (DoD)
1960	ALGOL is the result of work done by the ALGOL Committee in the ALGOL 60 Report.
1961	JOSS is originated by the RAND Corporation.
	GPSS (General Purpose Simulation System) is invented by Geoffrey Gordon with IBM.
	RPG (Report Program Generator) is unveiled by IBM.
	APL (A Programming Language) is designed by Kenneth Iverson with IBM.
1963	SNOBOL is developed by David Farber, Ralph Griswold, and Ivan Polonsky at Bell Laboratories.
1964	BASIC is originated by John G. Kemeny and Thomas E. Kurtz at Dartmouth.
	PL/I is announced by IBM.
	Simula I is produced by Kristen Nygaard and Ole-Johan Dahl at the Norwegian Computing Center.
1967	Simula 67 is created by Kristen Nygaard and Ole-Johan Dahl at the Norwegian Computing Center.
	LOGO is devised by Seymour Papert at the MIT Artificial Intelligence Laboratory.
1971	Pascal is constructed by Niklaus Wirth at the Swiss Federal Institute of Technology (ETH) in Zurich.

1973   C developed by Dennis Ritchie at Bell Laboratories.

Smalltalk is invented by Alan Kay at Xerox's PARC (Palo Alto Research Center).

1980   Ada is developed for the U.S. Department of Defense (DoD).

1985   C++ is created by Bjarne Stroustrup at Bell Laboratories.

1986   SGML (Standard Generalized Markup Language) is developed by the International Organization for Standardization (ISO).

1987   Perl is constructed by Larry Wall.

1989   HTML (HyperText Markup Language) is proposed by Tim Berners-Lee at CERN (Organization européenne pour la recherche nucléaire).

1991   Visual Basic is launched by the Microsoft Corporation.

1993   Mosaic is created by Marc Andreesen and Eric Bina for the National Center for Computing Applications (TSTCCA) at the University of Illinois-Urbana Champaign.

1994   A written specification of VRML (Virtual Reality Markup Language) is drafted by Mark Pesce, Tony Parisi, and Gavin Bell.

1995   Java is crafted by James Gosling of Sun Microsystems

1996   Javascript is developed by Brendan Eich at Netscape Communications co-announced by Netscape and Sun Microsystems.

1997   VRML (Virtual Reality Modeling Language), developed by the Web3D Consortium, becomes an international standard.

1998   XML (Extensible Markup Language) is originated by a working group of the World Wide Web Consortium (W3C).

2000   Microsoft publicly introduces the programming language C#.

2002   Perl 5.8 is released to the public.

2008   HTML5 is first introduced to the public as a working draft.

A

Accounting Software

Computers were developed to perform routine tasks over and over based on a set of instructions and data provided by the user. Accounting and bookkeeping consists of a series of routine tasks (transactions) performed over and over with new data. Given the automation provided by computers and the routine nature of accounting, it was inevitable that the two would match up. In fact, the earliest applications of computers were for accounting purposes. American inventor Herman Hollerith's (1860–1929) original tabulating machine was used to count the U.S. Census population numbers in 1890.

The first computer software designed for accounting purposes dealt with basic computations and accumulation of numbers. The large early computing systems added and subtracted numbers to help companies keep track of their financial information. As capabilities advanced, more complex systems were used for tracking customer transactions and related calculations.

Typical Applications

Accounting consists of some basic calculations and accumulation of numbers. Items such as loan interest computations, loan payment amounts, and tax due can be calculated with accounting software. In addition, there are several categories of general accounting tasks that any accounting software should support. These include general ledger, accounts payable, accounts receivable, payroll, inventory, job cost estimating, fixed assets, sales orders, and budgeting. Accounting software exists to serve various needs, with lightweight versions like Quicken to serve the home market, QuickBooks to serve small to medium businesses, and enterprise packages to serve the needs of large corporations.

General Ledger The general ledger is the final accumulation of financial data for an organization. It allows the organization to view the overall status of all accounting data.

Accounts Payable The accounts payable area handles payments to be made to vendors or others who provide goods or services to an organization. Data such as vendor information, payment amount, and related items are tracked by this software. Summaries of payments are posted to the general ledger on a periodic basis.

Accounts Receivable The accounts receivable area processes money due to an organization from customers or other parties. Data related to

Tax software for sale. © *AP Images/ ZAK BRIAN/SIPA.*

* **demographic** statistical data pertaining to a population

the reason for money due and the due date are contained in accounts receivable records. The accounts receivable software posts summaries of the data to the general ledger on a periodic basis.

Payroll Payroll deals with the calculation and payment of money to employees for work performed for the company. In addition, payroll records may also house demographic* information related to employees (human resources data). Payroll accounting involves a series of calculations for taxes, benefits, and other payroll items. The accumulation of payroll data is posted to the general ledger on a periodic basis.

Inventory Inventory software tracks the goods and supplies an organization keeps on hand to either supply customer needs or for internal use. The basic calculations handle additions and subtractions from the quantity in stock at any given time. More advanced inventory software can correlate the amount of raw materials required to make certain products and ensure that enough materials are on hand to meet varying levels of demand.

Job Cost Estimating Job costing helps project managers and others deal with the process of analyzing and estimating data to provide a cost estimate for a given project. Job costing software analyzes costs such as labor, equipment, supplies, and materials. Project costs can vary day-to-day or hour-to-hour depending on fluctuations in material cost, futures trading, or labor rates. Job costing software may be able to periodically retrieve updated costs for the components of a project to give a real-time estimate of the remaining cost.

Fixed Assets Fixed assets are the physical components of an organization—property, plant, and equipment. The purchase costs associated with each item, along with any improvements made to the item, would be tracked by accounting software. Also, depreciation of the item over the years would be calculated. The accumulation of fixed asset and depreciation data is posted to the general ledger on a periodic basis.

Sales Orders Sales orders can be tracked and credited to individual salespersons in an organization. Each order is entered to show details such as the quantity ordered, price, and other financial data. The accumulation of sales data is posted to the general ledger on a periodic basis.

Budgeting Budgeting software allows the organization and its managers to accumulate data on projected revenues and expenditures for a future time period. Usually, this period is a one-year look into the future. Budgeting software allows actual revenue and expenditure data to be posted so that fluctuations between budget and actual values can be reported.

Accounting software is available for use on various operating systems and for a wide variety of computer types, from stand-alone computers used for small business or home accounting needs to mainframe computers* that process accounting data for multinational corporations. Selecting the appropriate software for an organization is a matter of carefully matching the needs of the organization with an accounting software package that provides the functions and features needed by the organization at a price that is in proportion to the benefit to be gained.

 See also **IBM Corporation** • **Office Automation Systems** • **Tabulating Machines**

Resources

Books

Atrill, Peter, and E. J. McLaney. *Accounting and Finance for Non-Specialists*, 7th ed. Harlow, UK, and New York: Financial Times/Prentice Hall, 2011.

Bentham, Alan. *Guidelines on Obtaining and Implementing Accounting Software*. London: The Institute of Chartered Accountants in England & Wales, 2004.

Johnston, Randolph P., and Robert H. Spencer. *Accounting Software Solutions*. 4th ed. Hammond, LA: K2 Enterprises, 2006.

* **mainframe computers** large computers used by businesses and government agencies to process massive amounts of data; generally faster and more powerful than desktop computers but usually requiring specialized software

Meall, Lesley. *Online Accounting Software*. London: Information Technology Faculty of the Institute of Chartered Accountants in England and Wales, 2008.

Sebahar, Ken E. *The Executive Guide to Implementing Accounting Software: Over 100 Ways to Ensure the Success of Your Project*. North Charleston, SC: Booksurge LLC, 2007.

Agriculture

Agriculture is a vast industry that includes plant and animal production, comprehensive support and infrastructure systems, and food and fiber processing. Key application areas of computers in agriculture include record keeping, decision-making, control, and research. The diversity of agricultural enterprises and associated products require a variety of computer hardware and software solutions, from specialized software packages to computerized components for traditional machinery and equipment. A particular challenge to designers and manufacturers of computerized agricultural machinery is to make computers, analog/digital (A/D and D/A) converters, terminals, and connections unaffected by environmental conditions. Agricultural equipment experiences extremes of dust, rain and high humidity, vibration, and temperatures.

Recordkeeping

Recordkeeping is vital in any business. Agricultural enterprises use computers for common financial and business tasks such as inventory, payroll, accounting, and taxes. Because there are many differences between

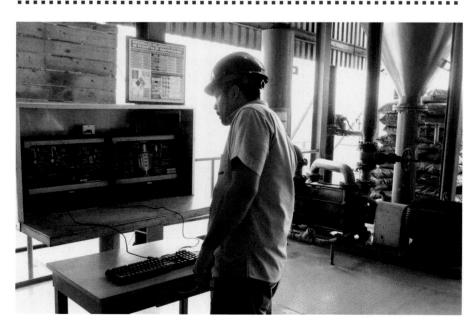

A worker uses a computer to monitor operations at a sugar-processing facility.
© *Juan Carlos/Bloomberg via Getty Images.*

agricultural businesses and other businesses (with regard to tax structure, labor management, insurance, and inventory, for example), software packages have been tailored specifically for agriculture. Spreadsheet and database templates are common, but specific application programs also exist.

Livestock and crop production farms have unique needs for records. For example, crop production fields have numerous descriptors and variables that should be recorded. Examples include soil type, drainage, slope, pH, and nutrient status. Databases have been developed to deal with this information. Precision agriculture (sometimes referred to as site-specific farming) requires such data to be recorded not only for fields but also for locations within fields. Because they provide a combination of database and drawing functions, Geographic Information Systems (GISs) are needed to handle the large amount of data. Global Positioning Systems (GPSs) work with computerized machinery in the field to correlate crop and soil conditions with exact locations on the globe. Because soil and crop conditions can vary tremendously within fields, this capability can improve the environmental friendliness of farming and improve profitability.

Similarly, livestock farms track individual animals, storing and evaluating information such as age, growth rate, milk production, health records, offspring productivity, and reproductive cycle status. Unlike with large corporations that employ computer scientists, farmers generally do not have or cannot hire the expertise to customize relevant software. Therefore, there is a market for software products suitable for those who are mostly novice computer users.

Decision-making

Computers can be used to assist agricultural decision-making through such tools and techniques as optimization, simulation, fuzzy logic*, expert systems, and computer aided drafting (CAD). A common problem to be solved on crop farms is the selection of the optimal field machinery set. Overly large equipment will result in poor use of capital and labor, while equipment that is too small may result in poor timing of operations and consequential loss of crop value. The equipment must function as an interdependent set; operations must flow in a sequential and timely manner. Simulations can model farm and machine events over time to predict what would happen if particular machinery sets were chosen. Weather, soil type, and desired field operations are important factors to consider. Optimization techniques such as linear or non-linear programming that minimize cost subject to reasonable constraints that include labor availability and frost dates can help improve profitability.

Increasing regulations require that nutrient management plans be developed, implemented, and monitored. While much of this is record-keeping in nature, decision tools are used to project future impact and profits, given past performance and conditions. Integrated pest management (IPM) also takes a holistic* view of production and optimizes the timing and rates of chemical application (if necessary) or the use of

fuzzy logic models human reasoning by permitting elements to have partial membership to a set; derived from fuzzy set theory

holistic looking at the entire system, rather than just its parts

* **algorithm** a rule or procedure used to solve a problem—most often described as a sequence of steps

alternative measures. IPM requires projection of consequences with various strategies so that the optimum strategy can be implemented. IPM models include simulation of pest population dynamics and rule-based expert systems techniques.

In poultry and livestock production, a major cost of production is feed, often exceeding 35 percent of gross receipts. Minimizing feed cost is a classic linear or non-linear optimization problem. Optimization methods can help determine the least costly ingredient package in a diet subject to constraints including energy, protein, intake limitations, minerals, and fiber requirements.

Landscape design and construction, which is also an agriculture-related enterprise, can benefit from computer aided drafting and drawing packages that help designers generate and illustrate concepts to clients. By providing projection of individual plant growth, good packages can show how plants on a site will look years after installation.

Control

Control of machinery by computers can provide consistency and reliability unmatched with human operation. Controller area networks (CANs) are common on tractors and self-propelled equipment. These CANs reduce wiring complexity and allow one or more on-board chips to control machine functions such as engine controls, transmission, and hydraulic power output. CANs use serial communications like other networks, but they have a specific data structure to facilitate interchange among vendors of CAN compatible devices and diagnosis of problems.

Computers are used increasingly to control seeding or chemical application rate automatically in fields. This requires GIS and GPS data input, computer algorithm*s to generate control signals (rule or formula based), and relays and amplifier cards to power mechanisms that perform the desired functions. Computerized control of these processes can help reduce costs by eliminating waste and improve the overall quality of the product by preventing over- or under-application of seeds or chemicals in any one area.

Support industries for agriculture inputs include manufacturing and delivery of machinery, feed, and fertilizer. After farms produce raw products, there is food and fiber manufacturing, which also uses computers for recordkeeping and industrial automation. Programmable logic controllers (PLCs) are used in all of these agricultural industries, as well as on farms. PLCs can perform intelligent on/off and proportional control on machines that meter, grind, weigh, blend, cut, and weld.

Computers are used for post-harvest sorting and quality control. Pictures of fruit and vegetables can be taken during processing and packing to allow different sized fruit to be sorted and to identify any physiological defects that would make each piece of fruit or vegetable unfit for sale. Prior to computer automation, this job would be performed by hand, which could lead to variations in how produce is categorized based upon different workers' judgment. Computer systems can also be used to maintain optimal environmental conditions in fruit, grain, and vegetable storage facilities, automatically obtaining readings from the air to determine temperature, humidity, and gas concentrations. Adjustments in humidity and temperature as well as the addition of nitrogen (N) gas can help prevent fruit ripening and slow the growth of bacterial or fungal disease that can spoil the harvested crops. For instance, a computer model has been developed that predicts the gas concentrations inside fruits and vegetables based on the incorporation of fruit or vegetable shape and fluid dynamics. Knowing this information makes it possible for storage facilities to make modifications in oxygen (O) and carbon dioxide (CO_2) concentrations to avoid internal browning, caused by low levels of oxygen, and slow ripening by increasing the carbon dioxide levels. Being able to determine the appropriate ratio of these gases is key to maintaining quality fruit and vegetables in storage. This model would allow fruits and vegetables to be stored for up to nine months post-harvest.

Research

Research in agriculture requires some uses of computers not utilized in other aspects of agricultural work. Very sophisticated simulation models address issues such as crop growth, animal nutrition, water flow in soil, thermal and physical behavior of agricultural products, machinery performance, and integrated farm systems.

As with most areas of research, good agricultural research requires computers for statistical analysis of data, generation of mathematical models, and control of research devices. Instrumentation to measure temperature, flow, pressure, electrical conductivity, and strain also requires computers or data loggers.

A recent new way to assist farmers and others in agriculture is e-agriculture, which uses existing information and methods but applies them for the Internet and electronic devices. E-agriculture uses computers, mobile computing, satellites, and other high-tech devices to improve the way that agriculture works in the overall cycle of raising crops and providing food for the world. One example of e-agriculture to add to agricultural efficiency is text messages or e-mails that inform potentially millions of farmers about such important subjects as new seed products, upcoming weather forecasts, and even the latest prices of corn, soybeans, and other farm commodities. Mobile applications (apps) are already in use to help farmers before, during, and after harvest.

 See also **Biology • Geographic Information Systems • Molecular Biology • Weather Forecasting**

Resources

Books

Brennan, L. E. *Using Computer-Based Technologies to Support Farmers' Decision Making: A Report for the Cooperative Venture for Capacity Building.* RIRDC publication, no. 07/104. Barton, A.C.T.: Rural Industries Research and Development Corporation, 2007.

Feeding Made Easy

Computer-based feeding systems can feed individual animals the specific amount they need. Tags identify individual animals, and then controllers dispense a customized feeding plan controlling feed type, quantity, and time of day. In addition to controlling the action of feeding, the program can also keep track of how much feed is used.

Bundgaard, Kristian, and Luke Isaken, editors. *Agriculture Research and Technology*. New York: Nova Science, 2010.

International Conference on Computers and Computing Technologies in Agriculture, and D. L. Swain. *Special Issue: Proceedings of the First International Conference on Computers and Computing Technologies in Agriculture (CCTA 2007), Held in Wuyishan, China, August 18–20, 2007*. Wellington, New Zealand: RSNZ Publishing, 2007.

Web Sites

E-agriculture.org. "Mobile Apps Targeting Post HHharvest Challenges in Agriculture." http://www.e-agriculture.org/news/mobile-apps-targeting-post-harvest-challenges-agriculture (accessed September 24, 2012).

FoodProductionDaily.com and Linda Rano. "New Computer Model May Improve Food Storage." http://www.foodproductiondaily.com/Quality-Safety/New-computer-model-may-improve-fruit-storage (accessed September 24, 2012).

Aircraft Flight Control

Aircraft in flight require adherence to a specific course for long periods of time, which can be tiring for the pilot. Likewise, steering ships on the water for hours is tedious and leads to crew fatigue. For more than

▶
Air traffic controller center in the Philippines. © *AP Images/Bullit Marquez.*

a century, ships have had auto-pilots or devices that maintain a heading without human operators. Controlling an aircraft is similar but more complex because an aircraft operates in three dimensions and travels at considerably higher speeds. In the air, small deviations can become large errors more quickly.

The automatic control of aircraft was not considered until aircraft were capable of practical long distance flight. In the 1920s when radio navigation became available for aircraft, air travel became practical, eventually leading to the development of auto-pilot systems for aircraft. The first aircraft autopilots were based on gyros* and were similar to those found in a ship. Such simple auto-pilots were capable of maintaining a set heading, but did not ensure the aircraft would follow a specific course. Heading is just what the word implies, the direction the aircraft is heading, which is not always the same as the path the aircraft actually flies. That path is called its "track." Its "course" is the desired path for the aircraft to fly. Because the medium in which aircraft fly, air, is not still, winds will blow the aircraft around in a somewhat unpredictable manner and the track and course may not agree. Flight crews needed to determine how much to change the heading in order keep the aircraft on course. The crew also had to adjust the power, ailerons*, and elevators to prevent the aircraft from gaining or losing altitude as well as keep it flying level.

When radio navigation and its accompanying electronics came along, auto-pilots became more sophisticated, allowing the auto-pilot to follow a radio beam. Auto-pilots could keep the aircraft at a constant altitude while also keeping the wings level.

Auto-Pilot Operation

An aircraft is said to have six degrees of freedom—up-down, left-right, forward-aft—and can rotate around three axes—roll, pitch, and yaw. Roll is rotation around the forward-to-aft line of the aircraft. Pitch is around the axis of the wing, and yaw is around the vertical. Auto-pilots used for en route travel can completely control an aircraft by changing only three of the six degrees of freedom: roll, pitch, and yaw. The most capable auto-pilots can actually land an aircraft, control engine power, and manipulate all six degrees of freedom.

An auto-pilot requires input information to control the motion of an aircraft. Gyros are used to sense motion while an altimeter senses altitude. Radio receivers provide information relative to the desired course of an aircraft. When the more sophisticated long distance navigation information is available, an aircraft may be controlled on a course to a specific point called a waypoint. Essentially, an aircraft could be programmed with a destination and automatically flown to that destination. When an auto-pilot reaches this level of sophistication it is called a "flight management system" (FMS). At the heart of an FMS is a "flight management computer" (FMC).

* **gyros** a contraction of gyroscopes; traditionally, a mechanical device that uses one or more spinning discs which resist changes to their position in space, which in turn is useful for identifying spatial orientation; newer, non-mechanical technologies use electronic or other means to measure spatial orientation

* **ailerons** control surfaces on the trailing edges of the wings of an aircraft—used to manage roll control

Microprocessors in Auto-Pilots

Although many auto-pilots existed before the introduction of the micro-processor, they were difficult to implement and required each aircraft type to have its own model auto-pilot. This is because each aircraft has its own characteristics and the auto-pilot reacts differently for each aircraft type. A programmable auto-pilot was the ideal solution and a perfect application of the microprocessor.

With the introduction of the microprocessor, an auto-pilot or FMS could be found even in small, private aircraft. However, the micropro-cessor also brought new challenges. The microprocessor must perform a series of operations, some of which jump from one address location to another and then return while keeping track of the entire process in what is called a stack. On some occasions, because of a software or hardware problem, the computer loses track and executes a bogus program. This situation can have catastrophic results.

Therefore, every piece of equipment that is installed in an aircraft registered in the United States must be certified by the Federal Aviation Administration (FAA) and similar agencies in other countries. All auto-matic flight control equipment must demonstrate that it is "fail-safe." This means that if the computer has a failure, the auto-pilot does not place the aircraft in a dangerous situation. It was difficult for the early microprocessor-controlled autopilots to demonstrate this characteristic.

Aircraft certification, until the introduction of the microprocessor, meant hardware. However, when microprocessor-based equipment appeared in aircraft, it became clear that software, like hardware, could also fail with serious consequences. Something needed to be done to insure the integrity of the software. The FAA developed certification pro-cedures for software, one of the first organizations to recognize this need.

Until then, while the microprocessor was revolutionizing the world, analog* auto-pilots were the mainstay in aircraft. Eventually, the new procedures adopted by the FAA to certify software were implemented and digital auto-pilots using microprocessors became common. The first microprocessor auto-pilots introduced in the late 1970s were programmed using assembly language*. This was necessary because of the small size of read-only memories of the time. It was not uncommon to find memories as small as 4K bits (not bytes). It was not long before 64K-bit read-only memory (ROM)* ROMs were available, but by modern standards that is very small. Also, many of the functions performed by the microprocessor involved switching the state of one bit of a port*. Assembly language pro-vided the closest connection to the actual inner workings of the hardware.

Flight Management Systems

In the late 1970s, the long range navigation system LORAN-C became fully operational. This navigation system provided aircraft position in latitude and longitude. The desired course was set by entering waypoint information, and deviation from the selected course was provided to the auto-pilot. This development led to the integration of the auto-pilot and the long distance navigation computer into one unit, and later, the integration of other navigation systems, such as short distance navigation and landing systems, into the auto-pilot as well. This is the concept behind a flight management system or FMS.

The FMS controls the aircraft and the navigation equipment. It contains databases for airways, airports, radio frequencies, and radio navigation aids. With the FMS, a desired course is entered and the FMS will automatically select the navigation equipment and radio frequencies. With so much stored data, changes occur regularly. Therefore, it is necessary to update the databases periodically to reflect the changes using a CD (compact disc), floppy disk, or a notebook computer.

Next Generation Air Transportation System

In 2003 the United States Congress created a charter for a new national air transportation system called the "Next Generation Air Transportation System" (NexGen). In 2007 the FAA released a statement describing NexGen as a sweeping transformation of the entire U.S. air transportation system with the central goal of substantially reducing aircraft gridlock, both in the skies and at the nation's airports. A prime component of NexGen entails transitioning away from ground-based radars and other systems to satellite-based technologies to achieve improved control of each aircraft within the overall air traffic system. For instance, "Automatic dependent surveillance-broadcast" (ADS-B) is a system for improved control of aircraft employing onboard Global Positioning System (GPS) equipment that utilizes satellite broadcasts to pinpoint the position and velocity of aircraft. The resulting data from each aircraft is broadcast to the air traffic control system, as well as to other aircraft, with the result that pilots and air traffic controllers will see the real-time positions and trajectories of aircraft throughout a given region. It is anticipated that such an improved, real-time flight control system will reduce air traffic congestion, travel time, fuel usage, and pollution, as well as increase overall air traffic safety. Despite expected delays, major milestones in the implementation of NexGen are scheduled to take place between 2012 and 2025. As early as 2010, airlines had saved thousands of gallons of fuel and thousands of hours of taxi time in some of the areas where airports had implemented NexGen.

▶ *See also* **Airline Reservations • Navigation • Satellite Technology • Telecommunications**

Resources

Books

Langton, Roy. *Stability and Control of Aircraft Systems: Introduction to Classical Feedback Control.* Chichester, UK, and Hoboken, NJ: Wiley, 2006.

Web Sites

United States Government Accountability Office "Next Generation Air Transportation System: FAA Has Made Some Progress in Implementation, but Delays Threaten to Impact Costs and Benefits" http://www.gao.gov/assets/590/585588.pdf (Accessed October 29, 2012).

Aircraft Traffic Management

In the early days of aviation, airplanes were mostly used as joy rides, in air shows, and for general tricks and stunts (barnstorming). Even into the 1920s, debate occurred regarding whether the airplane had a useful purpose, and one of the main concerns was the inability of planes to fly in bad weather. With the development of radio navigation aids, which would eventually lead to the flight instruments of today, radio landing aids were installed at larger airports. These airports became the first hubs for successful air travel and were connected to each other via airways,

Russia's prime minister, Vladimir Putin (2nd left), listens to explanations in the air traffic control operations room during a visit to one of the divisions of Russian aviation. © *ALEXEY DRUXHININ/ AFP/Getty Images.*

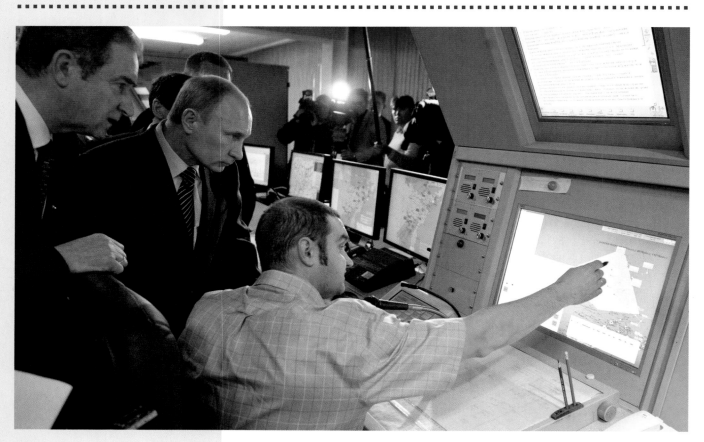

which are similar to highways that connect large cities. However, just as highways funnel traffic into a city, causing traffic congestion and possible collisions, airways also experience similar problems near airports, making methods of controlling air traffic necessary.

In the beginning, air traffic control (ATC) was mostly implemented via such tools as colored lights and flags. However, while lights and flags work well on the ground and therefore seem obvious choices for use at airports, they are only good for operations very close to airports and then only when the aircraft has a clear view of the airport. A system was needed to control the entire airway.

Early ATC systems were based on ensuring safe separation—that is, an aircraft departing an airport reported its position by radio. If the airplane was flying under poor visibility conditions, it would be difficult to determine its position with the crude radio navigation equipment of the time; the aircraft's altitude, which could be measured with reasonable accuracy even in poor visibility, was an important part of position reports. Other departing aircraft would then be held at the airport until the previous plane was sufficiently far from the airport to ensure that no collisions would occur. The key person in such ATC was the air traffic controller, who was in constant radio contact with the aircraft's crew. The problem with this type of ATC is that the required separation is so great, often more than twenty nautical miles (thirty-seven kilometers), that the capacity of the airport is diminished.

Primary and Secondary Radar

With the advent of radar*, aircraft could be located from the ground even in clouds, and accurate position reports were not required from the aircraft. The required amount of separation was reduced significantly and the airport was used at a higher capacity. However, alone was not enough to ensure flight safety. The controller saw only anonymous green blips on the screen, denoting the aircraft. Secondly, the screen, which is termed a plan position indicator, or PPI, is a two-dimensional display and aircraft are flying in a three-dimensional world. In order to control planes more accurately, a way was needed to identify the blips and to show their altitude. The system used is termed a secondary system, a communications system that operates in concert with the radar.

With these two tools, primary and secondary radar, air traffic controllers could monitor more aircraft in less airspace and increase the amount of aircraft on the airways. The air traffic controllers noted the pertinent information about an aircraft such as its flight number, aircraft ID number, assigned altitude, and destination on a small card. This card was placed in a holder referred to as a shrimp boat because of its shape; it held the card so that the data were easily visible to the controller. These data were a part of the flight plan, which was filed with ATC before the flight. As with the first ATC systems, constant communication with the aircraft was vital for safe separation.

* **radar** the acronym for RAdio Direction And Ranging; a technique developed in the 1930s that uses frequency shifts in reflected radio waves to measure distance and speed of a target

* **high-speed data links** digital communications systems that permit digital data to be reliably transferred at high speed

* **cathode ray tube (CRT)** a glass enclosure that projects images by directing a beam of electrons onto the back of a screen

* **algorithm** a rule or procedure used to solve a mathematical problem—most often described as a sequence of steps

Even with long distance radar, the controller can only handle a limited area of airspace, termed a sector. When an aircraft goes from one controller's sector into another, the shrimp boat is pushed along a track to the next sector's controller. This process is termed handing off.

Computers in ATC

ATC involves a large number of radar sites, information from flight plans, and controller-entered information. One of the first uses of large computers was gathering and displaying these data. Radar sites are connected to an en route air traffic control center, which is responsible for tens of thousands of square miles of air traffic. Smaller centers serve airports and are termed terminal radar control centers or TRACONs.

Radar data require reliable high-speed data links*. Data from several radar sites are combined and distributed to the sector displays. Even though air traffic control is accomplished with many controllers using data obtained from many radar sites, the entire system needs to be seamless; that is, there can be no gaps or areas not covered by ATC.

Historically the controller's PPI display would update in synchronism with the radar in real time. The image was not stored in a computer and was only displayed on the screen. The PPI cathode ray tube (CRT)* had a very long persistence, meaning that the image would fade away very slowly, allowing the controller to view it for a few seconds. Before the image faded completely, the radar would make another sweep and refresh the image. Because the image grew dim as it faded, it was necessary to make the radar room dark.

Modern air traffic control systems store the images digitally. The display is much brighter, can contain color, can be zoomed in or out, and can be scanned with a trackball or mouse. This improves the controllers' working conditions.

In the early part of the twenty-first century, air traffic control began a massive change to a totally different philosophy termed free flight. The existing air traffic control system funnels aircraft onto airways and then controls them from the ground. If aircraft were to choose their flight plan without using airways, the preferred route would be a direct route from departure to destination; separation would be automatic. Of course there is a chance that routes would cross and cause a collision. In a free flight system, aircraft choose a direct flight path and enter that flight path into a computer. A software algorithm* termed a conflict probe compares the flight plan to those of other aircraft, looking for potential collisions. If a potential collision does exist, the flight plan will be rejected and the aircraft will be requested to make a change. Another aspect of free flight is the use of global positioning system (GPS) technology that involves the use of coordinates to determine the location and position of other aircraft.

The computer also receives data from the air traffic radars and predicts future paths of aircraft already airborne. If the path of any aircraft projects a collision, the air traffic manager contacts the aircraft in question and requests a change of course. With this system, air traffic control becomes air traffic management or ATM.

The key to this system is a massive networked computer system with data from flight plans, en route radar data, and aircraft. Just as important as the computer is a network of data links, including air-ground-air links. A much smaller staff of air traffic managers would be able to ensure a higher level of safety for future air traffic.

New satellite technology, termed NextGen, will begin a testing phase in December 2009 in the Gulf of Mexico. The U.S. government is developing this satellite aircraft tracking system to eventually replace the current radar-based system. The satellite system will allow for more frequent take-offs, reduced airspace separation, more direct routes, and decreased inclement weather effects on flights. Using the satellite-based system, controllers will be able to observe the aircraft over bodies of water as opposed to the radar system in which controllers can only view aircraft over land. The government plans to fully implement this new technology as of 2013 with all aircraft being equipped with the necessary equipment as of 2020. By mid-2012, JetBlue planes flying into JFK airport in New York had adopted the system. This saved each plane eighteen gallons of fuel per flight, helped improve the time that passengers had to spend in transit, reduced the environmental impact, and contributed to keeping flights on time. Once this system spreads to more airlines and airports, it is expected to save the airline industry billions of dollars in terms of time as well as fuel, which will also result in reduced air pollution and greenhouse gas emissions.

 See also **Aircraft Flight Control • Global Positioning Systems**

Resources

Books

Duke, Graham. *Air Traffic Control.* 10th ed. Ian Allan abc. Hersham, UK: Ian Allan, 2009.

Learning Express. *Air Traffic Control Test Preparation.* New York: Learning Express, 2009.

Nolan, Michael S. *Fundamentals of Air Traffic Control.* 5th ed. Clifton Park, NY: Delmar, 2011.

Rider, David, and Jenny Beechener. *Jane's Air Traffic Control 2011–2012.* Coulsdon, UK, and Alexandria, VA: Jane's Information Group, 2011.

United States Federal Aviation Administration. *Instrument Flying Handbook*, revised ed. New York: Skyhorse Publishing, 2011.

Web Sites

Federal Aviation Administration "Start Spreading the News" http://www.faa.gov/nextgen/slides/?slide=8 (accessed October 31, 2012).

* **batch processing** an approach to computer utilization that queues noninteractive programs and runs them one after another

* **transaction processing** operations between client and server computers that are made up of many small exchanges that must all be completed for the transaction to proceed

Airline Reservations

Airline reservation systems (ARSs) originated in the mid–1950s as relatively unsophisticated internal systems to help with tasks such as seat assignments, maintenance scheduling, and aircraft loading. Modern ARSs are multi-faceted, full-service systems that assist with a variety of airline management tasks and service customer needs from the time of initial reservation through completion of the flight.

First Computerized Systems

American Airlines, an early pioneer in the use of commercial computer technology, developed a semi-automated customer reservation system termed Reservisor by 1960. It required considerable manual intervention and had a reservation error rate of eight percent, which was the lowest in the industry at the time. Recognizing that semi-automatic systems would not be capable of handling the rapidly increasing demand for air travel, American Airlines had already begun working with IBM, in the late 1950s, to develop the first automated, online, real-time computerized reservation system (CRS). The joint project would use interactive, real-time computing technology developed for a U.S. government air defense project referred to as Semi-Automatic Ground Environment (SAGE).

In 1964 the Semi-Automated Business Research Environment (Sabre) System was introduced. Sabre, a coast-to-coast telecommunications network, was the largest, private, online, real-time data processing system in the United States. Only the U.S. government had a larger working system. Most of the computing systems that existed in the 1960s were batch processing* systems, but Sabre was an early example of a transaction processing* system. It modified the content of the large databases containing flight and passenger information as a direct result of information entered directly from data terminals. For the first time, an airline was able to track passenger names on all connections of their flights.

When airline computers crash, it impacts flights and passengers across the country. © *AP Images/Charles Reex Arbogast.*

In the early years, American Airlines invested more than $350 million in this project, with $40 million spent for initial development. By comparison, a new jet cost $4.5 million during this time period. The immediate impact of the Sabre System implementation was a reduction in the reservation error rate to less than one percent, and a 30 percent savings on investment in personnel.

After investing $250 million in system development, United Airlines entered the CRS market in 1976 with the Apollo Reservation System. Other well-known traditional reservation systems originally developed by individual airlines include Worldspan LP, Galileo International Inc., which purchased Apollo in May 1997, and European competitor Amadeus Global Travel Distribution SA.

In 1976 Sabre and Apollo began placing their CRSs in travel agencies. Through office automation offered by the systems, travel agents could print both tickets and boarding passes for their customers. Travel agents were transformed into an extension of the airline industry, which significantly streamlined the ticketing process.

Expanding Reservations Services

Following deregulation* of the airline industry in 1978, the major CRSs such as Sabre and Apollo began listing airline reservations for all competing major carriers as well as for their host airlines. This networked a large number of travel agents with the major airlines and yielded a very profitable per ticket booking fee for the host airline.

Accusations of favoritism toward the host airline, based on the order in which available flights were listed on terminal screens, surfaced early in the 1980s. Since studies reveal that 90 percent of flights are booked from the first reservation screen, a favorable position can dramatically affect ticket sales. The U.S. Department of Transportation investigated this allegation and issued a ruling to prohibit favoritism toward the host airline by requiring that flight information be presented in a neutral order. Because of the prohibitive cost of developing their own CRSs, the airlines ultimately agreed to pay the per ticket booking fee to the major computerized reservations providers, and a code-sharing scheme was developed to help alleviate the screen order bias. Sabre, one of the most widely recognized information systems ever developed, was spun off as a private company by AMR Corporation in 2000. In October 2012, American Airlines sued Sabre accusing them of doubling the fees already charged for for displaying flight information. The airline also claimed that it had suffered $993 million in damages because of Sabre's favoritism. As of publication the lawsuit was unsettled.

Each CRS is networked with the global distribution system (GDS) to unify the reservations originating from different outlets into one system. There were three major GDS providers as of early 2009: Amadeus, Travelport (resulting from the Worldspan LP and Galileo International Inc. merger), and Sabre.

* **deregulation** the lowering of restrictions, rules, or regulations pertaining to an activity or operation (often commercial)

Impact of 9/11

The terrorist attacks on the United States on September 11, 2001, have affected all aspects of the airline industry, including airline reservation systems. The U.S. Department of Transportation is considering security measures that involve red-flagging a suspected terrorist's name in an airline reservation system. Such queries and retrievals from long-established mainframe-based systems would represent a very costly system overhaul. In addition to resolving technical and cost issues, various local, state, federal, and international government agencies must resolve privacy and data ownership issues associated with information sharing. The Transportation Security Administration (TSA) has received funds since 2004 to implement this type of flagging program. The Secure Flight program will serve to check passenger information from airline reservation systems against terrorist watch lists, the no-fly list of those people prohibited from boarding commercial airlines, and the list of people that require additional screening. As of late 2008, the air carriers were responsible for checking these lists against reservations. In January 2009, TSA began these checks for one airline and some other flights and will continue to increase their role in these checks until March 2010 when they assumed the function for all domestic flights. Air carriers submit passenger information to TSA through a web portal termed eSecure Flight for checks against the watch lists. TSA will also serve this function for international flights at some later date.

* **mainframe** large computer used by businesses and government agencies to process massive amounts of data; generally faster and more powerful than desktop computers but usually requiring specialized software

Full-Service Travel Management

CRSs have grown in sophistication and are able to offer customer services such as electronic tickets (e-tickets), wireless database access, hotel room reservations, rental car reservations, frequent flyer program mileage, and provision for special meal requests. As of June 1, 2008, the International Air Transport Association (IATA) required that all members issue e-tickets to replace paper tickets, saving $3 billion annually. The systems also provide airline management assistance by addressing financial, administrative, and staffing issues. These include crew management, flight operations, planning and scheduling airplane maintenance, loading aircraft to maintain balance, baggage tracking, decision support for control of overbooking, discount seat allocations, and yield management programs that dynamically adjust the number of special fare seats based on the number of reservations.

Enhancements are made to computerized reservation systems with the understanding that interruptions in service are not acceptable. To be successful, a reservation system must be reliable with a very low failure rate. Hardware and software redundancy for immediate backup in the event of a failure is an absolute necessity.

Impact of the Internet

In the mid–1990s an increasing number of consumers began purchasing airline tickets and other travel needs online. To meet rising customer interest in booking online air travel reservations, computerized reservation systems have evolved into convenient, user-friendly systems that are available via the Internet twenty-four hours per day. The long-established computerized reservation systems are experiencing a gradual technology migration away from traditional mainframe*-based systems and large databases in favor of client server systems with effective web-based interfaces. Search results that previously required an individual to interpret complex codes are now presented in straightforward, easy to understand notations.

In 1996 Sabre launched Travelocity.com, the first of the major comprehensive Internet travel sites. Travelocity.com and other systems, such as Expedia.com, allow consumers to gather information about flights using search criteria such as airline, lowest price, shortest flight, and departure and arrival times. Many airlines offer their own online ticket purchasing services. Also joining in the quest for online reservations is an airline collaborative named Orbitz.com, sponsored by American, United, Delta, Northwest, and Continental Airlines. Many online systems also allow for selection of hotels, rental cars, and other travel necessities, and may offer a discount if, for example, flight and hotel are booked together.

The wealth of customer data collected by these systems is used to target marketing and incentive programs that appeal to specific consumer interests. Internet-based systems offer many of the capabilities of the traditional CRSs, but in a customer-friendly format that is easy to use and understand.

▶ *See also* **Aircraft Flight Control • Internet • Office Automation Systems**

Resources

Books

Campbell-Kelly, Martin. *From Airline Reservations to Sonic the Hedgehog: A History of the Software Industry.* Cambridge, MA: MIT Press, 2004.

United States Department of Homeland Security. *Information Technology Management Needs to Be Strengthened at the Transportation Security Administration.* Washington, D.C.: Dept. of Homeland Security, Office of Inspector General, 2007.

United States Department of Justice, Office of the Inspector General. *Review of the Terrorist Screening Center's Efforts to Support the Secure Flight Program.* Washington, D.C.: U.S. Dept. of Justice, 2005.

Web Sites

Bloomberg Business Week. Harris, Andrew and Tom Korosec. "American Airlines Assails Sabre in Business Data Trial." http://www.businessweek.com/news/2012-10-24/american-airlines-assails-sabre-in-data-business-trial (accessed November 3, 2012).

Expedia. "About Expedia.com." http://www.expedia.com/daily/service/about.asp?rfrr=-950 (accessed November 3, 2012).

Nagesh, Gautham. "TSA Improves Program to Check Airline Passengers against Terrorist List." Nextgov.com (May 18, 2009). http://www.nextgov.com/nextgov/ng_20090518_1856.php (accessed November 3, 2012).

Orbitz. "Overview of Orbitz Worldwide." http://corp.orbitz.com/ (accessed November 3, 2012).

Sabre, Inc. "Sabre Holdings Corporation." http://www.sabre.com/ (accessed November 3, 2012).

Architecture

Architecture, which is generally defined as the art and science of designing and constructing edifices of any kind for human use, is one of the main design activities humankind has developed to modify its environment. Architecture is often cited among the oldest existing professions on Earth. Indeed, the way architects have approached their design problems, realized their designs through construction, and practiced their profession had not changed significantly over many centuries until the emergence of computers.

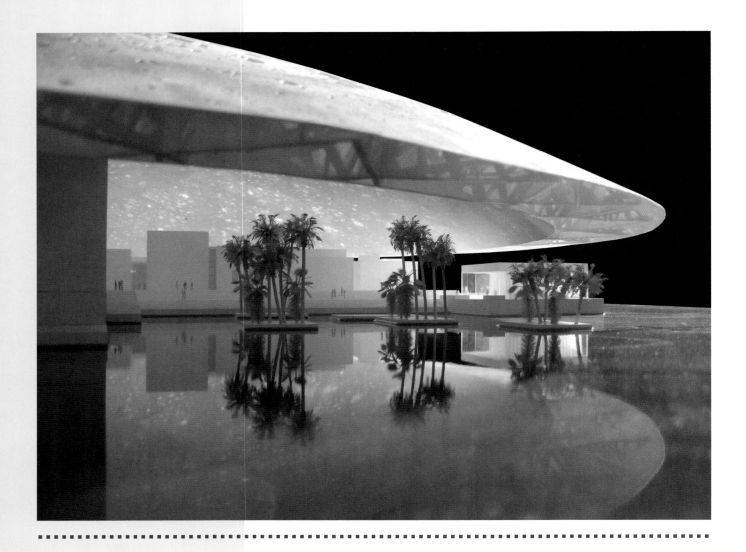

▲

A computer-generated image shows the Emirati version of the famous French the Louvre museum which will be built on a new artificial Island of Saadiyat in the United Arab Emirate of Abu Dhabi. The concept design of a classical museum, which is tipped to bear the Louvre's name and expected to cost 108 million dollars, was presented by representatives of French architect Jean Nouvel on February 1, 2007. © AFP/Getty Images.

Computers typically allow architects to create, store, and retrieve data describing design; to generate design solutions automatically; to test prospective solutions for their applicability; and to collaborate and communicate with clients, constructors, engineers, and other designers during design and construction processes. The early uses of computers in architecture and design did not come directly from the discipline itself, however.

The introduction of computer graphics commenced in the late 1940s through the U.S. Navy's Whirlpool project, a general-purpose flight simulator. However, incorporating computer graphics and usage with design activities took speed only after 1963 when American engineer Ivan E. Sutherland (1938–) developed the Sketchpad system for his PhD. thesis at Massachusetts Institute of Technology (MIT). Sketchpad allowed a mechanical engineer to generate designs by sitting at an interactive graphics terminal. The tool manipulated drawings displayed on the screen by use of a keyboard and a light pen—a selecting tool with a light sensing device, such as a photocell, which generates an electrical pulse to identify the portion of the display being pointed to. Sketchpad cleaned up rough drawings by straightening and connecting lines and constructing geometric patterns; therefore, it was conceived as the first computational drawing assistant. The techniques used in programming Sketchpad inspired the creation of object-oriented programming. Sketchpad was also the first program to feature a completely graphical user interface (GUI).

Although Sketchpad's major application domain was mechanical design, it opened the way to the development of computer-aided design (CAD) tools for architecture and other design disciplines. Most of the early CAD systems were applications for engineering design. Architecture lagged considerably behind, primarily due to economic reasons. As computers developed and the costs became more affordable for architectural firms and university-based research groups, utilization of the technology became an increasingly widespread reality for architects.

Software for Architects

The first milestone applications specifically developed for architectural usage were designed to help with planning and research of a project, using basic algorithm*s to draw shapes, to calculate engineering formulas involved in building design both correctly and automatically, and to help manage conflicting constraints. These computer tools mostly focused on the following areas of architectural design:

- Structural and mechanical calculations, such as those needed to determine what capacity of heating and ventilating equipment should be used;

- Cost estimation to determine the cost impact of design, materials, and construction decisions before the building is constructed;

- Documentation of building specifications (specs) that outline specifically which materials should be used, and how, and in what order for each building component;

- Automatic layout generation to figure out how spaces, equipment, or furniture should be allocated in a given area.

The widespread availability of personal computers starting in the early 1980s marks the beginning of the boom in commercial CAD software for architects. The major impact of these developments has been in the daily routines of how architects work in the office. Computerized drawing, three-dimensional modeling, and graphics editing applications have replaced paper, pen, and rulers, the traditional tool set of an architect. Architectural software offers speed, accuracy, ease of revision-making, and the ability to create rapid prototypes*. Moreover, some allow multiple users to work simultaneously on the same file, facilitating teamwork.

Computer-aided architectural design (CAAD) is a technology intensive field that is strongly dependent on processor capabilities, display technologies, and software and algorithm capabilities of the tools developed.

* **algorithm** a rule or procedure used to solve a mathematical problem—most often described as a sequence of steps

* **prototypes** working models or experimental investigation of proposed systems under development

Software for Architects

Examples of software commonly used by architects include FormZ by AutoDesSys Inc., for architectural three-dimensional modeling and drawing; ProjectBank by Bentley Inc., for versioning and real-time file sharing; AutoDesk 3D Studio Viz by AutoDesk Inc., for visualization, modeling and rendering; and Adobe Photoshop by Adobe Systems Inc., for graphics editing. Architects utilize Revit and AutoCAD for building information modeling. These advanced programs enable architects to draw on giant databases in order to determine variables that they formerly had to measure out physically, spatially, and visually.

Hardware technology has been capable of answering these demands for architects in their office environment with the introduction of devices such as high resolution and color printers, scanners, plotters, and advanced processors. CAAD software differs from typical CAD software in containing objects, techniques, and data specific to architecture as well as an integrated database and knowledge of construction and building parts.

On the construction site, tools increasing accuracy also help advance the quality of building design. For example, hand-held computers make it possible for users to access a central building database, whether they are architects on the building site or in the office. Increased and accurate communication via networked computers means that efficient revision management strategies can be employed to deal with worksite issues. Similarly, laser-scanning technology is used to collect data from existing buildings, which used to be done manually. Very high-resolution three-dimensional models are created using these data; the resulting drawings are used for renovation projects.

Specialized Tools

Architectural design is a special kind of problem-solving process with unique research and analysis needs. Computer-based research can help architects by providing automated decision-making tools. Generative systems, case-based design systems, and performance analysis tools are among the most popular application areas that aim to enhance an architect's design thinking pattern with the use of computer tools. A generative system explores alternative ways of solving the design problem by assembling various design elements in different combinations. Case-based design tools retrieve previously stored design information when a new problem is encountered. They function like a digital library where a previous design becomes the base for solving a new problem. Performance analysis tools complement these design tools by computationally supporting the evaluation of various design solutions according to how they behave under certain conditions such as daylight, noise, weight loads, and more.

Architectural software designers are now focused on developing computational tools and methods that are more streamlined and easier for architects to use. New sketching tools and applications that seamlessly handle the collection, processing, and dissemination of information take the lead in research and development. The pace of change in the computer industry often means that software applications are outdated before disciplines with unique problems such as architectural design can modify the programs to suit their needs. For that reason, there is always a considerable need for new software and devices to serve the needs of the architectural profession.

 See also **CAD/CAM, CA Engineering • Graphic Devices**

Resources

Books

As, Imdat, and Daniel L. Schodek. *Dynamic Digital Representations in Architecture: Visions in Motion.* Abingdon, UK, and New York: Taylor & Francis, 2008.

Bullivant, Lucy. *4dspace: Interactive Architecture.* Chichester, UK: Wiley-Academy, 2005.

Iwamoto, Lisa. *Digital Fabrications: Architectural and Material Techniques.* New York: Princeton Architectural Press, 2009.

Jefferis, Alan, and David A. Madsen. *Architectural Drafting & Design.* 6th ed. Clifton Park, NY: Delmar Cengage Learning, 2011.

Periodicals

Graves, Michael. "Architecture and the Lost Art of Drawing." *The New York Times*, September 2, 2012.

Asimov, Isaac
American Science Fiction Writer
1920–1992

Isaac Asimov was arguably the single most important fiction author to treat the subject of computers. Also one of the preeminent science writers in America during his lifetime, he applied discipline, intellect, smooth storytelling, and insight to all of his work. He wrote or edited more than 500 books and innumerable articles. His novels and stories dazzled the public with a visionary glimpse of the future of computing. He also changed forever the way that robots were imagined as a positive influence in human society.

A paradox in person, he was a gentleman who pretended to be a playboy, a witty and entertaining "life of the party," who led a fairly solitary writer's life—typing 90 words per minute, 10 hours a day, 363 days per year, and selling every word. He was a loving and loyal man, who became estranged from his son and his first wife. He had a profound understanding of the world, rarely traveled, and, though his fiction is filled with spaceships, he never once flew in an airplane.

Asimov was born January 2, 1920 (some sources cite October 4, 1919), in Petrovichi, Russia. He emigrated to the United States with his parents when he was three, and taught himself to read at the age of five. He exhibited an early interest in science and would later write voluminously on the topic. As an academic, Asimov earned a B.S. in chemistry from Columbia University in 1939, an M.A. in 1941, and a Ph.D. in 1948. He taught at Boston University School of Medicine in 1949, was

Russian-born American science-fiction author and biochemist Isaac Asimov (1991). © *Frank Capri/Hulton Archive/ Getty Images.*

associate professor of biochemistry from 1955 to 1979, and became full professor in 1979, although he stopped teaching full time in 1958.

In his work, Asimov was influenced by science writer, historian, and science fiction author H.G. Wells and by Jules Verne, whom he admired as one of the first writers able to make a living while specializing in science fiction. Asimov sought knowledge and success in multiple fields of interest. He almost majored in history, but settled on chemistry. He later published books on history, and his historical view colored both his nonfiction and fiction, especially in the fields of computers and robotics. Asimov's "Foundation" series, with a future human culture spanning 25 million planets, was explicitly modeled on Edward Gibbon's *The Decline and Fall of the Roman Empire.* His fictional "Psychohistory" proposes mathematical prediction of future human events; but his final stories show that he was skeptical of this idea.

Asimov ended his biochemistry professorship to become a full-time writer. As a nonfiction author, he covered dozens of fields, including astronomy, biology, chemistry, math, poetry, music, Sherlock Holmes, the Bible, and William Shakespeare. As a fiction author he concentrated on science fiction and on the mystery/detective genre, sometimes combining both in the same story.

Asimov wrote stories that are as thought-provoking today as they were when he wrote them. Among them is the 8,600-word short story, "A Feeling of Power," first published in 1958. In the work, Asimov predicted widespread use of a handheld programmable calculator, multicolored for civilians, blue-steel for the military. But he set the scenario 400 years in the future, after the art of doing arithmetic by pencil and paper had been lost. In the story a lone genius re-invents manual math, and then commits suicide when the military takes over his research. Interestingly, Asimov's prediction concerning the advent of handheld calculating hardware and software was flawless. But the technology was available within two decades, rather than in 400 years.

The "Multivac" stories of Asimov spin ideas about the infinite future of computing. Among several examples are: "The Last Question," a 5,400-word story from 1956, in which a computer ponders humans' ultimate question, and eventually merges with humanity, acquires god-like power, travels back in time, and creates the universe; "The Machine that Won the War," a 2,100-word story from 1961; and "The Life and Times of Multivac," published in 1975 by the *New York Times Magazine.* In the latter, the Multivac computer benignly takes control of all government and economic power, to save people from themselves.

Asimov once described science fiction as "that branch of literature which is concerned with the impact of scientific advance upon human beings." Asimov took that definition seriously, and wrote many millions of words to prove his point. He is credited with coining the word "robotics" from the word "robot," which was itself coined by the Czech playwright Karel Capek from the Slavic root for "worker," in the 1923 play "R.U.R."

(Rossum's Universal Robots). The word "robotics" is the accepted name for an actual academic and industrial discipline that focuses on the study, design, manufacturing, and application of robots in a variety of settings.

Numerous anthologies of computer and robot stories were published during the 1950s, including Isaac Asimov's *I, Robot,* 1950; Henry Kuttner's *Robots Have No Tails,* 1952; Martin Greenberg's *The Robot and the Man,* 1953; Groff Conklin's *Science Fiction Thinking Machines,* 1954; and Lester del Rey's *Robots and Changelings,* 1957. Yet today, it is Asimov more than any author who comes to mind when the word "robot" is spoken, in fiction or otherwise.

Asimov received numerous awards, including several Hugo Awards and multiple Nebula Awards. His novel *The End of Eternity* (1955) was selected and praised in *Science Fiction: The 100 Best Novels,* by David Pringle.

Asimov's Three Laws of Robotics

Asimov is arguably most famous and influential for what has become known as Asimov's Three Laws of Robotics, with credit to editor John Campbell, who codified them from Asimov's fiction. These edicts are as follows:

1. A robot may not injure a human being or, through inaction, allow a human being to come to harm.

2. A robot must obey the orders given it by human beings, except where such orders would conflict with the First Law.

3. A robot must protect its own existence as long as such protection does not conflict with the First and Second Laws.

Asimov explored the implications of these three laws in clever and meaningful ways, in at least twenty-nine short stories, spread over five short story collections, and in several novels. *The Caves of Steel,* which appeared in 1954, was a murder mystery that sketched a fascinating speculation on the utopian sociology of an automated future. In the 1945 story "Paradoxical Escape," everything people know about physics, astronomy, and "space warp theory" is input to a mechanical computer called the Brain. This robotic "character" invents Faster Than Light travel, but since it would be fatal to humans, the robotic computer wipes blank its memory. Other computers (robots) had also discovered this, as well, but Asimov's First Law of Robotics prohibited them from telling this to humans, as the knowledge—or rather, the likelihood that they would use it—would harm them. They burned out, rather than pass on the dangerous secret.

Isaac Asimov was not an inventor or creator of computer hardware or software. Nevertheless, his fictional portrayals of the relationship between computers and human beings had an impact on the development and integration of computer technology in modern society. His commentaries on the sociological and psychological effects of computerization on human society will, in all likelihood, continue to influence computer science scholars and enthusiasts.

Wells and Verne

H.G. Wells (1866–1946) is remembered for many works of fiction, including *The Invisible Man, The Time Machine,* and *The War of the Worlds.* His contemporary, Jules Verne (1828–1905), is also remembered for numerous works of fiction such as *Around the World in Eighty Days* and *Twenty Thousand Leagues Under the Sea.*

Mutual Admiration Society

It is reported that Isaac Asimov once shook hands on a "treaty" in a New York City cab with Arthur C. Clarke, author of *2001: A Space Odyssey,* in which they agreed that each would tell the public that Isaac Asimov was the world's number one science writer, and Clarke was the world's number one science fiction writer. In truth, the two rank side by side in both fields.

▶ *See also* **Artificial Intelligence • Fiction, Computers In • Robots**

Resources

Books

Asimov, Isaac. *Asimov on Science Fiction*. Garden City, NY: Doubleday, 1981.

Asimov, Isaac. *In Joy Still Felt: Autobiography of Isaac Asimov, 1954–1978*. Garden City, NY: Doubleday, 1980.

Asimov, Isaac. *In Memory Yet Green: Autobiography of Isaac Asimov, 1920–1954*. New York: Doubleday, 1979.

Asimov, Isaac. *Understanding Physics*. New York: Walker, 1966.

Bretnor, Reginald, ed. *Modern Science Fiction; Its Meaning and Its Future*. 2nd ed. Chicago: Advent Publishers, 1979.

Web Sites

Rothstein, Mervyn. "Isaac Asimov, Whose Thoughts and Books Traveled the Universe, Is Dead at 72." *New York Times*, April 7, 1992. http://www.nytimes.com/books/97/03/23/lifetimes/asi-v-obit.html (accessed November 2, 2012).

Astronomy

Astronomy is the scientific study of the universe as a whole and of objects that exist naturally in space, such as the Moon, planets, stars, and galaxies. The Sun is a rather typical star moving around the center of the Milky Way at a distance of 25,000 light years. This Milky Way, our galaxy, is made of hundreds of millions of stars with vast empty regions and diffuse gas in between all held together by gravity. There are at least another hundred billion galaxies in the observable universe.

Every day and night astronomers collect data on these objects in all bands of the electromagnetic spectrum of light. From radio waves through X-rays, small and large telescopes on the ground and in space record immense amounts of data. Analyzing these data is one of the major challenges of modern astronomy. Sophisticated time-dependent, three-dimensional models of astronomical objects and the universe as a whole are now routinely constructed to help astronomers interpret their observations.

In 1823, the president of the Royal Astronomical Society presented the society's gold medal to British mathematician Charles Babbage (1791–1871) for the invention of the first digital calculating machine. The president remarked: "In no department of science or of the arts does this discovery promise to be so eminently useful as in that of astronomy… The practical astronomer is interrupted in his pursuit, is diverted from his task of observation, by the irksome labour of computation;…" Before the first electronic computers became available to astronomers, many observatories employed humans referred to as computers for this "irksome labour of computation."

In the 1950s, theoretical astronomers began tapping the potential of programmable computing systems. Their first programs derived the solution of the restricted three-body problem* (the gravitational interaction of three massive bodies) and also the solution to the equations of stellar* structure. Model stellar atmospheres were also constructed from atomic data to be compared with observations of stellar spectra. The first practical applications were computations of precise apparent star positions and analysis routines transforming photoelectric observational data into meaningful scientific quantities.

By the 1960s, computers had become an integral part of research in astronomy. In particular, progress in the theoretical understanding of stellar structure and evolution was driven largely by results of numerical investigations.

Astronomical research stimulates new advances in computing. A prime example is SETI@home, a project that uses the computing power of idle home and office computers. SETI, which stands for Search for ExtraTerrestial Intelligence, involves the analysis of the many gigabytes of data collected daily at radio telescopes*. A freely distributed screensaver connects to a central data server and collects a small part of these data. When the home computer is otherwise idle, its processing power is used to look for extraterrestrial signals. Upon completion of the analysis, the results of the computation are relayed back to the central server. Although no alien life has been found to date, millions of SETI@home users are contributing to this scientific endeavor.

The rapid growth in computing technologies also enables new areas of astronomical research. The data obtained at telescopes are now all stored in large databases that can be accessed by astronomers around the globe. These archived data repositories act as virtual observatories. Scientists can retrieve (observe) data on the same astronomical objects in many different wave-bands in a very short time without even having access to a telescope. Any relevant scientific studies are cross-referenced with the observed objects and are readily accessible on the Internet worldwide.

Supercomputers* play an important role in astronomy today. Perhaps one of the most important uses of supercomputers is the physical modeling of the origin and evolution of astrophysical objects. Computational astrophysics has become a mature science in the past decades, driven not only by the ever-increasing power of computers but especially by new algorithm*ic breakthroughs. Novel techniques enable scientists to capture vast information about astronomical objects in the grand

Astrophotographer at work. © *Babek Tafreshi/SSPL via Getty Images.*

* **three-body problem** an intractable problem in mechanics that involves the attempts to predict the behavior of three bodies under gravitational effects

* **stellar** pertaining to the stars

* **radio telescopes** telescopes used for astronomical observation that operate on collecting electromagnetic radiation in frequency bands above the visible spectrum

* **supercomputers** very high performance computers, usually comprised of many processors and used for modeling and simulation of complex phenomena, like meteorology

* **algorithm** a rule or procedure used to solve a problem—most often described as a sequence of steps

Numerical Cosmology

Structures in the universe such as stars, galaxies, and clusters of galaxies are thought to arise from the collapse of initially diffuse matter via gravity. Regions in space, which were slightly more dense in the early universe than the average density, started to contract as early as 100 million years after the Big Bang—the beginning of the universe. Small objects formed first and merged into larger and larger galaxies. Cosmologists have been using supercomputers to follow this origin of cosmic structure in sophisticated, three-dimensional modeling. These models follow how gas and the mysterious dark matter, which is thought to constitute 84 percent of all the mass in the universe, clump into galaxies. The model universes are remarkably successful in matching observations, and they give novel insights into the sequence of events that occurred before the universe attained its present complexity.

space and time scales that they span. It has become possible to study in detail such difficult problems as the collision of black holes; the formation of planets, stars, and galaxies; and the large-scale structure of the universe.

In detailed three-dimensional models, computational astrophysicists follow the time evolution of magnetic fields, radiation, gas dynamics, chemistry, gravitational interactions, cosmic ray interactions, and many more physical processes. Physicists can experiment in laboratories to test their theories. Generally, only numerical experiments allow the astronomers and astrophysicists to test their theories in the quest to understand the nature of astronomical objects. However, as in the case of Sandia National Labs' Z Machine, scientists can run physical experiments, rather than just observe stars from afar. The Z Machine is able to produce substances very similar to white dwarf stars—a class of old, dense, faint stars—enabling astrophysicists to probe the properties of stars in a direct way.

Rapidly evolving computing facilities and sensitive observational technologies also have enabled astronomers to observe astronomical objects at new, finer resolutions. One example of these new technologies put to use is the push for the observation of planets outside Earth's solar system. Since the late 1990s, astronomers have developed new ways to detect extrasolar planets (also known as exoplanets). Like Earth, exoplanets do not shine with their own light, and are small and dim compared to the much larger and brighter stars they orbit.

In November 2007, astronomers announced the discovery of a distant solar system that resembles our own more closely than any found since the first extrasolar planet was confirmed in 1988. The star at the center of this solar system, named 55 Cancri, is 41 light-years away and is circled by at least five planets. The newly discovered system resembles our own in having a more massive planet farther out from the star and less-massive planets closer in. However, even the smallest of the 55 Cancri planets is several dozen times larger than Earth.

As of September 2012, more than 800 exoplanets had been discovered, via several types of detection. Some exoplanets are massive enough to exert a strong gravitational force on the star they orbit, causing the star to wobble back and forth. Others are large enough to block light from the star as the exoplanet passes between the star and the earth. Still others are detected by direct observation. Each of these techniques require the finest precision, which was not feasible until the last few years of the twentieth century.

These advancements and others in computing technologies fuel modern astronomical research and will continue to lead to profound new insights into the nature, origin, and evolution of the cosmos and the complex structures within.

 See also **Navigation • Physics • Weather Forecasting**

Resources

Books

Amico, Paola, et al, eds. *Scientific Detectors for Astronomy: The Beginning of a New Era.* Dordrecht, The Netherlands, and New York: Kluwer Academic Publishers, 2004.

Foust, Jeff, and Ron LaFon. *Astronomer's Computer Companion.* San Francisco: No Starch Press, 2000.

Wilson, Thomas L., Kristen Rohlfs, and Susanne Hüttemeister. *Tools of Radio Astronomy.* 5th ed. New York: Springer, 2009.

Web Sites

Astronomy Online. Astronomy Tools—Computers. http://astronomyonline.org/Science/Computers.asp (accessed October 9, 2012).

Exoplanet.eu. "The Extrasolar Planets Encyclopaedia." http://exoplanet.eu/ (accessed October 6, 2012).

ATM Machines

There was a time when people had to wait in line during a bank's limited hours to get money from their own accounts. The advent of the automated teller machine (ATM) changed the way consumers handle their money. The ATM also shows how technology can change traditional business and consumer practices.

People using an ATM machine.
© *NICHOLAS KAMM/AFP/ Getty Images.*

* **operating system** a set of programs which control all the hardware of a computer and provide user and device input/output functions

* **cathode ray tube (CRT)** a glass enclosure that projects images by directing a beam of electrons onto the back of a screen

* **graphical user interface (GUI)** an interface that allows computers to be operated through pictures (icons) and mouse-clicks, rather than through text and typing

* **interface** a boundary or border between two or more objects or systems; also a point of access

The evolution of the ATM reflects the technology of the time. As personal computers (PCs) and networks became more sophisticated, the ATM followed. The first ATMs were proprietary (i.e., the private property of a single individual or institution) and stand-alone (i.e., independent devices that did not connect to a network). These original ATMs were not PC-based; they did not have a PC processor or hard drive. They were based on a proprietary processing chip that was developed by the ATM manufacturer. Because the first generation ATMs were stand-alone devices, they had to be updated each day with account balances from the host bank. The magnetic strip on the back of the bank card recorded the customer's activity for the day to maintain an accurate account balance between updates from the host.

In the 1970s, the online network became part of the ATM. With a modem and phone line, the ATM could connect to the bank's computers to verify account balances. Banks realized they could reduce their hardware and expand their reach through shared networks (i.e., the once private networks of one bank communicated to another bank's network). Through the decade, these networks expanded regionally and later consolidated their interests into national networks, such as Cirrus and Plus.

Inside most ATMs in the early twenty-first century are PCs with an Intel processor chip running IBM's OS/2 Warp operating system*. Software and hardware developed by ATM manufacturers connects all of the peripheral devices of the ATM: card reader, currency dispenser, receipt printer, depository, and optional equipment such as an electronic audit printer or camera. At the application or software level, however, ATMs remain proprietary. Vendors have their own transaction processing language to direct the interaction of customer and machine, pass messages to and from the host processor, and handle any errors.

The input device for an ATM is a card reader, which initially identifies the account. A keypad is used to enter passwords and select transactions. A depository allows the user to deposit cash or checks. Some ATMs have a camera to record transactions, a useful tool to combat fraud. The output devices include a currency dispenser, receipt printer, speaker, electronic audit printer, and display screen.

Displays on some early ATMs used plastic letter wheels that would spin and form words. By borrowing the cathode ray tube (CRT)* technology from the television, text messages could direct a customer through the steps of a transaction. Early-twenty-first-century ATMs use a graphical user interface (GUI)* with sophisticated color display and dialogue.

The latest movement in ATM technology is to use a browser-based interface*, similar to what is seen on an Internet web page. This type of ATM connects to a host computer through a web server. The trend is moving away from proprietary application software to become more vendor independent.

Technology was not the only driving force behind the ATM phenomena. Two other changes created the incentive and opportunity.

First, the two largest regional networks changed operating procedures in 1996 and permitted surcharges on foreign transactions (i.e., transactions initiated on ATMs not owned by your bank could be charged with a service fee). Second, a federal law in the same year eliminated the requirement of a federal bank charter to establish an ATM. This allowed independent service organizations (ISOs) to enter the market.

Credit card companies introduced a new product, the debit card, to add utility for bank customers that, in effect, worked against the ATM. The debit card, like a credit card, allows one to purchase a product or service. Unlike the credit card, however, the funds for the purchase move immediately from the user's account to the merchant's account. Debit card users can also request additional cash at the time of purchase. The use of credit and debit cards and shopping on the Internet do not require constant trips to the ATM for physical currency.

These changes have affected the number of ATMs and the volume of activity in clear trends. In 1995 there were around 120,000 ATMs in the United States. By 1999 the estimate was 220,000. By 2012, that number has increased to 445,000. Despite the increased number of ATMs, ATM use is on the decline because of the increasing popularity of online banking. According to a 2009 survey, online banking had surpassed ATMs as the preferred method of banking for respondents under the age of 55.

An ATM's primary function is to dispense cash, but adding new features to an ATM can help challenge debit and credit cards. Features, such as selling stamps or display advertising, can be incorporated into the machine. New software features created by ATM vendors along with the development of web-enabled ATMs will make ticket purchases for concerts, theater, or sporting events possible through the ATM. An ATM receipt could be exchanged at the box office for the actual tickets. A web-enabled ATM could execute electronic trades over the Internet.

ATMs in convenience stores have already started to issue money orders, wire money, pay bills, print maps, deliver stock prices, and arrange video rentals. The applications that power the ATM continue to evolve. While technology and legislation spurred the growth of ATMs, technology, new applications, and a trend toward a cash-less society will certainly change and enhance their utility in the future.

ATM Hacking

Hackers are creating software for ATMs that will obtain account information, allowing them to withdraw cash from the machines. Malware, or malicious software, is software that is installed onto a computer without the owner's or administrator's knowledge in order to damage or infiltrate the system. A particular type of ATM malware, found on twenty ATMs running Windows XP in Eastern Europe in 2009, collects transaction information as well as PINs and contains instructions to print this information with the use of a special card. Unlike a computer virus, the malware is not self-replicating. The exact method of infection is not known,

ATM Card Thievery

Most people have not experienced problems using their ATM cards at ATMs. However, some ATM users have fallen prey to thieves who steal their information and raid their bank accounts. One of the ways that criminals gain access to bank accounts is by placing hidden cameras near ATM machines and recording people as they enter their PINs (personal identification numbers). Then the thieves use a device to record data from the magnetic stripe on their victims' ATM cards in order to create fake cards. Armed with the replica cards and PINs, the criminals gain access to accounts and withdraw funds. Thieves have also attempted to use cellular phones to take pictures of cards or record video of people entering their pins to obtain the necessary information.

but it is assumed that an ATM technician or keyholder for an ATM must install the malware. Inserting a special card into the ATM can print the information, transfer it to a storage device, and instruct the machine to dispense its cash holdings, which can be as high as $600,000.

▶ *See also* **IBM Corporation • Interactive Systems • User Interfaces**

Resources

Web Sites

Bowen, Jim. "How ATMs Work." http://money.howstuffworks.com/personal-finance/banking/atm.htm (accessed October 22, 2012).

Memphis Business Journal "Survey: Online Banking on the Rise" http://www.bizjournals.com/memphis/stories/2009/09/21/daily12.html (accessed October 11, 2012).

Zetter, Kim. "New ATM Malware Captures PINS and Cash—Updated." *Wired* (June 4, 2009) http://www.wired.com/threatlevel/2009/06/new-atm-malware-captures-pins-and-cash/ (accessed October 22, 2012).

BC

Biology

Computers play a significant role in biological research. An American physicist and biologist, Harold Morowitz (1927–) said, "computers are to biology what mathematics is to physics." Most people understand that computers are used to produce spreadsheets, help analyze data, graph results of experiments, and prepare final reports for presentations. Although computers are workhorses in these areas, computers and the Internet are considered vital in other ways to many different fields of biology and research. Computers and the Internet make it possible for researchers at different institutions or in different countries to collaborate on projects as well as making their research publications available through scientific journal websites. Many instruments used in biological research require a computer for operation of the machines and to receive results for analysis. In some cases, computer science and biology (along with chemistry, physics, and mathematics) are woven so tightly together they have become inseparable.

Scientific Organizations

The Centers for Disease Control and Prevention, or CDC, is a U.S. government agency headquartered in Atlanta, Georgia. The goal of the CDC is to protect the health and safety of U.S. citizens at home, work, and abroad through the detection, treatment, and prevention of health-related issues. The CDC has an integral role in the tracking of infectious diseases and uses computers in a multitude of ways.

This is illustrated by the Division of Parasitic Diseases (DPD), a branch of the CDC. The DPD extends knowledge and control of parasites and parasitic diseases primarily through the use of the Internet and extensive computer databases. At the agency's Internet web site, thousands of known parasites can be viewed (including microscopic slides). This aids in the identification of parasitic organisms and the diseases they cause.

The DPD supplies information to health care workers on how to recognize and treat possible cases of parasite-caused disease. Health care professionals can also find out how to get and submit samples for a diagnosis. Experts at the DPD will answer e-mailed questions and review digital images of slides of suspected parasites. Confirmed cases of parasitic infection are reported back to the DPD and are added to its extensive databases. Through the use of statistical analysis, trends of parasitic infections are tracked. Armed with this information, experts at the CDC are able to identify populations vulnerable to parasites. Steps can then

Graduate student looks at enlarged cell on a computer screen. © *AP Images/ RICH PEDRONCELLI.*

*algorithm a rule or procedure used to solve a mathematical problem—most often described as a sequence of steps

be taken to find infected individuals for treatment and limit exposure to others, keeping people healthy.

Originally, the CDC was founded to eliminate malaria. It now tracks a multitude of infectious diseases, from AIDS to the common flu. In 2001, the CDC was engaged in building a National Electronic Disease Surveillance System, which through the Internet creates a broad-based and comprehensive system linking local and national health departments regardless of differing computer platforms and software. This new system will allow faster detection of and more rapid intervention against public health threats.

The National Institutes of Health, or NIH, is another U.S. agency that extensively uses computers and the Internet in its collection and application of biological information. The National Center for Biotechnology Information (NCBI), a subdivision of the NIH, maintains expansive databases on their computers, including known gene sequences, for molecular biology researchers all over the world. The largest biomedical research facility in the world, the NIH is headquartered in Bethesda, Maryland.

Bioinformatics

One field that has proved essential to gene sequencing is *bioinformatics.* Researchers in this field develop algorithm*s and software to allow enormous amounts of biological information to be processed. Bioinformatics is essential to molecular biologists working on breaking genetic codes.

With only ten percent of the world's bacteria identified, gene sequencing is also being used to examine the deoxyribonucleic acid (DNA) of various bacteria. Scientists expect to use this method to identify previously undiscovered bacteria in what have always been considered inhospitable environments around the world, such as thermal springs, oil fields, or areas deep under the Earth's crust. Research on this amazing diversity of life contributes to humankind's knowledge of biological processes, and holds much promise for future researchers.

Bioengineering and Biomedical Engineering

Bioengineering is a new study that brings the science of engineering into the science of cell and molecular biology. Bioengineers use computers to study the structure and processes of living cells and organisms. The advances from bioengineering are seen in fields as diverse as manufacturing, chemical industries, defense industries, electronics, and agriculture. For example, through bioengineering one can detect harmful pollutants in the environment and harmful microorganisms in food.

Biomedical engineering, however, draws from many fields of engineering, such as electrical, mechanical, and chemical engineering. It is used to advance medicine and health care. Computers are used to analyze the functions of cells, and then to design mechanical reproductions to master that function. Computers are needed to use the components that result. One well-known example of biomedical engineering is the artificial heart.

Another result of biomedical engineering is the mechanization of lab tests. Routine lab tests used to be conducted by hand. The process of, for instance, checking a complete blood cell count required several time-consuming steps. Frequently the test was repeated to rule out possible lab error. Through biomedical engineering, the testing processing is done quickly, efficiently, and with very little likelihood of lab error. A blood sample is marked with the patient's bar code* moments after the blood is drawn from the patient. Once it is put in the automated machine, the computer takes over the processing. In some tests, computerized image analysis is used for a definitive diagnosis. The computer then directs the test results where needed. The use of automated lab tests lowers costs while vastly increasing efficiency, speed, and accuracy.

Environmental Biology

Computers are also valuable in environmental studies. Conservation agencies, such as the U.S. Fish and Wildlife Service, use computers in several ways. One key to successful conservation efforts is effective communication with local conservation groups, state officials, and local legislative bodies (who frequently decide upon important zoning issues). Through the Internet, a variety of educational materials are easily accessible.

Although the U.S. Fish and Wildlife Service's goal is to standardize equipment and provide reference material and electronic communication within the service, particularly to remote field offices, these efforts are seriously hampered by lack of funding for equipment upgrades. In other conservation efforts, computers are being used to model natural ecological systems for study. Satellite remote sensing, such as imagery and telemetry*, make regional and landscape mapping easier, more accurate,

* **bar code** a graphical number representation system where alphanumeric characters are represented by vertical black and white lines of varying width

* **telemetry** the science of taking measurements of something and transmitting the data to a distant receiver

Call to Action

In the fall of 2001, letters containing deadly anthrax spores were sent through the U.S. Postal Service to government and media employees. To bring authoritative information to the public as quickly as possible, the CDC put its web site into action. It posted information, including: facts and frequently asked questions about anthrax, smallpox, antibiotics, and vaccines; fact sheets on other types of biological and chemical agents; articles on treatment options and research findings; and instructions on how to handle mail. In addition, the web site offered the medical community information on how to test for anthrax exposure, what treatment options are available, and how to create a bioterrorism readiness plan. <http://www.bt.cdc.gov>

and cost effective. This helps environmental biologists gather information more effectively.

Researchers at the University of Ottawa in Canada are using computer modeling and satellite images to study the range of malaria-causing mosquitoes in Africa in an effort to understand and attempt to prevent the spread of this disease. Approximately 500 million people contract malaria from mosquitoes each year. The research is based on a theory that climate change is expanding the range of these mosquitoes into regions where human populations have little or no immunity. Nets treated with insecticide are effective means of malaria prevention. By providing nets for 60 percent of a community, the mosquito populations will decline and can result in as high as a 90 percent reduction in malaria transmission. By studying digital images of the terrain, computers can reveal areas with vegetation in which mosquitoes likely thrive. These images allow researchers to target areas that would most benefit from nets for reduced malaria transmission.

With the growing sophistication of research needs and resources and the increased use of the Internet to gather, share, and analyze scientific data, evidence suggests that computers will continue to play a vital part in the study of biology in its many applications.

 See also **Molecular Biology • Physics • Scientific Visualization**

Resources

Books

Campbell, Malcolm and Laurie J. Heyer *Discovering Genomics, Proteomics and Bioinformatics.* 2nd ed. San Francisco: CHSL Press, 2007.

Friedman, Yali *Building Biotechnology: Starting, Managing, and Understanding Biotechnology Companies.* Washington, DC: Logos Press, 2008.

Web Sites

Centers for Disease Control and Prevention (CDC). "Home Page." http://www.cdc.gov (accessed November 4, 2012).

Centers for Disease Control and Prevention (CDC), Division of Parasitic Diseases (DPD). "Identification and Diagnosis of Parasites of Public Health Concern." http://www.dpd.cdc.gov/dpdx/HTML/Aboutdpdx.htm (accessed November 4, 2012).

Stanford Center for Molecular and Genetic Medicine (CMGM). "Bioinformatics Resource." http://cmgm.stanford.edu (accessed November 4, 2012).

CAD/CAM, CA Engineering

At first a seemingly indecipherable collection of symbols, these acronyms are fairly easy to understand once one realizes that each "CA" stands for Computer-Aided (or Assisted). Thus, CAD is Computer-Aided Design; CAM stands for Computer-Aided Manufacturing; and the last acronym denotes Computer-Aided Engineering. Although presently interrelated technologies, they evolved separately.

The earliest to develop was CAD, originally termed Computer-Aided Drafting, a terminology still in use by approximately half the users of this technology mainly in the architectural, consulting, construction, mapping, and public utility fields. In many instances, the acronym is presented as CADD, signifying both applications. Invented by American engineer Ivan Sutherland, CAD was outlined in his seminal 1961 PhD dissertation. Sutherland described a computerized sketchpad in which he used a CRT* display and light pen to construct basic geometric entities such as points, lines, and arcs. Sutherland's initial concept resulted in the first commercially available CAD systems in the mid–1970s—systems that have evolved over the following decades, developing into the CAD software in use today.

* **CRT** the acronym for cathode ray tube, which is a glass enclosure that projects images by directing a beam of electrons onto the back of a screen

Airplane designed using CAD software.
© *Mark Elias/Bloomberg via Getty Images.*
▼

* **vector** an abstraction used in the physical sciences to model a quantity that has a magnitude (size) and a direction of action

* **raster** a line traced out by a beam of electrons as they strike a cathode ray tube (CRT)

In computer-aided drafting, the mouse, or "puck," on a digitizing tablet attached to the computer is used to trace or draw lines that are stored in the computer as graphic primitives. Combined with a digitizing tablet, which is basically an electronic drafting board, CAD represents the primary means for entering paper map documents into the computer. It should be noted that an alternative means is a scanner—basically a large, spatially accurate fax machine. However, the digital data produced by these two techniques is quite different. Digitizing (or drafting) with CAD produces vector* (points and lines) digital data while a scanner provides raster* data, which is essentially an accurate digital picture.

The basic drafting capabilities of CAD were supplemented through the addition of software tools allowing for the production of precise engineering drawings of intricate designs, such as complex machine parts or electronic circuit boards. A key development in CAD was the introduction of the graphic display terminal, which not only offered dramatically real displays of objects but also allowed the designer to interact graphically rather than through the keyboard or digitizer. In such a manner, designers could concentrate on decisions concerning the objects represented on the screen rather than focusing on the drawings. Indeed, the development of computer graphics is closely linked to that of CAD. Thus, in the manufacturing arena, CAD became an integral part of the design process, offering efficient and accurate creation, modification, analysis, and optimization of designs.

Computer-aided design applications enabling precise two-dimensional and three-dimensional designs to be implemented and graphically displayed are now routine parts of the manufacturing process for a wide variety of products in many fields, such as aerospace and automotive engineering. They are employed by such companies as Boeing, Ford, Toyota, and Volvo. AutoCAD and Microstation software are two of the standard products for industrial strength CAD for both two-dimensional and three-dimensional drafting and design.

If a design exists in the computer, then the next logical step would be to have the computer drive machine tools to produce the object indicated by the design. This is how CAM, or computer-aided manufacturing, was created. Since the mid-1980s, CAM has been closely linked with CAD, and the union is represented by the single acronym CAD/CAM. Although CAM actually includes various applications in the manufacturing process, such as production scheduling and inventory control, it is best illustrated by the integrated CAD/CAM systems within which a design can be developed and the manufacturing process controlled. In such a union, CAD software creates CNC/NC (computer numeric control/numeric control) codes, which are coded numerical instructions for automated control of machine tools such as lathes and mills, and are similar to the programming codes that drive plotters. Originally, paper tapes were produced to drive the machine tools, but newer tools are connected directly to the computer, so that the design and manufacturing process is seamless and computer-aided. This has resulted in faster, more efficient, and more accurate procedures.

A good illustration of the versatility offered by an integrated CAD/CAM approach is the design and development of printed circuit boards. A schematic* is created, using interactive graphics, to recall symbols from a database and place them in the appropriate locations. Once the design is completed, a circuit analysis program is used to test and verify the performance of the circuit board. The final step is to produce a photographic transparency directly from the CAD/CAM system, which is then used to manufacture the circuit board.

This basic feat of engineering, integrating computer capabilities with manual design, has recently been perfected by the integration of complex mathematical functions or analyses, such as finite element modeling and analysis, computational fluid dynamics*, boundary element analysis, and rigid body analysis, into the engineering design process, thereby establishing the field of computer-aided engineering.

CA engineering can basically be considered a set of numerical tools and processes to conduct numeric simulations. A good example is the analytic simulation* of the aerodynamics* of a body in a wind tunnel. Such an approach is used, for example, to make sure that a designed part is strong enough, or to simulate the operation of a designed feature before its manufacture. By providing analytic prototypes in the manufacturing process, CAE has reduced the need for physical prototypes, thereby speeding up the production process. Expert systems are also being added to extend the capabilities of the process. One such system presently under development is intelligent CAD, or IntCAD.

A practical application of these technologies occurred when the U.S. Civil War submarine *H. L. Hunley* was raised off the coast of Charleston, South Carolina, in October 2000. CAD and CAE techniques were used in this historic project to assess the submarine's structural weaknesses and to test and simulate various methods for raising the vessel. The final and successful method, fully tested in the system before application, was to place thirty-two nylon slings under the submarine, support it with a steel structure from above, and squirt foam along the side of the vessel to replace the sand that had supported it for more than a century.

 See also **Display Devices • Graphic Devices • Process Control**

Resources

Books

Visitainer, Randal, David Watts, et al. *CAE Methods and Their Application to Truck Design.* Warrendale, PA: Society of Automotive Engineers, 1997.

Zecher, Jack. *Computer Graphics for CAD/CAM Systems.* New York: Marcel Dekker, 1994.

Hunt for the Hunley

Scientists were eager to raise the Confederate submarine, the *H. L. Hunley*, from its watery grave near Charleston, South Carolina. Sunk in 1864 during the Civil War, the sub held the remains of eight sailors when it was raised in 2000. The *Hunley*, weighing 7.5 tons, disappeared after sinking the Union's U.S.S. *Housatonic* on February 14, 1864. The sub's location was discovered in 1995 and efforts began to recover the vessel in order to learn more about the people and technology of that era.

* **schematic** a diagrammatic representation of a system, showing logical structure without regard to physical constraints

* **fluid dynamics** the science and engineering of the motion of gases and liquids

* **analytic simulation** modeling of systems by using mathematical equations (often differential equations) and programming a computer with them to simulate the behavior of the real system

* **aerodynamics** the science and engineering of systems that are capable of flight

* **bandwidth** a measure of the frequency component of a signal or the capacity of a communication channel to carry signals

Periodicals

Franken, Stephanie. "Ansys Quietly Builds Business in Computer Aided Design." *Pittsburgh Post Gazette*, May 31, 2001.

Cell Phones

Of all consumer electronic devices ever invented, cellular telephones (cell phones or mobiles) have been the most popular in terms of the number of devices sold as a function of time. In early twenty-first century, cell phones have become more prevalent than wired phones (land lines).

The concept behind the working of a cell phone is based on what is known as *frequency reuse.* There is only so much of available *electromagnetic spectrum,* or frequency band, available for transmitting a voice call with a cell phone and this has to be shared by many users. Each voice conversation requires a certain amount of bandwidth*, which is a chunk of the available frequency band. In order to support the large number of subscribers, the service providers split the frequency band into smaller sub-bands and spread them over a given area. They install radio transmitters, called base stations that serve an area called a cell. Each cell utilizes a sub-band of the spectrum. Two cells that are sufficiently far apart can use the same sub-bands because radio signals lose their strength with distance and do not interfere. Thus, frequency sub-bands are spatially reused by the creation of several cells supported by base stations. The name "cellular telephony" comes from this architecture, but mobile phone-based communication is more popularly known as wireless communication technology.

▶ Mobile phone usage worldwide increases at high levels annually. © *AP Images/ Wang yunlong - Imaginechina.*

Each base station is connected to a mobile switching center that handles cell phone calls and also performs a very important function called mobility management. If a user makes a phone call to a wired telephone, a telephone switch will know how to route the call because the telephone device is fixed. If the caller is caller a cell phone, there must be a mechanism that keeps track of where the cell phone is and accordingly route the call. This mechanism is called mobility management. It is performed by the mobile switching center, with the assistance of two databases called the home location register and the visitor location register.

Every cell phone is registered with a home location register in its home calling area. For a call to a cell phone, the telephone switch contacts the mobile switching center associated with the home location register. The home location register contains information about the visitor location register with which the mobile phone is currently registered while roaming. From this point, the call is routed to the mobile switching center associated with the visitor location register and handled from there. As the person with the cell phone moves, the cell phone constantly updates its location with the visitor location register, which in turn updates the home location register upon a change in location.

Another important aspect of managing mobility is what is known as the process of *handoff.* As users move with their cell phones, they cross the coverage of one base station and enter the coverage area of another—that is they cross cell boundaries. At this point, the cell phone should switch its connection from the old base station to the new base station. This procedure is called handoff and it involves measuring and comparing the received signal strengths from multiple base stations.

Within a cell, multiple users may conduct phone conversations simultaneously, using the available frequency sub-band. They may do this in several different ways. The earliest technique was to further divide the sub-band into smaller chunks of frequency and use one chunk for one conversation. This is called *frequency division multiplexing* and was used in the analog cellular service first implemented in the early 1980s by AT&T. This was also adopted in Europe by several countries, each using its own standard. These systems were called the first generation cellular telephone systems. The frequency division multiplexing technique was inefficient and the resulting capacity to support subscribers was smaller than desired.

In the 1990s, there was a trend to move to *digital standards* to enhance the capacity of cellular systems. In Europe, all the countries agreed upon a common digital standard called the global system for mobile communications (GSM). In the United States, two major initial standards emerged called the IS-136 and IS-95 standards. These were the second-generation cellular telephone systems. They were replaced by latter-generation GSM and CDMA2000/WCDMA technologies.

The GSM and IS-136 standards are based on *time-division multiplexing* where users appear to talk continuously, but their signals are transmitted one after another. That is, their signals are separated in time and these are commonly called the TDMA (Time Division Multiple Access) standards. The IS-95 standard employed *code-division multiplexing* where the signals of all users are transmitted simultaneously using the same frequency band. Each user is assigned a unique code that is designed to enable easy separation of signals with minimum interference. This is called the CDMA (Code Division Multiple Access) standard and it has proved to provide a significant increase in capacity and other additional benefits. In the 2010s, there is a global evolutionary trend toward fourth generation (4G) systems, where most cell phones use some variation of GSM—or more limitedly in North America, CDMA—technologies.

Cell phones are becoming much more than simply tools used for voice conversations. The most modern "smartphones" are equipped with full Internet and World Wide Web access. GPS and app-enabled smartphones allow for a user experience tailored to specific interests, functions, and locations. People also use smartphones as portable music players and streaming media devices. Text messaging or short-messaging service (SMS) is extremely popular. This enables almost instantaneous exchange of very short messages between two cell phones. In summary, the cell phone is becoming a pivotal part of popular culture worldwide.

Additional Information

A major 2005 medical study found that driving while talking on a cell phone makes a driver four times more likely to be hospitalized by a traffic accident, and that headset use does not alter this statistic. Driving while texting has been shown to impair drivers as much or more than driving whilst intoxicated by alcohol (drunk driving).

 See also **Internet • Telecommunications • Wireless Technology**

Resources

Books

Goggin, Gerard. *Cell Phone Culture: Mobile Technology in Everyday Life.* London and New York: Routledge, 2006.

Web Sites

How Stuff Works. "How Cell Phones Work." http://www.howstuffworks. com/cell-phone.htm (accessed November 5, 2012).

Time. "A Photographic History of the Cell Phone." http://www.time. com/time/photogallery/0,29307,1636836,00.html (accessed November 5, 2012).

Chess Playing

The ancient, intellectually challenging game of chess originated in India and is played by two players on a checkerboard consisting of sixty-four squares, with thirty-two pieces divided equally by color. Each piece has its own role and ability to perform a unique function on the board. The game has enjoyed steady popularity and minor rule changes over centuries of time. With the development of computer technology, more and more players were able to improve their skills by playing against computers, using information stored in computer databases and even using computers as personal trainers.

How Chess Computers Work

There is no principal difference between a chess computer and a regular one. The computer programs evaluate chess positions on a virtual chessboard and select the best moves according to the specific criteria. Usually a computer calculates a numerical score for each position it evaluates, based on four variables. The highest score determines the move. These four variables include:

■ *Pieces.* Each piece is assigned a value at the start of the game. For example, a pawn gets a value of 1; a queen 9. These values may also be modified later as the game progresses.

■ *Position.* The computer observes all of the chess pieces on the chessboard and assigns them unit values based on how much territory they are able to attack.

■ *King safety.* The computer evaluates both kings' positions and attempts to put its own king on a safer square and to force its opponent's king to a more vulnerable square.

Visitors watch a chess game on a giant laptop. © *JOHN MACDOUGALL/AFP/ Getty Images.*

Figure 1. Possible moves when starting a chess game. *Reproduced by permission of Gale, a part of Cengage Learning.*

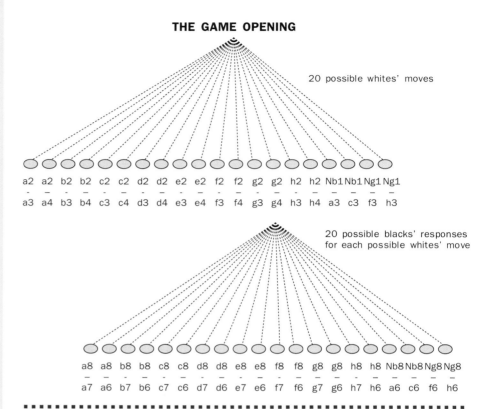

THE GAME OPENING

20 possible whites' moves

| a2 | a2 | b2 | b2 | c2 | c2 | d2 | d2 | e2 | e2 | f2 | f2 | g2 | g2 | h2 | h2 | Nb1 | Nb1 | Ng1 | Ng1 |
| a3 | a4 | b3 | b4 | c3 | c4 | d3 | d4 | e3 | e4 | f3 | f4 | g3 | g4 | h3 | h4 | a3 | c3 | f3 | h3 |

20 possible blacks' responses for each possible whites' move

| a8 | a8 | b8 | b8 | c8 | c8 | d8 | d8 | e8 | e8 | f8 | f8 | g8 | g8 | h8 | h8 | Nb8 | Nb8 | Ng8 | Ng8 |
| a7 | a6 | b7 | b6 | c7 | c6 | d7 | d6 | e7 | e6 | f7 | f6 | g7 | g6 | h7 | h6 | a6 | c6 | f6 | h6 |

* **artificial intelligence (AI)** a branch of computer science dealing with creating computer hardware and software to mimic the way people think and perform practical tasks

* **minimax algorithm** an approach to developing an optimal solution to a game or contest where two opposing systems are aiming at mutually exclusive goals

* **alpha beta pruning** a technique that under certain conditions offers an optimal way to search through data structures termed "trees"

* **supercomputer** a very high performance computer, usually comprised of many processors and used for modeling and simulation of complex phenomena, like meteorology

■ *Tempo.* The computer seeks to place its pieces on the intended squares to carry out its current plan faster than its opponents can counter.

The most popular opening chess move for the player of the white pieces is "e2-e4," which means the Whites move the pawn directly in front of the King 2 squares forward. This is only one of twenty possible first moves the Whites can make. Blacks' pieces have the same number of possible responses. So, there are 400 possible combinations for the first move alone. As the game continues, the number of possible positions keeps growing exponentially. All these possible moves may be presented in the form of a tree.

It is impossible for any computer to calculate all possible moves by brute computational force. Therefore, a computer estimates positions for only several moves ahead. Moreover, there are many well-developed artificial intelligence (AI)* strategies, such as minimax algorithm* or a technique termed alpha beta pruning*, that limit the search for the best move to an analysis of the most promising positions. In addition, computers use extensive databases of previous games for openings and endgames. For the endgames, when the number of pieces and thus the number of possible moves is reduced significantly, computers are able to calculate all possible positions when five or fewer pieces are left on a chessboard.

First-class chess computers also require very powerful hardware. IBM's Deep Blue supercomputer* uses a total of 512 microprocessors working in parallel to break down and analyze chess positions. Each processor simultaneously calculates and evaluates one possible sequence of moves, enabling the computer to examine 200 million positions a second!

History

The idea of a machine capable of playing chess was born long before computers. Historical annals mention Hungarian author Baron Wolfgang von Kempelen (1734–1804), who traveled around Europe in the eighteenth century with his Maezal Chess Automaton, nicknamed the Turk. The machine looked like a marionette that was able to make chess moves. The trick, of course, was that a tiny chess master was hidden inside the box.

The connection between modern computers and chess games began with a prophecy of British mathematician Alan Turing (1912–1954) that machines would compete in all purely intellectual fields including chess. Turing specified the first computer program for chess as early as 1947. American mathematician Claude Shannon (1916–2001) estimated the number of possible computer positions and proposed basic strategies for restricting the number of possibilities to be considered in a game of chess.

The first computer program for a full-fledged game of chess was written in 1957, and since 1966 computers have been playing in human chess tournaments, gradually increasing their rating and the level of tournaments over the years. Russian scientist and former world chess champion Mikhail Botvinnik (1911–1995) contributed to the development of computer algorithms for playing chess and to the creation of the Kaissa chess-playing computer program. Kaissa won the world computer chess championship in 1974.

As the result of a growing population of computer chess programmers the International Computer Chess Association (ICCA) was founded in 1977. The same year was marked with the first defeat of a grandmaster of chess by a computer. Since 1990, computers have occasionally beat the top players and even Russian world champions Anatoly Karpov (1951–) and Garry Kasparov (1963–). In 1997, the Deep Blue computer—coached by a research team of International Business Machines (IBM) scientists and engineers, and a grandmaster and U.S. chess champion Joel Benjamin (1964–)—defeated the reigning world champion (Garry Kasparov) in a classic chess match against a computer for the first time. Kasparov had won a prior match in 1996. Kasparov developed a method of playing chess termed Advanced Chess in 1998 in which a human-computer team played against another human-computer team. In 2005, British chess player Michael Adams (1971–) (ranked seventh at the time) was defeated by Hydra, a chess computer composed of custom hardware and sixty-four processors. In late 2006, the current world chess champion, Russian Vladimir Kramnik (1975–), was defeated by a German chess program termed Deep Fritz after a match in 2002 that ended in a draw. A number of computer programs now have a chess rating comparable with the top human players. One chess computer, Rybka, has an estimated rating (3200) exceeding the highest human rating (2851).

Computer Games

One of the founders of computer science and a leading scientist of Bell Laboratories, American mathematician Claude Shannon (1916–2001), estimated the number of possible computer games as 10^{120}. In comparison, there are thought to be 10^{75} atoms in the entire universe.

Recent Development: Internet and Chess

With the introduction of the Internet, millions of chess players and fans became a global chess community. Chess enthusiasts are able to play online with partners all around the world, browse through the latest chess news, download chess games from databases containing millions of games, and even play with the chess world champion. The "Kasparov versus the World" online chess tournament over the Internet lasted for more than four months from June to October 1999. More than 58 thousand individuals from seventy-five countries submitted their move votes and were able to give a respectable fight to the world champion. The game lasted sixty-two moves and was observed by more than 3 million web site visitors. The quality of the chess played throughout the game has been recognized by chess experts around the world as one of the best public chess games ever documented. In 2011, the IBM Blue Gene P supercomputer, which can reach operating speeds at the petaFLOPS level, or 10^{15} (500 trillion) floating-point operations per second, competed against Bulgarian chess grandmaster Veselin Aleksandrov Topalov (1975–) in preparation for Topalov's formal competition in the World chess championship held in Sophia, Bulgaria.

Growing proliferation of computers and the Internet gave an opportunity to masses of chess devotees to improve their expertise and chess literacy and to widen horizons by providing easy access to chess databases and other information. Used by grandmasters and novices alike, computers prove to be exceptionally handy tools to enjoy the ancient and popular game of chess. For instance, in 2012, chess players can use the chess-playing program called Pocket Fritz 4, which works inside Pocket PC personal digital assistants (PDAs). The commercial computer chess program called HIARCS (the acronym for higher intelligence auto-response chess system), which was developed by Mark Uniacke, works inside the Pocket Fritz 4. As an example of the extraordinary power of this program, three years earlier, in 2009, the Pocket Fritz 4 program inside a HTC Touch HD mobile phone won a category 6 chess tournament within the Copa Mercosur Grandmaster Tournament in Buenos Aires, Argentina. Then, in 2011, the HIARCS program won the World Chess Software Championship, one of two tournaments at the World Computer Chess Championship held in Tilburg, the Netherlands.

 See also **Artificial Intelligence** • **Games** • **IBM Corporation**

Resources

Books

Cook, Andrew. *Chunk Learning and Move Prompting: Making Moves in Chess*. Birmingham: School of Computer Science, University of Birmingham, 2008.

Hertan, Charles. *Forcing Chess Moves: The Key to Better Calculation.* Almaar, Netherlands: New in Chess, 2008.

Newborn, Monroe. *Beyond Deep Blue: Chess in the Stratosphere.* London: Springer, 2011.

Shenk, David. *The Immortal Game: A History of Chess or How 32 Carved Pieces on a Board Illuminated Our Understanding of War, Art, Science, and the Human Brain.* New York: Doubleday, 2006.

Web Sites

Chess Base. "Pocket Fritz 4" http://www.chessbase.com/shop/product. asp?pid=479 (accessed September 27, 2012).

Chess Base. "Topalov Training with Super Computer Blue Gene P" http://www.chessbase.com/newsdetail.asp?newsid=6361 (accessed September 27, 2012).

Computer History Museum. "Mastering the Game" http://www. computerhistory.org/chess/ (accessed September 27, 2012).

About the American Community Survey HIARCS. "World Chess Software Championship, Tilburg, The Netherlands, 24th-26th November 2011" http://www.hiarcs.com/Games/wcsc11/wcsc11.htm (accessed September 27, 2012).

HowStuffWorks.com and Marshall Brain. "How Chess Computers Work" http://electronics.howstuffworks.com/chess1.htm (accessed September 27, 2012).

Microchip manufacturing. © *AP Images/ ho/IBM*

* **transistor** a contraction of TRANSfer resISTOR; a semiconductor device, invented by John Bardeen, Walter Brattain, and William Shockley, which has three terminals; can be used for switching and amplifying electrical signals

Chip Manufacturing

Computer chips are at the heart of the modern technology revolution. But what are they made of and how are they made? They are made primarily of transistor*s, which act as electrical switches in digital circuits, and metal wires. The most significant type of, from an economic perspective, is the complementary metal oxide semiconductor (CMOS) . This is a three-terminal device consisting of a gate (metal), a source, and a drain. The gate is an electrical switch that controls the flow of electrons from the source to the drain. Applying a voltage turns "on" the gate, which directs an electric field across a thin silicon dioxide film, causing the semiconductor material to become conductive and thereby allowing electrons to flow. If the gate voltage is turned "off," the electrons go away. Transistors being "on" or "off" correspond to the binary "1" and "0."

So how are these transistors and wires made? The devices and wires on a chip are fabricated at the same time, alongside hundreds of other chips, using a process known as batch fabrication. It does not cost any more to fabricate 1,000 transistors than 100 transistors—or many million of transistors for that matter! This is known as batch fabrication and it results in substantial economies of scale that make chips inexpensive despite their complexity.

It all starts with silicon*—the primary constituent of sand, and therefore abundant and inexpensive. The is purified, and large cylindrical crystals one to two meters (three to six feet) long and up to one-third meter (twelve inches) in diameter are grown. These crystals are sliced into wafers 500–750 micrometers thick that form the substrate for the chips. The chip designer provides the chip manufacturer with a set of photomasks that contain a physical representation of the transistors and associated wires to be reproduced on the wafer. Photomasks are made of glass and chrome and define regions where light can penetrate (glass), and others where the light cannot penetrate (chrome), similar to a stencil. In a 0.18 micrometer, six metal layer process, up to twenty-five such photomasks are used.

One set of photomasks is used to define where dopant elements will be added. What are dopants? They are elements—such as boron, phosphorus, and arsenic—added to the silicon that allow the charge-carrying characteristics of the material to be altered in a controllable fashion, facilitating the formation of transistors. Another set of photomasks is used in a set of successive steps whereby a thin film (typically less than one micrometer, or 1 m) is deposited on the wafer, a thin photosensitive polymer film is placed on top, and the pattern from the photomask is transferred to the photosensitive polymer by shining light on the photomask. The thin film is etched where the photosensitive polymer has been removed, and finally the photosensitive polymer is removed. These steps are repeated to fabricate the transistor gate, the wires that connect the transistors together, and the insulating films that separate the metal wires from each other. After the circuits have been fabricated—a process that can take twenty to thirty days in a 0.18 μm CMOS production plant—the wafers are cut into small chips and individually packaged.

Now that these chips are ready, how fast will they run? The speed depends on the amount of time the transistors take turning on and off and the delay imposed by the wiring. The length of the gate determines the switching time of transistors: the shorter the gate, the faster the device can switch. Wiring delays come from two primary sources—the time it takes to charge the wire up to the necessary voltage and the time it takes for a signal to travel a given distance. The former is reduced when the size of the wire is shrunk, so as chip miniaturization progresses, this delay decreases. The travel time is set by the speed of light and the material properties. For typical materials, signals travel 15 centimeters (about 6 inches) in a billionth of a second, which means that it will take over a quarter of a clock cycle to travel across a 2 centimeter (about 3/4 of a inch) chip running at 2 GHz. Historically, the frequency at which microprocessors operate has doubled every two years!

The scaling of features to smaller dimensions (known as technology scaling) improves performance while decreasing cost. Technology scaling basically means more computing power is packed into increasingly smaller physical space. Scaling propels the semiconductor market growth, which in turn generates sufficient profit to develop increasingly aggressive technology generations—scaling begets scaling! This cycle fuels what is known as "Moore's Law," which states that the number of transistors per integrated circuit doubles every eighteen months. Since the length of the gate is a primary indicator of the speed of a process, it is associated with a generation of computer chip technology. Not only do microprocessors get faster as the gate length decreases, but if one is making memory chips, more memory can be packed on the chip.

Economics of Chip Manufacturing

Just as computer chips have decreased in size and increased in power in each generation, semiconductor sales as a percent of the Gross World Product (GWP) have doubled every three technology generations. The manufacturing capacity of the semiconductor industry is often measured in wafer starts per week, which is simply a tally of how many wafers are placed at the beginning of the manufacturing process. From 1998 to 2000, this figure increased by about 20 percent—from seven million to eight and a half million.

It is also important to understand that as miniaturization has occurred, the cost of the equipment necessary to fabricate the microelectronic devices has dramatically increased. This is because higher equipment quality is required to manufacture the increasingly small devices, as well as to control the dimensions of these devices within strict tolerances. Consequently, the cost of a factory has grown significantly each year, from ten million dollars in the 1980s, to almost two billion dollars in 1999. The expectation is that the cost of semiconductor manufacturing facilities will continue to increase—by about 3 percent per year due to productivity requirements and 5 percent per year for technology upgrades.

In late 2012, scientists at IBM made great strides in creating chips out of carbon nanotubes, fitting 10,000 carbon nanotubes onto a single silicone chip. Many scientists were worrying that Moore's Law would be stalled because making smaller chips was becoming increasingly difficult. With this breakthrough it will be possible to continue shrinking the size of chips.

Chip making is all about packing as many transistors in as small an area as possible, to produce fast microprocessors and large amounts of memory. Chip making employs economies of scale, because most process operations are performed for many wafers at once, and each wafer contains many chips, and each chip contains many transistors. This has resulted in a tremendous return on investment for manufacturers that has far outweighed the rising manufacturing costs. It is anticipated that such trends will continue until 2030 or so.

Computer Sciences, 2ⁿᵈ Edition

More on Moore

Moore's Law was a prediction made by Gordon Moore of Fairchild Semiconductor Corporation in 1965, and it has held remarkably true into the 2000s. In fact, rival companies, knowing Moore's Law, each set out to exceed it, making Moore's Law a self-fulfilling prophecy.

* **minicomputers** computers midway in size between a desktop computer and a mainframe computer; most modern desktops are much more powerful than the older minicomputers

* **central processing unit (CPU)** the part of a computer that performs computations and controls and coordinates other parts of the computer

▶ *See also* **Central Processing Unit • Microchip • Process Control**

Resources

Books

Jaeger, Richard C. *Introduction to Microelectronic Fabrication*. 2nd ed. Upper Saddle River, NJ: Prentice-Hall, 2002.

Streetman, Ben G., and Sanjay Banerjee. *Solid State Electronic Devices..* 6th ed. Upper Saddle River, NJ: Pearson/Prentice Hall, 1999.

Web Sites

IBM News Room "Researchers Demonstrate Initial Steps toward Commercial Fabrication of Carbon Nanotubes as a Successor to Silicon" http://www-03.ibm.com/press/us/en/pressrelease/39250.wss (accessed November 4, 2012).

Intel Corporation Web Site "Moore's Law and Intel Innovation". http://www.intel.com/content/www/us/en/history/museum-gordon-moore-law.html?wapkw=moore%27s+law (accessed November 4, 2012).

International Technology Roadmap for Semiconductors. http://public.itrs.net (accessed November 4, 2012).

Semiconductor Industry Association Web Site. "Industry Statistics" http://www.sia-online.org/industry_statistics/industry_statistics/ (accessed November 4, 2012).

Computer Assisted Instruction

Computer Assisted Instruction (CAI) is defined as the use of computers and software applications to teach concepts or skills. The International Business Machines Corporation (IBM) developed one of the first instructional computer systems in the 1960s using minicomputers*. From the 1960s to the 1980s, IBM produced a handful of these 1500 series computers for the military and several universities. These units, contained in special trailers, consisted of complete workstations: one large central processing unit (CPU)*, one instructor's station, and sixteen student terminals. The trailer was hauled from place to place as needed.

Pennsylvania State University (United States) and the University of Alberta (Canada) were two of the biggest advocates of the 1500 series stations and provided a great deal of early research on computer assisted instruction. Researchers from several universities, such as from the University of Pittsburgh's Learning Research and Development Center (LRDC), continue the effort to identify the best methods and tools for using interactive computer programs to enhance learning.

Computer assisted instruction, sometimes also called electronic-learning (e-learning), has changed radically since the 1500 series. Computers are found in the home and most schools, and a variety of applications exist to use the computer to teach. The military has continued to be a significant advocate of computer assisted instruction to teach large numbers of trainees a multitude of jobs, including teaching pilots how to fly with the use of flight simulators. The University of Phoenix provides higher education programs through online classes, offering associate's through doctoral degrees. They were one of the first institutions to offer online instruction in 1989. E-learning is a growing economic sector. In 2010, e-learning was an industry that generated over $50 billion in the United States. Worldwide, e-learning is also growing rapidly. In Latin American countries, e-learning revenues are projected to reach $2.2 billion in 2016, in U.S. dollars, while the western European market is expected to reach $8.1 billion that same year, according to the Ambient Insight report entitled "The Western Europe Market for Self-paced eLearning Products and Services: 2011–2016 Forecast and Analysis."

Learning Management Systems

One growing trend among schools is to use a powerful application termed Learning Management System (LMS). Some companies that sell LMSs provide a service to the schools. Students, using either the school-owned computers or computers in the schools provided by the company, connect to the service's Web site to access a curriculum chosen by the faculty. The students access the educational resources for a specific period of time over a specific number of weeks; the frequency and duration vary from program to program.

The advantages of using an LMS are compelling. Many students are eager to use such a site because of its trendy appeal (as compared with lecture- and textbook-based instruction), which may motivate them to do well. The curriculum can be adjusted to focus on specific areas of weakness, whether for the entire class or for an individual. Any or all students can be monitored for progress.

Among the disadvantages to implement an LMS, schools must have a reliable Internet connection with sufficient bandwidth for all students that will utilize the system, which can be a major and expensive project. Another disadvantage is that the programs themselves can cost up to $30,000, a price that might not include the cost of computers. The effectiveness of these programs, as compared to conventional instruction, is also still open to debate among critics and proponents of learning management systems.

A variety of LMSs are available from different manufacturers. Choosing among them can be quite difficult, as they have considerable variation of methodology and depth. They also work on several different hardware platforms. Construction of each course must be done on an individual basis, and so there are no plug and play options. Also, there are no universally accepted standards to compare programs. The Shared Content Object Reference Model, or SCORM (developed by the U.S. government), is one set of standards gaining acceptance.

Electronic Books

Electronic books, especially electronic textbooks, are another form of computer assisted instruction. E-textbooks offer several advantages over print textbooks. They can be updated quickly and easily at a far cheaper price than conventional textbooks. Complex images and concepts, such as molecular biology, can be illustrated in interactive, three-dimensional presentations, instead of traditional drawings or photographs on paper, to aid in understanding. A tablet, to which e-textbooks can be downloaded, weighs a fraction of several paper textbooks and occupies less space. Their use would address the growing concern about overweight backpacks for students of varying ages. Teachers could cut and paste curriculum text in a customized format for students. Assignments and homework could be posted on a server. Such a system would need little introduction or training for students, so many of whom are already media savvy and using online resources for learning-related activities.

There are drawbacks to using e-textbooks, however. The initial investment of computers and software can be costly. In some programs, graphics (such as maps, charts, graphs, and pies) might not be accessible to students with disabilities. Compatibility of programs with other learning software might be a problem. However, despite these concerns, the sales for e-textbooks were 3 percent of total textbook sales in 2010, according to the National Association of College Stores. That percentage is expected to increase to 10 to 15 percent by the end of 2012.

Electronic Performance Support Systems

Electronic Performance Support Systems, or EPSS, is another form of computer assisted instruction. Gloria Gery, an educational software expert in Tolland, Massachusetts, began developing EPSS in the early 1990s. The purpose of EPSS is to help automate a job. TurboTax is an example of an EPSS. Once TurboTax is started, the user is prompted to answer a series of financial questions. When finished, the program computes the complete tax return for the user. The program can print out a copy of the results for the user, and if directed to do so, will even send an electronic copy to the Internal Revenue Service (IRS).

EPSS has found uses in many fields. Auto mechanics use an EPSS to diagnose car trouble. Travel agents make reservations with one. Cornerstone, an EPSS used by the National Association of Securities Dealers, Inc. (NASD, a Wall Street self-regulatory organization) helps auditors do their jobs. The sale and leasing of cars is simplified with the help of an EPSS.

People often deem that their jobs are too creative or complex for EPSS, but in many cases they are mistaken. In jobs that require human judgment, EPSS offers a series of alternatives to which the user can refer. As a result, employees can assume more complex job responsibilities after much shorter training periods and with significantly higher accuracy than would be likely with traditional training or job support structures. Hiring employees becomes cheaper. Because employees do not need to be so highly trained, the pool of applicants is much bigger, which is a benefit for employers. There is a downside to EPSS. The reduced need for better-educated individuals and shorter training periods could reduce the need for highly educated employees, resulting in lower salaries in many job categories.

▶ *See also* **Educational Software • Library Applications • Logo**

Resources

Books

Dirksen, Julie. *Design For How People Learn*. Berkeley: New Riders, 2011.

Mayer, Richard. *Applying The Science of Learning*. New York: Pearson, 2010.

Halverson, Taylor. *Distance Education Innovations and New Learning Environments: Combining Traditional Teaching Methods and Emerging Technologies*. Amherst, NY: Cambria Press, 2009.

Web Sites

ASTD.org. "ASTD Learning System." http://www.astd.org/Publications/Books/ASTD-Learning-System (accessed October 1, 2012).

Cornell University, and Jon R. Miller, Andrew W. Nutting, and Lori Baker-Eveleth. "The Determinants of Electronic Textbook Use Among College Students." http://www.ilr.cornell.edu/cheri/upload/cheri_wp147.pdf (accessed October 1, 2012).

PR Newswire. "eLearning Market in Latin America to Reach $2.2 Billion by 2016." http://www.prnewswire.com/news-releases/elearning-market-in-latin-america-to-reach-22-billion-by–2016–167525175.html (accessed October 1, 2012).

PR Newswire. "Western Europe eLearning Market to Reach $8.1 billion by 2016." http://www.prnewswire.com/news-releases/western-europe-elearning-market-to-reach-81-billion-by–2016–171122561.html (accessed October 1, 2012).

RUSTICI Systems. "SCORM Explained." http://scorm.com/scorm-explained/ (accessed October 1, 2012).

Techscribe. "Electronic Performance Support Systems (EPSSs)." http://www.techscribe.co.uk/techw/epss.htm (accessed October 1, 2012).

Alternative Approaches to Learning

Learning management systems (LMSs) are also available that allow colleges and universities to construct their own courses for teaching non-traditional students. These include students who require flexible hours or live in distant locations. A professional team consisting of the subject matter expert (such as a faculty member), a curriculum expert, a graphics designer, and a programmer, usually works together to create these programs.

* **dot.com** a common term used to describe an Internet-based commercial company or organization

* **venture capitalists** persons or agencies that speculate by providing financial resources to enable product development, in the expectation of larger returns with product maturity

Computer Professional

As young people begin their search for a career, it is likely that many will consider one of the vast opportunities available in the computer industry. Skilled computer professionals are in steady demand, despite the normal fluctuations of the world economy.

Rise of the New Economy

In the first quarter of the twentieth-first century, widespread computerization of business, education, and entertainment means that virtually all aspects of the global economy are dependent, in one way or another, on the fortunes of the computer industry. This effect was heightened during the late 1990s when the so-called dot.com* market skyrocketed, boosting stock portfolios for investors worldwide. Young entrepreneurs backed with financing from venture capitalists* created multi-million dollar Internet companies based on ideas that were often untested against traditional business standards of profit and loss projections. Stock prices soared as hopeful investors jumped at the chance to capitalize on the tremendous wealth being made as these start-up companies created the latest software and Internet products and services.

Soon it became clear that many, if not most, of these new economy companies would not become or remain profitable to their stockholders. When the standard measures of business success were applied to the high technology market, the entire U.S. economy began to feel the impact. High tech consulting firms went bankrupt. Telecommunications networks designed to support the once-growing demand for digital services collapsed overnight. News reports of layoffs in major computer industry companies became common. The future suddenly appeared less positive for 'techies' who had come to expect high financial rewards in a short period of time. Economic analysts characterized this shift as a correction in the market; computer professionals considered it more of a disaster. However, the market for computer professionals remains strong, in part because every segment of the U.S. and world economy depends on fast, reliable computer networks and equipment. Professionals are needed to create and maintain this infrastructure.

Choosing and Preparing for a Career

There is a need for people to design, build, connect, and maintain computers and electronics; these jobs fall into the general category of hardware engineering. There is also a need for people who can conceptualize and create computer software; these jobs fall into the general category of computer programming. Professionals who design and maintain networks of computers are termed network engineers and often need to interact with hardware engineers and computer programmers. Within each broad type of computer-related work, there are many specialized technical functions, as well as the kinds of industry support jobs common to other market segments, including administration, sales and marketing, and customer service and support. Computer professionals also include the men and women who teach and perform research in academic settings.

Education   Individuals interested in pursuing a career as a computer professional should generally plan to earn at least a four-year degree (bachelor's level) in computer science or computer engineering. Fluency in multiple computer programming languages is vital for anyone interested in software development; the more languages learned, the more valuable the prospective employee. A solid understanding of hardware infrastructure is important, as well, especially for those interested in network creation or administration.

Not all computer professionals have an academic background in computer science or engineering, however. Often, people with advanced degrees in business, education, or something as seemingly unrelated to the computer industry as music, art, journalism, or criminology will find a niche as a computer industry professional. These individuals may not be involved in the technical aspects of software development or network configuration. However, their expertise may help provide unique services and help other computer professionals target hardware and software issues to solve problems within their domain.

Most American universities now offer a variety of academic programs that will prepare students to become computer professionals. Many well-known schools throughout the United States, such as the Massachusetts Institute of Technology (MIT), specialize in technology-related fields. There are also accredited certification programs available from industry giants such as Cisco Systems. As in all career fields, the selection of a training or preparatory program should be based on a match between student interests, strengths, and career goals, and the particular program and training options of any given school.

Hardware Engineers   Computer professionals who specialize in the hardware or infrastructure* aspect of the computer industry are the ones who design, build, test, and improve the computers and networks that support the economy. From the design of a mouse to the building of a supercomputer*, hardware engineers are needed to create the physical tools of the computer age. Some hardware engineers specialize in designing networks for computers to communicate with each other. Others focus on creating computer peripherals to meet the unique requirements of special needs users. Hardware specialists are needed to repair and modify equipment. Computer hardware engineers need to understand the technical aspects of computer design and connection; ideally, they will also learn to understand how people use and interact with computers, as well, which can help them create better equipment.

Computer Programming   Without software to operate the hardware, computer systems are useless. Computer programmers are charged with the duty of writing the code that creates user-friendly software.

* **infrastructure** the foundation or permanent installation necessary for a structure or system to operate

* **supercomputer** a very high performance computer, usually comprised of many processors and used for modeling and simulation of complex phenomena, like meteorology

Programmers are responsible for conceiving, designing, and building software applications. Sometimes they work alone. Often, teams of programmers apply their skills in a shared effort to create complex software. Computer programmers need to work methodically and analytically. Unlike some fields, where there is a range of acceptable solutions to a problem or small mistakes can be tolerated, if a computer program is not written correctly an array of undesirable behavior can occur, from incorrect calculations to crashes. Many programmers specialize in writing software for particular business, education, or entertainment purposes; the most adept programming specialists learn that it is important to communicate with users about what they want their finished software to accomplish.

Jobs in the Computer Industry

In addition to the people who create the tools—hardware and software—that one calls computers, there are professionals whose job it is to help businesses figure out the most effective way to use these tools. Many companies now have an Information Technology (IT) department. IT specialists work with a company to identify the best combinations of hardware, software, and networking to meet the company's needs. In some cases, this is done externally, on a consulting basis; in other companies this may be handled by in-house technology staff. The IT specialist must typically figure out how to use a company's limited resources to maintain a system of computer-based communications equipment from a vast array of vendors, always with an eye toward improving the firm's competitive edge in the market. After recommending hardware and software options, often the IT department is charged with ensuring the computer assets of the company are functioning correctly. This might entail replacing failed components, updating employee's computers, or managing the corporate network. For companies that do significant amounts of business on the Internet, IT professionals may have to maintain an externally facing Web site to ensure the company can continue to take on-line orders. Career paths for IT professionals start with entry-level positions and can lead to managerial and executive positions with titles such as IT director, chief information officer, and chief technology officer.

Many other jobs are available for computer professionals with the right combination of technical and other skills. Since people need to learn to use their company's technology resources, from hardware to software, there is a steady need for educators and training personnel. Repair specialists who can troubleshoot hardware and software problems on very short notice are in high demand wherever there are complex networks to maintain. Software companies need knowledgeable personnel to staff their customer support departments and help personal computer owners fix their problems by phone or by e-mail. There will always be a place for creative thinkers who can create and fill market niches with specialized software and hardware products and services.

According to TechMediaNetwork's "2012 Best Computer Careers Comparisons and Reviews," the computer position with the highest entry-level salary is software engineer, at $62,040. The five computer career areas in the United States with the most promising future are software engineering, telecommunications, systems analysis, network security, and network administration. These five computer areas range from $32,460 to $132,080 for entry-level positions coming out of college.

▶ *See also* **Computer Scientists**

Resources

Books

Farr, J. Michael. *Top 100 Computer and Technical Careers: Your Complete Guidebook to Major Jobs in Many Fields at All Training Levels.* Indianapolis: JIST Publishing, 2009.

Freedman, Jeri. *Careers in Computer Science and Programming.* New York: Rosen, 2011.

Institute for Career Research. *Careers in Computer Network Administration.* Chicago: Institute for Research, 2008.

McGraw-Hill editors. *Resume for Computer Careers.* New York: McGraw-Hill, 2008.

Wyckoff, Claire. *Computers and Information Technology.* New York: Ferguson, 2008.

Web Sites

ComputerCareers.net. "Computer Careers." http://www.computercareers.net/ (accessed October 1, 2012).

TechMediaNetwork. "2012 Best Computer Careers Comparisons and Reviews." http://computer-careers-review.toptenreviews.com/ (accessed October 1, 2012).

Computer Supported Cooperative Work (CSCW)

Computer Supported Cooperative Work (CSCW) results from the connectivity provided by modern computers via local area networks (LANs)* or the Internet, that allows multiple users to work together. In the early days of computing during the 1950s and 1960s, mainframe computers* executed business programs. They were given a stack of punched card*s, processed for a while, and eventually printed out an answer on long strips of folded green computer paper. End users never even saw these machines.

Hot High Tech Jobs

As of 2012, one of the hottest high tech job prospects is in the field of bioinformatics. The discipline, which combines the fields of biology and computer science, seeks ways to improve medical advances using supercomputers, huge data depositories, and medical knowledge.

* **local area networks (LANs)** high-speed computer networks that are designed for users who are located near each other

* **mainframe computers** large computers used by businesses and government agencies to process massive amounts of data; generally faster and more powerful than desktop computers but usually requiring specialized software

* **punched card** a paper card with punched holes which give instructions to a computer in order to encode program instructions and data

* **groupware** a software technology common in client/server systems whereby many users can access and process data at the same time

* **teletype** a machine that sends and receives telephonic signals

* **domain** a region in which a particular element or object exists or has influence; (math) the inputs to a function or relation

Only "operators" had access to the input and output devices. End users would usually hand a job request through a small window in the "computer center" to an operator, returning in a day or two to pick up the answer.

Then came the personal computer, or PC, which essentially did the same thing, except the computer center and the operators were no longer required. As a "personal" computer, this machine belonged to one individual, who no longer had to share processing time with others who also had access rights to the mainframe. Instead of punched cards and paper, keyboards and display screens became available. Ultimately WYSIWYG ("what you see is what you get") interfaces, such as Apple's Mac OS and the various releases of Microsoft Windows, became available, increasing the user's easy control of the machine's processes.

This focus on the solitary user changed with the development of the local area network (LAN), which allowed people to send e-mail around the office. It allowed people to access shared files and even to share applications. Chat and bulletin boards first appeared in these environments, and workflow programs and file servers started their lives on LANs. Many of these concepts have become the foundation for groupware* and multi-user programs, as they have developed into the twenty-first century.

By 2002, the Internet boosted the idea of working together that was pioneered in the time of the LAN. One of the major influences for groupware and multi-user applications on the Internet was games. In particular, multi-user dungeons (MUDs) pioneered many of the concepts that are leveraged today for collaborative applications in business, research, communications, and other endeavors.

Computer Supported Cooperative Work (CSCW) draws on these concepts. The view of what a computer is changes with it. While early computers were mainly viewed as "tools," they were later also seen as "documents." A word processor, for example, turns the computer into a tool. The file that is created with the word processor exists eventually independently of the word processor. Still, it is "in the computer." The computer therefore also serves as a "document."

With the advent of LANs and the Internet, a third view of computers was introduced: the computer as communication device. Very much like a telephone or a teletype*, the computer acts as the medium that transports messages. And although it is actually the network that transports the message, the computer is the terminal device, the access point to the communications network.

With these three perspectives on computers as tool, document, and communication device, one can start to look at the other issues that have an impact on groupware and multi-user systems.

Applications

CSCW and groupware can be categorized according to application domain*. A meeting system used in education will differ from a meeting system used in a business context. Engineering tasks usually require different tools than administrative tasks. The following list of task and application s will grow as new systems are built and applied to an ever-expanding set of s:

- Engineering
- Administration
- Manufacturing
- Research and development
- Banking and insurance
- Logistics and warehousing
- Decision making
- Teaching and learning
- Authoring
- Drafting
- Entertainment
- Software engineering
- Project management
- Military planning and operations.

Technology

In order to build, deploy, and use groupware, a number of enabling technologies must be in place. Among the most important technologies for the design and implementation of CSCW systems are:

- Networks
- Connectivity
- Naming and name spaces
- Mail and other communication protocols
- Multimedia technologies
- Hypertext and hypermedia
- Video technologies
- Cross-platform development tools
- Large bit mapped displays.

Synchronous/Co-located Applications

One example of a CSCW system is a synchronous/co-located application. To support teams in negotiating, decision making, brainstorming, learning, and other activities, a number of systems have been built to enhance a meeting room. Examples of such *electronic meeting rooms* are the *Capture Lab* at Electronic Data Systems, the *Electronic Meeting Systems (EMS)* at the University of Arizona, a commercial system by IBM, and the CoLab at Xerox PARC (Palo Alto Research Center). These systems usually consist of a room with special furniture that can be rearranged. The furniture

Xerox Parc's CoLab

Short for "collaboration laboratory," the CoLab project was conducted at Xerox PARC between 1987 and 1992. In part, the project evaluated the difference between meetings held without computer technology and those held with high tech tools available. CoLab offered each participant a computer and included a main electronic white board on which notes, diagrams, and discussion ideas could be displayed.

is also designed with the monitor under the surface of the desk. Users view the monitor through a glass surface on the desk, thus having an unobstructed view of other participants. The tables either form a circle or a semi-circle. Sometimes a large bitmapped device is used instead of the whiteboard or chalkboard. All devices are connected by a LAN. Special software can be written to take advantage of a configuration such as in Figure 1.

The motivation to create such meeting rooms is rather obvious: Media such as overheads and flip charts influence the way people communicate and how well they remember what was said in meetings.

Meetings can be classified along their functions: exploration, information sharing, brainstorming, problem solving, decision making, morale building, negotiating, planning, or social structuring. This diversity creates a wide range of design issues concerning the layout of the room, the capability of the software, the performance of the hardware, the selection of user interfaces, and many others.

 See also **Computer Professional • Office Automation Systems**

Resources

Books

Haring-Smith, Tori. *Learning Together: An Introduction to Collaborative Learning.* New York: Harper-Collins College Publications, 1993.

Weber, Aaron, and Scott Weber. *The Book of Evolution: Groupware for Linux Users.* San Francisco: No Starch Press, 2001.

Computerized Manufacturing

Computerization aids in the design of products, their fabrication, and the planning of manufacturing processes. Computerization of manufacturing began with the advent of computers after World War II, mainly in military-related applications. Now it is common in many commercial applications as well. The aerospace, automobile, chemical, electronics, and biomedical industries are among many that rely on computerized manufacturing.

Computer-Aided Design

In contemporary applications of computerized manufacturing, the process often begins with computer-aided design, more commonly known as CAD. In CAD, instead of drawing with pencils and a few drafting tools on paper, an engineer uses lines and curves stored in computer memory to produce a drawing that appears on a screen. The finished drawing can also be stored in computer memory.

It can actually be slower to produce a complex multiple layer drawing with CAD than it is to draw it by hand, especially when the drawing is in its initial stage. There are, however, several advantages to using CAD in the beginning stages. First, a CAD program allows an engineer to copy and paste portions of drawing, just as text can be manipulated in word processing, moving them and using them in as many locations on the screen as necessary. Secondly, just as changing numeric values in a spreadsheet cell alters the rest of the spreadsheet, accordingly an engineer can make size changes to a drawing without using pencil and eraser. Another advantage to using CAD even for preliminary drafts is that an engineer can recall previously drawn components from computer memory and use them in the drawing. Finally, CAD allows an engineer to transform a two-dimensional sketch into one that appears to be three-dimensional, and to rotate the image on the screen to evaluate it from different angles. For these reasons, using a CAD program can be much more efficient than drawing with pencil on paper.

Computer-Aided Engineering

CAD drawings can be incorporated into a computer-aided engineering (CAE) process. In CAE many hypothetical questions about material behavior can be answered by means of a computerized mechanical analysis of the effect of conditions such as stresses and deformations*. CAE also uses visualization* techniques such as computer animation to simulate a product's performance under various loads.

Instead of building expensive prototypes*, engineers can use CAE software to create numerous computer simulations that help them determine how machines and their parts will behave in different circumstances. CAE is used in many applications, but it is especially important in the aerospace and automobile industries where weight and size reduction is always a highly sought-after goal of engineering and where reducing the number of physical iterations needed to perfect a part by utilizing modeling and simulation can significantly reduce the cost to introduce a new product.

Computer-Aided Manufacturing

After the design and engineering processes are complete, manufacturing involves materials handling and product fabrication. These processes can also be automated by computerized technologies. In technical literature, these technologies are usually referred to as computer-aided manufacturing (CAM). When computer-aided manufacturing also uses computer-aided design, this is referred to as CAD/CAM.

Computerized materials handling focuses on automated storage and retrieval systems. These systems are automated warehouses where materials are stored on racks. The location of each stored material is registered in a database. Materials can be retrieved by conveyors, monorails, or computerized carts. The database keeps a continuous inventory of materials and their availability.

* **deformations** mechanical systems where a structure is physically misshapen, e.g., dented

* **visualization** a technique whereby complex systems are portrayed in a meaningful way using sophisticated computer graphics systems; e.g., chemical molecules

* **prototypes** working models or experimental investigation of proposed systems under development

* **embedded computers**
computers that do not have human user orientated input/output (I/O) devices; they are directly contained within other machines

Product Fabrication

Fabrication of products and their components is automated by means of flexible manufacturing systems, robots, and embedded computers*. The prevailing tendency in manufacturing is to shorten the time between conception of an idea and creation of a finished product so the consumer will get it as quickly as possible. Flexible manufacturing systems help achieve this goal. They often produce parts in small batches, just as they are needed for the rest of the manufacturing process.

Flexible Manufacturing Systems A flexible manufacturing system comprises equipment workstations connected by parts delivery routes. Parts are directed along those routes and are treated at the workstations. Each batch of parts might follow a different set of routes and workstations, according to production needs. In this way a manufacturing enterprise can quickly respond to ever-changing market demands and be ahead of the competition.

Delivery routes may employ motorized carts on tracks, or they may use motorized carts that follow wires embedded in the shop floor. Equipment workstations are the islands along delivery routes where tools for parts fabrication, assembly, and inspection are located. Most of those tools are automated and can be reprogrammed if the need arises. Each workstation is usually dedicated to the treatment of groups of similar parts.

Rapid Prototyping Rapid prototyping is a technique where raw materials can be manipulated by a computer controlled machine to form an object as directed by CAD drawing. Typical materials used in rapid prototyping are types of plastic, which can be extruded through a nozzle into various shapes. By controlling the rate of flow and repositioning the nozzle, the computer can create virtually any shape. After the plastic hardens, the newly created object can be removed and used for its intended purpose. Some uses of rapid prototyping are to verify the physical compatibility of CAD models, manufacturing limited quantity parts, or increasingly for home use. Several open source projects have sprung up that provide free instructions on how to assemble a rapid prototyping kit. The RepRap (replicating rapid prototyper) project is notable in that it has a stated goal of making the RepRap machine self-replicable, in that one RepRap machine can create all the parts necessary for a second machine. With the exception of electrical and motorized parts, the RepRap machine has been able to accomplish this feat of replicating itself. In addition, once a person owns a RepRap general-purpose self-replicating manufacturing machine it can operate as a three-dimensional (3D) desktop printer that is capable of printing 3D plastic objects.

Robots Another approach to the automation of production is the use of industrial robots. Contrary to popular early images of robots, industrial robots do not look like humans. Their main features are multifunctionality and reprogrammability. Paint-spraying robots in the automobile industry do not look at all human, but they help humans by doing their work in an environment that is hostile to human health.

Robots are also employed in the spot welding of automobile bodies. Because of the heat and bright light involved in spot welding, it is difficult for humans to perform this task with consistent quality. Not only is the job adaptable to robotics, it is better suited to computerization than to human performance. Other manufacturing processes suited to the multi-functionality of robots include the automated loading and unloading of heavy objects, the application of adhesives, the assembly of aircraft parts especially with rivets, the drilling and fastening of metal panels, and the sanding of missile wings, to name just a few.

The ability to reprogram a robot is an important advantage of using robots over other types of automated manufacturing equipment. A robot is made up of a controller, a manipulator, and sensors. The controller is a device through which a robot is programmed. Robots employ programs of varying complexity, from programs with multiple if ... then conditions to artificial intelligence (AI)*. An example of artificial intelligence is a program based on an expert system. Such a system is usually constructed by gathering information from human experts. Out of this information, a program is developed. It encodes a set of rules mimicking human intuition. The robot is programmed to act according to this set of rules.

The robot's manipulator usually comprises electric, hydraulic, or pneumatic* mechanisms that move an industrial robot's arms. An arm has a number of joints that determine its capability to fulfill the numerous functions the robot is designed to perform.

Not all robots are equipped with sensors, but the most versatile ones are. Of course, robots with sensors usually are much more expensive than those without. Sensors vary depending on tasks. If an industrial robot is used for inspection, its sensors may detect flaws in manufactured parts. A robot used to assemble electronic circuit boards is usually equipped with sensors that enable it to put components into proper places on the board.

Embedded computers are extensively used in many manufacturing applications, especially for the control of production processes. The most advanced of them are linked to sensors and have some kind of networking capability. They might receive remote commands and send this information to enterprise management system databases.

Computer-Aided Process Planning (CAPP)

Detailed planning is needed in order to implement a successful computerized manufacturing project. Once a design is finalized, an engineer prepares a detailed process plan. The plan comprises step-by-step instructions that include how to set up equipment, how to make a part, and last but not least, how to assure quality by inspecting the part after it is made. Routings between equipment workstations must also

* **artificial intelligence (AI)** a branch of computer science dealing with creating computer hardware and software to mimic the way people think and perform practical tasks

* **pneumatic** powered by pressurized air, supplied through tubes or pipes

Multifunctionality

Multifunctionality means that a robot can fulfill as many tasks as possible within the scope of its operation. For example, spray painting is a hazardous and monotonous job. It requires the consistent ability to follow various shapes and cover them with numerous protection layers. Using a paint-spraying robot reduces health risks to human beings, and it also provides a higher level of repetitive consistency than human beings can achieve.

* **synergistic** relating to synergism, which is the phenomenon whereby the action of a group of elements is greater than their individual actions

be determined. The plan is usually supplemented with drawings of the tools necessary to make the part and detailed instructions about how to operate the tools. Process planning is a tedious and time-consuming job. In a manufacturing environment, where it is always desirable to reduce time from idea to finished product, the computer-aided process planning (CAPP) can speed up the planning process and help ward off the competition.

There are two approaches to computer-aided process planning: variant and generative. The variant CAPP system is based on parts classification. As in biological classification, parts to be manufactured are combined into families. Parts that belong to a certain family have similar shapes, attributes, and parameters. They should also have similar production processes. This assumption is true in the majority of cases. The determination of which family a new part belongs to is made either manually by an engineer or by an appropriate artificial intelligence method. Once the family is established, a generic process description can be pulled from the program's database and an engineer may start modifying it to comply with the actual characteristics of the part.

One drawback of the variant CAPP is that the generic family process may not be suitable for a particular new part. The generative CAPP system does not have this drawback because it is based on an entirely different principle than variant CAPP. Instead of retrieving a generic family process and editing it, a process plan is created from scratch by using a set of decision rules that define the selection of proper operations, the sequence of operations, the treatments, the tools, and the delivery routes to be used in creating the part.

Computer Integrated Manufacturing (CIM)

The most advanced computerized manufacturing system is termed Computer Integrated Manufacturing, or CIM. The goal of CIM is to combine synergistic*ally all the computerized manufacturing technologies described earlier. At a slightly less comprehensive level, there are many manufacturing enterprises that include islands of automation—materials handling, for example—as well as manufacturing processes that are not automated. Integration of those islands into one system is another approach to CIM.

While integrating computerized manufacturing technologies into CIM, it is important to keep in mind that an enterprise might use different brands of equipment, process controllers, conveyors, robots, and other components. An engineer should always exercise common sense and evaluate profits versus costs while making a decision about what level of computerized manufacturing automation is appropriate in each particular case.

 See also **Chip Manufacturing** • **Image Analysis: Medicine** • **Process Control** • **Robotics** • **Robots**

Resources

Books

Chang, Tien-Chien, Richard A. Wysk, and Hsu-Pin Wang. *Computer-Aided Manufacturing.* Upper Saddle River, NJ: Pearson Prentice Hall, 2006.

Holmstrom, Jonny, Mikael Wiberg, and Andreas Lund, editors. *Industrial Informatics Design, Use, and Innovation: Perspectives and Services.* Hershey, PA: IGI Global.

Jiang, Pingyu, and Shuichi Fukada, eds. *E-Manufacturing Towards Global Engineering.* Bradford, England: Emerald Group Publishing, 2007.

Nasr, Emad Abouel, and Ali K. Kamrani. *Computer-Based Design and Manufacturing: An Information-Based Approach.* New York: Springer, 2007.

Sawhney, G. S. *Fundamentals of Computer Aided Manufacturing.* New Delhi, India: I. K. International Publishing, 2007.

Xu, Xun. *Integrating Advanced Computer-aided Design, Manufacturing, and Numerical Control: Principles and Implementations.* Hershey, PA: Information Science Reference, 2009.

Web Sites

ComputerIntegratedManufacturing.com. "Computer Integrated Manufacturing." http://www.computerintegratedmanufacturing.com/ (accessed October 2, 2012).

MB Info. "The History of CAD." http://mbinfo.mbdesign.net/CAD-History.htm (accessed October 2, 2012).

RepRap.org. "Welcome to RepRap.org." http://reprap.org/wiki/Main_Page (accessed October 2, 2012).

Statistics Studies of Peer Production. "Manufacturing in Motion: First Survey on 3D Printing Community." http://surveys.peerproduction.net/2012/05/manufacturing-in-motion/ (accessed October 2, 2012).

Sir Godfrey Hounsfield. © *Central Press/Hulton Archive/Getty Images.*

* **computer-assisted tomography** the use of computers in assisting with the management of X-ray images

Allan Cormack and Godfrey Newbold Hounsfield

Developers of Computer-Assisted Tomography
1924–1998
1919–2004

Allan McLeod Cormack and Godfrey Newbold Hounsfield won the Nobel Prize in physiology or medicine in 1979 for their work in the development of computer-assisted tomography* (CAT).

* **Harvard Cyclotron** a specialized machine (cyclotron) developed in 1948 at Harvard University; it is used to carry out experiments in sub-atomic physics and medicine

Allan Cormack

Allan Cormack was born in Johannesburg, South Africa, in 1924. His parents had emigrated from Scotland to South Africa shortly before World War I (1914–1918); his father was a civil servant, who worked as an engineer for the post office. The family migrated through South Africa until 1936, when they settled in Cape Town after the death of Cormack's father. Cormack attended the Rondebosch Boys High School in Cape Town, and subsequently received both bachelor's and master's degrees in physics from the University of Cape Town. However, he initially studied electrical engineering in a department headed by B. L. Goodlet, who believed that engineers needed a good grounding in physics and math. Cormack was already interested in these subjects, having earlier studied astronomy, a field which requires a solid background in physics and math. Thus, he eventually abandoned engineering for physics.

After obtaining his degrees at Cape Town, he went to St. John's College, Cambridge, England, as a research student and worked in the Cavendish Laboratory under Professor Otto Frisch (1904–1979), a renowned physicist. Frisch, along with his aunt Lise Meitner, had performed fundamental work in the area of nuclear fission. Cormack later worked on problems connected with Helium-6 (He-6, Helium of atomic weight 6).

Cormack later married Barbara Seavey, an American, whom he had met at a quantum dynamics lecture. Cormack sought a teaching position in the physics department at the University of Cape Town. Offered a position as lecturer, Cormack returned to Cape Town with his wife in 1950. His first sabbatical, however, was spent at Harvard University, where he worked on the team connected with the Harvard Cyclotron*. During his stay at Harvard, Cormack was offered a position in the physics department at Tufts University, which he accepted in 1957, remaining there for the duration of his career. Having officially retired in 1995, Cormack continued working at Tufts.

While in Cape Town in the 1950s, Cormack also served as a medical physicist in the department of radiology at Groote Schuur Hospital. It was there that he began to think about the possibility of using X rays for diagnostic purposes, particularly in the treatment of cancer patients. X rays are absorbed by dense material, such as bone, hence obscuring the view of the tissue in question. Reasoning that multiple X rays projected at different angles, but in a single plane, would yield a more detailed image, he developed a set of equations to describe the process. However, his findings, published in 1963 and 1964 in the *Journal of Applied Physics,* went largely unnoticed.

Godfrey Hounsfield

Godfrey Hounsfield was born on August 28, 1919, in Newark, Nottinghamshire, England, and raised on a farm. He attributed his interest in mechanical and electrical gadgets, especially experimentation, to his days and experiences on the farm, uncluttered by the distractions of a "larger" and "busier" civilization. He suggested that this was at the expense of his more formal schooling at Magnus Grammar School in Newark, where he claimed to respond only to math and physics with any "moderate" enthusiasm. He joined the Royal Air Force (RAF) as a volunteer reservist at the outbreak of World War II (1939–1945), and became interested in radio and then radar*. He became a mechanic instructor and was moved to the Royal College of Science in South Kensington and then to the Cranwell Radar School.

After the war, one of his superiors, Air Vice-Marshall Cassidy obtained a grant for him to attend the Faraday House Electrical Engineering College in London, where Hounsfield earned a diploma. In 1951 Hounsfield joined the staff of EMI, Ltd., in Middlesex, England, where he worked on radar and guided weapons. He later became interested in computers, creating drums and tape decks from scratch, experimenting with core memory, and, in 1958, leading a design team to construct the first all-transistor computer built in Great Britain, the EMIDEC 1100.

When this work was finished, he transferred to EMI Central Research Laboratories in Hayes. It was there that he became interested in pattern recognition*. Through this interest in, he happened upon the work that would eventually lead to computerized tomography.

Hounsfield got the initial idea in 1967, after which he carried on experimentation, finally developing and designing several prototype*s, some of which went into production. EMI introduced the first commercial scanner in 1972. In this period, 1970 to 1972, Cormack became aware of the developments in CT-scanning and became, once again, more involved in these problems.

Both Cormack and Hounsfield developed interests in biology late in their careers. Cormack died in 1998; Hounsfield continued to work and live in Great Britain. The first heart transplant was performed at Groote Schuur Hospital by Dr. Christiaan Barnard in 1967. This is, of course, where Cormack worked. Cormack and Hounsfield had worked independently in the same area, and were both honored for the body of their work.

Hounsfield also won the Gardiner Foundation Award for achievement in biomedical research in 1976, and the Lasker Award for research in the biological sciences in 1975. He was knighted in 1981. The two scientists met for the first time in Stockholm, as Nobel Prize laureates.

 See also **Graphic Devices • Image Analysis: Medicine • Medical Systems**

Resources

Web Sites

Nobel e-Museum. http://www.nobelmuseum.se/en (accessed November 2, 2012).

CAT Explained

Computer-assisted tomography is a means of taking X-rays of difficult to observe portions of the body. This is achieved by taking multiple images from various angles and then combining the results.

* **radar** the acronym for RAdio Direction And Ranging; a technique developed in the 1930s that uses frequency shifts in reflected radio waves to measure distance and speed of a target

* **pattern recognition** a process used by some artificial-intelligence systems to identify a variety of patterns, including visual patterns, information patterns buried in a noisy signal, and word patterns imbedded in text

* **prototype** a working model or experimental investigation of proposed systems under development

Cray, Seymour
American Computer Designer
1925-1996

Seymour Cray, widely regarded as the father of supercomputer*s, was born in Chippewa Falls, Wisconsin, on September 28, 1925. He died on October 5, 1996, after a car accident. A man of unerring focus, Cray maintained a single goal throughout his lifetime—to build the fastest computer possible.

After obtaining a bachelor's degree in electrical engineering and a master's degree in applied mathematics from the University of Minnesota, Cray started his career with Engineering Research Associates, which became Remington Rand, then Sperry Rand. Here Cray designed his first computer, the ERA 1101. He also helped design the UNIVAC (Universal Automatic Computer) 1103. When the UNIVAC shifted its focus away from supercomputers, Cray did not. Instead, he left to start Control Data Corporation (CDC), leading the first design team to abandon vacuum tube*s and produce the first commercial transistor*-based computer, the CDC 1604, in 1958.

Within a few years, Cray decided that the administrative duties associated with running a successful business interfered with his concentration on computer design. With CDC's blessing, he left for home and solitude in Chippewa Falls. CDC built Cray's laboratory close to his home. His time there proved productive, and in 1963, CDC released the Cray-designed CDC 6600. To reduce heat build-up in the compact unit, Cray installed a freon* cooling system inside the computer. This machine was not only three times faster than its IBM counterpart, but was also smaller and a bargain at $7.5 million each. Customers for the 6600 included the U.S. Atomic Energy Commission, which used it to to study thermonuclear explosions, and the U.S. Weather Bureau, which used it to to assist in weather predictions.

In 1969 CDC released the Cray-designed 7600, which could perform twenty megaflops, or twenty million calculations (floating point operations* or FLOPS) per second. Many believe the 7600 was the first supercomputer.

When CDC declined to market Cray's next machine (the 8600), instead expanding into other commercial ventures, Cray again chose to focus on supercomputer design. He started Cray Research in 1972. The Cray 1, released in 1976, was the first computer to master successfully vector processing* and at the time was the fastest scalar processor* in the world. This single-processor, 160 megaflop computer had 1 million, 64-bit words of central memory, and used three types of integrated circuit*s. The computer itself was an 8 × 6 foot (about 2.4 × 1.8 meter) cylindrical structure. With a maximum wire length of 4 feet (1.2 meters), it still required a total of 60 miles (18.3 meters) of wire. Each unit cost $8.8 million. Cray Research went public in 1976, a month before its first sale (to Los Alamos National Laboratories in New Mexico). The sale of stock raised $10 million, helping the company to survive.

By 1984 Cray Research owned 70 percent of the supercomputer market. Cray himself was worth $17 million. In November of 1981, Cray resigned as CEO of Cray Research to become an independent contractor. Again, he sought solitude to build what he called "simple, dumb things." While he worked on the Cray 2, Cray Research, led by Steve Chen, revised the Cray 1. Chen's resultant Cray X-MP was the first multi-processing computer, able to perform 500 megaflops. The resultant rivalry between Cray and Chen eventually led to Cray's departure from the company in 1989. Cray then founded Cray Computer Corporation of Colorado Springs.

Cray wanted the Cray 2 to be four to six times more powerful than the Cray 1. When finished in 1985 with four processors, the Cray 2 doubled that expectation. This supercomputer had the largest internal memory capacity of any computer (two million bytes) and 256 million words of central memory. It could perform 1.2 gigaflops (or 1.2 million FLOPS per second). Cray fit the entire structure in a C-shaped cabinet 53 inches (136 centimeters) across and 45 inches (115 centimeters) high. To diffuse heat, he immersed the circuits in the coolant Fluorinert. Its cost was $17.6 million. What the Cray 2 accomplished in one second had taken a year to accomplish by hand in 1952. This computer was used to study intense magnetic fields associated with fusion reactors and to help design heat shields for space exploration.

In 1985 Cray began work on the Cray 3, using 16 processors. This machine was based on gallium arsenide* instead of silicon*, but the design was eventually dropped due to its high development cost. He then began work on the Cray 4, which would have had 64 processors. This project, too, was dropped. Cray Computer filed for bankruptcy protection in 1995.

Still, Cray was convinced that he could design a high performance, low cost system. By the time of his sudden death in 1996, he had established another new company, SRC Computers, toward this goal.

Two factors are cited in the decline of the supercomputer market. First, competition with cheaper and increasingly powerful microprocessors, and the ability for minicomputers to be networked, helped reduce the demand for very expensive machines. Second, with the end of the "Cold War," military budgets were slashed. New supercomputers for military use were no longer a practical consideration, reducing the already exclusive market.

▶ See also **Minicomputers • Physics • Supercomputers**

Resources

Books

Slater, Robert. "Seymour Cray: The Hermit of Chippewa Falls and His Simple, 'Dumb Things.'" In *Portraits in Silicon*. Cambridge, MA: MIT Press, 1987.

More Power

The evolution of supercomputers has continued along divergent paths. Less than five years after Cray's death in 1996, Apple Computer's G4 series of supercomputers became the first desktop systems to deliver a sustained performance of more than one gigaflop, with a theoretical peak performance of 5.3 gigaflops. The G4 Cube takes up less than eight square inches of desk space, and costs less than $2,000. By 2001, the world's most powerful supercomputers, from companies like Cray, Inc. and NEC, could deal with trillions of calculations per second and MPPs (massively parallel processors). They cost millions.

* **gallium arsenide** a chemical used in the production of semiconductor devices; chemical symbol GaAs

* **silicon** a chemical element with symbol Si; the most abundant element in the Earth's crust and the most commonly used semiconductor material

Periodicals

Markoff, John. "Seymour Cray, Computer Industry Pioneer and Father of the Supercomputer, Dies at 71." *New York Times*, October 6, 1996, p. 1.

Web Sites

"Cray History." Cray Inc. http://www.cray.com/About/History.aspx (accessed November 2, 2012).

"Power Macintosh G4 Cube." Apple Computer, Inc. http://apple-history.com/g4cube (accessed November 2, 2012).

D

Data Processing

Everyone is familiar with the term "word processing," but computers were really developed for "data processing"—the organization and manipulation of large amounts of numeric data, or in computer jargon, "number crunching." Some examples of data processing are calculation of satellite orbits, weather forecasting, statistical analyses, and in a more practical sense, business applications such as accounting, payroll, and billing.

The story of the development of the computer reveals that for centuries people created and used a variety of mechanical devices to simplify the calculation and processing of numeric data. One of the most relevant occurrences in the development of the computer was the work done by American engineer Herman Hollerith (1860–1929) in 1889. In seeking to develop an easier and quicker method to count the U.S. Census, he decided to use punched card*s to record the data and then use the cards as input into a calculating machine designed to tabulate the data. The technique worked and Hollerith eventually founded the Tabulating Machine Company. In the 1920s, this company became the International Business Machines (IBM) Corporation.

Another important phase in the computer's development also involved seeking a simpler solution for calculations involving large amounts of numeric data. During World War II, the accurate targeting of large artillery guns required frequent solutions of many complex mathematical formulae. The first electronic, general purpose digital computer—known as the Electronic Numerical Integrator and Computer (ENIAC)—was developed to produce such calculations. ENIAC eventually lead to the development of the Universal Automatic Calculator (UNIVAC) series of computers that for many years rivaled those produced by IBM in the field of data processing.

Subsequently, computers have been the mainstay of data processing, particularly for the business world where they long ago replaced tabulating machines. Computers now allow for the automation of functions such as payroll and billing that previously required an army of clerks and a room full of filing cabinets. Indeed, the data processing needs of the business world were as influential in the development of computer technology as were the government's need for accurate census enumeration and the military's need for faster ballistic trajectory calculations.

One of the most significant developments in data processing for business needs was computer data storage and retrieval, or databases and database management systems. A database is an organized collection of logically related data, which can be shared by different computer programs

* **punched card** a paper card with punched holes which give instructions to a computer in order to encode program instructions and data

The ENIAC

The Electronic Numerical Integrator and Computer (ENIAC) was developed by J. Presper Eckert Jr. and John Mauchly. It was first used in ballistics testing for the military following World War II. The huge ENIAC was nothing like a personal computer as it weighed about thirty tons and contained about 18,000 vacuum tubes.

* **relational database** a collection of records that permits logical and business relationships to be developed between themselves and their contents

known as application programs. A database management system (DBMS) is a computer program that creates, maintains, and accesses the database. The database approach has many advantages over simply storing data directly in computer programs. Database systems originated in the late 1950s and early 1960s, largely by research and development personnel at IBM in response to the needs of the business community. Today, one of the most popular database and program combinations is the relational database* and the management system (RDBMS).

With today's personal computers, many data processing applications developed for business use are now routinely available to everyone. Some examples include spreadsheets, personal finance software, and database programs. Although they can be used in other ways, spreadsheets were developed for accounting and are basically automated ledger books. They utilize columns and rows to display numbers and text, and allow calculations to be performed on the data. Some typical spreadsheet software packages include Excel (produced by Microsoft), Lotus 1-2-3 (Lotus Software), and QuattroPro (Borland Software). Personal finance software such as Quicken (Intuit) can help people manage money and budgets as well as aid in calculating taxes

Database and database management systems are valuable data processing tools. Oracle (Oracle Corporation), MySQL (now owned by Oracle Corporation), and Access (Microsoft) are database programs readily available today. Microsoft's Access database program, and its Excel spreadsheet program, are both typically bundled in Microsoft's "Office" suite of interrelated desktop programs; the latest version is Office 2010.

Data processing is a vital function of business and personal computers, and the desire to find easier ways to handle large amounts of numeric data was one of the major driving forces in the development of the digital computer. Indeed, numeric calculations are the backbone of computer operations since all operations are based on binary digits (0,1), or simple numbers. Consequently even when an application is functioning as a "word processor," or a user is playing games, the computer is, in fact, performing data processing.

 See also **Abacus • Hollerith, Herman • Office Automation Systems • Tabulating Machines**

Resources

Book

Kroenke, David, and David Auer. *Database Processing: Fundamentals, Design, and Implementation*, 12th ed. Boston: Pearson, 2012.

Web Site

University of Iowa. "Punched Cards: A Brief Illustrated Technical History." http://homepage.cs.uiowa.edu/˜jones/cards/history.html (accessed November 4, 2012).

Data Visualization

* **filter queries** queries used to select subsets from a data collection, e.g., all documents with a creation date later than 01/01/2000

"A picture is worth 1,000 words." Data visualization is based on this old adage, pointing out the value of displaying quantitative information as images or graphs. The idea is to convey the meaning of the data in a simple and intuitive manner. This is achieved by mapping quantity into geometric attributes, length, area, color, symbols, positions, curves, or other visual cues. Common graphs are *histograms* or *bar charts*, displaying quantity as length; *pie charts* for presenting parts of a whole; *time series*, which show the development of a variable over time; and *scatterplots* showing the relationships between two variables by marking pairing quantities. These graphs are abstract, but use real-world properties to support intuitive understanding. A pie diagram makes associations to bakery goods, time series to mountains and valleys, and scatterplots may be discussed using terms such as position, closeness, distance, groups, and outliers or individuals.

The physical connection is more direct in maps, where the information space itself is a real-world representation. Maps are an ideal information space for displaying any type of geographically based data, using concrete or abstract symbols. Depths and heights may be converted into color, for example, on a scale from dark blue, to shades of greens, to dark brown to symbolize the highest mountains. Other geographical data may be presented in different layers on the same map, as when lines represent borders, arrows visualize winds and currents, and symbols show the presence of hospitals or churches. More abstract data can be displayed by positioning pie and bar charts on the map or by using color-coding or shading of areas.

Although the first geographical maps were drawn on clay tablets more than 5,000 years ago, data maps and other visualizations were first created in the seventeenth century. With a few exceptions, such as seismograms from earthquake detectors and electrocardiograms from heart monitors, the graphs had to be made by hand and handled separately from text through the printing process. This changed with the advent of the computer, which made it easy to collect and organize large amounts of data, to create graphs automatically through spreadsheet programs, and to integrate text and graphics in modern word processing software. With laser printers, copying machines, and offset technology, graphics can be printed as easily as text. Data visualization has therefore become an important part of many documents, whether a student paper, scientific journal, or newspaper.

For online presentations, it is possible to create dynamic visualizations. Here the user may set up filter queries* that select the data to be displayed, choose display methodology, select values to be presented on different axes, and so on. The most advanced systems may also present simulations, showing how data sets change over time. In online systems the visualization may act as an interface to an underlying database, for example by letting the user retrieve an object by clicking on its representation on the display.

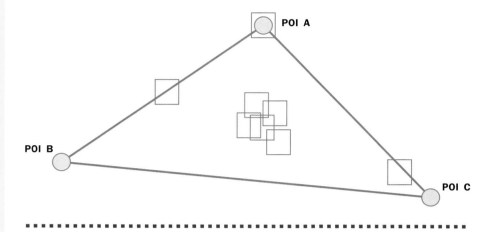

POI A

POI B

POI C

Figure 1. VIBE display space with three POIs. *Reproduced by permission of Gale, a part of Cengage Learning.*

Visualizing More than Two Dimensions

Most common visualization techniques are based on one or two variables, but different techniques can be used to visualize higher dimensions. For instance, shadowing techniques may give depth to the display, adding a third axis, or the user may be able to rotate a multidimensional display, looking at it from different viewpoints. Visual Information Browsing Environment (VIBE), an experimental system, uses a different approach based on relative position of data objects with regard to a user-defined visualization space. The metaphor behind this system is a bookshelf, for example where books on geography may be stacked to the left, books on history to the right. A book on historical geography may then naturally be inserted in the middle.

A VIBE display space is shown in the accompanying figure. It is defined by three Points Of Interest (POI)s, shown by circles in the diagram. Data objects are represented as rectangles and will be positioned according to the score they have on each POI. For example, an object that gets a score on A only, will be positioned on top of A; an object that gets a score on A and B, but a zero score on C is positioned between A and B, closest to the POI with the highest score; an object that get a similar score on all three POIs will be positioned in the middle of the space. The coordinates for the documents are calculated as an average of the POI coordinates, weighted by the POI scores. See Figure 1.

VIBE works with any type of data. A manufacturer, for example, may use VIBE to display its products in a space defined by POIs such as a price, weight, or volume, while a student may wish to present readings in a space with POIs defined by terms such as "history" or "geography." In the latter case, a function will be needed to map the concept into a numerical score, which may be as simple as counting the frequency of the POI terms within each document. VIBE allows for any number of POIs in a multidimensional display. However, with more than three POIs, the display may become ambiguous, and the user may need to assign colors to POIs or move POIs around to see the correlation between the objects. An advantage with visualization over statistical methods is that all data objects will be shown. VIBE has been used with as many as several thousand objects. The display may then show clusters, positions where most of the objects fall, but still be able to present icons for individual data objects.

Pitfalls with Visual Displays

A picture does not always say more than 1,000 words! Graphs may use so many visual effects that they become confusing for the reader, hiding the meaning of the data. Ideally, the size of the effect shown in the graphic should be similar to the size of the effect in the data. Typical distortions are found in time series of monetary data, where values are not adjusted for inflation or where a special scale is not made apparent to the reader. In a three-dimensional pie chart, the sector in front may look bigger than the one in the back, even if the quantities are identical. It is interesting to see that publications that take accuracy very seriously often fail in their graphics. In addition to controlling the effects of the graphic, it is important to consider if a graphic is needed at all! A few numbers may often be presented better directly in the text or as a table than in a pie chart.

▶ *See also* **Database Management Software • Image Analysis: Medicine • Scientific Visualization**

Resources

Books

Fry, Ben. *Visualizing Data: Exploring and Explaining Data with the Processing Environment.* Beijing, China, and Sebastopol, CA: O'Reilly Media, 2008.

Web Sites

Vitaly Friedman. "Data Visualization: Modern Approaches." *Smashing Magazine*, August 2, 2007. http://www.smashingmagazine. com/2007/08/02/data-visualization-modern-approaches/ (accessed November 4, 2012).

Database Management Software

Databases are software applications designed to store and retrieve information. Databases have long been employed as a vital tool by government and business to store, organize, and locate information. Modern database management systems are complex software applications that combine information from discrete sources, allowing information to be quickly

What Is A Histogram?

A histogram reveals statistics in the form of a bar graph. It is used to indicate variations in the topic being studied. Histograms can provide data on the success or failure of a product, process, or procedure. For example, by studying the sales revenue of a new computer system over the course of several years via a histogram, the manufacturer can determine the success of the product.

* **data mining** a technique of automatically obtaining information from databases that is normally hidden or not obvious

* **relational database** a collection of records that permits logical and business relationships to be developed between themselves and their contents

located and displayed to the user. Perhaps the most elementary example of a database is a simple list of names and their associated phone numbers.

Databases are used for problem solving by all types and sizes of organizations, as well as by consumers, often also referred to as end users. Businesses commonly employ electronic databases to store and retrieve lists of customer names, addresses, phone numbers, billing information, and other data valuable to the organization. Databases are used to solve problems and to answer important questions, such as how much money the company owes, to whom, and to flag when the account becomes past due for payment. They can be also used for data mining* to query large knowledge bases, making them vital in helping organizations achieve financial goals, increase customer satisfaction as well as efficiency, and reap profits.

With the advent of the personal computer, database software has become standard in business, government, and even private individuals' work to store, sort, and retrieve information. The Internet has proven to be a valuable backbone for allowing users to access vast databases from remote locations using a personal computer equipped with a modem and communication software. Business and government organizations rely on computer networks and the Internet to distribute databases to their workers and customers. Consumers utilize stand-alone personal computers to create and access databases to store and retrieve information. Common consumer database applications include storing lists of names, addresses, phone numbers, recipes, videos, compact discs (CDs), digital versatile discs (DVDs), etc. Databases can be used to store a wide variety of information in various formats and can also be used to store and retrieve graphics, sounds, text, or a mixture of these formats.

Database Structure

Databases are computer files that store information. These data can be of many different types and formats, depending on the mission. All databases store data in tables or groups of tables. Each table consists of rows and columns, not unlike a grid or graph. Vertical columns of a table are called fields, and the horizontal rows are called records. Each field has a label at the top, and each record has a number at the left margin.

Relational Databases

When two or more tables are related in a database, it is known as a "relational database*." Relational databases allow records from more than one table to be searched and displayed. The two or more tables must share a common field, like name, phone number, etc. If two tables contain a field that is common to both tables, then the data from two tables can be searched in a single query.

SQL

Structured Query Language (SQL) is becoming the standard dialect for accessing database management systems. SQL permits users to perform a wide variety of functions, including creating databases, adding information, updating or altering information stored in the database, deleting data, searching for specific information, and displaying that information once it has been located by a query. SQL can be utilized to search more than one table at a time and can then construct new tables of information. SQL also permits users to change the structure of an existing database and to modify security settings.

SQL command statements are entered via the keyboard and are executed like a software program. Assume that a company has a database table called "employees." This table contains the complete list of all employees with their name, address, city, and phone number. If a list is needed of all the names and phone numbers in this table, one would write the SQL statement as follows:

Select FirstName, LastName, Phone

From EmployeeTable;

The preceding statement tells the database to display all the entries in the table because no specific search condition is specified. If the scope of the search is limited to employees living in a specific city, then one would write the following SQL statement using the Where command.

Select FirstName, LastName, Phone

From EmployeeTable

Where City = "Boston";

SQL was first formally standardized by the American National Standards Institute (ANSI) in 1986. Since that time, several upgraded standards for SQL have been created. The latest SQL standard—as of 2012—was published in 2011 and is denoted as "SQL:2011."

Commercial Database Products

There are numerous database development software packages on the market, and they meet a wide variety of end user and commercial applications. These packages support a wide variety of operating systems and computer platforms, including Windows, Macintosh, Linux, and others. Each is intended either for commercial or consumer applications.

Microsoft produces the Access database development software. This package runs under the Windows operating system and is intended for both business and consumer applications. It also offers SQL Server for large database projects. Oracle is a database development software package for creating powerful applications for large-scale database applications in sizable organizations and government agencies. File Maker Pro is a Macintosh-based database development package for commercial and consumer sized applications.

Security

The security and integrity of information systems is of vast importance to organizations, and significant resources are often deployed in this area. The overall integrity and security of the database is the joint responsibility of the network administrator and the database administrator.

If the database resides on a network, which is typical, network security is the first line of defense to protect the database and the information stored within it. Network administrators can limit access to the directory or files where the actual data and program files are stored. This denies access to those who would delete, modify, or corrupt these files.

Working in concert with the network administrator, the database administrator is responsible for ensuring that the database system is secure from unauthorized use and access. Additional responsibilities include modifying the database and upgrading or maintaining the system. The database administrator secures the database application by applying the security settings offered by the particular database package to prevent unauthorized access. The administrator accomplishes this by assigning user names and passwords to everyone in the organization.

Such a system forces users to log onto the system with a valid user name and password before gaining access. The user name and password tell the database software what type of access to grant to the user. This prevents data stored in the database from being altered, deleted, or copied without permission. Access rights are arranged in a hierarchy, with some users having limited access, while trusted users have expanded access. Groups of users can be confined to a "read only" mode that allows them to read information stored in the database but prevents them from making any alterations.

Database management software systems have created the ability to store and retrieve large quantities of information. They have allowed data from widely dissimilar sources to be correlated in order to solve problems and answer questions. They allow companies to maintain lists of their customers, suppliers, inventory, financial records, trade secrets, and other valuable information. Databases can be used to store and retrieve information in many different formats: graphics, sound, text, and mixed modes. The SQL allows databases to be created, populated, updated, and searched. Database management systems can be accessed using stand-alone computers, office networks, and the global Internet, and are undergoing constant evolution and expansion.

▶ *See also* **Computer Supported Cooperative Work (CSCW) • Productivity Software • SQL • SQL: Databases**

Resources

Books

McFadden, Fred R., Jeffrey A. Hoffer, and Mary B. Prescott. *Modern Database Management.* 8th ed. Upper Saddle River, NJ: Prentice Hall, 2007.

Web Sites

ISO "ISO/IEC 9075-1:2011" http://www.iso.org/iso/home/store/catalogue_tc/catalogue_detail.htm?csnumber=53681 (accessed October 8, 2012).

Decision Support Systems

Computer systems that provide users with support to analyze complex information and help to make decisions are called decision support systems (DSSs). In some cases, such systems may predict the impact of decisions before they are made.

Decision support systems are an advancement of management information systems, whose main purpose is to supply information to managers. Although the functions of management information systems are limited mostly to control of storage, organization, retrieval, and maintaining the security and integrity of data, decision support systems include model building and model-based reasoning capabilities. Decision support systems do not have the problem-solving competence of expert systems, however, which are programmed with the knowledge of human experts and can make some final decisions without human intervention. Decision support systems generally help human beings solve complex problems, and provide data that can lead to non-predetermined solutions that are beyond the limitations of expert systems.

The concept of decision support systems originated in the late 1950s and early 1960s, when researchers at Carnegie Institute of Technology located in Pittsburgh, Pennsylvania, conducted pioneering studies of organizational decision-making. Some time later Tom Gerrity and a team of scientists performed research on interactive computing at the Massachusetts Institute of Technology. One of their projects was dedicated to supporting investment managers in the administration of their clients' stock portfolios. These original studies were mostly done by graduate students and professors at leading engineering and business schools who had access to the most advanced computer systems of that time. It became obvious at the time that the emerging computer technology could serve as an excellent tool for the development of decision support systems.

Later on, scientists and computer programmers applied analytical and scientific methods for the development of more sophisticated DSSs. They used mathematical models and algorithm*s from such fields of study as artificial intelligence (AI)*, mathematical simulation and optimization, and concepts of mathematical logic.

In recent years, decision support tools like data warehousing* and online analytical applications have enhanced the capabilities of decision support systems. Joint efforts of scientists and programmers resulted in the development of the DSS generator—software for the building of decision support systems customized to the user's requirements.

Applications

Over the years DSSs have gained popularity in such areas as business management, medicine and health care, the military, environmental policy, and other areas that involve risk management, proper resource allocation, and similar tactical and strategic decisions. Decision-making is particularly important in the areas of business and finance. Very often,

algorithm a rule or procedure used to solve a mathematical problem—most often described as a sequence of steps

artificial intelligence (AI) a branch of computer science dealing with creating computer hardware and software to mimic the way people think and perform practical tasks

data warehousing to implement an informational database used to store shared data

* **meteorological** pertaining to the study of the atmosphere and weather phenomena

distribution of valuable resources and large sums of money are based on human intuitive judgment. DSSs provide aid in such tasks as cash flow analysis, break-even analysis, scenario analysis, and inventory techniques. The number of working DSSs demonstrates the necessity of such systems. The Taxpayers' Assistant System of the U.S. Internal Revenue Service helps its personnel give correct tax information to taxpayers. Also, DSS programs assist credit card company employees in allowing or disallowing certain charges, and advise bank officers regarding loans and mortgage approvals.

In manufacturing, decision support systems are solving design problems by using analytical, statistical, and model-building software, especially in the car- and aircraft-making industries. Such giants of automotive industry as General Motors and Ford Motor Company use comprehensive decision support systems.

Systems for scheduling and customer support are universally available for use in different fields. Their use helps bring down costs and increase service efficiency. American Airlines developed a system to schedule airplanes for required maintenance. As people deal with increasingly complex machinery and sophisticated instrumentation, DSSs become an important component in service and customer support, particularly providing expertise in troubleshooting and systems operation.

Decision support systems are also widely used in environmental science, particularly in air quality impact analysis. For example, a model developed by the Stanford Research Institute computes hourly averages of carbon monoxide for any urban location, while a program developed by the Argonne National Laboratory of Illinois provides meteorological* data and classifies sources of emission for the Federal Aviation Administration (FAA).

Healthcare professionals are assisted by decision support tools in determining the prognosis of individual patients based on an analysis of clinical data, and in determining whether a patient is eligible for clinical research based on the patient's clinical history. Applications such as alerting systems, critiquing systems, and diagnostic suggestion systems are utilized in hospital operating rooms, intensive care units, laboratories, and other medical facilities. Implementation of these tools can significantly improve the quality and reduce the cost of health care.

These and other DSSs may work actively or in a passive mode. Passive systems are mostly used by physicians for reference purposes, while active systems give advice in certain situations, such as alerting medical personnel when a parameter being monitored in a patient—such as temperature or heart rate—exceeds its designated threshold value.

Whether they are active or passive systems, healthcare decision support systems are limited to the role of advisor to clinicians and other healthcare professionals. They do not act as expert systems. Only physicians themselves are responsible for decisions made concerning human health; DSSs act as information tools in this and other circumstances.

Components

An effective decision support system requires reliable data and usually includes an interactive user interface*, a knowledge base, and an inference (reasoning) engine.

The knowledge base is the component of a DSS that contains both well-established facts and results obtained by trial-and-error methods. It may include such different elements as formulas (algebraic, logical, or statistical expressions), guidelines, and knowledge of risk and cost of operations. Often knowledge is presented in the form of rules.

The inference engine is a complex computer algorithm, which uses the data in the knowledge base to obtain a solution to a problem. There are two approaches for decision-making systems: under certainty and under uncertainty. Decision-making under certainty most often utilizes a mathematical model that gives an unambiguous response. On the other hand, decision-making under uncertainty uses statistical approaches, such as Bayesian networks*, neural networks*, and other methods of AI.

The advancement of decision support systems would be impossible without its interaction with a number of related fields. Business analysts and mathematicians develop mathematical models for use in DSS, software engineers provide tools for knowledge maintenance and data mining, and psychologists assist in DSS design by conducting behavioral decision-making research.

As the need for more sophisticated decision-making will increase in the future, it is probable that decision support systems will become more intelligent and user friendly, and applicable to a broader spectrum of professions.

 See also **Information Systems • Integrated Software • Medical Systems**

Resources

Books

Berner, Eta S., ed. *Clinical Decision Support Systems: Theory and Practice.* 2nd ed. New York: Springer, 2007.

Marakas, George M. *Decision Support Systems in the 21st Century.* 2nd ed. Upper Saddle River, NJ: Prentice Hall, 2003.

Turban, Efraim, and Jay E. Aronson. *Decision Support Systems and Intelligent Systems.* 7th ed. Upper Saddle River, NJ: Prentice Hall, 2005

Periodical

Krol, Marina, and David L. Reich. "Development of a Decision Support System for Detecting Critical Conditions during Anesthesia." *Journal of Medical Systems* 24, no. 3 (2000): 141–146.

Xplaining One's Options

Decision support systems provide people in various trades and occupations with data to help them make informed judgments. In the field of medicine, DXplain is one such system. Culling data from a depository of 2,000 diseases and 5,000 clinical probabilities associated with those ailments, DXplain offers information on symptoms and treatment options. The system is used at hospitals and in medical schools as a reference tool.

* **interface** a boundary or border between two or more objects or systems; also a point of access

* **Bayesian networks** structures that describe systems in which there is a degree of uncertainty; used in automated decision making

* **neural networks** pattern recognition systems whose structure and operation are loosely inspired by analogy to neurons in the human brain

Desktop Publishing

Desktop publishing (DTP) refers to the practice of producing high quality printed output, fully paginated including graphics, using personal computers, page layout software, and printers designed to create near typeset-quality pages. This technology is vital to printers, publishers, designers, and authors who use it to reduce drastically the time it takes to design and publish print products with minimal labor and a shorter revisions process. It also enables people who wish to publish a work to do so independently from a publisher and without a typesetter or printing press.

The core technologies (the personal computer, WYSIWYG—"what you see is what you get"—text processing, page description languages, and high-resolution laser printing) were developed at the Xerox Palo Alto Research Center (PARC) in the 1970s. However the particular configuration that launched the commercial phenomenon of DTP in 1985 consisted of Apple Macintosh personal computers running Aldus Publishing's PageMaker page layout software, connected to Apple's 300 dpi Laserwriter laser printer with the Adobe Postscript page description language.

DTP has significant differences from word processing, and requires different software packages to be truly effective. A popular DTP title for home and small business use is Microsoft Publisher, which allows text and graphics to be placed in arbitrary regions of a page. Compared to Microsoft Word, a comparable word processor, text and images can be placed in a document, but the layout of a document always starts from the top of a page. Carriage returns can be inserted to move the cursor down the page and text justification and tabs can be used to move from the left-hand side of the page to the right-hand side, but this does not equate with the layout options provided by DTP software. Complex image manipulation and layering is also not feasible in word processing software. Just as word processors cannot replace DTP software for complex layout tasks, DTP software is not equipped to replace word processors for creation of large documents. Choosing the right tool for the job is an adage, which still holds true for software assisted tasks.

The emergence of DTP was a major event in the history of publishing technology because it allowed almost any small organization, even individuals, to easily and inexpensively produce hardcopy printed pages suitable for use as printing masters. These had the potential to be nearly comparable in aesthetic appearance and typesetting features to what had previously required far more costly, time consuming, and hard-to-use technologies, expertise, and workflows. DTP also positioned its users to take advantage of digital inputs, which was important as word processing became the routine method for document creation.

Historical Context of Communication Technologies

The social and technological significance of DTP can be best seen by placing it in historical context as an innovation in communication technology.

Many historians and anthropologists consider the emergence of writing to be an absolutely necessary condition for the legal, commercial, and religious systems that characterize civilized societies. Although writing had appeared by 2000 BCE, few important innovations occurred for the next 3,500 years. This was the period of scribal transmission, when texts were published by laboriously copying them by hand. A key advancement during these centuries was the development of phonemic (alphabetic) writing systems that were far easier to learn and use than previous word-based systems or syllabic systems. Other innovations included the development of paper and the codex book (rather than scroll), cursive script, and the development of social organizations to manage copying (such as the scriptorium of western medieval Europe). Despite these innovations, by the end of the Middle Ages* books were still extremely rare and expensive to produce, publishing remained a sophisticated specialist practice, and writing and reading were rather rare abilities.

The dramatic emergence of printing press technology in late fifteenth-century Europe made it possible to reproduce texts far more easily, and with greater fidelity, than was possible with scribal transmission. The consequences of this invention radically affected all aspects of our social, political, religious, and cultural lives. Printing is now recognized by historians as perhaps the single most influential technological event for western civilization.

A Walk Through Mid-Twentieth Century Printing

Contemporary life involves an immersion in printed material: newspapers, magazines, textbooks, scientific journals, instruction manuals, technical documentation, charts, tables, contracts, receipts, business proposals, catalogs, junk mail, brochures, flyers, product packaging, and so on. But the production of the visually pleasing pages that support this flow of information has until very recently been an expensive and time-consuming process, requiring specialized expertise of many kinds and very costly equipment.

The steam operated presses and hot type of the nineteenth century gave way to phototypesetting and computer composition by the mid-twentieth century. However, the publishing process of the 1970s and early 1980s was still an extremely complicated and expensive process.

Consider for example a relatively simple book with black and white line art. Designers prepared written specifications for typography and layout. These were delivered to editors who, perhaps after several revision cycles, used them to mark up typewritten or word-processed manuscripts. The marked up copy then went to a composition house where computer compositors entered, usually by hand, texts and formatting commands into computer files in order to implement the instructions expressed in the markup.

Next, in a separate step, these files were batch processing* by composition software to create data files in the specific language used by

* **Middle Ages** the time period that lasted from around the fifth century AD through the middle of the fifteenth century AD

* **batch processing** an approach to computer utilization that queues noninteractive programs and runs them one after another

a particular phototypesetting machine. Samples of the phototypesetting (imaged on film) were sent back to the compositor and editor for approval. Note that with no previewing capability, this was the first opportunity the compositor had to see the actual visual effects of the formatting codes.

When samples finally appeared correct to the compositors, they were sent back to the editor who verified that they met the original design specifications. Several iterations might be involved, and given the nature of the process, even the purely mechanical part of the iteration could take as long as twenty-four hours, especially if either composition or typesetting were outsourced to another company, which was quite a normal procedure. Moreover, if several computers were involved (e.g., the copyeditor's computer, the composition computer, and the typesetting computer), removable media such as eight-track tapes had to be prepared and delivered physically.

Once the samples seemed to be correct, a complete set of galleys (un-paginated formatted text) were produced, along with sets of captions, page numbers, running titles, and other features needed to make up the printed page. All of these, along with needed artwork, were sent to paste-up specialists who used razor tools, paste, and hot wax to physically compose each individual page on special paste-up boards by cutting the galleys of type into columns and pages, adding the artwork (prepared separately), and adding the individual running titles, page numbers, captions, etc. Indexes, in-text references to pages or numbered figures, variable running titles, and other page-based apparatus could not be constructed until pagination was known, so they could only now be composed by the compositors and processed by the layout artists. The completed paste-up boards (termed mechanicals) were then stacked and transported to the printer. From these boards were created printing plates.

Corrections or changes required time-consuming repetitions of this process, and, in particular, any changes that resulted in a change in pagination were enormously expensive. The final product could not be easily revised, updated, or repackaged for other uses or for other delivery formats, whether analog (anthologies, abridgements, new editions) or digital (CD-ROMS, databases, e-books, web pages).

While it is true that systems were eventually developed that allowed text to be composed into pages interactively and previewed in a WYSIWYG ("What you see is what you get") environment by the compositor, these were expensive, typically could not accommodate artwork, and in any case were not widely used, even by the early 1980s.

The Emergence of Desktop Publishing

In the mid–1980s, a revolution occurred which radically changed the publishing process. This change was the result of two things, each itself a combination of recently developed hardware and software:

- WYSIWYG page layout software running on a personal computer;
- a high resolution all-points-addressable matrix printer with high-function page description software.

The revolutionary personal computer was the Apple Macintosh. The page layout software was PageMaker, released by Aldus Publishing. The printer was the Apple Laserwriter, and the page description software was termed Postscript, by Adobe. The marketing of these components in 1985 marked the commercial debut of DTP.

Problems with Desktop Publishing

This new, widely accessible, generally affordable technology for mass producing typeset-quality pages, complete with graphics, offered many improvements over previous technologies. However DTP also brought with it some problems.

Quality Concerns   The low cost of equipment and the ease with which software could be learned seemed to suggest that anyone who could acquire and operate the tools could create and produce typeset-quality pages. The graphics specialists who knew how to design pleasing pages were rapidly replaced in many organizations by clerical workers or by professionals in other disciplines whose chief qualification for DTP was their expertise in operating an office computer. Because it was assumed that DTP software could be implemented with little or no training, organizations eliminated whole departments and discarded traditional processes of design and production.

Without a framework of policies and procedures to oversee the use of DTP tools, the result was very frequently a loss not only of visual quality (the ransom note effect one gets from ugly combinations of fonts and bad composition practices), but also—and much more importantly—a loss of accuracy and effectiveness of the printed materials. Ironically, many organizations discovered that the money-saving potential of DTP tools actually led to an overall loss of efficiency, as tasks that had once been done by professional designers became time-consuming additions to the workload of people with other primary responsibilities.

Information Management Concerns   During the late 1970s and early 1980s another major revolution in publishing was underway. The descriptive markup approach organized digital documents into structures of logical components (such as chapters, sections, titles, paragraphs, lists, block quotations, and other similar items), and then separately associated formatting rules with each type of component. This approach turned out to have many advantages over directly inserting formatting codes into the document, making it easier to create documents, globally alter formatting, support information retrieval, print on a variety of output devices, convert to different file formats, or customize output for a variety of purposes. Documents created this way could be flexibly repurposed for different products and delivery systems. This way of managing a document as a database is based on fundamental principles of information management.

The creators of DTP systems rarely followed these insights, however, preferring instead to focus on the intuitive ease-of-use and composition

The Scriptorium

In the days before the printing press, copies of books had to be created by hand. To assist in this endeavor, scriptoria (copying rooms) were established. These rooms were often cold and ill-lit, as heat and artificial light from candles were perceived to be fire hazards. In some scriptoria, someone would read the text aloud while others copied it. In monastic scriptoria, monks worked alone.

* **XML** the acronym for eXtensible Markup Language; a method of applying structure to data so that documents can be represented

capabilities of the software. As a result, early DTP products were generally far less versatile and functional than they might have been. It was hard to import data easily from other, more structured formats. Even more significantly, it was difficult to use content that had been processed by DTP systems for anything other than the original intended printed products: DTP files could not be easily repurposed for delivery on CD-ROMs (compact discs-read only memory) or the web. It was also difficult to access files by information retrieval tools, import them into databases, or integrate them with emerging networked information systems.

Today these problems are being addressed. In particular, the descriptive markup approach to creating and managing content is increasingly integrated with DTP tools and practices, due in part, perhaps, to the recent near-universal acceptance of XML* as the standard language for describing publishing content. It is now recognized that the production of effective high-quality publications requires carefully thought-out processes and compliance with fundamental principles of information management. There is no substitute for expertise and carefully defined systems. And there is no substitution for principles and best practices.

DTP is now common in business, government, and education. It continues to be based on the same basic components found in the original configuration of 1985: high-resolution all-points-addressable matrix printers, personal computers, interactive page-layout and graphics software, and page description printing software—each easy-to-use, powerful, and relatively inexpensive. The challenge now is to integrate DTP into the wider process of creating, managing, and delivering information in the networked world.

 See also **Document Processing • Integrated Software • Markup Languages • Technology of Desktop Publishing**

Resources

Books

Hinderliter, Hal. *Desktop Publishing Primer*. Pittsburgh: GATF Press, 2004.

Lake, Susan E. L., and Karen Bean. *Digital Desktop Publishing*. Mason, OH: Thomson/South-Western, 2008.

MacRae, Kyle. *Desktop Publishing Manual*. Sparkford, Yeovil: Haynes, 2006.

Redmond, Kate, Claire Thompson, Julie Wakeling, and James Paul Wallis. *13 Desktop Publishing Projects for Beginners at Home*. Millom, UK: Helpful Book Company, 2007.

Weixel, Suzanne. *Desktop Publishing Basics*. Boston: Thompson Course Technology, 2004.

Distance Learning

The terms distance learning, distance education, and distributed learning often are used interchangeably, though some authors make sharp distinctions between their meanings. Distance education typically refers to distributed learning resources in academic settings, whereas distance learning is commonly defined as the acquisition of knowledge and skills through mediated information and instruction. The focus of the former term is on the process of teaching and its supporting systems whereas the focus of the latter is on the process of learning.

Distance learning can take a wide variety of forms, but generally it means that the instructor and learners are in different places or the teaching and learning occur at different times. Interaction among participants and with the learning resources usually involves some form of electronic media or mediated communication. Distance education can be online courses or hybrid/blended online, meaning that some portions are on-site while others are on-line.

Distance learning has been a feature of higher education in the United States for more than a century. Since 1890, an estimated 130 million Americans have taken distance or correspondence study courses. These courses are not offered exclusively by colleges and universities, but also by businesses, nonprofit organizations, trade associations, and the military, among others. According to the U.S. Department of Education, the percentage of undergraduate students enrolled in at least one distance-learning class increased from 8 percent in 2000 to 20 percent in 2008. Further, in the same period the percentage of students enrolled in a degree program through distance learning increased from 2 percent to 4 percent. In addition, 27 percent of students were found to be studying computer

Students taking online courses via Florida's Virtual School. © *AP Images/ John Raoux.*

* **bandwidth** a measure of the frequency component of a signal or the capacity of a communication channel to carry signals

science and taking distance-learning classes, as opposed to 20 percent of students studying other fields and taking distance-learning classes. Eight percent of these computer science students were in degree programs, as compared to all other students, who came in at 4 percent. According to statistics from the Chronicle of Higher Education, the number of students using online learning is expected to grow in the future. Enrollment in higher education for online course was approximately 780,000 in 2011. Experts expect that number to increase to 3.97 million in 2014. The growth for online courses is so great that many institutions, based on community college surveys, are reporting that they are unable to meet the needs of students wanting such courses. Distance learning is also an international phenomenon. For example, the pioneering United Kingdom's Open University estimated that it had served more than two million people in its first thirty years.

Accreditation

The Distance Education and Training Council (DETC), founded in 1926, is a nonprofit (501 c 6) educational organization that is acknowledged by the U.S. Department of Education as the "nationally recognized accrediting agency" for distance learning institutions. Headquartered in Washington, D.C., the DETC provides distance learning institutions with the most current, practical, and relevant services available.

Technology in Distance Learning

Technology has played an increasingly important role in the delivery of distance education and in the distribution of distance learning resources. In 1890, distance education equated to correspondence (home) study where students worked through specially prepared self-instructional print materials, submitted assignments, and received feedback from their instructors via mail. This model is still the prevalent form of distance education throughout the world. The advent of radio and television brought another dimension to distance learning, and for a time they were heralded as replacements for the classroom.

During the 1980s, interactive television (ITV) emerged as an effective tool for engaging students studying at a distance. ITV connects multiple classrooms by way of two-way audio and video communication. An instructor teaching a class at the home site can see and talk with students at far site classrooms, as they can with the students in the room at the home site. ITV uses hardware and software solutions to compress the video stream so more information can be sent over relatively low bandwidth* communications lines. For example, three Integrated Services Digital Network (ISDN) lines can provide 384 kilobits per second (Kbps) of dedicated between sites, enabling full-motion (30 fps [frames per second]) video and quality audio transmission.

More recently, the Internet has emerged as the preferred technology to support students studying at a distance. Along with this trend, a new breed of integrated Web-based tools supports the creation and

* **groupware** a software
technology common in client/
server systems whereby many
users can access and process
data at the same time

delivery of instructional materials and provides a variety of communication capabilities. Products such as *Blackboard* (http://www.blackboard.com/) and *WebCT* (https://vista.unm.edu/webct/) exemplify these course management systems.

Four Distance Learning Models

A wide variety of technologies support learning and the delivery of education. To understand them, consider two dimensions of learning—time and location. Learning technologies can be divided into four quadrants, defined by whether the teacher and learner share the same location (local) or are separated (distant) and by whether the teaching and learning activities take place at the same time (synchronous) or at different times (asynchronous). The case of local/synchronous learning refers to forms of traditional face-to-face instruction and all others refer to distance learning scenarios.

Local/Synchronous The local/synchronous option utilizes the traditional classroom technologies supplemented with computers, VCRs, DVD players, and data/video projection systems that allow the entire class to view videos, presentations, and demonstrations simultaneously. Educational institutions increasingly are building smart classrooms with network access, touch-sensitive display screens (such as *Smart Boards*), and groupware* to support collaborative work in the classroom. Many instructors also prefer to teach in classrooms that are configured with networked computers at every seat or workgroup and with hardware or software technologies that provide computer input and output monitoring and control capabilities. These enable the instructor to grab any student's screen image and display it on all computers in the class or on the large screen. In addition, many institutions are supporting laptop/tablet use in the classroom, either by providing network ports at each seat or providing wireless network access throughout the campus.

Distant/Synchronous The distant/synchronous option is supported by technologies such as Interactive Television. Satellite downlinks and broadcast television provide a higher level of quality and wider reach, but entail greater costs and allow less interaction, typically providing telephone lines for questions from the recipients. As higher-bandwidth access to the Internet becomes more widely available, desktop videoconferencing will become an increasingly effective solution, in either point-to-point or multi-point mode. This option, characterized by software such as Microsoft's *GoToMeeting* (www.gotomeeting.com/) and Internet MegaMeeting's *MegaMeeting* (http://www.megameeting.com/), provides a video and audio link, along with file sharing, application sharing, chat tools, and whiteboards, allowing multiple attendees to view and edit graphic material simultaneously in a shared space. Synchronous chat tools are common components of Web-based course management systems.

Local/Asynchronous The local/asynchronous option has learners physically present in the same place but performing different learning activities. This is characterized by computer lab and small group activities and is supported by technologies such as streaming video, ported classrooms, wireless network access, and computer-based applications.

Distant/Asynchronous The distant/asynchronous model is the oldest and most common form of distance learning model. It uses self-instructional learning materials in forms ranging from paper and pencil to multimedia content posted on Web-based course management systems. Computers are proving to be extremely useful tools in providing active learning experiences, feedback, and communications capabilities. Multimedia enhanced computer-based training (including games and simulations), though difficult and costly to develop, can utilize CD and DVD technologies to great advantage. The Internet also has enabled the effective use of e-mail, list servers, and threaded discussion groups, as well as a host of emerging groupware applications.

Open Learning Initiative

In 2002, Carnegie Mellon University launched the Open Learning Initiative (OLI, http://oli.cmu.edu/), which is a Web-based learning program focused on monitoring students' progress and virtual tutoring. The program helps students by pointing out what concepts are understood from the online work and provides professors with the information necessary to modify lectures for concepts with which students are having trouble. OLI was used in conjunction with a course at a large state university, resulting in a 99 percent course completion rate. The same course conducted without OLI, had a completion rate of only 41 percent. In 2012, OLI at Carnegie Mellon offered, for example, the class Probability and Statistics, which introduced students to the general concepts and logic within statistical reasoning. Many other colleges and universities also provide OLI. For instance, Harvard University offers free OLI classes through its Harvard Extension School's Open Learning Initiative.

In 2011, Stanford University, in California, introduced a novel concept in distance learning that adds to the OLI concept. It is offering its class *Introduction to Artificial Intelligence* free of charge to anyone who is interested and has a solid understanding in linear algebra and probability. Completion of the online course, which is taught by two experts in artificial intelligence, will result in a Certificate of Achievement.

In addition, several U.S. universities are partnering in a not-for-profit online course learning platform called edX. The edX platform provides a way for anyone in the world with an Internet connection to participate in college courses designed by professors. Founded by Harvard University and the Massachusetts Institute of Technology, the edX Universities as they are called, have been joined by the University of California at Berkeley and the University of Texas System (nine universities and six health institutions). The edX Web site is found at https://www.edx.org/.

Job Demand

Whereas distance learning is greatly enhanced through technology, one should not equate it with technology nor associate it exclusively with a single delivery mode (correspondence, telecourses, computer assisted instruction, ITV, or the Web). The essence of distance learning is that it increases dependence on self-instructional course materials and learning activities. This fact has resulted in a dramatically increased job demand for instructional designers (professionals trained in learning and instructional theory and their application) and instructional technologists (professionals experienced in computer, graphics, and multimedia applications).

Some of the leading distance learning schools in the United States are Kaplan University (http://getinfo.kaplan.edu/index.aspx), the University of Phoenix (http://www.phoenix.edu/), Grand Canyon University (http://www.gcu.edu/), and Capella University (http://www.capella.edu).

▶ *See also* **Computer Assisted Instruction** • **Educational Software** • **Telecommunications**

Resources

Books

Bailey, Edward P. *Focus on Distance Education Developments.* New York: Nova Science Publishers, 2007.

Donnelly, Peter, Joel Benson, and Paul Kirk. *How to Succeed at E-learning.* Chichester, UK, and Hoboken, NJ: Wiley-Blackwell, 2012.

Hogan, Robert, ed. *Transnational Distance Learning and Building New Markets for Universities.* Hershey, PA: Information Science Reference, 2012.

Information Resources Management Association, ed. *Virtual Learning Environments: Concepts, Methodologies, Tools, and Applications.* Hershey, PA: Information Science Reference, 2012.

Moller, Leslie, and Jason B. Huett, eds. *The Next Generation of Distance Education: Unconstrained Learning.* New York: Springer, 2012.

Moore, Michael G. *Handbook of Distance Education.* 2nd ed. Mahwah, NJ: L. Erlbaum Associates, 2007.

Morales, Arelene V., ed. *Distance Education Issues and Challenges.* New York: Nova Science Publishers, 2007.

Ruhe, Valerie, and Bruno D. Zumbo. *Evaluation in Distance Education and E-Learning: The Unfolding Model.* New York: Guilford Press, 2009.

Schlosser, Lee Ayers, and Michael R. Simonson. *Distance Education: Definition and Glossary of Terms.* 3rd ed. Charlotte, NC: IAP/Information Age Publishing, 2010.

Essence of Distance Learning (DL)

In distance learning, the instructors and learners are in different places or the teaching and learning occur at different times. While it is greatly enhanced through technology, DL should not be equated with technology nor associated exclusively with a single delivery mode. The essence of distance learning is that it increases dependence on self-instructional course materials and learning activities.

Simonson, Michael R. *Teaching and Learning at a Distance: Foundations of Distance Education*. 5th ed. Boston: Allyn & Bacon, 2012.

Web Sites

Distance Education and Training Council. "About DETC." http://www.detc.org/about.html (accessed October 2, 2012).

DistanceLearningNet.com. "The History of Distance Learning." http://www.distancelearningnet.com/the-history-of-distance-learning/ (accessed October 2, 2012).

Get Educated Inc. "Online Learning on Steroids—Growth Statistics Skyrocketing." http://www.geteducated.com/online-education-facts-and-statistics/latest-online-learning-news-and-research/395-online-distance-education-grows (accessed November 9, 2012).

Harvard Extension School, Harvard University. "Harvard Open Courses: Open Learning Initiative." http://www.extension.harvard.edu/open-learning-initiative (accessed October 2, 2012).

U.S. Department of Education. "Learning at a Distance Undergraduate Enrollment in Distance Education Courses and Degree Programs." http://nces.ed.gov/pubsearch/pubsinfo.asp?pubid=2012154 (accessed November 9, 2012).

E

Economic Modeling

As computing technologies have become more and more sophisticated, economists have come to rely increasingly heavily on computers for a variety of tasks. Today, economists use computers to analyze large quantities of statistical information, to create simulations or scenarios of what might happen to an economy if a particular economic variable, such as the price of oil, changes, and to solve complex mathematical problems that advance our knowledge of economic processes.

Perhaps the most common use of computers in economics is for the analysis of statistical information. Economists refer to this type of analysis as econometrics. Using the large amounts of statistical economic information that are now easily available on the Internet and elsewhere, economists can test simple but important questions about economic behavior. For example, based on data for the past two decades for the fifty states in the United States, these statistics can provide information about how an increase in the price of a pack of cigarettes will affect the number of packs of cigarettes that people buy and how this will reduce the incidence of such health problems as lung cancer and tooth loss. In order to analyze such questions, economists must have access to information on how many packs of cigarettes are sold at any time, and at what price. They must also know the relationship between the number of people who smoke cigarettes and the number of people who end up getting sick. In addition, they must have powerful computers in order to analyze such large quantities of statistical information. And finally, they must have the methods and software that enable them to answer such questions.

The most widely used method in economics for analyzing relationships between two or more variables (such as the price of a pack of cigarettes and the number of packs bought) is termed regression analysis. In a regression, the economist specifies the relationship he or she is trying to analyze. In the preceding example, the regression analysis indicates the effect of the price of cigarettes on their consumption, and the effect of the consumption of cigarettes on the health of populations. Using a regression, the economist is able not only to tell whether or not cigarette consumption falls due to price increases, but also predict the amount by which consumption is decreased due to the price increase. Similarly, the economist may be able to estimate the effect of an increase in the price of a pack of cigarettes on the number of people who develop lung cancer or who lose their teeth as a consequence. Such information is of enormous value to policymakers. In the cigarette example, this information could enable people in the federal or state governments to determine a level of taxation that would reduce the consumption of cigarettes due to an increase in price, without being so large as to be burdensome to cigarette smokers.

Because computers are so integral to the analysis of economic data, a number of software packages are now available that enable economists to run regressions and to answer questions about economic behavior. Microsoft Excel, for example, has a regression tool that allows the researcher to do very basic kinds of economic analysis. Professional economists, however, use more sophisticated statistical software packages for their analyses. Among the most popular analytics and statistics packages are SAS and SPSS, which are used by businesses, government agencies, and academic researchers alike for the analysis of economic statistics. Depending on the particular kind of analysis to be done, other packages such as RATS, Stata, TSP, Limdep, Nlogit, and Matlab, are also very useful.

Computers also enable economists to run simulations, in which a possible scenario for the future is created, allowing economists to answer important economic questions about this scenario. For example, an economist might ask what would happen to smoking in the United States if the price of a pack of cigarettes were to triple over the next year. Because this may never have happened in the past, the economist may not be able to use any single example from previous years to estimate the effect of this change in price on the change in consumption. The economist can, however, make an informed guess as to what might happen with the help of software.

Economists use a variety of software packages to simulate scenarios about which there is no prior statistical information. These include the General Algebraic Modeling System (GAMS) and Wolfram Mathematica, both of which enable the economist to write down explicit relationships between variables that will play a role in the final outcome of the simulation. To extend the cigarette example, we know that a tripling in the price of cigarettes will cause many smokers to cut back on smoking because they have limited income to spend on cigarettes. But perhaps this will only affect casual smokers, for whom it is, presumably, easier to stop smoking. Addicts, on the other hand, may continue to smoke the quantities they did prior to the increase in the price. Depending on how we think addicts and casual users behave, we may want to model their behavior differently, making the simulation more complex. Fortunately, as computers have become increasingly powerful, economists have been able to analyze increasingly complex economic problems. It is common, for example, for economists at universities and government and policy institutions to simulate the workings of an entire economy using hundreds of mathematical equations written in the GAMS software. The increase in networking speed has been almost as important to economic modeling as the increase in computing power. Faster network speeds enable economic simulations to be spread out over multiple computers (termed a cluster), enabling more data to be processed in a given amount of time than one computer could accomplish. In complex simulations, many variables are dependant on each other so data about the simulation frequently needs to be distributed to the other computers in the cluster. Without faster networks, clustered modeling would be limited quickly by the bottleneck of transmitting data.

Given the rapid development of economic modeling and the increasing availability of statistical economic information that can be used to understand the way the economy works, it is difficult to not be optimistic about the future of economic modeling

▶ *See also* **Decision Support Systems** • **Image Analysis: Medicine** • **Mathematics** • **Pattern Recognition** • **Simulation**

Resources

Books

Christensen, Bent J., and Nicholas M. Kiefer. *Economic Modeling and Inference.* Princeton: Princeton University Press, 2009.

Giovanini, Enrico. *Understanding Economic Statistics.* Paris: OECD Publishing, 2008.

Gujarati, Damodar N., and Dawn C. Porter. *Basic Econometrics.* 5th ed. Boston: McGraw-Hill Irwin, 2009.

Pindyck, Robert S., Daniel L. Rubinfeld, and Frank A. Wolak. *Econometric Models and Economic Forecasts.* 5th ed. London: MacGraw-Hill Education, 2008.

Educational Software

Educational software, or computer applications developed for the purpose of teaching and learning, arrived with virtually the first desktop computers. Education professionals recognized this potential early, and many schools acquired computers long before they were found in most American homes. Educational applications then greatly increased.

Educational software encompasses a variety of forms, costs, and purposes. Programs exist to teach individual preschoolers letter names, sounds, and grammar in English as well as other languages. Other programs introduce mathematical concepts for all grades, or are aimed at helping to develop good writing skills. Some programs, such as flight simulators, teach professionals the details of their jobs. Still other programs, called Learning Management Systems (LMSs), are designed for use by certain grades in entire school districts for teaching or evaluation purposes; these often include access to a software company's Web site for comprehensive services.

Economics and the Economy

Economists rely heavily on computers to analyze economic statistics and models of the workings of the economy. As computers become increasingly powerful, economists will be able to use increasingly sophisticated methods to study economic relationships. This, in turn, will greatly enhance people's understanding of economic relationships and the economy.

At the college and university level, LMSs are powerful application management systems that offer courses via the Internet for non-traditional students. These tools allow institutions to design entire online courses. The projects require a team, consisting of the subject-matter expert (usually a faculty member), a graphics artist, a curriculum designer, and a programmer, to put the complete package together.

Selecting Educational Software

Choosing an educational application to integrate into a curriculum can be difficult. Curriculum materials are generally selected for use over the course of several years. One drawback to using educational software programs in this way is that the applications often change from year to year, thus requiring frequent upgrade purchases. Sometimes the latest edition of a program has been modified to run on more powerful computers than a school can afford to use. Sometimes favorite applications are absorbed into other programs or disappear entirely. Another drawback is that there are no universally accepted standards or recognized independent organizations (such as the Food and Drug Administration for medications) for evaluating these programs.

Some LMSs are designed to accommodate hundreds of students. These programs require Internet access, which offers several advantages. Content, such as political maps, can be updated easily when needed. The programs allow individuals to work at their own pace and can be adapted to concentrate on an individual's particular weak area. The progress of the students can be evaluated at any time. Most of these programs offer technical support for the faculty if needed, and some offer teacher tutorials.

The cost of these services varies depending on the equipment (for example, computers may supplied by the company or the school), the time required per week per student, and the total number of weeks needed by each student to complete the program. For instance, a commonly used program designed to help elementary students read costs $30,000 per year, not counting the price of the computers.

Effective Evaluation and Implementation

Educational software is evaluated by many of the same standards used for evaluating other educational materials. Some commonly asked questions are: Is the program appropriate for the age and development of the user? Are the graphics attractive and do they lead to better learning? Is the depth of the program appropriate? Is the method for teaching effective? Is the software entertaining enough to keep the user interested? Does the program stimulate further learning of the subject?

Once software is selected, it must be effectively implemented. The environment around the computer is important. Is the computer located in a computer lab or is it in the classroom? How often during the week, and for how long, does the student have access to the computer? Is the area inviting? Is it designed to accommodate a single student at a time, or can multiple students access the computer together and learn from each other? Software should be compatible with the environment in which it will be used. If daily use is recommended to meet the learning objectives of a software program, but students will have only weekly access to the program, another program should be selected, or computer access should be increased. Likewise, software designed to be used by two or more students working cooperatively is best used in a setting that comfortably accommodates more than one student at each computer.

Market Issues

Educational software companies, especially ones that produce LMSs, face unique challenges. First, the consumer, generally educators at a school district or a large institution, must be sold on the program. Second, in order for schools to implement the Internet systems mentioned previously, reliable networks must be installed; this takes time and money, especially in older buildings. Third, schools usually have budgets that are settled well ahead of time and followed strictly. School boards must approve the thousands of dollars that many of these programs cost. Further, financing may need to be found. The entire process of implementing an LMS can take years! Software companies might not have the financial means to survive between the time a school or district agrees to buy a system and the point when the system is actually purchased.

Companies that develop educational software, such as the Learning Company that produces the widely recognized Carmen San Diego (http://www.carmensandiego.com/) and Reader Rabbit (http://www.reader-rabbit.com/) series, are easily affected by downturns in the computer software and Internet industries. Some have been sold and resold, leaving in question the future of both the companies and the content, quality, and variety of their products. The overall number of compact disc-read only memory (CD-ROM) educational software programs available has fallen due to major changes in the software market since 2000.

Software Effectiveness Factors

Surprisingly, many experts agree that the quality of the software is not the most important consideration in how successful it is; the expertise and comfort level of the person helping the student is the single most critical factor. Many software programs offer technical support and tutorials to help teachers become more comfortable with the system. If the software is school-based, another important success factor is the ability of children to access the software from home and the parents' comfort level in assisting the student. Some school districts have programs that provide laptop computers or tablets to students so they can be used outside of school.

There is also controversy about the effectiveness of educational software in general. Many school districts have seen increased test scores after implementing educational software systems. Others claim that the cool factor is largely responsible for these results, and that students do at least as well if the same energy is spent in well-planned conventional instruction. Few argue that educational software programs may

Computer Sciences, 2ⁿᵈ Edition

SCORM Standards

The U.S. federal government has developed a set of standards known as Sharable Courseware Object Reference Model (SCORM). These standards have been designed to help build a platform for integrating learning technology into Department of Defense education programs. The SCORM standards, which help procurers evaluate curriculum and infrastructure compatibilities of various educational software programs, are gaining acceptance for evaluating Learning Management Systems (LMSs).

be a student's first introduction to computers. For those already familiar with computers, educational software prods them to use computers for more than just surfing the Internet. This might prove to be the biggest benefit of all.

▶ *See also* **Computer Assisted Instruction • Integrated Software • Library Applications • Office Automation Systems**

Resources

Books

Bennett, Maggie. *Team Gamer: Designing an Educational Computer Game to Teach Chesapeake Bay Ecology.* 2007.

Cooper, Linda, and David Barber. *Using New Web Tools in the Primary Classroom: A Practical Guide for Enhancing Teaching and Learning.* Milton Park, England: Routledge, 2012.

Dainter, Jason. *A Collaborative Educational Computer Game That Enhances Learning Skills for Key Stage 1 Citizenship Skills.* Leeds: University of Leeds, School of Computing, 2006.

Holt, Dale, Stephen Segrave, and Jacob L. Cybulski, editors. *Professional Education Using E-simulations: Benefits of Blended Learning Design.* Hershey, PA: Business Science Reference, 2012.

Jia, Jiyou, editor. *Educational Stages and Interactive Learning: From Kindergarten to Workplace Training.* Hershey, PA: Information Science Reference, 2012.

Polly, Drew, Clif Mims, and Kay A. Persichitte, editors. *Developing Technology-rich Teacher Education Programs: Key Issues.* Hershey, PA: IGI Global, 2012.

Web Sites

JCA Solutions. "SCORM—Shareable Content Object Reference Model." http://www.scormsoft.com/scorm (accessed October 2, 2012).

Embedded Technology (Ubiquitous Computing)

Do walls have ears? Not right now, but it will not be long before walls not only have ears, but will also be able to see what we are doing and even tell us things that are relevant to our activities. Traditionally, when people said that walls have ears, they suspected that someone was spying. In the modern context, the walls will be a lot friendlier. They will sense who is in their vicinity, but only to determine the occupants' needs and to help them by adjusting the room light and the window shades to suit their tastes or by performing similar tasks.

Such service is an illustration of embedded technology (or ubiquitous computing) at work. In simple terms, ubiquitous computing allows computing architecture to be embedded into the environment. Artifacts in the environment can then sense different aspects of their surroundings as well as the user's ongoing activities, reason about them, and act accordingly.

Types of Ubiquitous Computing

Ubiquitous computing can take various forms. A sampling of some of those forms follows.

Portable Computing   Laptops and handheld computers have made computing portable. You can carry your computer with you everywhere, but your experience is only slightly different than in your office—you still must interact with the computer through a more or less traditional interface*.

Pervasive Computing   Smart devices* have computing technology in unexpected places. At first this will be in information appliances such as phones, personal digital assistants (PDAs), and pagers. Later, pervasive computing is expected to expand to include more traditional appliances such as toasters, refrigerators, washing machines, ovens, home security systems, and so on. Still later, the infrastructure* will develop so that will include equipment like you might find on the road, in an automobile, in a hotel, or in an airport. For example, you might be able to pay tolls or buy airline tickets with your phone-based electronic wallet. Prototypes* demonstrating such capabilities already exist, but their widespread usage will require a universal infrastructure with increased computing and communications power. As of 2012, the popular smartphones Android and iPhone had applications such as Google Wallet and PayPass, which allowed users to pay from their phone at participating stores and restaurants.

Smart buildings are buildings that are well networked and equipped with smart appliances and have a personal computer based system that can control the ambient* conditions within the building. The "smarts" are needed to start and stop different appliances to maximize the users' comfort or security and to minimize cost. For example, a smart house could run the water heater whenever energy prices are low; it could select the best times to turn on the heat or air conditioning within the premises, based on which rooms are currently occupied or are likely to be occupied shortly.

Calm Computing   This technology carries out the idea of computing fading into the background. With this technology, the artifacts are intelligent, but do not require focused interaction—we just live with them

* **interface** a boundary or border between two or more objects or systems; also a point of access

* **smart devices** devices and appliances that host an embedded computer system that offers greater control and flexibility

* **infrastructure** the foundation or permanent installation necessary for a structure or system to operate

* **Prototypes** working models or experimental investigation of proposed systems under development

* **ambient** pertaining to the surrounding atmosphere or environment

* **virtual reality (VR)** the use of elaborate input/output devices to create the illusion that the user is in a different environment

and they work unobtrusively to make our lives simpler. An example of this is the "dangling string" network monitor. A traditional user interface for monitoring computer network traffic would capture a lot of data and try to present it on a computer screen. By contrast, the dangling string hangs from a hallway ceiling and is controlled by a small motor. Network activity causes the motor to kick the string ever so slightly. Activity in the network is thus presented as the literal hum of the swaying string.

The basic concept behind calm computing is to develop user interfaces that are not based on symbols. Although symbols can convey a lot of detailed information, people have to focus on them to extract that information. In contrast, humans can capture a lot of non-symbolic information in a manner that does not require their explicit attention. Although your main current task can be successfully carried out in a symbolic mode, you can be peripherally aware of a lot of other activities without concentrating on them. The hum of a string, the shadows cast by a ceiling fan, the reflections cast by a shimmering pool of water all fall into this latter category. You will probably be aware of the flickering shadows and reflections and how fast they are changing even though you might be concentrating on your word processor or a phone conversation. Now imagine if these shadows and reflections and other changes in environment were used to convey specific meanings such as "All's well in the plant" or "There seems to be a lot of relevant activity in one of the chat rooms I visit" or "Suddenly, the stock market is seeing a lot of trades in the technology sector."

Wearable Computing In this opposite of calm computing, instead of having computers embedded in the environment, you carry the computers on your person. One main difference from regular computers is in the user interface. Wearable computers are designed for hands-free operation. Often, the intended user would be walking about or in an awkward posture, such as atop an electric utility pole or inside a narrow submarine engine room. Equipment repair was one of the earliest applications for wearable computing. It allows the user to give commands by voice and view information through a head-mounted display that projects an image on to the user's glasses.

The earliest wearable computers were quite bulky: the user literally had to carry a backpack with a computer in it. However, with advances in technology, it is possible to have wearable computers embedded in wristwatches or pendants or even sewn into clothing. These miniature computers are usually designed for specific applications, such as displaying text and pictures and giving online directions as the user walks about. In another application the wearable computer provides an interface to a three-dimensional information space where the user's head, neck, and eye movements can be interpreted as desires to probe some aspect of the space in more detail. Instead of traditional virtual reality (VR)*, the user may be engaged in the "real" reality and only occasionally looking into the information space when a specific need requires it.

Related Technology

The techniques involved in ubiquitous computing are as diverse as its applications. Many of these techniques, however, deal with peripheral technologies. We need motors to drive the changes in environment that calm computing requires. We need head-mounted displays for certain kinds of wearable interfaces. For the wearables, we need lightweight processors that consume low power and small batteries that can feed them. Certain kinds of pervasive applications—for instance, those fixed in a tollbooth or a smart home—may have no restrictions on size, power, or communication ability; for applications that entail mobility, all those restrictions apply. For wearable computers, there are significant challenges in materials to weave conducting channels into fabrics. Some researchers are developing techniques to generate power from the normal actions of a human body, such as the impact of the heel on the ground in walking.

Interestingly, although the basic programming required to build ubiquitous applications is the same as programming for other applications, the abstractions involved tend to be quite different. The interface modalities* of desktop computing are not much use in calm and wearable settings. Another special feature of calm computing is that its effectiveness relies on a lot of reasoning to infer the user's desires. Unlike desktop computing, users do not simply type in or use their mouse to indicate their commands—the system has to figure out if users would like the light to be turned down ever so slightly to adjust to their mood. Thus artificial intelligence (AI) techniques will help here.

Ubiquitous computing tends to require a significant infrastructure. Depending on the needs of a specific application, the infrastructure should include the ability for different components to communicate on wireline or wireless networks; the components should be able to discover each other's presence as do the Java-based Jini services and other registration services; the components should be able to move around physically while retaining their identity and address as in mobile IP and 3G (third generation) wireless networks. An application might require the ability to authenticate participants through the public key infrastructure (PKI)*, or the ability to make secure payments through SET, the secure electronic transaction protocol. The exact requirements from the infrastructure will vary with the application, but broad-based capabilities are likely to be needed in many cases. For example, buildings should have location sensors so that they can detect users; users' wearable computers should be able to talk to the buildings and to the computers of other users. Computers in automobiles should be able to talk to computers at tollbooths and be able to pay for the privilege of going through the booth.

Most of the technologies necessary for ubiquitous computing exist and the infrastructure is spreading more widely every moment. Although it is still unknown exactly what forms ubiquitous computing will take when it becomes a commercial reality, we can be sure it will be something both challenging and creative.

Computer Sciences, 2nd Edition

Mark Weiser of the famed Xerox research facility PARC in Palo Alto, California, is credited with coining the term "ubiquitous computing," originally meant to signify computing that would occur in the background. Later the term was used more broadly to include all shades of computing everywhere. In this article we address, ubiquitous computing in its broadest sense.

* **modalities** classifications of the truth of a logical proposition or statement, or characteristics of an object or entity
* **public key infrastructure (PKI)** the supporting programs and protocols that act together to enable public key encryption/decryption

▶ *See also* **Ergonomics • Microchip • Operating Systems • User Interfaces**

Resources

Periodicals

Ishii, Hiroshi, Sandia Ren, and Phil Frei. "Pinwheels: Visualizing Information Flow in an Architectural Space." In *Proceedings of the Conference on Human Factors in Computing Systems,* Seattle, Washington, March 31–April 5, 2001.

Shenck, Nathan S., and Joseph A. Paradiso. "Energy Scavenging with Shoe-Mounted Piezoelectrics." *IEEE Micro* 21, no. 3 (May June 2001).

Want, Roy, Bill N. Schilit, Norman I. Adams, Rich Gold, Karin Petersen, David Goldberg, John R. Ellis, and Mark Weiser. "An Overview of the PARCTAB Ubiquitous Computing Experiment." *IEEE Personal Communications* 2, no. 6 (December 1995): 28–43.

Web Sites

PC Magazine "7 Ways to Pay Using an iPhone" http://www.pcmag.com/slideshow/story/301548/7-ways-to-pay-using-an-iphone (accessed October 13, 2012).

Expert Systems

Expert systems, also called "rule-based systems," are computer programs or sets of programs that use knowledge of a domain (a specific field or discipline) to act as an expert in that domain. Expert systems have been built for dozens of sub-fields in medicine, business, and science, making this one of the most successfully commercialized branches of artificial intelligence (AI)*.

History

During the early years of artificial intelligence, computer scientists primarily developed programs that solved well-defined, self-explanatory problems (e.g., game playing, machine translation, or symbolic integrations). These programs required clever reasoning techniques to manipulate the logical and mathematical problems they were presented, but they did not require much knowledge beyond those techniques.

In the 1960s researchers began to realize that to solve many interesting problems, the programs would not only need to be able to interpret the problems, but they would need background knowledge to understand them fully. Through the late 1960s and early 1970s, Bruce Buchanan developed DENDRAL at Stanford University as an attempt to address that problem. DENDRAL was one of the first expert systems written. It was designed to use mass spectrometry* and other chemical information to deduce the molecular structure of chemical compounds. DENDRAL's knowledge of chemistry consisted of hundreds of rules describing the interactions of chemical compounds. These rules were the result of more than ten years of collaboration between chemists, geneticists, and computer scientists.

Applications

Users of expert systems are often knowledgeable in the domain of the system, but are not experts themselves. The expert system gathers information by presenting the user with a series of questions. That information is integrated with its stored rules (knowledge) to generate more specific questions. In some cases (e.g., medical diagnosis), the expert system can suggest actions for the user to take (e.g., a culture or blood test) to gather more information. Eventually, the expert system delivers a decision or conclusion, often accompanied by an explanation of how it was reached.

Expert systems allow users to leverage the knowledge of experts without requiring their presence. These systems, though limited to fields where questions can be precisely stated, are useful in any field where experts are rare, expensive, or inaccessible. They can both automate a lengthy decision process and deal with large quantities of data that might overwhelm a human.

Even the broad categories to which expert systems have been applied are too numerous to list, though a particularly comprehensive, if dated, list can be found in the *Expert Systems Catalog of Applications* (1993). In medicine, systems have been applied to ECG (electrocardiography) interpretation, cancer prognosis, athlete health monitoring, infant development, antimicrobial therapy, depression therapy, skin disease diagnosis, and many other domains. Industrial applications include air traffic control, automobile diagnostics, supply chain planning, blast furnace control, power grid management, automobile design, elevator design, locomotive repair, agriculture, and manufacturing facility layout. Scientific systems have also been designed for weather prediction, analytical chemistry, electronic circuit design and analysis, space shuttle maintenance, and hazardous waste management.

While there are many full and partial successes, expert systems have limitations. Though they no longer cost $500,000 to develop as they did in the 1970s, they are still expensive to design. Their development requires the careful, long-term attention of both the programmers encoding the knowledge and the experts providing it. They tend to work only in very narrow domains, and their accuracy can degrade* without warning if a problem approaches the limits of the system's knowledge. Finally, they are only as good as the experts from whom they were programmed; unlike experts, they cannot advance the state of the art or reach novel conclusions (though they can often reach surprising conclusions that an expert might overlook). If rules are programmed incorrectly, the engine

* **mass spectrometry** the process of identifying the compounds or elemental particles within a substance

* **degrade** to reduce quality or performance of a system

* **Heuristics** procedures that serve to guide investigation but that have not been proven

will reach incorrect conclusions or fail without warning and sometimes without indication.

Technologies

Expert systems consist of two primary components: a knowledge base and an inference engine. The knowledge base is a set of rules encoding the expert's knowledge of the field. The inference engine is the set of techniques that manipulates that knowledge with respect to user input.

To develop an expert system, programmers and experts collaborate, often for several years, to develop the knowledge base. The rules are then extensively tested on problems with known solutions and field-tested on new problems under an expert's supervision. The team then determines which rules are responsible for problems or errors in the system's conclusions, and corrects those rules. This process is repeated until the system is considered reliable enough to be used by non-experts.

Although the knowledge base must be developed from scratch for any given problem, the inference engine can often be adapted in whole or in part from previous systems. One popular category of tools is the "expert system shell," a pre-packaged engine that is ready to run with the "simple" addition of a rule set. Other tools only provide parts of engines that a programmer can assemble to build a custom engine quickly.

Inference engine techniques have been an active research topic since 1970. In the "brute-force" approach, the engine literally tries every possible answer to the problem until it finds a solution. This only works in domains where a program can list all of the possible solutions (e.g., checkers or certain logical problems) and is often prohibitively slow.

The "heuristic search" method is an improvement that uses heuristics* to narrow down the list of possible answers before trying them. While this often allows the system to find the solution substantially faster, heuristics are, by definition, not always correct. In some cases, a heuristic will actually eliminate the correct answer. Once the system realizes that the correct answer was eliminated, it will retrace its steps, reversing the narrowing effect of each heuristic it used, until it finds the answer.

In many cases, it is not possible to check an answer for correctness; the only way to find a solution is to show, using strict logic, that the input the user provided proves a conclusion. For these cases, "production systems" are used with rules encoded as if-then statements (e.g., "if it is a bird, then it has wings"). The system can then trigger rules using information provided by the user (e.g., "it is a bird") to reach provable conclusions. By taking those conclusions and using them to trigger other rules, the system can reach more complex conclusions. In some cases, the system can use heuristics to "guess" a possible conclusion. In these cases, the system works backward from the guessed conclusion by trying to find a chain of rules to prove it.

There are many variations on these broad categories of systems. Most current systems keep track of how conclusions were reached so that they can provide plain-English explanations. These explanations assist the user in evaluating the conclusions. Some systems can work with rules that are not always correct by assigning them a certainty (probability of being correct). By combining these certainties as rules are chained, the system can produce a conclusion (or several) and tell the user how certain those conclusions are. Fuzzy logic* allows a system to deal with qualitative information (e.g., "the fish is large") by interpreting the qualitative statement as several possible quantitative meanings, each with some amount of certainty. For example, the statement "the fish is large" might be interpreted as "there is an 80 percent chance that the fish is larger than 20 pounds, a 90 percent chance that it is larger than 10 pounds…" "Predicate logic" systems can manipulate logical rules far more complex than if-then statements to reach conclusions. Beyond logical rules, more advanced systems can store knowledge as "semantic nets," "frame systems," or "structured objects," among other representations.

*fuzzy logic models human reasoning by permitting elements to have partial membership to a set; derived from fuzzy set theory

Current Research

The widespread commercial applications of expert systems have given rise to research topics focusing on both system effectiveness and usability. Better plain-English explanations lead to more reliable systems. Techniques for accelerating the encoding of knowledge into rules reduce the time-consuming process of creating a knowledge base. Alternative methods for representing those rules, even by using multiple methods within a single system, increase the representative power of a rule set. Inference-engines with improved techniques for manipulating rules can reach more complex solutions, and engines that use multiple techniques can use them to complement and check each other. Inference techniques designed for reuse can simplify the complex and labor-intensive process of creating engines.

Internet Availability

As the numbers of both businesses and individuals connected to the Internet increased dramatically from the late 1990s through the 2000s, so too did the availability of expert systems via the Internet. Some expert systems are available to the user at particular websites, while other systems can be downloaded to the user's PC or other device. These Internet-based and Internet-available expert systems cover a broad range of fields, such as business, medicine, education, and science.

 See also **Artificial Intelligence** • **Decision Support Systems** • **Lisp** • **Neural Networks**

Resources

Books

Giarratano, Joseph C. *Expert Systems: Principles and Programming.* 4th ed. Boston: Thomson, 2005.

Nguyen, Hung T., and Elbert A. Walker. *A First Course in Fuzzy Logic.* 3rd ed. Boca Raton, FL: Chapman & Hall/CRC, 2006.

F

Fashion Design

In the high-profile world of fashion design, the emphasis is increasingly placed on selling a dream rather than on describing the cut and construction of garments. The fashion press excels in presenting whimsical creations on models known for their beauty, poise, and exposure. Technological advancements within the field of fashion design are rarely mentioned. When one takes a closer look at the fashion industry, however, one sees how computer technology has changed the landscape and possesses the ability to transform it further.

The design and production of garments usually is the work of a team of individuals, each of whom specializes in a different process. A designer, or design team, will first produce sketches of garments or drape fabric on a dressform to obtain different styles. The artistic rendering of a garment is there to create a mood and is typically supplemented with precise line drawings that are known as flats. With computer-aided design (CAD) software, a designer can scan a sketch and manipulate the result with image-editing software or draw directly onto the computer's interface* with a sensor-equipped pen and special tablet.

Although numerous sketches are still done by hand, their precise renderings in line drawings are increasingly achieved through the use of computers. Since software programs can store and project various styles, fabrics, and colors that can be interchanged at the click of a button, the design of clothing is now accessible to many business-minded individuals who may not have the previously required refined drawing skills. As a result, product-development teams and other merchandisers have become more involved in the design process. The ease, convenience, speed, and versatility offered by image-editing software has thus helped to make it an essential design tool.

In conjunction with CAD software, the business-driven fashion industry also uses computer applications that allow cost-analysis of garments from their earliest stages. Once a garment is sketched, its cost can be projected by using programmed data that estimates the amounts of fabrics, notions*, and assembling complexity, depending on stylistic features.

After the styles have been determined, the designer gives the renderings to patternmakers, who engineer ways to build the garments. Although garments draped on a three-dimensional form can be transposed to paper, the prevalent way to construct a garment is by making a flat pattern that is then cut into fabric and assembled into a three-dimensional sample. Patternmakers use basic pattern shapes that they modify according to

* **interface** a boundary or border between two or more objects or systems; also a point of access

* **notions** small items used in making clothing, like buttons and trim

A designer uses a shape-shifting robotic mannequin. © *PRIIT SIMSON/AFP/ Getty Images.*

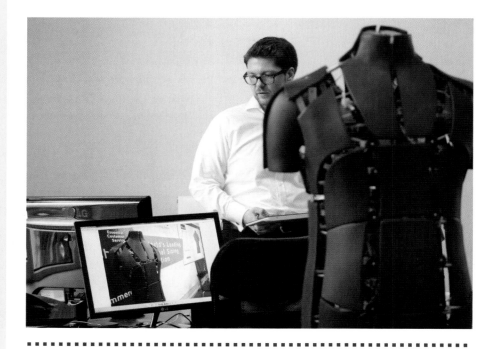

design specifications. Essentially, they try to fit a three-dimensional body using a two-dimensional medium. By placing such elements as darts, gathers, and pleats or by breaking down larger flat pieces into several smaller sections, they can improve a garment's fit.

Although the fibers and weave structures influence the drape of a fabric and cannot be easily estimated through computer simulation, the mathematical operations and geometrical nature of the work involved in flat pattern-making make it a perfect candidate for computerization. Basic pattern shapes are now digitized and manipulated directly on the computer. Where the human hand loses precision in cutting and measuring every segment of a pattern, the computer can ensure that all the pieces of the puzzle fit together precisely and conform to the measurements of the body it is to cover quickly and with greater accuracy.

From this pattern, a sample is sewn and adjustments are made to comply with the drape of the fabric and to ensure that proportions are respected. Using the computer, the corrected patterns are positioned in various ways in order to utilize the bolts of fabric with greatest efficiency. Once this placement is determined, the fabric is piled up and the patterns can be cut with a computer-guided laser beam or knife.

Fashion design software also is used for creating portfolios and catalogs. These images are uploaded to company or designer websites for greater distribution and viewership of clothing lines, which can affect current fashion trends. For aspiring designers, numerous versions of fashion design software are available for purchase and can be used to create designs and print pattern pieces.

Where the fashion industry needs these precision-bound tools to increase productivity and accuracy, the same technology can also allow for greater fit. Although the computerized sector of the industry caters to the masses and produces garments based on standardized measurements, some companies have started offering custom-tailored garments by entering individual customers' measurements into software programs and creating garments according to these specifications.

With the advancement of technology, new applications are devised that offer even greater potential to the field of fashion design. Many CAD programs for designing and constructing clothing emplay what are termed orthogonal* projections to create patterns. These consist of graphic projections of objects on a grid-like surface or set of perpendicular intersections. These two-dimensional, manually-drawn flat patterns have been around since the eighteenth century, producing a wide range of fashions until settling on our present simple late twenty-first century styles.

Orthogonal projection has limitations. Architects and designers have adapted computer tools developed for neurosurgery, software developed for the aerospace industry, and digitized three-dimensional animation using next-generation CAD and other design systems. Although some architects still start with orthogonal projection, others have abandoned it completely or relied heavily on digitized animation in the development and projection of their architectural designs. Providing that the variables found in textiles can eventually be analyzed like those of building materials, this could prove very influential in the cutting and production of clothing.

To advance even further beyond the two-dimensional flat pattern approach to clothing design, digital three-dimensional animation can be employed. Designers and retailers can display their products in three-dimensional animated settings that simulate the various body types of online customers.

▶ *See also* **Animation • CAD/CAM, CA Engineering • Graphic Devices**

Resources

Books

Berry, Kathleen M., and Lois F. Hennes. *The Fashion Design System: Pattern Engineering for the 21st Century*. Nambour, Queensland, Australia: The Fashion Design System, 2008.

Nugent, Laura. *Computerized Patternmaking for Apparel Production*. New York: Fairchild Publications, 2009.

Film and Video Editing

When most people think about what makes great movies and television programs, they might consider the importance of a well-written script, or the magical collaboration between a first-rate director and

Cutting Edge Technology

Many schools offer coursework in CAD for fashion design majors. As CAD technology improves, more and more potential employers in the fashion industry require applicants to have knowledge of the latest technology available.

* **orthogonal** elements or objects that are perpendicular to one another; in a logical sense this means that changes in one have no effect on the other

Putting the finishing touches on a video for use on a blog. © *Bob Levey/Getty Images. For Montblanc.*

high-powered actors. But many people outside the entertainment business do not know much about the world of post-production, the sophisticated crafts and technologies that turn miles of raw footage into finished products that can teach us, motivate us, and make us laugh or cry.

Computers play a role in many aspects of post-production, including animation and special effects, but one area in which they have brought about enormous change is editing—the art and craft of arranging pictures and sound to tell the story envisioned by the writer, producer, and director.

Background

Moving images were first captured on photographic film in the late nineteenth century, and for decades film—an optical/chemical medium—was the only way to record and preserve moving images. With the delivery of the first practical videotape recorder in 1956, it became possible to capture moving images electromagnetically, eliminating the expensive and time-consuming process of developing and printing film.

Until the early 1980s, film and videotape had separate, well-defined uses in the worlds of news and entertainment. Film's strengths were seen to be excellent picture quality, long shelf life, portability, and a technology that was widely used around the world. Traditionally, film has been used for theatrical presentation, prime-time network TV production, high-end commercials (in 35 mm), and documentary (in 16 mm).

The strength of videotape has been economy, speed of production and post-production, and a "live" look. Originally, tape was used for non-prime television such as soap operas, talk shows, and game shows, and for low-end commercials.

During the 1980s and 1990s, the differences between film and video gradually became less pronounced. As video technology grew more reliable and less expensive, videotape became important in news and documentary production, in corporate communications, and eventually in consumer products. Videotape's picture quality also improved greatly, to the point where low-budget feature films like *The Blair Witch Project* are being shot on video and transferred to film for theatrical distribution. High definition—the highest quality of video—allows image quality that equals that of film. Production costs in "high-def" are lower than in film, and elaborate special effects are easier and less expensive than with traditional film optical effects.

Use of Computers in Editing

For most of the twentieth century, film was cut by hand. Editors were talented craftspeople who worked directly with their material—they assembled scenes by splicing together separate picture and sound rolls, and had great flexibility in rearranging and trimming shots for optimum on-screen impact. The technology was simple, and although the process was labor-intensive, it allowed great creative control.

By contrast, as videotape editing evolved from the 1960s through the 1980s, it was relatively clumsy and needed rooms full of expensive equipment. The process required playing back scenes from two or more video players, and recording them in the desired sequence onto another recorder. Specialist technicians had to operate the equipment, so editors had less creative control over their material. Worse, video editing was "linear"—that is, scenes had to be assembled in order from the beginning of the program, and if a change was desired everything had to be rebuilt from that point on. The technology made the process a lot faster than film editing, but there was less opportunity for subtlety and creativity.

Then came the computer revolution. Starting in the early to mid-1990s, personal computers became powerful enough that production footage (whether it was shot on film or tape) could be transferred to hard disc arrays, and editors working with Mac- or Windows-based editing systems could have the best of both worlds. Computerized systems gave them the precision, random-access ability, and "hands-on" feel of film editing, but, since the systems were electronic, they offered the speed and low cost of the video world.

Use of these computer-based "non-linear editors" or "NLEs"—so-called to distinguish the new style of editing from traditional linear video editing—has totally changed the way content is organized in many media. For example:

- News organizations like CNN use huge amounts of computer storage to keep video materials online, allowing several editors simultaneous access to the footage so they can work on multiple versions of the story for different programs.

- All TV shows and commercials, and most movies, are now edited on NLEs.

- Consumers are buying low-cost, easy-to-use hardware and software to edit their home movies.

The Process

This is how non-linear editing is accomplished on a professional level. The original footage can be shot on film or videotape; footage shot on film is transferred to video in an expensive, carefully controlled process. Then the videotape is digitized, or "loaded in," to the NLE's hard drive.

As the footage is being transferred into the computer, it usually goes through a compression process, so it will need less storage space on the NLE's hard drives. Video files are very large—one minute of "broadcast-quality" picture and sound can consume about two gigabytes of disc storage; high definition footage requires approximately nine gigabytes per minute of material. Editors often need many hours of footage available to them as they edit a project, and digitizing that much footage without compression would require massive and expensive storage systems. But when footage is compressed, at a typical ratio of five to one, a two-minute video clip that might require 4 gigabytes (or 4,000 megabytes) if it is digitized uncompressed will need only 800 megabytes.

The trade-off with compression is that video quality is somewhat reduced (typically, the images are not as crisp and the color fidelity is not as good as the original). But the editors choose a compression ratio that gives them a picture that is good enough to make their decisions. And the reduced quality is temporary—the final product will be made using the high-quality original footage.

As the footage is digitized, the NLE's software helps the editor organize the material. The editor or an assistant "logs in" each shot, writing a description of the shot and what scene it is intended for. The system's visual interface generates a "bin" to hold all the shots that belong in a given scene. A database management system keeps track of where everything is, and allows the editor to sort and retrieve information quickly.

Once the footage is in the system, the creative part begins—building the program scene by scene. That means not just selecting the best shots to tell the story, but also developing a pace and rhythm that propel the story forward, and selecting visual transitions to blend the scenes together. The software provides an easy-to-use graphical display, and gives the editor a variety of tools to arrange the materials, including drag-and-drop, keyboard commands, and placement of scenes on a visual timeline—very much the way word processing software allows a writer to rearrange words.

The NLE's software precisely tracks all the editor's changes, remembers which shots originated where, keeps picture and sound synchronized, and makes an "edit decision list" which describes exactly the portion of each shot that has been selected to be shown in a particular order. The computer plays back the edited scenes in real time, showing the editor, director, producers, and others exactly how scenes will look in the final product. Changes can be made easily, and different ways of organizing the material can be tried out. Because the original material is not being cut or changed during this process—the computer is just displaying the editor's choices of shots in the right sequence—the editing is said to be "non-destructive." The process proceeds over and over, with scenes being continually refined until the creative team agrees that the best possible choices have been made about how to use the materials. This decision point is often called "picture lock."

Once the picture is locked, the process moves in one of three directions. First, if the production originated on film, and the final product is to be a film print (for instance a movie to be shown in theaters), the NLE generates a "negative cut list." The cut list describes exactly what portions of which shots from the original production footage have been selected. Then craftspeople physically cut or "conform" the original negative, splicing it together in the order the editor specified. Finally, traditional optical/chemical film printing techniques are used to make the prints that will be distributed to theaters.

Second, whether the production was originally shot on film or tape, if the final product is to be released on DVD, as television programs are, a "video master" is prepared. This can be done in one of two ways:

- In an "online conforming session," the edit decision list prepared by the NLE software controls a video editing system, using two or more playback videotape machines and one recorder. The high-quality videotapes containing the original footage are automatically played back in sequence on two or more videotape players and assembled onto a new videotape, with transitions and special effects generated by a video "switcher."

- Alternatively, the finished product can be generated completely within an NLE. First, the selected shots—which had originally been compressed to save on storage space—are re-digitized from the original videotapes into the NLE at the full resolution. Then the NLE plays them back in sequence to be recorded on a videotape recorder, with transitions and special effects generated and added by the software on the NLE. The finished product can be exported from the NLE to a variety of different digital media: DVD, hard drive, or server, or converted to high-quality files.

The third way the edited material can be released is directly to broadcast. For instance, once a news story has been edited, it can be transferred immediately from the NLE over a high-speed network to an "air server," from which it is played as often as needed.

Sound Tracks

Audio can be edited within the NLE and released with the video as a final product without any further effort. Often, though, only basic sound editing is done within the NLE, and a separate team of specialists does audio mixing and "sweetening" using a similar computer-based system that is optimized for audio work.

In an audio-editing computer, multiple sound tracks are constructed for dialog, narration, music, and sound effects. The sound mixing team listens to these tracks while watching the edited picture, and carefully

A Technically Demanding Effort

Video editing requires extensive computer resources. High-end professional non-linear editing systems rely on expensive separate video boards with sophisticated video capture chips. All systems require fast processors—the most advanced use multiprocessing to manipulate the torrent of digital data. Video and audio are both best handled in memory-heavy systems with hundreds of megabytes of RAM (random access memory). Editors always want access to more material at higher resolutions, increasing the pressure for more hard drive space. Higher-resolution video requires high-speed interconnections capable of moving data between devices at speeds of between four hundred megabits and one gigabit per second.

blends and enhances the separate tracks to tell the audio portion of the story in the most effective way. Once the sound track is finished, it can be "laid down" on digital audio tape or it can remain within the audio computer; either way it is synchronized by computer with the picture from the NLE as the final video master is produced.

What is the result of all this creativity, effort, and technology? A movie or a television program that—the creative team hopes—is so skillfully prepared that it will entertain us for a little while, or even teach us something about ourselves and our world.

The Future

Technology and economics are driving the evolution of film and video editing. Computer-based video editing at all levels will continue to become less expensive, more powerful and easier to use. This process lowers the barriers to entry for the novice filmmaker, the enterprising journalist, and the consumer who just wants to make better home movies.

The Internet is only beginning to have an effect on editing, but the possibilities are intriguing. Accessing the same materials from anywhere in the world, multiple editors will be able to collaborate on a program. Producers, directors, and executives will screen and comment on the work in progress from anywhere, and highly specialized work like sound mixing and effects generation will have no geographic limitations.

On the high end, both broadcast television and theatrical features are moving away from film and toward high-definition video—a process that will push technical requirements higher as editing systems are built to handle the extreme demands of high-def. Next up is the replacement of traditional 35 mm film projection in theaters with high-definition video taken directly from satellite or fiber optic cable—one more major step in the journey from the film medium to the electronic one.

 See also **Animation • Graphic Devices**

Resources

Books

Ohanian, Thomas A. *Digital Nonlinear Editing*. 2nd ed. Boston: Focal Press, 1998.

Zettl, Herbert *Television Production Handbook*. 11th ed. Boston: Cengage Learning, 2012.

G

Geographic Information Systems

Many difficult decision-making processes in geographic planning, environmental, and social studies arise because they require the manipulation and integration of large volumes of spatially-indexed data. Computerized geographical information systems (GIS) provide the key to the efficient use of such data sets because they can efficiently perform such functions on vast quantities of spatially addressed data. These powerful systems acquire data from many sources, change the data into a variety of useful formats, store the data, retrieve and manipulate the data for analysis, and then generate outputs required by a given user.

Underlying each GIS is a powerful spatial database management subsystem that provides such functions as efficient data storage, retrieval and updating, as well as security, integrity, and redundancy control. Within the database, a variety of mappable characteristics associated with any given geographical location are organized as a series of spatially-registered maps, or "overlays." Each of these overlays describes a single theme of geographical features (such as water features, geology, or vegetation), and is stored as a separate data layer. Each feature in a map layer is described by the linking of two components: geometry and attributes.

For example, a road is represented geometrically as a line linked with attributes describing road type, name, and conditions. A land parcel has an interior and a boundary, and is represented by a polygon* associated with attributes describing ownership, value, and tax. Additional topological or metric information (such as neighborhood, connectivity, distance, and directions) may also be computed from geometry and stored for fast response to topology-related queries.

A GIS can integrate information from a variety of sources and formats. Common geographical feature maps that describe administrative boundaries, hydrologic* features, land use, parcels, transportation, and population data, are widely available from government agencies and private data vendors. Additional data can be captured through field measurement, use of GPS (global positioning system), and direct interpretation of remotely sensed images. There are also common data standards for sharing digital geographic data among users and producers. In order to answer queries that require combinations of multiple data inputs, source data must be pre-processed (converted for consistent format and scale and errors corrected) to achieve consistency and compatibility in data types, scales, spatial reference systems, spatial units, and coverage.

* **polygon** a many-sided, closed, geometrical figure

* **hydrologic** relating to water

* **artificial intelligence (AI)** a branch of computer science dealing with creating computer hardware and software to mimic the way people think and perform practical tasks

* **synergistic** relating to synergism, which is the phenomenon whereby the action of a group of elements is greater than their individual actions

* **cartography** map making

A typical GIS is capable of performing a variety of data analysis procedures that involve access to both spatial and non-spatial information of one or more geographical feature classes. As a generic spatial analysis engine, a GIS provides a number of primitive operations that can be combined to implement a given analytical procedure.

Map *reclassification* operations merely repackage information from an existing map layer into a new one that has feature classes and attribute categories different from the original one. Map *overlay* operations involve the creation of a new map layer from two or more existing map overlays. It begins by finding point-by-point or region-based spatial coincidence among input maps, and then assigns a new value to each location based on the spatial coincident values of input overlays. An overlay operation requires that input map layers must be compatible in scale, coordinate systems, error characteristics, and data coding methods.

Other analytical functions of GIS include buffer zones, neighborhood characterization, and connectivity measurement. A particular feature of GIS is the ability to calculate more realistic distance measures among objects based on actual geometry, travel time, and cost, rather than straight-line distance. The trend in developing GIS analytical functions is to better integrate GIS with other software in statistical analysis, operations research, and artificial intelligence (AI)* tools.

In the decades since their first appearance in the 1960s, geographical information systems have experienced phenomenal growth in sophistication, size, and popularity. In the early twenty-first century, GIS is a multi-billion dollar industry and has become part of a basic information infrastructure for private enterprises, government agencies, and academic institutions. The majority of the operational GIS are used for thematic mapping, handling spatial queries, and decision-making support.

Thematic mapping involves making special purpose maps that provide appropriate content, context, symbolization, and illustrations. Geographic information systems provide utilities to make all stages of map-making faster, more accurate, and easier to do. *Spatial query* processing selects objects based on the combination of their locational, topological, and descriptive attributes. *Decision-support* functions of GIS allow users to ask "what if" questions to evaluate alternative actions.

In terms of practical applications, GIS programs assist with resource inventory, administrative recordkeeping, communication or transportation infrastructure and facility management, emergency response, and environmental monitoring preservation. Examples of GIS applications include understanding the process of water and nutrient flows over the land surface, identifying potential markets for a product in the local area, and deciding on the fastest route over which to send a fire truck to a downtown restaurant. All these tasks utilize the functionalities of a GIS to deal with complex spatial data sets.

Geographical information systems represent a synergistic* development of multiple technical fields, including computer cartography*, computational geometry, spatial and relational database*s, and information visualization. Fast retrieval of spatial data is made possible by using efficient indexing schemes such as quadtrees* or R-trees. The processing of spatial queries (e.g, point-in-polygon) relies on computational geometry algorithm*s such as line sweeping, Voronoi diagrams, and convex hulls. The increasing trend to build spatial data types and spatial operators in database engines make it possible to model the complexities of spatial data with object-relational or object-oriented approaches. Computer graphics and visualization techniques have increased the effectiveness of communicating spatial information to users.

Looking into the future, geographical information systems will likely become more user-friendly. With the development of web-based GIS, there is an evolution from single-user systems to more open, multiple-user systems. There has been much cross-fertilization between the fields of artificial intelligence and spatial information systems due to increased needs to deduct new information from retrieved data. Knowledge-based geographic information systems that incorporate deductive reasoning and learning facilities will be more powerful in modeling human spatial intelligence in the environment. An object-oriented, intelligent, dynamic, multimedia geographical information system will revolutionize people's views of the spaces and worlds in which we live.

▶ *See also* **Embedded Technology (Ubiquitous Computing)** • **Satellite Technology** • **Telecommunications**

Resources

Books

Laurini, Robert, and Derek Thompson. *Fundamentals of Spatial Information Systems*, 7th printing. London: Academic Press, 1999.

Longley, Paul A., et al., eds. *Geographic Information Systems &amp Science*. 3rd ed. Hoboken, NJ: Wiley, 2011.

Periodical

Berry, J. K. "Fundamental Operations in Computer-assisted Map Analysis." *International Journal of Geographical Information Science* 1, no. 2 (January 1987): 119–136.

Gross, Alfred J.
American Inventor
1918–2001

Alfred J. Gross was the inventor of several handheld communication devices, including the first walkie-talkie. Gross began his life-long romance with wireless communications at age nine during a cruise on

Research Sharing

The *International Journal of Geographical Information Science* is a scholarly publication that brings together the latest information on GIS technology from around the globe. The publication is geared to professionals involved in GIS applications, and is available online for a fee.

* **relational database** a collection of records that permits logical and business relationships to be developed between themselves and their contents

* **quadtrees** data structures resembling trees, which have four branches at every node (rather than two as with a binary tree); used in the construction of complex databases

* **algorithm** a rule or procedure used to solve a problem, most often described as a sequence of steps

* **ham radio** a legal (or licensed) amateur radio

Lake Erie. While exploring the ship, Gross met the radio operator and was invited into the radio room to listen to the transmission. The sound of wireless telegraphy fascinated him so much that he begged his parents to buy him a crystal set, an early radio.

Shortly thereafter, Gross began to build a ham radio* from scavenged junkyard materials. By age fifteen he was fabricating his own metal radio chassis in a metal working class. A year later he earned his amateur operator's license. He was now a operator. The next step for Gross was to build a handheld device—the walkie-talkie—to communicate. He wanted to talk with other ham operators while on the move.

His hobby began to develop into a potential career. By 1938, while a student in electrical engineering at Case Western Reserve, in Cleveland, Ohio, Gross had succeeded in inventing a two-way handheld radio using miniaturized components. He then started exploring ways to use frequencies above 100 MHz. By the end of the 1930s, he had built two models that operated at 300 MHz and could transmit a distance of 38 kilometers (30 miles). As World War II began, Gross' invention would take on a critical function.

In 1941 Gross was invited to demonstrate his walkie-talkie to the Office of Strategic Services (OSS), the forerunner of the U.S. Central Intelligence Agency (CIA). That meeting resulted in citizen Gross becoming Captain Gross and the initiation of the Joan/Eleanor project, a two-way ground to air radio system for military and espionage use. This system would enable personnel on the ground and behind enemy lines to communicate with high-flying airplanes. These transmissions could not be intercepted by the enemy as the radios operated at higher frequencies then the standard available transceivers. This feature enabled undetected gathering and reporting of enemy military movements.

Long after the war, Gross received recognition for his work. His contribution was cited as significantly shortening the war through the successful gathering of intelligence. The net result was the saving of countless lives. This "Top Secret" project was not declassified until 1976.

After the war, Gross set up two companies: Citizens Radio Corporation, which focused on the designing, development, and manufacture of personal wireless transceivers; and Gross Electronics, which designed and manufactured other communications products. Both companies were based in Cleveland, Ohio.

For the next twenty years, Gross developed circuitry for various wireless devices. In 1948 the Federal Communications Commission (FCC) approved the two-way radio, "Citizens' Band," for personal use. Initially, these radios were used by farmers and the U.S. Coast Guard. A year later, Gross invented and patented circuitry that responded selectively to specific signals for use as a pocket-sized receiver, the pager. Physicians were his targeted audience for the use of such pagers. However, the initial reaction of the medical community was unenthusiastic because the device beeped. Medical professionals anticipated that the noise would annoy patients and might even interrupt the physician's golf game. However, Gross lived to see his pager not only accepted but also become a necessary device for many professionals and service providers.

Gross's invention also received unexpected fame when it was featured in the Dick Tracy comic book series, developed by Chester Gould. The cartoonist incorporated Gross' idea of a miniaturized two-way radio into the series as a two-way wrist radio. Then, in the late 1950s, the U.S. Navy parachuted an unmanned battery-operated weather station into the Antarctic that was designed and manufactured by Gross Electronics. Gross continued to develop and patent various cordless and portable telephonic devices through the 1960s.

After closing his companies, Gross did not retire but continued to conduct research as a specialist in microwave communications for Sperry Corporation, General Electric, and Westinghouse as well as other large corporations. At seventy-two he became the senior principal engineer for the Orbital Science Corporation while also continuing to work on personal projects. He also continued to give presentations to elementary and high school students on technology and inventions.

Although his numerous patents expired before Gross could realize the full material rewards for his efforts, he is quoted as observing, without rancor, that, "If I still had the patents on my inventions I would be as rich as Bill Gates." For Gross the true reward was the ability to continue being productive throughout his life. He never lost his zest for exploring and expanding wireless technology and sharing his knowledge and enthusiasm with others.

▶ *See also* **Bell Labs • Cellular Technology • Internet • Telecommunications • Wireless Technology**

Resources

Periodicals

Saxon, Wolfgang. "Al Gross, Inventor of Gizmos with Potential, Dies at 82." *New York Times*, January 2, 2001.

Honorable Career

Throughout his career, Gross received recognition for his inventions. Among these are a commendation from U.S. President Ronald Reagan, the Institute of Electrical and Electronics Engineers (IEEE) Century of Honors Medal, and the Marconi Memorial Gold Medal of Achievement.

H

Hacking

For years, "hacker" was a positive term that described computer enthusiasts who had a zeal for computer programming. Those who hacked took pride in their ability to write computer programs that stretched the capabilities of computer systems and find clever solutions to seemingly impossible problems. Although many computer enthusiasts still ascribe to this definition, the everyday usage of the word has changed significantly. Today, "hacking" generally refers to individuals who break into computer systems or use their programming skills or expert knowledge to act maliciously. (Traditional hackers [the good kind] prefer to use the term "cracker" to refer to these individuals.)

Some of the most common types of hacking include:

- Breaking into computer networks;
- Bypassing passwords or copy protection in computer software;
- Defacing and/or damaging Internet web sites;
- Causing a denial of service attack on a web site or network (preventing legitimate users from accessing a web site);
- Stealing valuable information such as passwords and credit card data.

A Systematic Process

Although portrayed otherwise in Hollywood films and in television shows, hacking is a systematic, tiresome process in which the attacker attempts methodically to locate computer systems, identify their vulnerabilities, and then compromise those vulnerabilities to obtain access. Experts have identified six steps that are generally followed in the hacking process. These include (1) footprinting (reconnaissance); (2) scanning; (3) enumeration; (4) penetration; (5) advance; and (6) covering tracks.

Footprinting The first technique often used by hackers is called footprinting. The objective is to gather information essential to an attack and enable an attacker to obtain a complete profile of an organization's security posture. During this phase, the hacker might gain information about the location of the company, phone numbers, employee names, security policies, and the overall layout of the target network. Often, hackers can perform this work with a simple web browser, a telephone, and a search engine. Unfortunately, humans are often the weakest security link in a corporation. A clever phone call to the technical support department can

Computer Sciences, 2ⁿᵈ Edition

* **ping sweeps** technique that identifies properties belonging to a server computer, by sending it collections of "ping" packets and examining the responses from the server

* **port scans** operations whereby ports are probed so that information about their status can be collected

* **Trojan horse** potentially destructive computer program that masquerades as something benign; named after the wooden horse employed by the Acheans to conquer Troy

often compromise critical information: "Hi, this is Bill and I forgot my password. Can you remind me what it is?"

Scanning Next, hackers perform scanning to gain a more detailed view of a company's network and to understand what specific computer systems and services are in use. During this phase, the hacker determines which systems on the target network are live and reachable from the Internet. Commonly used scanning techniques include network ping sweeps* and port scans*. A ping sweep lets the attacker determine which individual computers on the network are alive and potential targets for attack. Port scanning can be used to determine what ports (a port is like a door or window on a house) are open on a given computer, and whether or not the software managing those ports has any obvious vulnerabilities.

Enumeration The third phase is the process of identifying user accounts and poorly protected computing resources. During the enumeration stage, the hacker connects to computers in the target network and pokes around these systems to gain more information. While the scanning phase might be compared to a knock on the door or a turn of the doorknob to see if it is locked, enumeration could be compared to entering an office and rifling through a file cabinet or desk drawer for information. It is definitely more intrusive.

Penetration During the fourth phase, penetration, the attacker attempts to gain control of one or more systems in the target network. For example, once an attacker has acquired a list of usernames during enumeration, he can usually guess one of the users' passwords and gain more extensive access to that user's account. Alternatively, once the attacker has determined that a target computer is running an old or buggy piece of software or one that is configured improperly, the hacker may attempt to exploit known vulnerabilities with this software to gain control of the system.

Advance In the advance phase of hacking, the attacker leverages computers or accounts that have been compromised during penetration to launch additional attacks on the target network. For instance, the attacker can break into more sensitive administrator root accounts, install backdoors or Trojan horse* programs, and install network sniffers to gather additional information (for example, passwords) from data flowing over the network.

Covering Tracks In the final phase of hacking, the hacker eliminates any records or logs showing his malicious behavior. By deleting log files, disabling system auditing (which would otherwise alert the administrator to malicious activities), and hiding hacking files that the hacker has introduced, he can cover his tracks and avoid detection. Finally, the hacker can install a root kit, which is a series of programs that replace the existing system software to both cover his tracks and gather new information.

Attacks, Countermeasures, and Motivations

Since the late 1990s, the number of hacking attacks has grown dramatically. Both private companies such as Microsoft, Yahoo, Amazon.com, Buy.com, and U.S. government entities like the Federal Bureau of Investigation (FBI) and the White House have been targeted by hackers. In the vast majority of incidents, hackers have attempted to either launch denial of service attacks or deface Internet web pages with inappropriate content. However, some of the attacks are far more insidious. In January of 2000, a nineteen-year-old Russian hacker, using the pseudonym Maxim, threatened to publish more than 300,000 customer credit card numbers (obtained by hacking into a popular e-commerce site) if he was not given $100,000 cash.

Another notorious hacker is Israeli-born Ehud Tenenbaum (1979–). At the age of nineteen, Tenenbaum, otherwise known as "The Analyzer," made international headlines when he was arrested in 1998 along with several other Isrealis and a pair of American teenagers. The group was accused of penetrating government computer systems in the United States and Israel. In the U.S., the government organizations that were victims of the group's hacking included NASA and the Pentagon. Tenenbaum was penalized for those crimes with a fine, a suspended prison sentence, and probation. Later, as a computer security consultant, Tenenbaum seemed to have turned his talents to work for the benefit of society. However, in 2009 Tenenbaum plead guilty in New York City to participating in a scheme that hacked into two U.S. banks, as well as other financial institutions, in order to steal upwards of $10 million. Beyond these highly publicized cases, it is unclear how many corporations have been hacked successfully; however, from all accounts, the number is definitely large and growing.

In May 2012, security analysts at Kaspersky Labs, a computer security company, announced the discovery of one of the most complex and sustained cyberattacks in history. Following a joint investigation with the United Nations' International Telecommunication Union, Kaspersky revealed that malware, known as Flame, had infected government, university, business, and individual computer systems in Iran, Israel, Sudan, Syria, Lebanon, Saudi Arabia, and Egypt since at least 2010. Flame collected private data and sent the information to the attackers. Flame was even capable of secretly recording video and audio using a computer's webcam and microphone before sending it back to the attackers. Kaspersky security analysts claim that the complexity of the malware and the systems targeted indicate that the cyberattack was state-sponsored. Computer security experts will spend years analyzing data from the attack in an attempt to identify the attackers.

A number of technologies are available to companies to prevent hacking attacks. The most popular tools are Internet firewalls, anti-virus software, intrusion detection systems, and vulnerability assessment tools. Firewalls are used to set up a virtual wall between the Internet and the

Hackers and Climategate

A notorious case of hacking was at the core of the scandal known as "Climategate." In late 2009 a server at the Climate Research Unit (CRU) at the University of East Anglia in England was breached by unknown hacker(s). Over a thousand e-mails, as well as many other documents, were publicly leaked from the CRU's web server. Many of the e-mails consisted of correspondence between prominent British and American climate scientists. Some skeptics of man-made global warming claim that the leaked e-mails indicate a conscience effort to skew climate research in order to reinforce the notion that humans are responsible for recent climate change, a charge the scientists involved denied. The ensuing controversy prompted official reviews in both the United States and Britain to address the charges of scientific misconduct on the part of the climate scientists. This case highlights the dramatic effects that hacking can produce when the data that is hacked involves a controversial topic such as climate change.

company's internal network to repel attackers. Anti-virus software detects and removes computer viruses, worms, and Trojan horses. Intrusion detection systems watch over critical networks and computers looking for suspicious activities, and can alert administrators in the event of an attack. Finally, corporations use vulnerability assessment tools to inventory their computing infrastructure and better understand the existing vulnerabilities.

Contrary to popular belief, most hackers are not international or industrial spies with evil motives and a desire to rule the world; most hackers have a simpler agenda. Among hackers, one of the most frequently cited motivations is that hacking is fun and is like solving a game or a puzzle. Many hackers perceive their activities to be harmless and they do not believe that they are victimizing anyone. In addition, the thrill of doing something illegal or the ability to access data unavailable to the public can be a tempting motivator. The chance to earn recognition from within a hacker group also offers strong incentive for up-and-coming hackers who have yet to gain a reputation. Finally, many hackers justify their actions by explaining that they are doing a service for other computer users by identifying new security holes.

Judicial, Criminal, and Civil Implications of Hacking

The following federal statutes offer computer crime and hacking protection:

- 18 U.S.C. § 1029. Fraud and Related Activity in Connection with Access Devices;
- 18 U.S.C. § 1030. Fraud and Related Activity in Connection with Computers;
- 18 U.S.C. § 1362. Communication Lines, Stations, or Systems;
- 18 U.S.C. § 2511. Interception and Disclosure of Wire, Oral, or Electronic Communications Prohibited;
- 18 U.S.C. § 2701. Unlawful Access to Stored Communications;
- 18 U.S.C. § 2702. Disclosure of Contents;
- 18 U.S.C. § 2703. Requirements for Governmental Access.

As this list suggests, there is a substantial body of statutory law that applies directly to computer crime and hackers. Hacking of government computers, computers that are used by or for the government, and private computers used "in interstate commerce or communications" can be prosecuted under existing statutes. The existing statutory framework also provides for civil liability for unauthorized interception of communications. Finally, federal statutes exist to protect federal records, property, or public money. Consequently, bank, credit records, and electronic fund transfers are all protected by federal laws. In recent cases, prosecuted hackers have been incarcerated, sentenced to home detention, and/or ordered to pay restitution; some hackers have been ordered to pay thousands of dollars in fines.

▶ *See also* **Hackers • Privacy • Security • Security Hardware • Security Software**

Resources

Books

McClure, Stuart, Joel Scambray, and George Kurtz. *Hacking Exposed: Network Security Secrets & Solutions.* 5th ed. Emeryville, CA: McGraw-Hill/Osborne, 2005.

Hewlett, William

American Executive
1913–2001

William Hewlett teamed with David Packard to create one of the largest and most successful technology businesses in the world, the Hewlett-Packard Company. After an initial investment of $538 to set up shop in a garage, Hewlett and Packard worked to see their organization grow into a multi-billion dollar enterprise. The pair also became known for their management style, called "management by walking around," which was copied by other technology companies. In their walks, they made inpromptu visits and talked to employees of all levels, including non-management personnel.

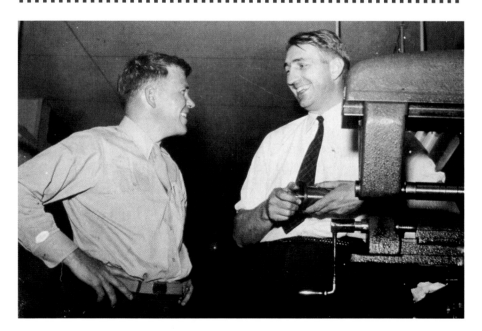

Hackers and Y2K

As the new millennium approached, concerns about the Y2K (year 2000) bug surfaced. At that time, many computer programs stored dates as two digits (e.g., "99" for "1999"). People worried that a date of "00" might be read by computers as "1900" rather than "2000" and cause computers to malfunction or shut down. As business and government agencies scrambled to patch these programs, concern grew that terrorists would try to take advantage of the situation and hack into such systems. However, corporations and government bodies, including the Federal Bureau of Investigation, took steps to secure programs, preventing hackers from crashing vital services, such as the distribution of social security checks.

Hewlett (left) and Packard set up shop in Silicon Valley. © *AP Images/HO/ Hewlett Packard.*

* **oscillator** an electronic component that produces a precise waveform of a fixed known frequency; this can be used as a time base (clock) signal to other devices

* **Silicon Valley** an area in California near San Francisco, which has been the home location of many of the most significant information technology orientated companies and universities

Hewlett was born on May 20, 1913, in Ann Arbor, Michigan, and grew up in San Francisco. Dyslexia prevented him from reading well, so he approached learning by disassembling common objects such as door locks and other mechanical devices and conducting experiments in chemistry. In 1930 Hewlett entered Stanford University, graduating with a bachelor of arts degree in 1934. It was during this time that he and David Packard began a friendship that would last for sixty years.

Hewlett continued his education at Massachusetts Institute of Technology, earning a master of science degree in engineering. The last phase of his education was an advanced degree in engineering from Stanford, which he completed in 1939. That was also the year that he and Packard decided to form an electronics company in Palo Alto, California. With their initial $538 investment, a garage for a shop, and lots of ideas, the Hewlett-Packard Company (HP) was born. The name of the company (i.e., the order of their names) was determined in a coin toss. Hewlett took charge of product development, while Packard assumed marketing duties.

HP's initial products included a tuner for harmonicas, a self-flushing urinal, a shock machine to induce weight loss, and a foul line indicator for bowling alleys. The first successful product, the audio oscillator*, was based on Hewlett's graduate research at Stanford. The provided a cheaper, easier way to generate audio frequencies, which made it useful for geological and medical instruments and military equipment. Walt Disney Studios, HP's first customer, used the to develop the unique sound track for the animated movie *Fantasia,* starring Mickey Mouse. The business was profitable and growing, and by the 1950s HP would become the dominant provider of electronic testing and measurement equipment.

During World War II, Hewlett served on the staff of the U.S. Army's chief signal officer, and then became head of the electronics section of the New Development Division of the War Department Special Staff. In this capacity, he was part of a special team that inspected Japanese industries at the end of the war. One benefit from his military service was meeting first-rate engineers whom he later recruited to work for his company. When he returned to HP at the end of the war, he became vice president of the company.

His military experience gave Hewlett insight into management styles. With Packard, he developed employee-oriented polices. The company pioneered such ideas as profit sharing, flextime, catastrophic health insurance, decentralized decision-making, open offices, and management by objective. When former employees started their own companies in Silicon Valley*, they often instituted these same practices.

Steve Jobs, cofounder of Apple Computer, credits Hewlett for his own start in life as an entrepreneur as well as for his own management style. Jobs contacted HP as a twelve-year-old looking for spare parts to construct a frequency counter. Not only did Hewlett provide the parts, but he also hired Jobs for a summer position in the division that produced frequency counters. There are numerous other anecdotes about Hewlett and his generosity with others.

The first HP computer, Model 2116, was an automatic controller for measurement systems. Introduced in 1966, it was redesigned from a freestanding model to desktop size, marketed and sold as a calculator. Hewlett then challenged his engineers to further shrink the size to allow the device to fit into a shirt pocket. The resulting HP scientific calculator quickly replaced the slide rule* as the computational device for scientists and engineers. Today the company is best known for its laser printers and scanners.

Hewlett's own interests went far beyond engineering. He was a modern-day renaissance man. He and his wife, Flora, established the William and Flora Hewlett Foundation which supports educational, environmental, arts and other programs. After Hewlett's death on January 12, 2001, the foundation was to receive a major portion of his estate in order to continue supporting these causes.

Hewlett was also instrumental in the founding of the Public Policy Institute of California, which researches economic, social, and political issues that impact the state. His interest in conservation led to his purchase of land on the shore of Lake Tahoe (located between California and Nevada) and deeding it to the U.S. Forest Service in order to prevent development along the pristine lake front. Hewlett was also an amateur botanist, and he photographed and catalogued many California wild flowers.

Hewlett held honorary degrees from numerous American colleges and universities, was a member of the National Academy of Engineering and the National Academy of Sciences, and served as trustee for various educational institutions. He also served as a member of the President's General Advisory Committee on Foreign Assistance Programs and the President's Science Advisory Committee during the Lyndon Johnson Administration. In 1985, he was awarded the National Medal of Science by President Ronald Reagan.

 See also **Computers, Generations • IBM Corporation • Watson, Thomas J., Sr.**

Resources

Books

Packard, David, David Kirby, and Karen R. Lewis. *The HP Way: How Bill Hewlett and I Build Our Company.* New York: Collins Business Essentials, 2005.

Tracy, Kathleen. *William Hewlett: Pioneer of the Computer Age.* Dear, DE: Mitchell Lane Publishers, 2003.

David Packard

A cofounder of Hewlett-Packard, David Packard (1912–1996) was president of HP from 1947 to 1964. Then he became chairperson of the board and chief executive officer. In 1969 he was appointed as deputy U.S. secretary of defense. In addition to establishing the David and Lucile Packard Foundation, he served on various boards devoted to environment and conservation issues.

* **slide rule** invented by Scotsman John Napier (1550–1617), it permits the mechanical automation of calculations using logarithms

Home System Software

One of the principal reasons that the personal computer (PC) has become a universally used appliance is that there is a wide array of software designed to support the needs and interests of home users. The personal computer is not only a workstation for word processing, accounting, and Internet access. It is also a reference library providing direct access to atlases, dictionaries, encyclopedias, and other reference works; an entertainment system providing recorded music, movies, and games; and occasionally a medium for controlling other automated home systems.

The software commonly installed on home systems falls into the following categories:

- Productivity applications, including office suites, personal financial management, and hypertext markup language (HTML) composer/editor applications;
- System and disk management utilities;
- Anti-virus software;
- File compression, decompression, and archiving applications;
- Digital document and eBook readers;
- Internet connectivity and Web browsing;
- Reference tools;
- Streaming audio and video players;
- Compact disc-rewritable (CD-RW) and digital versatile disc (DVD) tools;
- Games.

Office Suites

The office suite is at the core of most home systems. The suite generally consists of a set of applications supporting word processing, presentations, electronic mail, spreadsheets, and database creation, typically outfitted with a common interface, and usually designed to provide inter-application communications. The most popular suite is Microsoft *Office*, with versions for both Windows and Macintosh operating systems. The most recent version (as of 2012) for the Windows operating system is *Office 2010*, which was released by Microsoft in June 2010. Besides Microsoft *Office*, there are other commercial suites with modest shares of the market, most notably Corel's *WordPerfect Office*.

There is also competition from the open source software environment. Three open source office suites include Apache OpenOffice (formerly called Oracle OpenOffice), Calligra Suite (an advanced version of KOffice), and LibreOffice.

Personal financial software is another popular productivity application. These programs are designed to manage personal finances—including checking, credit card accounts, and investment accounts—and some enable users to update their personal bank accounts interactively. Banks and investment brokerages also frequently provide customers with software specially designed to manage personal accounts. Intuit's Quicken is a popular personal finance software program.

Yet another popular productivity application is the Hypertext Markup Language (HTML) composer/editor. In some cases, the HTML composer/editor is part of an office suite—for example, Microsoft's *FrontPage* is included in certain versions of Microsoft *Office*, and Microsoft Word is also capable of composing and editing HTML files. Other popular HTML composing and editing tools, such as Macromedia's *Dreamweaver*, are standalone development environments incorporating many other features and utilities, including remote website management.

System and Disk Management Utilities

Because the data capacity of hard disks has continued to grow larger while at the same time becoming less expensive, and the number of programs installed on home systems has generally continued to become more numerous, utilities aimed at managing disks and how files are written to disks have become increasingly important. Most of the applications written in this area are designed to scan hard disks for physical defects, detect fragmented files, and reorganize file systems.

Disk defragmentation tools re-write the files on a disk to increase the efficiency and reliability with which programs and other files are called from the disk. Tools of this type are important to many users, because disk fragmentation is a common problem on systems that enjoy heavy usage, and because highly fragmented file systems can have a significant and adverse effect on performance of a computer. These programs cannot actually fix physical defects, but most of them are able to preserve the integrity of systems and user data by identifying and marking defective clusters.

Disk management tools are often the core of a much larger set of tools included in a number of popular systems utilities packages. Such sets commonly include utilities intended to correct minor errors in the configuration of the operating system and/or applications, identify and mark redundant files for deletion, clear system and application caches, and restore deleted files.

Anti-Virus and Firewall Software

Anti-virus and firewall software is arguably the most important of the utilities that may be installed on a personal computer. Computer viruses are common, and they can be transmitted in a number of different ways, including infected flash drives or other portable storage media; through file transfers; and via electronic mail (e-mail). Most of the viruses that circulate are designed to corrupt and destroy file systems. Some viruses in circulation are especially dangerous, because they are designed to copy personal information, such as the information in an electronic address book, and then use the data as the basis for propagating the virus and infecting

* **algorithm** a rule or procedure used to solve a mathematical problem—most often described as a sequence of steps

* **de facto** as is

other systems by sending copies of the virus to other users via e-mail. Anti-virus software is designed to scan local file systems, on-demand or on a scheduled basis, and check incoming e-mail, with particular attention to the contents of attached files. Firewall software is used to keep a computer network secure.

A key to the effectiveness of anti-virus and firewall software is the frequency and thoroughness with which it is updated. The most effective anti-virus programs obtain updates frequently via the Internet. The company Symantec provides a popular anti-virus software package called Norton 360.

Adobe Acrobat Reader and eBook Readers

Files rendered in Adobe's Portable Document Format (PDF) are one of the most popular ways of publishing formatted documents, because PDF enables authors to preserve formatting beyond the framework of the application in which the document was created, and because Adobe has elected to make the Acrobat *Reader* available free of charge and for a number of different computer platforms. So, the Acrobat *Reader* is a common part of the software installed on home systems. In addition, Adobe makes available *eBook Reader*, which supports PDF files and the Electronic Book Exchange (EBX) digital rights management standards.

Microsoft makes several document viewers available without charge, including viewers for *Access, Excel, PowerPoint*, and *Word* as well as its *Reader*, which supports Microsoft's own eBook format. Microsoft *Reader* supports text, images, and audio, as well as other media, including streaming video.

Archiving and Compression Utilities

Archived and compressed files are a common element of file management, storage, and exchange. There are a number of relevant methods for archiving and compressing (or uncompressing) files in the personal computer environment, distinguished mainly by the efficiency of the underlying algorithm*s, but the most widely used in the personal computer environment are utilities that incorporate the compression/decompression developed by Phil Katz. Recognizable by the de facto* standard file extension,*.zip, this archiving and compression format is used to store and transmit programs and documents. WinZip (http://www.winzip.com/) is a popular compression and data backup utility.

Reference Tools

PC vendors recognized early on that they could capture a significant part of the then-lucrative market for home encyclopedia sales if they included compact disc-read only memory (CD-ROM) based encyclopedias and other reference works as part of the installed software bundle that shipped with their systems, or sold reference works of this type as a low-priced addition. As a result, large numbers of systems include a multimedia encyclopedia. (In the beginning, the multimedia encyclopedias were decidedly inferior to most printed encyclopedias, but eventually, encyclopedias such as Microsoft's *Encarta* achieved much greater editorial authority.) In addition, such systems often include other reference works, such as an atlas, a dictionary, and a thesaurus, and in many cases these reference works are supplemented by Internet-based updating services. Between 2009 and 2011, Microsoft discontinued its *Encarta* due to increasing on-line competition, such as from Wikipedia.com.

Internet Connectivity

Hundreds of millions of personal computer users connect to the Internet from home, and many of them use third-party applications to connect with an Internet Service Provider (ISP)*, connect to remote systems via telnet, read and send e-mail, and upload and download files. ISPs, most notably America Online, make such software available without charge to customers paying for online access through their services. As of 2012, America Online, now known as AOL, serves about 3.1 million customers, both paying and free, in the United States.

Internet-connected users employ web browsers such as Microsoft's *Internet Explorer* to view and interact with the World Wide Web. Because web browsers also support various other functions, including remote login, file transfer, and access to remote services, including e-mail services, the web browser is not only an almost-universal application, it is also one that plays a multiplicity of roles on many home systems.

Streaming Audio and Video

In recent years, streaming audio and video have become important sources of information and entertainment for Internet-connected users, particularly users with broadband access (via digital subscriber line (DSL) or cable modem services). Because there are competing technologies—Microsoft uses technologies based on the WAV file format, whereas almost all of the other application developers in this area rely on relevant aspects of the Moving Pictures Experts Group (MPEG)* standards—many users have two or more applications to support streaming audio and video installed on their systems. Today, it would not be unusual for a home system to host both Microsoft's *Windows Media Player* and Real Networks' *Real Player*, each of which may be downloaded free-of-charge over the Internet.

Optical Disc Technologies: CD, DVD, and Blu-ray

Most home systems are equipped with CD and/or DVD drives that are capable of recording CDs (CD-R) and addressing rewriteable CDs (CDRW) and/or DVDs (DVD±RW). Such systems include utilities that are designed to write to blank CDs and DVDs and/or format and read rewriteable discs. DVDs are often used for recording movies or other data-intensive applications, and utilize the MPEG file and compression standard. In an expanded format, DVDs can hold up to 17 gigabytes (GB) of video, audio, or other information. The higher-density Blu-ray optical disc technology features up to 25 GB for single-layered discs, and 50 GB for dual-layered discs.

* **Internet Service Provider (ISP)** a commercial enterprise which offers paying subscribers access to the Internet (usually via modem) for a fee

* **MPEG (Moving Pictures Experts Group)** an encoding scheme for data files that contain motion pictures—it is used in the same way as JPEG (Joint Photographic Experts Group) encoding

Games

Home systems commonly include games of various types. There are many types of games available, but the most popular games fall into the following categories: action; adventure and fantasy; military; and sports simulation. Internet-based games, using Java, Shockwave, or some other distributable media, are increasing in popularity, as are interactive, multi-player games. Computer games are distinctive among the applications installed on home systems because games commonly require more sophisticated or specialized hardware. For example, many games require comparatively more powerful graphics adapters; others require special physical controllers.

 See also **Animation • Embedded Technology (Ubiquitous Computing) • Integrated Software • Music**

Resources

Books

Gralla, Preston. *How the Internet Works*. 8th ed. Indianapolis: Que Publications, 2007.

White, Ron. *How Computers Work*. 9th ed. Indianapolis: Que Publications, 2008.

Web Sites

Microsoft. "Welcome to Office." http://office.microsoft.com/en-us/ (accessed October 3, 2012).

Symantec. "Norton 360." http://buy.norton.com/mf/productDetails/ productSkuCode/21236413/productShortName/norton-360/ sourcePageType/Category/categoryCode/All_In_One_Security_ Sub_Category/priceGroupId/1000000/slotNo/1/.

I

Image Analysis: Medicine

The evolution of computers has dramatically affected the quality of human life in the field of medicine. Many developments during the last thirty years of the twentieth century and into the first two decades of the twenty-first century have taken place in the field of diagnostic radiology, which is used to diagnose and sometimes treat illnesses. Among the image analysis tools now available that are derived from advances in computer technology are the ultrasound, computed tomography, nuclear medicine, and magnetic resonance imaging.

Ultrasound

Ultrasound is an example of technology that was first developed to serve military purposes. The principle behind ultrasonography was first used during World War II. Called SONAR, an acronym for SOund Navigation And Ranging, it helped detect the presence of underwater submarines. Ultrasound was not widely used in medicine until the early 1970s. Diagnostic ultrasound uses sound waves that are too high for the human ear to detect (between one million and 20 million cycles per second). These sound waves are used to evaluate the soft tissues of the body, such as muscles and organs.

The method is simple. First, a piezoelectric crystal* is pulsed with electricity, making the crystal vibrate in a hand-held unit, called a transducer. The result is a sound wave. When the transducer is applied to the skin with a special electrophoretic gel, the sound waves are sent through tissue until they encounter acoustical resistance. (Electrophoretic concerns the movement of dispersed particles relative to a fluid that is under the action of a spatially consistent electric field.) Such resistance makes some portion of the sound wave reflect back to its source. After pulsing, the transducer stops and acquires (listens for) the sound waves reflected back to the crystal. Once that happens, the crystal vibrates again, producing electricity to indicate the pressure, amplitude, frequency, and speed of the returning wave. The computer then records the results. With this information, the computer is able to construct an image of the variety and depth of tissues through which the wave has passed. The use of ultrasound is limited, however. Tissues with too much acoustical resistance, for example bone and air, make this tool useless when the tissue to be examined lies behind a bone or a lung.

* **piezoelectric crystal** an electronic component that when subjected to a current will produce a waveform signal at a precise rate, which can then be used as a clock signal in a computer

Computer screens showing high resolution medical imagery. © *Spencer Pratt/Getty Images.*

* **pixel** a single picture element on a video screen; one of the individual dots making up a picture on a video screen or digital image

Computed Tomography

Computed Tomography, or CT, which became widely used in the late 1970s, would be impossible without computers. In CT, x rays are transmitted through a body at various angles. The x rays are then measured on the other side of the body by detectors. Depending on the percentage of x rays that are successfully transmitted through the body, the computer is able to create a matrix defining the structure of tissues that absorbed the x rays. The resulting images are usually displayed as slices; however, complex two-and three-dimensional images may be constructed by the computer if additional information is needed by physicians. The CT scanner usually takes multiple slices that are a prescribed distance apart, from millimeters to centimeters.

Modern CT scanners use slices made up of millions of pixel*s. These are assigned a number on the grayscale somewhere in between very black and very white, and given a numerical value. With CT, the computer can adjust the grayscale after the study is complete to allow the trained observer to study a particular tissue density. For instance, the grayscale is adjusted to a very low level to look inside the lung, which is mostly air. With slight differences of grayscale, the image could show subtle differences in lung tissue, but with that particular scale, muscle and bone surrounding the lung would both look white. Conversely, if the goal of the study is to look for a small metal fragment imbedded in the spine, the grayscale would be adjusted to allow the image to differentiate between the density of metal versus the slightly less dense bone. Air, muscles, and other tissues in that study would look uniformly black. Both examinations can be done, without repeating the study, simply by varying the grayscale level of a given result.

Nuclear Medicine

Nuclear medicine is another type of diagnostic study that requires computers. These studies deal with the body's function more than with evaluating anatomy. Special radioactive molecules are tailored to target an organ's function. These radioactive materials are usually injected into the patient. After a given period of time, the patient is examined with a special device that measures radioactivity from the body. The computers measure the amount of radioactivity, help determine the source of that activity, and most importantly, are used to filter out misleading radioactivity.

Magnetic Resonance Imaging

Magnetic resonance imaging, or MRI, is very different. A strong magnet is utilized to align protons in the human body. The MRI machine then briefly sends radio waves through the body, exciting the protons. The unit then listens for the radio waves that the excited protons emit. The machine measures the number of hydrogen nuclei, or protons, in a given part of the body. Different body tissues, and even the different chemicals in the tissues, emit different radio waves.

After the study is done using the desired frequency, the information is collected and digitized by the computer, so the information can be presented and analyzed. Since the frequency of the radio waves is chosen for a specific task, the process might be repeated several times using different frequencies in a single study.

Evolution of Medical Technology

All of these techniques would be impossible without advances in both physics and computers. The results from these technologies, as well as regular (called plain-film) x rays, can be digitized, and therefore analyzed, manipulated, transported, stored, and presented in multiple ways.

When these tools were first introduced, the computers that ran them were mainframe computers* requiring their own customized room with extensive cooling systems. Over the years, they became smaller as computers became more powerful. By the end of the twentieth century, most of these studies were being done with computers only slightly larger than personal computers (PCs). As with everything else in the computer field, these tools, software applications, and technologies continue to evolve in the twenty-first century.

Besides the abovementioned medical applications for computers, other tools used in computer-assisted medicine include functional MRI (fMRI, which scans the brain), single-photon emission computed tomography (SPECT, a nuclear medicine tomographic imaging technique that uses gamma rays), photoacoustics (a hybrid imaging tool based on the photoacoustic effect), and breast thermography (an infrared imaging thermography tool to analyze breast cancer). With great technological advances, uses for computer image analysis are limited only by the imagination. Computer color analysis is used to measure the success of bleaching teeth.

* **mainframe computers** large computers used by businesses and government agencies to process massive amounts of data; generally faster and more powerful than desktop computers but usually requiring specialized software

Examining the Ocean Floor

Ultrasound technology (SONAR), first used during World War II to detect enemy submarines, is still used to locate submersed objects. In 1998, a team of scientists, led by American underwater archaeologist Robert Ballard (1942–), went in search of the USS *Yorktown*, an aircraft carrier that was sunk during the Battle of Midway in 1942. Using a SONAR sled and a robot, the team developed digital images of the Pacific Ocean floor; after analyzing the images, they pinpointed the remains of the ship.

It is also used to analyze lesion borders in various types of skin cancer as well as to examine the back of the eye through digitized retinal analysis. Image analysis can be used to evaluate wound healing that is undetectable to the human eye. Also, image analysis computer programs are invaluable in guiding surgeons in microscopic surgery.

Outside of medicine, uses for image analysis abound in the sciences, from the development of agricultural products, to the study of the activity and reproduction of plant and animal cells. Image analysis tools are used for the genetic analysis of various living entities. Computer image analysis is also becoming an economical and accurate method in the teaching of biology, microbiology, and other fields of science.

▶ *See also* **Medical Systems • Molecular Biology • Scientific Visualization**

Resources

Books

Bushong, Stewart Carlyle. *Radiologic Science for Technologists: Physics, Biology, and Protection*. 10th ed. St. Louis: Elsevier Mosby, 2013.

Frank, Eugene D. *Merrill's Atlas of Radiographic Positioning & Procedures*. 12th ed. St. Louis: Elsevier Mosby, 2012.

Ramesh, Chandra. *Nuclear Medicine Physics: The Basics*. 7th ed. Philadelphia: Wolters Kluwer Health/Lippincott Williams & Wilkins, 2012.

Web Sites

Medline Plus. "Ultrasound." http://www.nlm.nih.gov/medlineplus/ultrasound.html (accessed October 4, 2012).

National Cancer Institute. "Computed Tomography (CT): Questions and Answers." http://www.cancer.gov/cancertopics/factsheet/detection/CT (accessed October 4, 2012).

WebMD. "Magnetic Resonance Imaging (MRI)." http://www.webmd.com/a-to-z-guides/magnetic-resonance-imaging-mri (accessed October 4, 2012).

Integrated Software

Much of the developed world's population now requires computer technology to perform a host of tasks. People rely on computers when they go shopping, schedule meetings, create presentations, balance checkbooks, make car payments, or seek entertainment. Many Americans use computers at home, at school, at the library, and at work. People expect all computers to be able to communicate to one another and allow them to transfer documents without errors between computers so that they can share their work with others. Integrated software, which is defined as computer software that consists of the most commonly used functions of the major productivity software programs–functions that include database management, data communications, spreadsheets, and word processing–makes it easy to do such tasks.

One type of integrated software is the business office suite, which is now a staple in many home offices, small businesses, and large enterprises. These suites typically include word processing, spreadsheets, databases, e-mail, appointment scheduling, electronic slide capability, and Web browsing programs, all of which can create and exchange information quickly and easily. Microsoft Office 2010, for the Microsoft Windows operating system, and Microsoft Office 2011 for the Apple Macintosh (Mac) operating system, are two of more popular office suites currently on the market.

Another example of integrated software is the developer's office suite for those who create new software. These packages offer programs including word processing, Hypertext Markup Language (HTML)* editors, Web navigation tools, e-mail, bulletin board managers, application builders, scripting languages*, directory browsers, help browsers, and program editors.

A suite of programs for home computer use can include software that a home user would find helpful, such as word processing, money management, e-mail, a Web browser, an encyclopedia, and a dictionary. A lawyer's office suite typically includes a combination of word processing, proofreading, document assembly, research, Web navigation, and e-mail programs.

A variety of manufacturers offer these integrated software packages, and each has its own unique advantages depending on the needs of its targeted customer base. This article describes the typical business office suite.

History

The integration of powerful business software occurred in the late twentieth century. In the early 1980s, Lotus 1-2-3 was the only software available to create spreadsheets; Gopher protocol (commonly called gopher), developed at the University of Minnesota, was the single application to read e-mail; and there were only a few word processing options, including WordStar, WordPerfect, or a line editor such as *vi*. Overhead slide presentations could not be created on a computer. Appointment scheduling was done using paper and pencil.

At that time, each piece of office software was an independent entity. That is, without expert assistance, files could not be shared across platforms or combined into one document. Therefore, users could not import WordStar documents into a Lotus spreadsheet, or access files on a Unix (trademarked as UNIX) operating system from a disk operating system (DOS). By the 1990s, however, a variety of software manufacturers offered business professionals complex integrated packages that gave them the ability to create complex, format-rich documents.

* **Hypertext Markup Language (HTML)** an encoding scheme for text data that uses special tags in the text to signify properties to the viewing program (browser) like links to other documents or document parts

* **scripting languages** modern high-level programming languages that are interpreted rather than compiled; they are usually cross-platform and support rapid application development

The first efforts to combine capabilities resulted in integrated programs, such as Microsoft Works and Claris Works. Each was a single program that combined several software functions, such as simplified versions of word processors, spreadsheets, and databases. Early versions of these programs created documents that could not be exported into more sophisticated full-sized word processing or spreadsheet applications. Their primary benefit to the user was that multiple office functions could be accomplished using one piece of software.

Microsoft Office 97 and Lotus SmartSuite 97, released in the last half of the 1990s, were both fully functional integrated software packages, each being composed of several individual programs. When they were introduced, they were immediately adopted by many businesses because they allowed several applications to share data easily. Each suite included word processing, spreadsheet, organizer/scheduler, database, graphics, and e-mail programs—all designed to work seamlessly together. They allowed users to create complex documents that incorporated information generated by two or more of the applications, such as a word processing document that included diagrams, graphs, spreadsheets, and hyperlinks.

Pasting, Linking, and Embedding

Integrated software offers users a variety of cut and paste tools to share data among applications. On the simplest level, information can be cut or copied from the source application (for example, a block of cells from a spreadsheet) and pasted into the target application (such as a word processing document). With the paste tool, a user can place a snapshot of the desired section of the spreadsheet in the document. The cutting and copying tools save the desired spreadsheet cells in multiple formats so that the paste process will be successful with a display of the added material in the format that works best. Although the cut, copy, and paste tools are the simplest way to share information, the data in the target document is not kept current if changes are made in the source location. The old data remains until the new data is pasted in its place.

Object Linking and Embedding (OLE) helps resolve this limitation by pasting an embedded link or object in the target application. This process requires the paste link or paste special tools, instead of paste. OLE works only with OLE-enabled applications. When a link is pasted into a target document, it becomes a compound document. All compound documents require the cooperation of all linked applications to create the final product and require that all source applications be kept in their original location. If one of the source applications is moved, or if the compound document is moved, the link is broken and the document remains incomplete until the link is reestablished. As long as the link is intact, all changes made on the source applications are displayed on the compound document.

For example, if the compound document is an analytical paper created on a word processor that includes links to a drawing and a spreadsheet, all three applications (the word processor, the drawing program, and the spreadsheet software) must cooperate to display and print the finished paper. Once the document is created, all subsequent changes made on the spreadsheet or to the drawing are tracked by a system of reminders. The next time the paper is opened using the word processor, the reminders deliver the changes, which then appear in the document.

A second kind of compound document is one that includes embedded objects, which are created by using the paste special tool. The successful use of embedded objects requires that all source applications remain in their original locations. Embedded objects can be edited directly from within the compound document, without the need to open the source document first. To make changes to an embedded spreadsheet, for example, the user first opens the compound document and then double clicks on the cells that are embedded on the page. This causes a small window to open so changes can be made directly on the page. However, these changes are not transmitted to the source document. Likewise, any changes made to the original spreadsheet are not reflected in the word processing document.

Another option, called paste as hyperlink, creates a hyperlink of the pasted object, such as the cells of a pasted spreadsheet. By double clicking on a hyperlink, the user opens the source application for easy editing. As long as the link remains valid, all changes made on the hyperlinked file are reflected in the compound document.

▶ *See also* **Database Management Software • Office Automation Systems • SQL • SQL: Databases**

Resources

Books

Bott, Ed, and Carl Siechert. *Microsoft Office 2010 Inside Out*. Redmond, WA: Microsoft Press, 2010.

Newby, Timothy J., and Judith Oates Lewandowski. *Teaching and Learning with Microsoft Office 2010 and Office 2011 for Mac*. Boston: Pearson, 2013.

Summers, Boyd L. *Effective Methods for Software and Systems Integration*. Boca Raton, FL: CRC Press, 2013.

Web Sites

Microsoft. "Office 2010." http://office.microsoft.com/en-us/products/ (accessed October 8, 2012).

A Word About WordStar

Those who were around when word processing software was in its infancy remember how they marveled when WordStar hit the market. Introduced in 1979, the program allowed the user to generate and manipulate text, store the data for later retrieval and revision, and print out the document. Sound like today's word processing software? It does, but WordStar was the first such program to be a commercial success.

K

Kemeny, John G.
Mathematician, Educator, and Philosopher
1926-1992

Devoting his career to mathematics and education, John G. Kemeny served as president of Dartmouth College for more than a decade. He also taught at the school for many years and is remembered for his books. Skilled in the field of mathematics, he teamed with fellow professor Thomas E. Kurtz to create the BASIC programming language.

Kemeny was born in Budapest, Hungary, on May 31, 1926. He and his family were Jewish and fled Hungary in 1940 to escape the Nazis. He immigrated to the United States and finished high school in New York City, becoming a U.S. citizen in 1945.

In 1943 Kemeny was admitted to Princeton University, where he majored in mathematics and minored in philosophy. His studies were interrupted when he joined the U.S. Army's Manhattan Project* at Los Alamos in New Mexico, but in 1947 he graduated from Princeton and began work on a doctorate in mathematics. During his work on the atom bomb project at Los Alamos, Kemeny worked with mathematician John von Neumann (1903–1957). At Princeton his colleagues included physicist Albert Einstein (1879–1955) and mathematician Alonzo Church (1903–1955). In 1949 at the age of twenty-three, Kemeny completed his doctorate and joined the faculty at Princeton. He taught in both the department of mathematics and the department of philosophy.

Kemeny took a professorship at Dartmouth College in 1953 and served as chairperson of the department of mathematics from 1954 to 1967. In 1964 he and fellow professor Thomas E. Kurtz created the Beginners All-purpose Symbolic Instruction Code (BASIC) programming language. BASIC was designed so that computer novices could quickly become proficient in the writing of computer programs. The BASIC language was adopted by high schools and colleges throughout the world. It is the language that many contemporary computer professionals credit with sparking their initial interest in computers.

Kemeny's *Introduction to Finite Mathematics* sold more than 200,000 copies in the United States and has been translated into several languages. He also wrote *A Philosopher Looks at Science* and *Random Essays on Mathematics, Education and Computers* and is the coauthor of nine other books on mathematics.

* **Manhattan Project** the U.S. project designed to create the world's first atomic bomb

John G. Kemeny demonstrates an early technique of networking computers in 1970. Later, as president of Dartmouth College, Kemeny pioneered the integration of computers into university education. © *Emory Kristof/National Geographic/Getty Images.*

BASIC's Other Creator

Thomas E. Kurtz (1928–) was a professor of math and computer sciences at Dartmouth University. He was instrumental in establishing the first time-sharing computer system for use by college students.

* **algorithm** a rule or procedure used to solve a mathematical problem—most often described as a sequence of steps

In 1970 Kemeny was named president of Dartmouth at the relatively young age of forty-three. His tenure as president was marked by a genuine concern for the teaching mission of the college as well as a clearly liberal political viewpoint.

Kemeny's presidency began during a period of student unrest across the United States, related to the treatment of minorities and U.S. involvement in the Vietnam conflict. When four students at Kent State were killed by National Guard troops during a protest of the war, Kemeny showed solidarity with the antiwar protestors by temporarily suspending all academic activities at Dartmouth.

Kemeny was president of Dartmouth when it first admitted women in 1972. As president he withstood criticism from alumni when he abandoned Dartmouth's Native American mascot, which he found offensive.

By 1981 Kemeny perceived a shift in the political winds. In his final commencement address as president, he warned the students against "a voice heard in many guises throughout history, which is the most dangerous voice you will ever hear. It appeals to the basest of instincts in all of us, it appeals to human prejudice. It tries to divide us by setting whites against blacks, by setting Christians against Jews, by setting men against women. And if it succeeds in dividing us from our fellow beings, it will impose its evil will upon a fragmented society."

Kemeny served as president of Dartmouth for eleven years before returning to the department of mathematics to continue teaching. The mathematician, educator, and philosopher died of a heart attack on December 26, 1992. He was survived by his wife, two children, and two grandchildren.

▶ *See also* **Decision Support Systems • Mathematics • Procedural Languages**

Resources

Books

Kemeny, Jean Alexander. *It's Different at Dartmouth: A Memoir.* Brattleboro, VT: S. Greene Press, 1979.

Kemeny, John G. *Man and the Computer.* New York: Scribner, 1972.

Knowledge-Based Systems

A knowledge-based system is a computer program that reasons and uses knowledge to solve complex problems. Traditionally, computers have solved complex problems using arithmetic algorithm*s created by programmers. With knowledge-based systems, human knowledge is captured and embedded explicitly within a program in a symbolic format.

Expressing knowledge as rules and heuristics* has two particular advantages over previous software development technology. Not only can explicit knowledge be trapped in the computer, but so can implicit knowledge, which is useful and potentially very profitable. The other advantage is that knowledge that exists in the form of rules can be captured in that form, without having to be converted by teams of analysts and programmers into data definitions and procedures.

Types of Systems

One way that knowledge-based systems can be classified is by the kind of conclusions they produce. Some interpret the available evidence and produce diagnoses—for example, to explain the reason for a machine breakdown. Others interpret the available evidence but offer a prediction, such as the likelihood of a particular applicant for a loan becoming a slow-payer or a defaulter. Some systems address design questions, proposing the form or layout of a product or the configuration of components. Some are related to industrial engineering matters such as the procedure for assembling the components.

However, not all knowledge-based systems are so ambitious. Many use the captured rules to determine the class to which a particular example belongs. For example, a system might determine whether a particular person is, or is not, entitled to a particular government benefit, an entry visa, or permanent residence.

Development Techniques

During the development of a knowledge-based system, knowledge is extracted from one or more domain specialists, or people who have specialized knowledge in the relevant domain. The knowledge is commonly expressed in the form of antecedent-consequent (IF THEN) rules. In some cases it may be possible for the domain specialist to feed the knowledge directly into the system, but usually an intermediary knowledge engineer captures it using supporting software.

Once the system is developed, a user consults it to find information about some event or situation within a problem domain. The software draws inferences by applying the explicit rules elicited by the expert and the more general implicit rules derived by the system. A result is provided to the user in the form of a diagnosis, prognosis, recommendation, or decision, depending on the nature of the application. In addition, the user may request an explanation of the argument the software used to reach its conclusion.

Knowledge-based systems usually contain three components: a human-computer interface*, a knowledge base, and an inference engine program. The human-computer interface is where the user formulates queries, which the knowledge-based system uses to solicit further information from the user and explain to the user the reasoning process employed to arrive at an answer. The knowledge of one or more human experts in a specific field or task is stored in the knowledge base. The knowledge base is set up as an intelligent database—it can usually manipulate the stored information in a logical, natural, or easy-to-find way. It can conduct

* **Heuristics** procedures that serve to guide investigation but that have not been proven

* **interface** a boundary or border between two or more objects or systems; also a point of access

*__inference__ a suggestion or implication of something based on other known related facts and conclusions

searches based on predetermined rules of defined associations and relationships, as well as by the more traditional data search techniques.

The knowledge base is usually made up of factual knowledge, and sometimes even heuristic knowledge. Factual knowledge consists of information that is commonly shared, found in textbooks or journals, or agreed upon by humans knowledgeable in a specific field or task. Heuristic knowledge, on the other hand, is experiential knowledge of performance; it is the knowledge behind an educated guess.

The inference* engine of an expert system is usually set up to mimic the reasoning, or problem-solving ability, that the human expert would use to arrive at a conclusion. The inference engine simulates the evaluation process of relating the information and rules in the knowledge base to the answers to a series of questions given by the operator. Following this model, an expert system will receive propositions, or answers to a certain line of questioning, and then try to use its inference engine to process the information into rules. It will compare the propositions to facts and rules registered in its knowledge base.

Current and Future Uses

The primary goal of knowledge-based systems is to make expertise available to decision-makers who need answers quickly. Expertise is often unavailable at the right place and the right time. Portable computers loaded with in-depth knowledge of specific subjects can bring years' worth of knowledge to a specific problem. The first knowledge-based or expert system, Dendral, was developed in 1965 by Edward Feigenbaum (1936–) and Joshua Lederberg of Stanford University in California and was used to analyze chemical compounds. Since 1965, knowledge-based systems have enhanced productivity in business, science, engineering, and the military. They also attempt to predict the weather, stock market values, and mineral deposit locations; give a medical diagnosis; dispense medication; and evaluate applications and transaction patterns.

Knowledge-based systems appear to have a great deal of potential, but they also face some challenges. Most knowledge-based systems operate within very specific problem domains, and therefore do not undertake or support a complete activity, but rather one or two tasks within a sequence or cluster of tasks. The benefit that such software offers is not necessarily to automate the process completely and cut costs drastically, but to assist the user to complete the activity faster, somewhat more cheaply, and probably more accurately.

 See also **Artificial Intelligence • Neural Networks**

Resources

Books

Akerkar, Rajendra, and Priti Sajja. *Knowledge-Based Systems*. Sudbury, MA: Jones and Bartlett Publishers, 2010.

L

Laser Technology

Laser devices use light to store, transfer, or print images and text; they are also used in a wide range of other applications, including surgery and weaponry. The coherent radiation of the laser gives it special strength. The laser (Light Amplification by Stimulated Emission of Radiation) started as an extension of the maser, or "Microwave Amplification by Stimulated Emission of Radiation." As its name indicates, the maser is an amplifier, which was originally used for amplifying weak radio signals from space. The light waves for lasers are very much like radio waves but with a much shorter wavelength.

The laser generates light energy by converting the energy states of a material. The energy level of an atom is a function of its temperature. Its lowest energy level is called its "ground state." The application of additional heat, light, or electric field can raise its energy level. The familiar neon sign, which is glass tubing filled with low-pressure neon gas, works on this principle. Two electrodes are inserted in the ends of the glass tubing and a high voltage is applied to the electrodes to raise the energy levels of the gas atoms.

Neon light results from the gas's natural endeavor to return to its lowest energy state, emitting photons of energy as it does so. A photon is the smallest unit of energy (or quantum) of electromagnetic radiation. The energy of a photon is inversely proportional to the wavelength of the associated electromagnetic wave, so shorter wavelengths correspond to higher energy photons. Smaller energy transitions within atoms emit photons with longer wavelengths such as infrared light, while larger energy transitions produce photons of shorter wavelengths, such as visible light.

In the neon sign, the extra energy added by passing electricity through the neon gas is first stored in the atoms of the neon gas in the tube by raising them to a higher energy state. As the neon atoms return to lower energy states, they give up the excess energy as photons.

From Neon Signs to Lasers

One form of laser contains a gas, in which the energy level of the atoms in the medium can be increased above their ground state using a high voltage similar to a neon sign. The majority of atoms are forced to an enhanced energy state or a situation called population inversion*. But, in order to make a laser, the elevated energy state must be *metastable,* as described in the following paragraph.

In the neon sign, the increased energy state is unstable. The gas returns spontaneously to a lower energy state and eventually to the ground state.

* **population inversion** used in quantum mechanics to describe when the number of atoms at higher energy levels is greater than the number at lower energy levels, which is a condition needed for photons (light) to be emitted

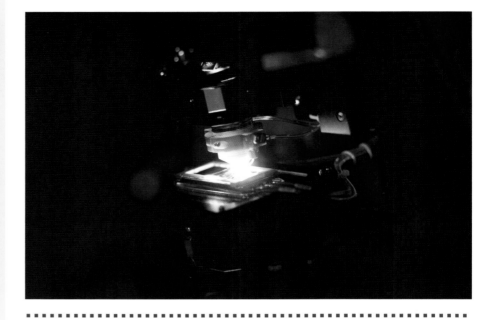

A laser light sequences slides in a lab at a research facility in Mountain View, California. © *David Paul Morris/ Bloomberg via Getty Images.*

* **milliwatt** a power measurement indicating one-thousandth (or 10^{-3}) of a watt

A metastable state implies that the atoms will remain in an elevated energy state for a period of time, on the order of one one-thousandth of a second or so, and can be encouraged to change to the ground state by the application of a stimulus. Not all materials have this metastable state, but those that do are suitable for lasers. Pure neon is used to generate light in a neon sign, but a mixture of helium and neon can be used to create a laser because the mix has a metastable state.

An atom that has emitted a photon stimulates other atoms to return to a lower energy state from the metastable state. The laser has mirrored ends so the photons bounce between the mirrors and cause other atoms to emit photons. Before long, a large number of photons are bouncing between the mirrors and a very large amount of light energy is generated. One of the mirrors is only half-silvered so that some of the photons pass through to form a beam of light instead of being reflected.

Laser Light

In the laser, every atom that releases a photon from the metastable state produces exactly the same color or wavelength of light. Also, the waves associated with the photon are all "coherent," meaning they are in step with each other. This produces a light beam that is very pure, having a beam of only one color (that is, a monochromatic beam).

Laser light can be very intense. Even though a laser has a relatively low total power, the power is concentrated in a very small area. The common laser pointer has a power output of only one or two milliwatts*, but the power is spread over an area of only about a millimeter in diameter. The intensity of the laser pointer is greater than the intensity of a projected image and is easily visible. Large lasers can produce a total power of more than a kilowatt with an intensity that can cut metal. In fact, scientists have built lasers that produce a total power of more than a petawatt (10^{15} watts).

Semiconductors and Lasers

A number of materials have been developed that have the necessary characteristics for lasers. Among them are semiconductors, which are materials, like silicon, whose electrical conductivity is between that of a conductor and that of an insulator. Many semiconductor diode lasers produce an infrared wavelength longer than the deepest red visible to the human eye. It is generally more difficult to generate shorter wavelengths using a laser of any type.

Semiconductor lasers are particularly useful because they are very inexpensive and are quite small. They are suited for connecting directly to thin optical fibers with little loss of light energy. Special laser diodes are made that produce wavelengths in the infrared that produce the lowest loss in glass fiber. Without the semiconductor laser, long-distance fiber optic* communications would not be possible.

Harnessing Laser Technology

Just as important as the generation of pure light energy is the detection of light photons. A number of semiconductor devices, diodes, transistors, and integrated circuits* are capable of sensing light energy. Some of these devices, particularly diodes called photo diodes, can handle very high-speed data and are the receiving end of fiber optic communications systems. The field of generating and detecting light energy is called electro-optics.

When laser light is used for communications, it is necessary to "modulate" or change the light in some way so that it can be used as a carrier of information. The same is true for radio communications. While there are two basic ways to modulate a radio carrier: amplitude* and angle (i.e., phase). Phase and modulation are also both used to modulate a laser signal.

Amplitude modulation can be achieved by changing the electrical power delivered to the laser or by the use of special light modulators. The disadvantage of modulating the electrical power applied to the laser diode is that it causes changes in the wavelength of the light. External light modulators do not cause this change. These modulators are made of non-linear material and are used for very short pulses of light of less than one nanosecond*.

When laser light is used for producing a display or for scanning an object such as in a checkout counter bar code reader, the laser beam is deflected using mirrors. The mirrors are very small so that they can be deflected without the application of a large force. Special electric motors that turn only a few degrees are used. Deflected laser beams are used to generate images and can generate spectacular light shows. The most intriguing display produced by laser light is the hologram, a true three-dimensional image.

* **fiber optic** transmission technology using long, thin strands of glass fiber; internal reflections in the fiber assure that light entering one end is transmitted to the other end with only small losses in intensity; used widely in transmitting digital information

* **integrated circuits** circuits with the transistors, resistors, and other circuit elements etched into the surface of a single chip of semiconducting material, usually silicon

* **amplitude** the size or magnitude of an electrical signal

* **nanosecond** one-thousand-millionth (one billionth, or 10^{-9}) of a second

Laser light is used for reading optical discs as well as for scanning bar codes, measuring distances, and detecting objects. The "laser printer" alters the charge on a photoconductive drum to which charged ink particles, called "toner," are applied. High-power lasers can be used for cutting, burning, surgery, and even as weapons of war. Lasers are used in any application where an intense, monochromatic, and coherent light source is needed.

▶ *See also* **Internet • Telecommunications • Telephony**

Resources

Books

Chang, William Shen-chie. *Principles of Lasers and Optics.* Cambridge, UK, and New York: Cambridge University Press, 2005.

Csele, Mark. *Fundamentals of Light Sources and Lasers.* Hoboken, NJ: J. Wiley, 2004.

Hecht, Jeff. *Beam: The Race to Make the Laser.* Oxford and New York: Oxford University Press, 2005.

Marshall, Gerald F. *Handbook of Optical and Laser Scanning.* 2nd ed. New York: Marcel Dekker, 2002.

Nair, K.P. Raiappan. *Atoms, Molecules, and Lasers.* Oxford, UK: Alpha Science, 2006.

Svelto, Orazio. *Principles of Lasers.* 5th ed. New York: Springer, 2010.

Quimby, Richard S. *Photonics and Lasers: An Introduction.* Hoboken, NJ: Wiley-Interscience, 2006.

Periodical

Dunne, Mike. "Laser-Driven Particle Accelerators." *Science.* 312, no. 5772 (April 21, 2006): 374–376.

Web Sites

National Aeronautics and Space Administration (NASA). "Laser Interferometer Space Antenna." http://lisa.nasa.gov/ (Accessed October 21, 2012).

Legal Systems

As in many areas of business and professional practice, the use of computers in the legal sphere had become widespread by the beginning of the 1990s. In some realms of law practice, such as research and office management, computer automation had a major impact a decade or two earlier. Automated systems have affected everything from the way courtroom trials are undertaken to the way lawyers prepare documents.

Legal Research

The heart of an attorney's work is research. One must be able to locate the primary sources, the cases, statutes, and regulations that make up the law, before clients can be advised, contracts prepared, or litigation brought to trial. This is the area of legal practice that has been most radically affected by the introduction of computer technology.

The earliest experiments with computer-aided legal research were undertaken by John Horty at the University of Pittsburgh in the early 1960s. Horty encoded the text of state public health statutes into a digital form that could be read by a computer. A researcher could run simple searches by matching language submitted by the researcher against the statutory text using Boolean logic*.

By the mid-1960s, Horty's research had attracted the attention of several key members of the Ohio Bar Association. They wanted to take automated legal research to the next level by developing a system that would allow massive amounts of legal information to be stored and then retrieved by searching the full text of each document. By 1973, the system, now named LexisNexis, was ready for commercial marketing. The earliest version of LexisNexis was rather primitive; it mostly contained just state and federal case law. Communication problems were frequent and complicated searches were slow, often taking longer than thirty minutes.

By 1975, West Publishing Company was marketing a competing product, Westlaw, to attorneys. West Publishing originally built its product to work solely as an indexed system utilizing the topic and key number indexing employed in their print compilations of cases. Within a few years Westlaw was redesigned as both a full-text and an indexed system.

In the 2010s, both LexisNexis and Westlaw are powerful research tools containing hundreds of databases incorporating millions of legal, news, and public record documents. Besides full-text searching, both LexisNexis and Westlaw now allow for indexed and natural language searching. Both systems enable users to extract case citations from legal documents, such as a brief, and verifying that the cases are still current and valid law.

The success of both LexisNexis and Westlaw has led to several complementary online and software-based products. Numerous smaller companies have developed more modest research systems and tools. These CD and online-based products offer relatively low-cost searching compared to LexisNexis and Westlaw. In addition, with the advent of the Internet, many courts, legislatures, and regulatory agencies have made their documents available via the World Wide Web.

Document Assembly

The popular image of an attorney is usually based on television characters making heroic gestures in front of a jury. The truth is that many attorneys have never spent a working day in a courtroom. Legal work such

* **Boolean logic** a system, developed by George Boole (1815–1864), which treats abstract objects (such as sets or classes) as algebraic quantities; Boole applied his mathematical system to the study of classical logic

* **spreadsheet** an accounting or business tool that details numerical data in columns for tabulation purposes

as preparing wills, filling out tax forms, incorporating businesses, and handling real estate transactions can at times require shrewd analysis and attention to detail. Just as often, though, they are routine processes that can be automated to save time.

Beginning in the 1980s with the introduction of the personal computer, software engineers developed programs to assist with document assembly. At first these were simple routines, which provided help in such tasks as drafting wills, based on word processing software. More sophisticated products, such as those that compute taxes or prepare trusts, were soon built around database or spreadsheet* programs. These software packages quickly gained favor with the legal profession, with the result that now there are dozens of companies offering a wide range of document assembly products.

Case Management

A successful law practice involves more than good research skills and thorough knowledge of the law. There are business components that can be time-consuming, but many of these can be handled with computer technology. Storing client data, keeping track of timesheets, and debt collection are all business functions that are easily automated. One of the most important innovations in this area is software that functions as an electronic calendar. These programs enable the busy attorney to track and maintain filing deadlines. The most sophisticated of these are keyed into state or federal court rules and automatically compute the date that a filing or court appearance is due. Companion smartphone and tablet computer applications enable users to sync office calendars with all of their computing devices and access information while away from the office.

Litigation Support

Complicated trials involving large corporations can require enormous numbers of documents. Paralegals and other research assistants may have to examine, index, and code boxes full of business records and depositions from potential witnesses, and store the documents in a manner that allows for rapid retrieval. Up until the 1980s, microfilm was the storage vehicle of choice; computers were relegated to an indexing role. Low-cost scanning technology and cheap, abundant electronic storage—either physical or on a remote "cloud" server—have enabled the entire process to be automated. More businesses and government agencies are keeping electronic records as well, requiring lawyers to become familiar with computer archiving and document location. These records are assigned codes that capture identifying information such as date, author, title, addressee, and type of document; each record is also given a unique document number.

Another way computer technology provides litigation support is through the creation of graphics, videos, and other visual aids for courtroom use. The most sophisticated of these are simulations that can recreate an accident scene or show the path of a bullet.

Communications

Fueled by the communications potential of the Internet, courts of all types are implementing systems that enable attorneys to file and retrieve documents in pending cases electronically. The potential is there for all parties in a case to receive filings simultaneously and without delay. Electronic docketing or registration of legal proceedings also allows attorneys to take note of other cases that were filed against a particular party within a specific period of time. Land records, deeds, judgments, wills, divorces, and other such legal records have been made available online in most jurisdictions.

Courtroom Practice

The judiciary, as a whole, traditionally has not been eager to embrace new technology. Little by little changes have been working their way into the courtroom. In many U.S. counties it is possible to receive real-time transcription of the proceedings of an ongoing trial. The court stenographer utilizes a system that converts shorthand to a transcript format that is distributed through multiple channels in the courtroom. This nearly simultaneous record can benefit deaf or blind jurors and participants.

The paperless trial is another reality that is being played out in a few selected courtrooms around the country. Jurors can view video clips, computer simulations, and exhibits on video screens or monitors in the jury box. The reported advantages have been faster and cheaper trials and the ability to focus the jury's attention in a more direct fashion.

▶ *See also* **Information Retrieval • Medical Systems • Security**

Resources

Books

Putman, William H. *Pocket Guide to Legal Research*. Farmington Hills, MI: Cengage, 2008.

Sloan, Amy, and Steven D. Schwinn. *Basic Legal Research Workbook*. 4th ed. New York: Wolters Kluwer Law & Business, 2011.

Library Applications

Computers are used in libraries all over the world to provide access to a range of electronic information resources and to manage materials (books, journals, videos, and other media) held in particular collections. For many people, barriers of income, age, gender, or race can limit their access to computer technology and thus to the wealth of information that is available to others. The public library, with its history of providing free information, may offer access to the Internet and make a range of

Project Gutenberg

The love of the printed word is evident in Project Gutenberg, which was begun in 1971 by Michael Hart. Project Gutenberg seeks to make books—those that have fallen into the public domain—readily available to people throughout the world. The organization, staffed mainly by hundreds of volunteers, captures texts in electronic form, including many classic works of literature. The group reports making one more e-text available each day. For more information, see the PG Web site <http://www.gutenberg.net/>.

* **digital divide** imaginary line separating those who can access digital information from those who cannot

* **transistor** a contraction of TRANSfer resISTOR; a semiconductor device, invented by John Bardeen, Walter Brattain, and William Shockley, which has three terminals; can be used for switching and amplifying electrical signals

* **minicomputers** computers midway in size between a desktop computer and a mainframe computer; most modern desktops are much more powerful than the older minicomputers

* **relational database** a collection of records that permits logical and business relationships to be developed between themselves and their contents

information sources available to everyone. Computers are made available in public libraries so as to minimize this digital divide*.

The huge size, complexity, and cost of early computers in the 1940s and 1950s meant that they were unsuitable for use in library and information work. However by the 1960s when transistors* started to replace the original valves, and codes had been developed so that alphabetic characters as well as numbers could be input, stored, and output, work on library applications started. For instance, a study on automation at the U.S. Library of Congress (LC) was undertaken in 1963. A major problem faced was how best to "describe" a book to the computer. Following much debate, which also involved colleagues in Great Britain, a format known as MARC (Machine Readable Cataloging) was developed and is still being used for bibliographic records in libraries all over the world.

Now, the LC not only offers access to printed materials via its reading rooms in Washington but also makes available a wide range of electronic information resources. Many libraries, especially national libraries, digitize material in their collections so that anyone in the world who has access to the Internet can explore the wealth of these collections. Copyright clearance must be acquired where necessary.

Electronic Library Catalogs

During the early 1970s, many public and academic libraries began using computer systems to help manage and control the basic processes of acquisition, cataloging, and the circulation of items (both books and journals) in their collections. At first programs were written locally, but by the end of the 1970s a number of organizations started to offer integrated software and hardware packages using the minicomputers* that were then under development. In some instances libraries came together to form cooperatives and to develop shared databases of MARC records so that individual libraries did not have to create their own catalog records.

Online Public Access Catalogs (or OPACs) started to appear in the 1980s. The OPAC module of an integrated library management system makes use of the techniques developed within online information retrieval systems. Library patrons can search the catalog by entering an author's name, the title of a book, or a subject term on a keyboard and view the results on a screen rather than looking through trays of catalog cards. The OPACs of many libraries in the world can be searched using the Internet. During the 1990s many of these library management systems were developed using software programs based on standard relational database* management systems, standard operating systems, and client/server technology.

Networks

Libraries have used computer networks to link workstations in remote branches to centralized systems, enabling multiple sites to share facilities such as information databases and printers. In addition libraries utilize networks to access external services. In the 1970s, ARPANET (the forerunner to the Internet) and the commercial packet-switched network* Tymnet were used by European libraries to access online information retrieval systems in the United States. The rapid developments of the Internet and the World Wide Web greatly influenced the services provided by libraries. Many libraries all over the world provide access to information on the web for their users.

* **packet-switched network** a network based on digital communications systems whereby packets of data are dispatched to receivers based on addresses that they contain

Digital Resources

Librarians in the 2010s still need to select, acquire, and organize quality information resources for their patrons. A new challenge is that much information is published digitally as well as, or instead of, in print. Electronic journals, newspapers, magazines, and information databses are common and many books, including student textbooks, are available as e-books. As "e-learning" and virtual learning environments become more commonplace, the concept of a teacher/lecturer imparting knowledge in a classroom is yielding to less centralized approaches to education. Students are being given more responsibility for managing their educational resources through technology and new media formats. Librarians, therefore, in consultation with teachers, increasingly are involved in making appropriate quality learning resources available for students.

Technological developments supporting the collection, creation, management, and preservation of digital resources, and the implementation of electronic mechanisms for searching a range of resources, have given rise to the phrase "digital library" to describe this new world of library science.

▶ *See also* **Database Management Software • Educational Software • Information Retrieval**

Resources

Web Sites

LibDex: The Library Index. "Welcome to LibDex." http://www.libdex.com (accessed November 3, 2012).

Library of Congress. http://www.loc.gov (accessed November 3, 2012).

M

Magnetic Stripe Cards

A magnetic stripe card is a card (e.g., a credit card) that contains a stripe of magnetically-encoded data. These cards are paired with readers and writers, and are used in a wide variety of applications for storing information.

Usage

Most identification, credit, automated teller machine, and membership cards have a thin magnetic stripe across one side of the card. By "swiping" the card through or inserting the card into a reader, a computer can read the data on the stripe. Magnetic stripes make card usage much less prone to error because the data are not entered manually. The data cannot be read without a correctly programmed machine, and the cards must be created with special equipment, both of which make cards hard to falsify. The stripes can also contain encrypted information and information not printed on the card which can only be created or read by specialized computers.

Technologies

The magnetic stripe is actually an area of dense microscopic bar magnets, of which there are approximately 200 million per square inch. The magnets can be used to encode the data in an infinite number of ways. High security cards encode the data in proprietary, undisclosed formats that prevent intruders from even reading the data. However, all credit, banking, and automated teller machine cards use the same type of encoding. Most other cards use this encoding as well.

Like larger bar magnets, one end of each microscopic magnet is a north pole (N) and the other a south pole (S) (see Figure 1). In an empty, horizontal stripe, all of the bars are aligned left to right so that the north poles are facing one direction and the south poles the other. The north pole of each magnet is therefore adjacent to the south pole of the next magnet and, like other bar magnets, all of the aligned magnets act as one larger magnet.

Unlike usual bar magnets, these tiny magnets can be made to reverse their polarity. If a single or a continuous group of bar magnets is reversed, the stripe will act like three opposing bar magnets (see Figure 2).

If several sections of magnets are reversed, the stripe looks like a series of opposing magnets (Figure 3).

The like poles of two magnets repel each other. This results in a strong magnetic field at those junctions. A magnetic stripe reader has a head,

Figure 1: A horizontally aligned row of bar magnets *Reproduced by permission of Gale, a part of Cengage Learning.* ▶

Figure 2: A horizontally aligned row of bar magnets with one reversed section *Reproduced by permission of Gale, a part of Cengage Learning.* ▶

Figure 3: A horizontally aligned row of seven sections, each reversed with respect to its neighbors *Reproduced by permission of Gale, a part of Cengage Learning.* ▶

Figure 4: The analog signal, with peaks, induced by the magnets in Figure 3. *Reproduced by permission of Gale, a part of Cengage Learning.* ▶

Figure 5: The digital signal, created from the analog signal in Figure 4. *Reproduced by permission of Gale, a part of Cengage Learning.* ▶

Figure 1: A horizontally aligned row of bar magnets

Figure 2: A horizontally aligned row of bar magnets with one reversed section

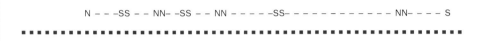

Figure 3: A horizontally aligned row of seven sections, each reversed with respect to its neighbors

Figure 4: The analog signal, with peaks, induced by the magnets in Figure 3.

Figure 5: The digital signal, created from the analog signal in Figure 4.

much like the one in an audio tape player, which can detect that field. The head senses the field at a north-north junction as a positive voltage and the field at a south-south junction as a negative one (Figure 4).

The reader converts the analog signal into a digital one by turning positive peaks into transitions from low to high and negative peaks into transitions from high to low (Figure 5).

Finally, the reader measures the length of each high/low pair. Each pair is interpreted as a bit—a short pair as a binary "1" and a long pair as a binary "0." In this way, the preceding sequence of magnets encodes the bits "110."

The difficulty in this system is that it depends on the reader measuring the distance between the peaks. The card is usually swiped through the reader by a person's hand, and it is difficult or impossible to regulate the specific speed at which the card should be swiped. At a low speed, a single high/low pair will look longer than it actually is. At a high speed, the same pair will look shorter. So, long pairs (zeroes) are exactly twice as long as short pairs (ones). In this way, no matter how rapidly or slowly the user moves the card, so long as the card is moved at a relatively constant speed, the machine reader can differentiate a one from a zero.

These bits are used to represent letters and numbers just as they are in a computer. On most cards, there are actually three independent stripes. The first stripe contains letters in the American National Standards Institute/International Organization for Standardization (ANSI/ISO) ALPHA format, and can contain a name or other text. The second and third stripes contain credit card or identification numbers, and are in binary coded decimal (BCD)* format. While the first and second stripes contain "read-only" data, the third stripe is designed to be both written to and read while it is being swiped. This feature is rarely used, however.

These stripes can be made of several different materials, but can all be damaged by strong magnets. A strong magnet will align all of the magnets in the stripe, effectively erasing it.

In the 1990s so-called smart cards* were widely introduced into the European consumer market. Later on, in the 2000s, smart cards became readily available to U.S. consumers. Smart cards contain embedded computer chips, and come in "contactless" and "contact" varieties. Contact-type smart cards are read in much the same way as cards with magnetic stripes—that is, they are swiped through, or inserted into, readers—but smart cards are capable of holding substantially more information. The chips embedded in smart cards can also perform calculations, allowing the cards to act "intelligently."

Stack of U.S. visas is sorted at the U.S. Consulate in Tijuana, Mexico. © *AP Images/Denis Poroy.*

* **binary coded decimal (BCD)** an ANSI/ISO standard encoding of the digits 0 to 9 using 4 binary bits; the encoding only uses 10 of the available 16 4-bit combinations

* **smart card** a credit-card style card that has a microcomputer embedded within it; it carries more information to assist the owner or user

 See also **Embedded Technology (Ubiquitous Computing) • Input Devices • Security**

Resources

Books

Poslad, Stefan. *Ubiquitous Computing: Smart Devices, Environments and Interactions.* Chichester, UK: Wiley, 2009.

Rankl, Wolfgang, and Wolfgang Effing. *Smart Card Handbook..* 4th ed. Chichester, UK: Wiley, 2010.

Mathematics

The invention and ideas of many mathematicians and scientists led to the development of the computer, which today is used for mathematical teaching purposes from preschool through college-level classrooms.

* **commodity** raw material or service marketed prior to being used

* **cryptography** the science of understanding codes and ciphers and their application

With its ability to process vast amounts of facts and figures and to solve problems at extremely high speeds, the computer is a valuable asset to solve the complex math-laden research problems of the sciences as well as problems in business and industry.

Major applications of computers in the mathematical sciences include their use in mathematical biology, where math is applied to disciplines such as medicine, making use of laboratory animal experiments as surrogates for a human biological system. Mathematical computer programs take the data drawn from the animal study and extrapolate it to fit the human system. Then, mathematical theory answers the question of how far these data can be transformed yet still preserve similarity between species. Mathematical ecology tries to understand the patterns of nature as society increasingly faces shortages in energy and depletion of its limited resources. Computers can also be programmed to develop premium tables for life insurance companies, to examine the likely effects of air pollution on forest productivity, and to simulate mathematical model outcomes that are used to predict areas of disease outbreaks.

Mathematical geography computer programs model flows of goods, people, and ideas over space so that commodity* exchange, transportation, and population migration patterns can be studied. Large-scale computers are used in mathematical physics to solve equations that were previously intractable, and for problems involving a third dimension, numerous computer graphics packages display three-dimensional spatial surfaces. A byproduct of the advent of computers is the ability to use this tool to investigate nonlinear methods. As a result, the stability of our solar system has been checked for millions of years to come.

In the information age, information needs to be stored, processed, and retrieved in various forms. The field of cryptography* is loaded with computer science and mathematics complementing each other to ensure the confidentiality of information transmitted over telephone lines and computer networks. Encoding and decoding operations are computationally intense. Once a message is coded, its security may hinge on the inability of an intruder to solve the mathematical riddle of finding the prime factors of a large number. Economical encoding is required in high-resolution television because of the enormous amount of information required. Data compression techniques are initially mathematical concepts before becoming electromagnetic signals that emerge as a picture on the TV screen.

Mathematical application software routines that solve equations, perform computations, or analyze experimental data are often found in area-specific subroutine libraries which are written most often in the computer programming languages Fortran or C. In order to minimize inconsistencies across different computers, the Institute of Electrical and Electronics Engineers (IEEE) standard is met to govern the precision of numbers with decimal positions.

The basic configuration of mathematics learning in the classroom entails the usage of stand-alone personal computers, or alternatively, networked microcomputers utilizing shared software programs. The computer is valued for its ability to aid students to make connections between a verbal word problem, its symbolic form (such as a function), and its graphical form. These multiple representations usually appear simultaneously on the computer screen. For home and school use, public domain mathematical software and shareware* are readily available on the Internet and there is a gamut of proprietary software written that spans the breadth and depth of the mathematical branches (arithmetic, algebra, geometry, trigonometry, elementary functions, calculus, numerical analysis, numerical partial differential equations, number theory, modern algebra, probability and statistics, modeling, complex variables, etc.). Often software is developed for a definitive mathematical maturity level. In lieu of graphics packages, spreadsheets are useful for plotting data and are most useful when teaching arithmetic and geometric progressions.

Mathematics, the science of patterns, is a way of looking at the world in terms of entities that do not exist in the physical world (the numbers, points, lines and planes, functions, and geometric figures are all pure abstractions of the mind) so the mathematician looks to the mathematical proof to explain the physical world. Several attempts have been made to develop theorem-proving technology on computers. However, most of these systems are far too advanced for high school use. Nevertheless, the non-mathematician, with the use of computer graphics, can appreciate the sets of Gaston Julia and Benoit B. Mandelbrot for their artistic beauty.

Mathematical theory is important to the efficient functioning of the Internet. The Internet is an enormous, worldwide network linking together government, business, and academic networks; in turn, those smaller networks consist of linked computers, servers, and associated equipment. A branch of mathematics called *network theory* is useful for describing and analyzing the flow of information over the complex systems that compose the Internet. The insights provided by network theory can provide for a more efficient flow of information through real-world networks, including the Internet. Network theory (which itself is part of the more-general graph theory) also finds application in many other disciplines, including particle physics, economics, and biology.

To conclude, an intriguing application of mathematics to the computer world lies at the heart of the computer itself, its microprocessor. This chip is essentially a complex array of patterns of propositional logic (p and q, p or q, p implies q, not p, etc.) etched into silicon*.

▶ *See also* **Data Visualization** • **Decision Support Systems** • **Interactive Systems** • **Physics**

Resources

Books

Bali, N., M. Goyal, and Christopher Watkins. *Advanced Engineering Mathematics: A Computer Approach*. Hingham, MA: Infinity Science Press, 2007.

Julia and Mandelbrot Sets

Gaston Julia (1893–1978), a French mathematician, studied the iteration of polynomials and rational functions in the early twentieth century. A strikingly beautiful picture is produced from function iterations: a, $f(a)$, $f(f(a))$, $f(f(f(a)))$, etc. Mandelbrot sets, named after mathematician Benoit B. Mandelbrot (1924–), are whole families of functions parameterized by a variable. These sets have become something of an art form.

* **shareware** a software distribution technique, whereby the author shares copies of his programs at no cost, in the expectation that users will later pay a fee of some sort

* **silicon** a chemical element with symbol Si; the most abundant element in the Earth's crust and the most commonly used semiconductor material

*__microprocessor__ the principle
element in a computer; the
component that understands
how to carry out operations
under the direction of the
running program, the central
processing unit (CPU)

Biggs, Norman. *Codes: An Introduction to Information Communication and Cryptography.* London: Springer, 2008.

Bogart, Kenneth P., Clifford Stein, and Robert L. Drysdale. *Discrete Mathematics for Computer Science.* Emeryville, CA: Key College Pub, 2006.

Buchmann, Johannes. *Introduction to Cryptography.* 2nd ed. New York: Springer, 2004.

Burton, David M. *The History of Mathematics: An Introduction.* 7th ed. New York: McGraw-Hill, 2011.

Deem, Bill R. and Tony Zannini. *Electronics and Computer Math.* 8th ed. Upper Saddle River, NJ: Prentice Hall, 2005.

Jeffrey, Alan. *Mathematics for Engineers and Scientists.* 6th ed. Boca Raton, FL: Chapman & Hall/CRC, 2005.

Kamath, Chandrika. *Scientific Data Mining: A Practical Perspective.* Philadelphia: Society for Industrial and Applied Mathematics, 2009.

O'Leary, Dianne P. *Scientific Computing with Case Studies.* Philadelphia: Society for Industrial and Applied Mathematics, 2009.

Speyer, Jason Lee, and Walter H. Chung. *Stochastic Processes, Estimation, and Control.* Philadelphia: Society for Industrial and Applied Mathematics, 2008.

Medical Systems

Medical systems help doctors and nurses diagnose and treat patients. Hospitals and clinics rely extensively on computer technology to examine patients, cure disease, advance the science of medicine, and conduct the business of health care. During the early development of computers, the health industry recognized their usefulness. In the decades from the 1960s to the 1990s, computers primarily were used in business-related endeavors such as with financial accounting, insurance, inventory management, and administration. In the 2010s, computer systems were highly essential in various medical systems. Medical computer systems is also sometimes referred to within the broader heading of health informatics (additionally called by such names as health care informatics and medical informatics), which is a medical discipline involving the use of computer science, health care, and information science. Some of the topics within medical systems are: embedded systems, desktop computing and databases, and tele-health.

Embedded Systems

Many visits to a hospital start in the emergency room, which may be filled with electronic devices that look nothing like desktop computers. However, most of these devices rely on an embedded microprocessor*, the same type of chip that powers other computers. Instead of using a stethoscope, a nurse may depend on an embedded chip in a blood pressure machine to measure a patient's pulse and blood pressure. Another embedded processor may help take the patient's temperature or deliver controlled amounts of a drug through an intravenous tube at regular intervals. These types of systems ease the burden on medical workers and improve the quality of care.

Other devices tackle more complex tasks such as constantly determining the amount of oxygen in the patient's blood. Some doctors use personal digital assistants (PDAs) such as Palm Pilots to help retrieve information about drugs and diseases, as well as to write drug prescriptions and to store information about patients. Even smaller devices known as smart card*s, which are the same size as a credit card, can store medical information on an embedded chip.

Often, desktop and laptop computers are used to consolidate information from embedded systems. For instance, in a critical care unit designed to treat very sick patients, desktop computers may alert a nurse if an electronic sensor determines that a patient is having difficulty breathing. Desktop computers also help people to use smart cards and PDAs.

Desktop/Laptop Computing and Databases

Health care organizations use desktop and laptop computers to accomplish administrative tasks required of any large business, such as routing e-mail, tracking supplies, paying employees, and keeping track of customers—in this case, patients. One of the key tools used to accomplish these tasks is a database. A database is a system that allows an organization systematically to store, process, and retrieve large amounts of data. One can think of a database as the nervous system for an organization, because the database provides the information needed to coordinate the actions of its members.

Paper-based databases typically employ standardized paper forms, folders, and filing cabinets. An electronic database is a software program that runs on one or more computers. Electronic databases offer many advantages over paper databases. However, because people are so comfortable with paper forms and because it is difficult and expensive to create an electronic database that can track everything that paper systems track, medical institutions have been slow to change from paper-based systems to electronic databases. Most health care organizations today rely on a combination of paper and computer-based systems.

Medical scientists use databases to conduct research on hundreds or even thousands of patients at a time. For example, to study the effectiveness of a new prescription drug, it is not enough to look at only a small number of patients. Instead, a large number of patients, usually at least 100, must be evaluated. This way, if the patients get better after taking the drug, the scientist can be sure that the drug was responsible for the good results. Databases also help hospital administrators to identify trends and improve the efficiency of health care organizations.

Cybertherapy

Can psychological therapy—also called cybertherapy—be conducted successfully via the Internet? The issue is highly debated due, in part, to the fact that psychiatrists need to be licensed in any state in which they practice. Another important consideration is that doctors traditionally consider their patients' facial expressions and body language before making diagnoses. If cybertherapy is conducted via e-mail, those clues are lost. However, some advocates of online therapy suggest videoconferencing as a possible solution.

* **smart card** a credit-card style card that has a microcomputer embedded within it; it carries more information to assist the owner or user

The most important information tracked by a medical database is a patient's medical record. The medical record contains the history of the patient's health and treatments. The medical record may contain prescriptions, doctor's notes, x-ray films, immunizations, and the results of various laboratory tests. Doctors review the medical record whenever they need to make an important decision about how to treat the patient.

Because electronic systems make it very easy to retrieve and copy information, one of the concerns with electronic databases is patient privacy. Patients expect that their personal medical information will be kept confidential. Hospitals must be sure that each part of the medical record is protected so that only authorized personnel are able to view confidential data.

Computers and databases are also very important when patients are prescribed drugs. One of the important issues with prescription drugs is that some of these drugs can interact, or combine harmfully when taken together. For example, some patients have become sick and even died after taking a combination of prescription drugs that produced harmful side effects. Another problem is that doctors have difficulty remembering the recommended dosage for each of the hundreds of drugs available. With so many prescription and non-prescription drugs on the market and new drugs entering the market constantly, databases help doctors and pharmacists to be sure that they are prescribing drugs in the proper dose and that the drugs will not interact harmfully with each other. The best drug dispensaries require the pharmacist to enter all prescriptions into an electronic database that warns of a potentially harmful drug interaction before the patient receives the medication.

Tele-Health

When a patient far away from a medical facility needs expert medical advice, tele-health technology enables doctors to evaluate patients even though they may be separated by hundreds, or even thousands, of miles. Tele-heath is made possible by the same technology that runs the Internet. It could involve the electronic transmission of an x-ray image to a distant radiologist, who can diagnose the patient by examining the x ray. Tele-health could also involve setting up a computer and camera in a patient's home so that a health care provider can see and talk with the patient without traveling to the patient's home.

Further advancements in tele-health may one day enable a surgeon in one hospital to operate routinely on patients located in different hospitals. Sophisticated robots could allow the physician to see the patient and even have the sensation of touching him or her. Called remote surgery, or telesurgery, these robotic surgical systems have been developed, for instance, through Intuitive Surgical's da Vinci Surgical System. Three of the robot's arms hold medical objects such as a scalpel, scissors, or other such instruments. A fourth arm holds an endoscopic camera to provide stereoscopic vision for the surgeon. As of 2012, physicians used the system primarily for cardiac valve repair, gynecologic procedures, and prostatectomies (surgeries on the prostate gland). However, before these telesurgeries can happen on a routinely safe basis, information technology must improve and be extremely reliable so that the electronic connection between the surgeon and the remote control robot will not fail.

▶ *See also* **Biology • Data Visualization • Image Analysis: Medicine**

Resources

Books

Röcker, Carsten, and Martina Ziefle, eds. *Smart Healthcare Applications and Services: Developments and Practices*. Hershey, PA: Information Science Reference, 2011.

Staudinger, Bettina, Victoria Höss, and Herwig Ostermann, eds. *Nursing and Clinical Informatics: Socio-technical Approaches*. Hershey, PA: Information Science Reference, 2009.

Web Sites

Intuitive Surgical. "The da Vinci Surgical System." http://www.intuitivesurgical.com/products/davinci_surgical_system/ (accessed October 9, 2012).

University of Illinois at Chicago. "The History of Health Informatics." http://healthinformatics.uic.edu/history-of-health-informatics/ (accessed October 9, 2012).

Molecular Biology

Molecular biology is the branch of biology that studies biological activity at the molecular level (within and around molecules). It is mainly concerned with understanding what goes on between the various systems of a cell, including the interactions between the biological phenomena known as deoxyribonucleic acid (DNA), ribonucleic acid (RNA), proteins, and other macromolecules as well as learning how these intricate interactions are controlled. Within molecular biology, computers place a large role in this molecular study, research, and understanding.

DNA is located in the nucleus of all living cells. DNA dictates which creatures walk, fly, or bore through the soil. Each DNA strand is constructed from combinations of four nucleotides or building blocks: adenine, cytosine, guanine, and thymine. A given sequence of three nucleotides, in turn, codes for an amino acid, and a sequence of amino acids bind together to form proteins. The strands of DNA, made up of bonded nucleotide pairs, are very long. Molecular biologists have worked

Chemical company employee controls samples in the molecular biology department. © *AP Images/Merck*.

* **algorithm** a rule or procedure used to solve a mathematical problem—most often described as a sequence of steps

toward breaking the genetic code by identifying the nucleotides in order and searching for patterns.

Nature gave scientists one big hint: adenine always binds to thymine, and guanine always binds to cytosine. In the past, researchers found fluorescent molecules that mimic the natural nucleotides. When the known fluorescent molecule bound to an unknown nucleotide, scientists could identify that particular nucleotide pair of the DNA strand. The process took a decade or more. Researchers can speed up this painstaking work with help from computers, so they can accomplish such tasks in hours instead of years.

The challenges are formidable. Scientists must isolate and copy genes. DNA sequencers are able to read the genetic sequence of DNA in a prepared sample through detection of fluorescence. The fluorescence emitted for each nucleotide is recorded as a peak and the information is transmitted into a computer program for visualization. The computer program is then able to determine, based on the series of peaks, the sequence of nucleotides that constitute the DNA strand. The monitoring equipment must be fast enough, or the process slowed enough, to allow for an accurate identification of these bonded molecules. Finally, researchers must have computer programs that employ algorithm*s to help them process the multitude of data they would receive from even one single strand of DNA, which could have 70 thousand nucleotides. Computers are then needed to transmit and compare the sequence of the genes being studied with known gene sequence databases, a monumental task for which computers are particularly well suited.

The benefits of such research are profound. The study of human genetics is the first most obvious benefit, since these findings will aid research in fields as diverse as inherited diseases and anthropology. Since DNA holds the key to every aspect of the human body, genetic studies could potentially be used to mimic how different cells work. This would allow researchers to develop and experiment with the effect of medications on the body without using living subjects. Disease processes, such as various forms of cancer, could potentially be duplicated in an electronic model and studied. This kind of understanding would aid in the development of successful treatments. Scientists also hope to use DNA sequences to identify and classify organisms, from the discovery of new bacteria to tracing the evolution of animals. Models of bacterial DNA could help in the study of the spread of diseases.

Gene therapy is a field in which the genes of living things are manipulated and even exchanged with one another to provide a beneficial result. For instance, potatoes have produced spider silk, one of the strongest materials on earth. In addition, frogs and earthworms have been genetically modified to produce proteins that allow them to glow in the dark. A type of corn has been modified to fight tooth decay effectively. Vitamin A has been added to rice, making the grain more nutritious. Many of these applications of gene therapy have met controversy, since the long-term effects of gene manipulation in food are unknown.

Bioinformatics is the field in which software is developed to aid in the study of molecular biology. Many of the studies currently being conducted in molecular biology would be impossible without the help of computers and computer software. This software comes from various places. One researcher developed a basic bioinformatics software application and posted it on the Web for others to download and improve upon, as did the creators of the Linux operating system*, resulting in a versatile software application. Other firms have hired professionals to develop and copyright applications, which are then sold to researchers and private firms.

The U.S. government has played a pivotal role in the quest for information by establishing the National Center for Biotechnology Information, or NCBI. The NCBI is a division of the National Library of Medicine (NLM), which stores biomedical (such as gene sequence) databases. The NLM itself is a division of the National Institutes of Health (NIH). With all of the resources of the NIH, it is considered the largest biomedical research facility in the world. The NCBI is the result of a cooperative effort. Researchers, academic institutions, and similar agencies from other countries around the world access and contribute to the databases available at the NCBI.

Molecular biology and computers are also finding uses within the medical field. For example, scientists have developed a device that electronically smells the presence of bacterial infections in the lungs. Breath samples are taken from patients and put into an aroma-detection device. The machine measures the electrical resistance of the molecules in the sample of air. The results are then displayed in a two-dimensional map. Different bacteria produce distinct characteristics on this map. This is a potentially life-saving tool because it allows physicians to treat patients immediately with the correct antibiotic for pneumonia instead of

* **Linux operating system** an open source UNIX operating system that was originally created by Finnish-American software engineer Linus Torvalds (1969–) in the early 1990s

waiting two or three days for sample cultures of the bacteria to be grown and identified.

Although the use of computers is rapidly advancing the field of molecular biology, there is growing evidence that molecular biology is also important to computer science. Researchers at Harvard Medical School in Massachusetts are working with a purple protein termed bacteriorhodopsin, produced by a type of bacteria native to salt marshes. This protein is quite stable, readily produced, and easily processed. Many assert that it will eventually replace silicon (Si) microchips. Bacteriorhodopsin changes shape upon exposure to light. One shape is designated as binary 0, and the other shape is designated as binary 1. Bacteriorhodopsin is suspended in organized layers within a polymer gel. Because an individual protein changes shape upon reacting to different colors of lasers, the shape of an individual protein within the cube can be manipulated.

CD-ROMs (compact disc-read only memory), hard drives, and flash drives are different forms of memory that operate on a two-dimensional basis. The bacteriorhodopsin gel would be a type of three-dimensional memory. Researchers assert that a DVD-sized disc coated with this bacteriorhodopsin protein/gel will be able to store up to fifty terabytes (50 thousand gigabytes, where giga stands for 1 billion) on a single disc. Dr. Venkatesan Renugopalakrishnan of Harvard Medical School and Northeastern University (Boston, Massachusetts) is collaborating with the NEC Corporation to develop this protein-coated disc technology.

Experts agree that future molecular biology studies would be unthinkable without computers. Perhaps in the future, computers will be equally dependent upon molecular biology. As such, the branch of computing called DNA computing is being researched increasingly for its important applications in many areas. For instance, a programmable molecular computer, what is sometimes called a biocomputer, already has been developed that uses DNA molecules and enzymes instead of the traditional silicon microchips. Medical researchers have used such computers to diagnosis cancer in patients, and then to administer the correct amount of medicine to fight the disease. Although biocomputers are still in their infancy, their potential in the future is great for many medical applications. However, as of 2012, the brain is still the most powerful biocomputer in existence.

 See also **Binary Number System • Biology • Image Analysis • Molecular Computing • Pattern Recognition**

Resources

Books

Agutter, Paul S., and D. N. Wheatley. *About Life: Concepts in Modern Biology.* Dordrecht, Netherlands: Springer, 2007.

Bray, Dennis. *Wetware: A Computer in Every Living Cell.* New Haven, CT, and London: Yale University Press, 2009.

Forbes, Nancy. *Imitation of Life: How Biology Is Inspiring Computing.* Cambridge, MA: MIT Press, 2004.

Helms, Volkhard. *Principles of Computational Cell Biology: From Protein Complexes to Cellular Networks.* Weinheim, Germany: Wiley-VCH, 2008.

Ramachandran, K. I., G. Deepa, and K. Namboori. *Computational Chemistry and Molecular Modeling: Principles and Applications.* Berlin: Springer, 2008.

Web Sites

News-Medical.net. "What is Molecular Biology." http://www.news-medical.net/health/What-is-Molecular-Biology.aspx (accessed October 12, 2012).

New York University Medical Center. "Using Computers in Molecular Biology." http://www.med.nyu.edu/rcr/rcr/course/index.html (accessed October 12, 2012).

Music Composition

Computer-assisted music composition is an exciting field. Some of the most interesting possibilities of such composition are depicted in Figure 1, where the possibilities of musical information flows are illustrated. The traditional way of using the computer to compose music is to use software to produce music written in Common Music Notation (CMN),

Individual using software to compose music. © *Rebecca Sapp/WireImage/Getty*

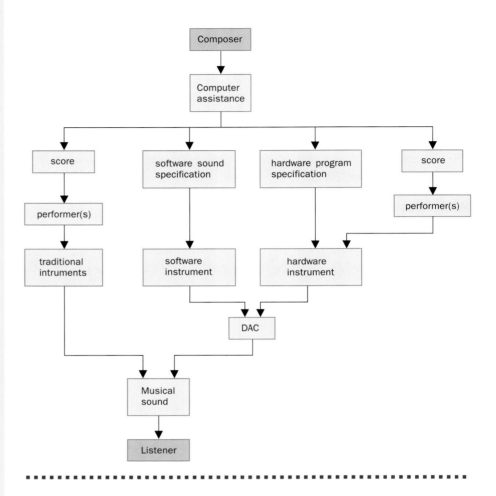

Figure 1. The main paths of computer music composition, from composer to listener. *Reproduced by permission of Gale, a part of Cengage Learning.*

or so-called Western Music Notation, that can be printed and given to human performers who execute music using traditional instruments such as piano, guitar, or violin.

However, the computer also can produce a music score automatically. In this case, the composer becomes a programmer and builds a computer program rather than a music score. A significant example of this may be found in the early work of American composer and teacher Lejaren Hiller (1924–1994), who wrote programs that composed most, if not all, of such scores as the *Illiac Suite for String Quartet* (1956) and *Computer Cantata* (1964).

Another path from the composer to the listener consists in using direct audio synthesis via specific computer programs (e.g., CSOUND, FM synthesis) that integrate the power of a programming language (like "C") with specialized functions to treat audio signals. The elaborated signals are played through a Digital to Analog Converter (DAC). Significant examples of this method may be found in works like *Turenas*, by American inventor and composer John Chowning (1934–), that utilize only purely synthesized sounds. This kind of processing on audio data can also be done directly in hardware if real-time interaction is needed. These features can be executed by human performers through the use of computer peripheral hardware, including electronic synthesizers, workstation keyboards, and effect generators. This last option is largely used in popular or light commercial music. These various methods of composing and performing music using the computer can be combined in multiple ways. For example, *Répons*, by French composer and conductor Pierre Boulez (1925–), combines the programmable real-time capabilities of a digital synthesizer with a sizable ensemble of traditional instruments.

Languages for Music Modeling

Music is one of the most complex languages. Many elementary operations are necessary to create a music score; these include editing, saving, loading, visualizing, executing, coding grabbed sounds, printing, and analyzing data. Specific music models and languages have been defined to perform these functions. These can be classified into three main categories: sound-oriented, notation-oriented, and analysis-oriented models.

Sound-oriented models address music modeling by considering the sounds produced, regardless of the visual representation issues of music notation and multiple visualization modalities. Classical examples of sound-oriented models are MIDI (Music Instrument Digital Interface) and CSOUND. Of these, MIDI, first developed in 1982, is the most common. MIDI uses a limited number of music notation symbols (e.g., notes, rests, accidentals, clefs, ties, and dots). MIDI is a protocol* designed to allow computers and electronic instruments of different manufacturers to work together. MIDI provides a set of common functions such as note events, timing events, pitch bends, pedal information, and synchronization. It is one of the most used s for the interchange of music information because it allows storing music in a compact form.

Notation-oriented models focus on representing scores on the screen and printing them on paper by using a set of notation symbols. Software examples include Finale, Sibelius, Igor, and Score.

Analysis-oriented models such as EsAC, Humdrum, and MusicData are used to describe music for its further analysis at the level of harmony, style, and melody. These models tend to code music with numbers in order to make metric analysis easier while neglecting several detailed interpretation symbols.

A new category of music languages has been proposed in order to exchange music on the Internet. Samples of this type of language include SMDL, WEDELMUSIC, and Music XML. Some of these are based on the XML (eXtensible Markup Language) programming language currently in use for much Internet content.

Software such Apple's GarageBand combines a sound-oriented model with a notation-oriented model, seeking to simplify both the creation and distribution of music. GarageBand is also notable in that it is distributed free with new Apple computers and tablets. This has enabled music hobbyists to enter the world of computer-aided composition.

* **protocol** an agreed understanding for the sub-operations that make up a transaction, usually found in the specification of inter-computer communications

Notational Music Composition

Common music editors allow the composer to write music in different ways by using specific input devices such as tables, light pens, or special keyboards. Many allow users to edit with a mouse, import files from other music languages, and use optical music recognition techniques (wherein music information is extracted from a scanned printed or hand-written sheet) or audio recognition (detecting the pitch and rhythm from an audio source). Innovative solutions for music composition have benefited from the increasing presence of distributed systems. For example, MOODS is a cooperative system for editing and manipulating music. The most common input method is using a MIDI keyboard to enter the notes. The composer plays the keyboard, producing the melody for a specific voice or track (typically an instrument), which is translated by the device into MIDI codes and sent to the computer where the codes are converted into music notation. The composer is thus able to see the played notes on the monitor, to store the music, and to print it. Another typical feature is related to the output of music: after the music input phase, the composer can choose the instrument associated with each track and listen to the execution or use it as accompaniment. To do this, the computer sends MIDI commands to drive external (e.g., keyboards, tone and effects generators, controllers) or internal (e.g., software synthesizer) reproducers.

Algorithmic Composition

In algorithmic composition, the composer builds a program rather than a score. This form of composition is totally led by the computer. Two main methods for computer-driven composition have been developed: deterministic and probabilistic. The first approach generates notes without random selection. The variables supplied to such a process may be a set of pitches, a musical phrase, or some constraints that the process must satisfy. The other approach integrates random choice into the decision-making process, generating musical events according to probability tables, which estimate the occurrence of certain events.

Audio Music Composition

Computer-based audio music composition is based on the elaboration of sound samples. Composers combine synthetic or digitized sounds using specific editing programs (e.g., groove machine, audio editing) or hardware instruments (e.g., sampler keyboard, sequencer) that provide support for functions such as:

- Multi-track recording or sequencing, to manage several audio tracks simultaneously for playback or recording process;
- Time stretching, which allows for changing the length of audio data duration without affecting the pitch;
- Pitch shifting, in which sound samples are modified in order to transpose the pitch of notes;

■ Effect applying, to add reverberation, delay, modulation, and dynamics effects.

Audio editor and electronic devices provide the composer with several sound generation techniques like:

■ Additive sound synthesis. This common technique merges and filters signals with different wave-forms, different frequencies, phases, and amplitudes to produce new sound signals.

■ Subtractive sound synthesis. In this technique, a complex audio signal is modified through filtering so as to modify the frequency contents.

■ Physical modeling synthesis (PhM). This begins with mathematical models of the physical acoustics of instrumental sound production. The equations of PhM describe the mechanical and acoustic behavior of an instrument being played.

■ Frequency Modulation (FM) Synthesis. This is based on the theory underlying the FM of radio-band frequencies. This form of synthesis was introduced by Yamaha in 1983 with the DX7 synthesizer. In the basic modulation technique, a carrier oscillator is modulated in frequency by a modulator oscillator. This allows the computer to modify amplitude and create harmonics that generate the new signal.

▶ *See also* **Animation • Film and Video Editing • Music • Music, Computer**

Resources

Books

Cope, David. *Computer Models of Musical Creativity*. Cambridge, MA: MIT Press, 2005.

Hewitt, Michael. *Composition for Computer Musicians*. Boston: Course Technology, 2009.

Hugill, Andrew, ed. *Internet Music*. Abingdon: Routledge, 2005.

Loy, D. Gareth. *Musimathics: The Mathematical Foundations of Music*. Cambridge, MA, and London: MIT Press, 2006.

Miranda, Eduardo Reck. *Composing Music with Computers*. Oxford, UK, and Boston: Focal Press, 2001; reprint. Amsterdam: Elsevier, 2006.

Miranda, Eduardo Reck, and Al Biles. *Evolutionary Computer Music*. London: Springer, 2007.

Nierhaus, Gerhard. *Algorithmic Composition: Paradigms of Automated Music Generation*. Vienna and New York: Springer, 2009.

Rapid Growth

Music composition technology via computer is evolving rapidly. New paradigms and solutions are ready to be used by large groups of people.

N

Navigation

Navigation is the art of finding one's way from one location to another. This appears pretty simple in the age of interstate highways and well-marked street intersections: follow the road signs or a map and the task should be easy. It is even easier with GPS, which is short for Global Positioning System. However, imagine being in an aircraft or a ship and all that can be seen is the blue sky above and the clouds below, or nothing but waves. Now, imagine it is night and nothing at all can be seen! In this computer-centered society, digital means are available to use satellite technology and other electronic tools to help figure out positions and destinations. Long before these were available, however, mathematical navigational systems were devised to guide ship captains and travelers of centuries past; these time-tested tools provide the foundation upon which today's sophisticated, electronic navigational tools are built.

Early Navigational Foundations

To aid in navigation and mapmaking, a coordinate system was created using virtual lines of latitude and longitude that cross at 90 degree angles. Latitude is referenced to a circle circumscribed around Earth called the equator, and designated as zero latitude. North of the equator, the latitude lines are parallel to the equator and are called north latitude. The geographical North Pole is 90 degrees north latitude and the circle at that latitude has such a small radius it is virtually a point. The South Pole is 90 degrees south latitude. The angle of latitude is the angular difference between two lines: one drawn from the center of Earth to the equator and one drawn from the center of Earth to the latitude in question.

Longitude lines also run around Earth but through the North and South Poles. The reference line, the zero meridian, runs through the Royal Observatory in Greenwich, just outside of London, England. Lines of longitude are designated east and west from the zero meridian. Time zones are also a function of longitude and the reference time zone from which all others are measured is called Greenwich Mean Time (GMT). This brings up an important subject: the inseparable relationship between time and navigation.

Time Zones, Sundials, and Longitudinal Calculations

Nearly everyone is familiar with the sundial, which uses the shadow of its angled center piece, called the *gnomon,* to indicate (tell) time. The sundial tells local time, based on its relationship to the sun in any given place.

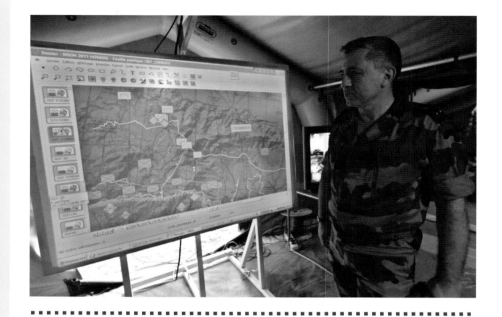

General looking at a computer-generated map showing the field of an exercise as part of a training ahead of the squad's departure for Afghanistan. © *PATRICK HERTZOG/AFP/Getty Images.*

As an example, at exactly high noon the gnomon produces no shadow as the sun is precisely midway between sunrise and sunset. However, high noon occurs at different times at different places on Earth. This is why there are time zones.

There are generally 24 time zones corresponding roughly to the one-hour segments of a 24-hour Earth day. There are some odd time zones with half-hour and even smaller increments, but these are rare. The actual time of high noon does not jump in one-hour steps, of course, but changes gradually as one travels around Earth. If the sundial is adjusted so the gnomon points to true north, the sundial will show true solar time. The difference between true solar time at some location and the true solar time at the zero meridian can be used to calculate longitude.

In order to use the sundial to determine longitude in relationship to the zero meridian, however, a traveler must have an accurate mechanical clock set to precise GMT before traveling. The English government offered a substantial reward in 1761 for the invention of an accurate clock that would operate on a ship for precisely this reason. Whereas the latitude of a ship could be determined by measuring the position of the sun at its highest point, without a reference to time, determining longitude without an accurate GMT reading required lunar observations and time-consuming, difficult mathematical computations. Trade and exploratory ships could travel more safely, accurately, and economically with the use of reliable time-keeping technology.

The requirements for navigation became much more stringent when humans began to travel by air. A ship traveling on open water is relatively slow, so finding a fix, or position, every few hours was sufficient. Even if fog or other bad weather prohibited taking fixes, the ship could slow down or stop until conditions improved. This is not possible with aircraft!

Accurate position fixes must be available continuously. Clock and sundial technology could not perform this complex task!

From Radio Beacons to On-Board Computers

One of the first aircraft navigation systems, invented in the 1920s, used radio beacons. The aircraft could hop from one beacon to another on what were called airways. Position could be determined from these airways but this involved tedious procedures that were not only difficult but time-consuming as well. The beacons were strategically located so that the airways passed directly over airports to simplify the navigation. Similar homing beacons were used for ships but only near shore due to the limited range of the beacon's radio signal.

Later, more sophisticated radio navigation systems for both air and sea actually measured the vessel's latitude and longitude, which was plotted on a navigation chart. This was acceptable for ships at sea, but unfolding a large navigation chart and plotting a course in an aircraft cockpit was not particularly convenient. However, because it was the best option at the time, it was done.

What would have been ideal would be a computer that took the latitude and longitude information and automatically calculated steering information. Some ship navigators had access to such a computer, which worked with the first long-range radio navigation systems during World War II. These computers were huge mechanical monsters that were acceptable for a battleship but not suited for aircraft.

It was not until small digital computers became available that long-range navigation became commonplace in aircraft. The aircrew could enter the desired final or intermediate destinations, called waypoints, into the computer, and the computer would calculate the steering information, which was displayed with an indicator. It was even possible to use the steering information in the form of electrical signals to control a ship or aircraft with an autopilot.

Long-Distance Navigation Systems

Since World War II, several improved long distance radio navigation systems have been developed. The first was LORAN, which stands for long range navigation. Shortly after LORAN was Omega, which was followed by a much-improved LORAN called LORAN-C. Finally, in the late 1970s, the satellite-based Global Positioning System (GPS) was developed. GPS can provide navigation anywhere on Earth, and for the typical consumer it can indicate position to within a 15 meters (about 50 feet) of error, which is superior to any previous navigation system.

The GPS navigation system consists of a constellation of at least 24 satellites in well-known orbits. A network of ground stations controls the orbits and functions of the satellites. The satellites transmit radio signals that are used to measure the distance from the user to each satellite. A computer solves the geometry problem and determines the user's position.

Computer Sciences, 2nd Edition

GPS depends on the very accurate atomic clocks located in the satellites and ground control stations. It is fascinating to realize that the secret to accurate navigation in 1761 was precise clocks, and the same remains true today.

In addition to a radio receiver, the GPS user equipment has a rather extensive computer. It is necessary to separate the signals from the individual satellites. The computer knows which satellites are present and where they are in their orbits. It inserts a number of calibration factors and calculates the position of the user equipment in latitude, longitude, altitude, and precise time. Most GPS receivers used for aircraft have large databases, which include the locations of airports, radio navigation aids, airways, and so on.

GPS products for consumer use have become increasingly popular since the late 1990s. In addition to providing convenience and security to people driving in unfamiliar areas, GPS technology such as the General Motors OnStar navigational system, which connects drivers to assistance operators via GPS satellites, can help save lives by directing drivers to hospitals or police stations near where they are, should an emergency arise. Throughout the 2000s and now into the 2010s, more and more consumer electronic devices incorporated navigation hardware and software of one sort or another. For instance, GPS has been incorporated into smartphones and tablet personal computers (PCs). Examples of smartphones with built-in GPS are the Samsung Galaxy Beam, Nokia Pureview 808, and Sony Xperia Ion. Each of these smartphones contain GPS with assisted GPS (A-GPS), which is a system that helps to improve startup performance of the satellite-based GPS system on the phones.

Improving Aircraft Navigation with NexGen

According to a 2007 press release by the Federal Aviation Administration (FAA), the entire U.S. air transportation system will be radically overhauled by the Next Generation Air Transportation System (NexGen). A central goal of NexGen is to substantially reduce gridlock in the skies and at the nation's airports. NexGen will transition away from ground-based radars and other systems, and instead migrate to satellite-based technologies that will improve control of each aircraft within the overall air traffic system. For instance, "Automatic dependent surveillance-broadcast" (ADS-B) is a system for improved control of aircraft using onboard GPS. The resulting navigation data from each aircraft is then broadcast to other aircraft, and to the air traffic control system, so that pilots and air traffic controllers can see the real-time positions and trajectories of all the aircraft throughout a given region. The resulting improvement in aircraft navigation should reduce passenger travel time, fuel usage and pollution, and air traffic congestion, while at the same time improving safety. According to the June 29, 2012, FAA article *Start Spreading the News*, the airline Jet Blue began NextGen procedures at the John F. Kennedy International Airport in New York City. Such improvements provide for a much more efficient path for landings, which saves time and fuel expense. In fact, the article states, "As is the case with other NextGen routes, the new approaches create more predictability into one of the busiest airports in the country. It allows the airlines to move passengers in and out of the airport faster while also reducing the environmental impact of each flight. The airline is predicting that it will save about 18 gallons per flight by lying the precision satellite route." Major milestones in the implementation of NexGen are scheduled to take place between 2012 and 2025.

▶ See also **Aircraft Traffic Management • Geographical Information Systems • Global Positioning Systems • Satellite Technology**

Resources

Books

Clausing, Donald J. *The Aviator's Guide to Navigation.* 4th ed. Boston: McGraw-Hill Professional, 2006.

El-Rabbany, Ahmed. *Introduction to GPS: The Global Positioning System.* Boston: Artech House, 2002.

Hofmann-Wellenhof, Bernhard, Herbert Lichtenegger, and Elmar Wasle. *GNSS—Global Navigation Satellite Systems: GPS, GLONASS, Galileo, and More.* Vienna and New York: Springer, 2008.

Kennedy, Michael. *The Global Positioning System and ArcGIS.* Boca Raton, FL: CRC, 2010.

Web Sites

Federal Aviation Administration. "Start Spreading the News." http://www.faa.gov/nextgen/slides/?slide=8 (accessed October 15, 2012).

Jaxov.com. "Top 10 Smartphones of 2012." http://jaxov.com/2012/04/top-10-smartphones-2012/ (accessed October 15, 2012).

Neural Networks

Since its inception in the 1940s, when it was hailed as The Electronic Brain, the digital computer has been expected to replicate cognitive* functions; that is, mental processes found in the human brain that involve such activities as memory, perception, and independent thinking. Although developments in hardware technology and software techniques have enabled limited successes in this direction, many capabilities remain uniquely human. The field of artificial intelligence (AI)* seeks to infer general principles of intelligence by analyzing human processes, and then to encode them in software. The standard approach to AI is grounded in the assumption that human cognition is based on the ability

Universal Skill

Animals do it! Humans do it! Do what? Navigate! The ability to travel successfully from one location to another is a skill nearly as old as life itself. Modern navigation has reached such a level of sophistication that aircraft can fly half-way around the globe and land perfectly on a runway using only electronic navigation.

* **cognitive** pertaining to the concepts of knowing or perceiving

* **artificial intelligence (AI)** a branch of computer science dealing with creating computer hardware and software to mimic the way people think and perform practical tasks

to manipulate symbols using logical operators. An alternative approach, generally known as neural networks, is motivated by the observation that the biological brain is the only device capable of intelligent behavior.

Thus, the neural network framework is rooted in principles abstracted from human knowledge of neurobiological function. Some of these follow:

- Computation is performed by a network of interconnected units, each representing a neuron or a set of neurons.

- Each unit generates an output signal that is a simple parametric function of the signals on its input lines, which can be either output signals from other neurons or external signals (environmental input to the network).

- A given unit cannot transmit different signals to different units; its output signal is broadcast to a set of units that can comprise the entire network or any subset.

- Each input line to a neuron has a corresponding weight parameter, a value that determines the influence of that line on the neuron's output.

- The function ultimately computed by a network is determined by the connectivity of the units, their individual input-output functions, and the weights among them.

A diagram of a neural network is shown in Figure 1. The nine units in the diagram are numbered, and the curved lines with arrows indicate the connectivity of the network. Units 1 and 8 receive no input from other units in the network; their activity values are set by stimuli external to the network, like the light detecting cells in the retina, for example. Similarly, units 3, 5, and 7 are output units; these units do not activate any other units. Generally, output units generate the ultimate result of the network computation. Biologically, they would correspond to *effector* cells in the nervous system; that is, cells that directly influence the environment, like motor neurons that directly stimulate muscle tissue.

The thickness of the links is meant to represent the weight of the connection, and dashed links denote negative values to the links. An N by N matrix is a more precise (and for a computer program, more useful) representation of the connectivity in a network with N units.

The network computation proceeds by computing activity values for each unit according to a function that combines its inputs multiplied by the connection weights. Once the modeler has selected the unit function and set the connectivity of the units, the function computed by the network is determined by the weight values. These values can either be set by the modeler or learned by the network to give a function that is extracted from observations.

Hard-Wired Neural Networks

Consider the task of adjusting several interdependent parameters of a complex system so that its output function is optimal. An example is scheduling classes at a large university, so that conflicts among classroom

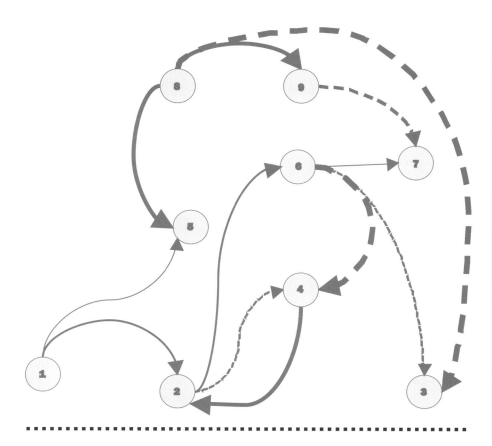

Figure 1. Diagram of a neural network. *Reproduced by permission of Gale, a part of Cengage Learning.*

use, student course choices, and faculty teaching times are minimized. Another is the simultaneous function of the many muscles in the human body in performing a complex task like riding a bicycle or juggling. For a task with multiple simultaneous constraints among the variables, it is often impossible to find a solution that is guaranteed to be optimal (as in, the absolute best). But, there are several approaches to finding very good solutions, and for many real-world situations this is sufficient.

A neural network can be designed to approach such a problem by defining each unit to represent the truth value of a specific hypothesis. For example, in the class-scheduling task, a unit may represent the plausibility that *English 101 will be taught in Room 312 by Professor Miller from 10 a.m. to 11 a.m. on Monday, Wednesday, and Friday.* Another unit would represent another hypothesis, such as *Psychology 400 will be taught in Room 312 by Professor Wu from 10 a.m. to 11 a.m. on Monday, Wednesday, and Friday.* Because there is a conflict (both classes cannot meet in the same room at the same time) between these two hypotheses, the connection between them would have a negative value. Thus, a network can represent hypotheses as nodes and constraints among hypotheses as weight values between pairs of nodes. The success of this approach depends on the skills and intuitions of the network designer. While there are some guiding principles to network design, it remains very much an art form.

Computer Sciences, 2ⁿᵈ Edition

* **heuristic** a procedure that serves to guide investigation but that has not been proven

Neural networks have been applied to many problems of this kind, often providing a better solution than other heuristic* techniques. A classic example of a difficult (NP complete) problem is the so-called traveling salesperson problem (TSP). Given a set of N locations, the goal of the TSP is to find the shortest path that goes to every point and returns to the starting location. A neural network can be used to find a *pretty good* path; that is, the solution is good, though not guaranteed to be the best. Experiment results published in 1985 by American scientists John J. Hopfield (1933–) and David W. Tank showed that a neural network finds a path that is very close to optimal.

Learning in Neural Networks

One of the most attractive features of neural network models is their capacity to learn. Since the response properties of the network are determined by connectivity and weight values, a learning procedure can be expressed mathematically as a function that determines the amount by which each weight changes in terms of the activities of the neurons. Most neural network learning procedures are based on a postulate put forward by Canadian psychologist Donald O. Hebb (1904–1985) in his classic book, *The Organization of Behavior*: "When an axon of cell A is near enough to excite a cell B and repeatedly or persistently takes part in firing it, some growth process or metabolic change takes place in one or both cells such that A's efficiency, as one of the cells firing B is increased."

Various mathematical and computational enhancements to Hebb's original theory have led to many approaches to machine learning. Of these, a technique known as backpropagation, originally discovered by American scientist Paul J. Werbos (1947–), in 1974, has been the primary driving force in neural networks since the mid-1980s.

Typically, a network that acquires information (*learns*) is trained to learn the relationship between a set of input and output variables that have been independently measured across many examples. For example, the input might be a set of blood test results and the output might be a binary value that indicates whether the patient was later found to have a particular form of cancer. A learning network could be defined as a set of input units (each representing a blood test result) which activate a set of intermediate units, which then activate a single output unit (representing the development of a tumor). Initially, the weights are randomly assigned, and so the network output is not useful for medical diagnosis. Training proceeds by presenting input data to the network and comparing the resulting network output to the target value (the corresponding output value in the data). The backpropagation technique specifies how to adjust the network weights based on the network error (target minus network output) and the input activation values.

This technique is broadly applicable to problems involving pattern recognition, spanning a broad spectrum of domains. These include military applications, such as detecting submarines from sonar signals;

financial applications including stock market prediction; medical diagnosis; and speech recognition. Neural network learning algorithm*s have also shed light onto the neurobiological mechanisms underlying human learning.

Neural networks can be built and evaluated by computer programs that are commercially available. For instance, the Neural Network Toolbox™, by MathWorks, models complex nonlinear neural network systems. The Toolbox contains the ingredients necessary for designing, training, simulating, and visualizing neural networks. Among its important features is the ability to create supervised networks such as learning vector quantization, nonlinear autoregressive, and radial basis, along with the capability to generate unsupervised networks such as competitive layers and self-organizing maps. Its Simulink⁻ feature enables the user to build and evaluate neural networks.

▶ *See also* **Artificial Intelligence • Expert Systems • Pattern Recognition**

Resources

Books

Hernández, Carlos, et al., eds. *From Brains to Systems: Brain-Inspired Cognitive Systems 2010*. New York: Springer, 2011.

Hebb, Donald O. *The Organization of Behavior: A Neuropsychological Theory*. New York: Wiley, 1949. Reprint. Mahwah, NJ: L. Erlbaum Associates, 2002.

Zeng, Zhigang, and Jun Wang, eds. *Advances in Neural Network Research and Applications*. Berlin: Springer, 2010.

Periodicals

Hopfield, John J., and David W. Tank. "'Neural' Computation of Decisions in Optimization Problems." *Biological Cybernetics* 52, no. 3 (July 1985): 141–152.

Werbos, Paul J. "Beyond Regression: New Tools for Prediction and Analysis in the Behavioral Sciences." Ph.D. Thesis, Harvard University, 1974.

Web Sites

MathWorks. "Neural Network Toolbox " http://www.mathworks.com/products/neural-network/index.html (accessed October 16, 2012).

Werbos, Paul J. "Welcome to the Werbos World!" http://www.werbos.com/ (accessed October 16, 2012).

Predicting Stock Market Trends

Can a neural network predict which stocks will rise or fall? Various companies claim success with their systems, which analyze previous trading trends. Some of the factors taken into consideration include current stock values and net change in specific stocks during the previous week.

* **algorithm** a rule or procedure used to solve a mathematical problem—most often described as a sequence of steps

O

Open Source

There are three dimensions to the concept of *open source* as it applies to computing. First, open source is a philosophy about computing and sharing programming code to improve the quality of computing. The term open source also refers to a wide array of OSs and applications that have been developed under this philosophy, and, finally, it represents a general approach to the treatment of intellectual property*, usually in reference to licensing software or related documentation.

Origins of Open Source Computing

The idea of sharing the source code* for computer programs so that the programs can be debugged, modified, or improved is a practice that began in the late 1950s, when International Business Machines (IBM) provided programmers employed by their customers with access to the for applications running on their mainframe computers*. The idea of creating source code for the purposes of sharing it can be traced to the early days of the Internet, when programmers wrote and shared source code for the applications that have been fundamental to the development of the Internet. The establishment and workings of the Free Software Foundation (FSF) have also promoted this approach.

The emergence of the Internet provided a global medium through which programmers could exchange source code, documentation, and other information about programming. The FSF, which was founded in 1985 and is "dedicated to promoting computer users' right to use, study, copy, modify, and redistribute computer programs," provided not only software (under its GNU Project), but also a social and political framework for advancing knowledge in the field. The foundation promoted the development and use of free software and documentation (not necessarily free of charge, but freely accessible as intellectual property) and campaigned to increase what its members believe to be the ethical and political issues of freedom in the use of software.

The General Public License

One of the key contributions made by the FSF has been to establish the legal basis for free software under U.S. intellectual property law, in the form of the General Public License (GPL). Under the GPL, software is licensed to ensure the freedom to make derivative works, may be distributed without charge, and the original source code must be disclosed or distributed with the binary representation. The essential purpose of the

* **intellectual property** the acknowledgement that an individual's creativity and innovation can be owned in the same way as physical property

* **source code** the human-readable programs that are compiled or interpreted so that they can be executed by a computing machine

* **mainframe computers** large computers used by businesses and government agencies to process massive amounts of data; generally faster and more powerful than desktop computers but usually requiring specialized software

Students participating in an Open Source Education project. © *AP Images/ San Angelo Standard-Times, Kimberley Parker.*

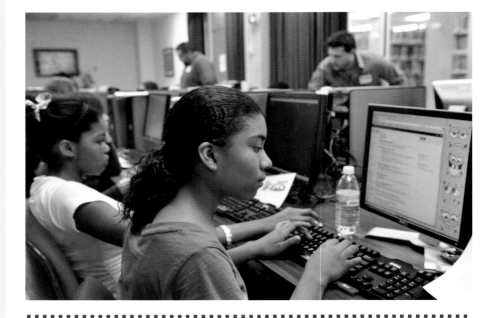

* **proprietary software** software created by an individual or company that is sold under a license that dictates use and distribution

GPL is to create a legal environment that is hospitable to the exchange of source code and programs, and which tends to promote efforts to study, change, or improve computer software. Related or variant licensing schemes include the Lesser GPL (LGPL), the Apache license, the Artistic License, the FreeBSD copyright, the Mozilla Public License, the Netscape Public License, the Sun Community Source License (SCSL), and the Sun Industry Standards License (SISL). The Creative Commons License has been developed to provide similar legal protection to non-source code intellectual property (e.g., images or music).

There is considerable controversy in regard to the benefits of the GPL. Its proponents argue that software developed and issued under the GPL is less expensive and ultimately more powerful than proprietary software*, because development and testing are open processes to which anyone can contribute. Critics of the GPL claim that open software diminishes incentives to create better software, because it weakens the business models on which the industry has been based. Furthermore, there are critics of the GPL within the open source community who claim it does not promote free software, but forces users of GPLed software to conform to the FSF philosophy. Other licenses, such the Berkeley Software Distribution (BSD) license, grant permission to freely redistribute licensed source code without requiring derivative works to be similarly licensed.

Because of the connotations of free software, and owing to the anti-business stance of American software developer Richard Stallman (1953–), the founder of the FSF, a less pejorative term, open source, was adopted during the 1990s. In order to further clarify the circumstances under which open source software is distributed, a group referred to as the Open Source Initiative has formulated the Open Source Definition, which effectively reconciles different licensing schemes, and the Open

Source Certification Program, which is aimed at preventing misuse of the phrase open source and identifying software that is developed or made available under a license that meets the Open Source Definition.

Open Source Development Models

The open source community is divided, at least philosophically, into two factions. The first faction is united by the belief that there is civic, economic, and moral value in the free development and exchange of software. The second faction is defined mainly by a business model, under which open source development is used to reduce the costs of research and development, accelerate the rate at which systems and applications are developed (and debugged), and create open distribution channels that engender broader interest in the software. For some companies, like Red Hat, open source software is the primary basis of their business. For other companies, such as IBM, open source software is employed to create or maintain a product line while lowering direct investment. For many more firms in the software industry, including Microsoft, public domain and open source software is employed to supplement proprietary products and services.

Open Source Computing and the Emergence of Linux

The Free Software Foundation has exerted considerable influence since its establishment, but the emergence of the Linux operating system (OS) is the main reason that open source software has become a significant factor in computing. Developed by a Finnish student named Linus Torvalds (1969–) (and modeled on a UNIX-like operating system, MINIX, but without MINIX source code), Linux was initially released in 1991. Owing largely to continued work by Torvalds on the kernel of the OS and an integration of the operating system with a suite of utilities developed by the FSF's GNU Project, Linux has matured into a sophisticated OS that now constitutes a legitimate alternative to proprietary systems on the market for server software. In addition, there are several major open source projects, including the GNOME and KDE projects, that are intended to create graphical desktop environments for Linux that allow it to challenge both Microsoft Windows and Apple's OS X as an OS for personal and corporate desktops.

Other Important Open Source Projects

Linux has received the most attention, but there are a number of other important open source projects, including the GNU Project's compilers, libraries, utilities, and its Emacs editor; the Perl and Python languages; the FreeBSD OS; the Apache web server; the MySQL database; and sendmail. Of these initiatives, the Apache Project, which began in 1995 with a small group of programmers working collaboratively to transform the CERN Web server software into a more reliable application, is arguably the most important, because the Apache web server has played a pivotal role in the growth of the World Wide Web, through the continuous development and distribution of a powerful open source application and an array of modular functions and services. The combination of Linux, Apache, MySQL, and the PHP scripting language is known as LAMP, and provides a completely free environment for developing dynamic websites, which has fueled the growth of web applications on the Internet. Sendmail is the core service for most of the e-mail transported over the Internet.

Open Source Documentation

An important factor in the development of open source computing has been the application of the open source philosophy to the development and distribution of documentation. Commercial developers and vendors have moved to reduce the amount and quality of documentation that is distributed with OSs and applications, effectively abandoning the provision of documentation for their products to an expensive but ineffectual aftermarket. At the same time, the application of the open source model to documentation has led to the widespread availability of guides and manuals that are accurate, thorough, and up-to-date.

For example, the Linux Documentation Project (LDP) has played a key role in the development of Linux. The purpose of the LDP is to promote and coordinate the publication of guides and manuals that support both systems administrators and end users. The LDP serves as a central distribution point for a number of independently produced guides. The LDP also promotes the creation and maintenance of so-called HOWTOs, briefer guides to specific topics, such as disk partitioning, the configuration of proxy servers, and security.

 See also **Codes** • **Coding Techniques** • **Programming**

Resources

Books

Berry, David M. *Copy, Rip, Burn: The Politics of Copyleft and Open Source.* London: Pluto Press, 2008.

Chopra, Samir, and Scott Dexter. *Decoding Liberation: The Promise of Free and Open Source Software.* Routledge studies in new media and cyberculture. New York: Routledge, 2008.

Deek, Fadi P., and James A. McHugh. *Open Source: Technology and Policy.* Cambridge, UK, and New York: Cambridge University Press, 2008.

Feller, Joseph, ed. *Perspectives on Free and Open Source Software.* Cambridge, MA: MIT Press, 2005.

St. Amant, Kirk, and Brian Still, eds. *Handbook of Research on Open Source Software: Technological, Economic, and Social Perspectives.* Hershey, PA: Information Science Reference, 2007.

Weber, Steve. *The Success of Open Source.* Cambridge, Mass.A: Harvard University Press, 2004.

Organick, Elliot

Engineer and Pioneering Computer Scientist
1925–1985

* **thermodynamic** relating to heat energy

Best remembered for his easy-to-understand textbooks about computers, programming, and operating systems, Elliot Organick was a pioneer computer scientist who was also passionate about making advances in technology simple and easy to understand. According to J. A. N. Lee in *Computer Pioneers,* one of Organick's most quoted remarks when hearing about new advances in technology was: "This is great stuff, but does it have to be so complicated?"

Organick was born in Brooklyn, New York, on February 25, 1925. After high school in Manhattan, he began studies in chemical engineering at the University of Michigan in 1941. He graduated in only three years, going on to work as a chemist for the Manhattan Project, the U.S. government's secret effort to develop an atomic bomb during World War II. He returned to academics shortly afterward, however, earning a master's degree from the University of Michigan in 1947 and a doctorate in chemical engineering in 1950.

In those days there were no specialized "computer scientists." Instead, mathematicians, physicists, engineers, and other researchers often used computers to perform numeric computations faster and to get more accurate results. Organick was one of those innovators when he used an IBM Card Programmed Calculator to carry out his chemical engineering thermodynamic* calculations. He soon became intrigued with using computers to enhance teaching and learning, and by the late 1950s was one of the first true computer scientists.

While Organick worked for the United Gas Pipeline Company from 1950 to 1955, his interest in computers helped advance the development of computer applications in the petroleum industry. For a short time after leaving that job, he worked as a consultant in computer applications. However, on the advice of his doctoral adviser, Organick returned to academia and joined the Computing Center at the University of Houston. Within five years he was its director.

In 1959 the Ford Foundation established a major project to induce the engineering faculty of the University of Michigan to use computers in engineering education and teaching. After a nationwide search, the director of the project invited Organick to return to Ann Arbor as associate director. While in Michigan, Organick was able to convince the National Science Foundation (NSF) that all educators needed to know how to use computers. With NSF funding, he organized several courses in 1960, and taught them to engineering faculty and high school science and math teachers during the summers until 1963.

Since good computer science study materials were not available in the early 1960s, Organick undertook to write some himself, with enduring success. His first, *A Fortran Primer,* was initially published in 1961 and later revised in 1966. In 1974 he and L. P. Meissner transformed it into the well

Michigan Algorithm Decoder (MAD)

MAD was a computer language based on Algol 58 developed at the University of Michigan to teach programming to undergraduate students. It was very efficient, which meant that the programs were returned to the students rather quickly, and it provided good diagnostics, which helped the students find their errors.

Multics

Multics (Multiplexed Information and Computing Service) was a general purpose computing system developed by MIT, Bell Labs, and General Electric. The system was meant to support hundreds of timesharing users, which was a significant innovation at that time. Although the system was not a commercial success, its operating system introduced significant concepts in computer design.

known *Fortran IV*. During his stay in Michigan, Organick also explored the Michigan Algorithm Decoder (MAD), which led to his book, *The MAD Primer*. Although this work was not as widely circulated as the Fortran title, programming language designers of that generation admired it.

Between 1968 and 1969, Organick went to the Massachusetts Institute of Technology (MIT) on sabbatical to work on its MAC project. The result of this experience was a textbook on the Multics operating system. In keeping with his reputation as a writer who could explain technical ideas in the computer field clearly and precisely, Organick developed an exceptionally clear description of how the Multics system works.

In 1971 Organick was recruited by the University of Utah as professor of computer science. There, he shaped a ground-breaking undergraduate computer science curriculum. His design was so thorough and farsighted that the program was not restructured until 1985.

By the mid-1970s, Organick had become the leading writer of computer science texts. *Computer Science: A First Course,* which he wrote with A. I. Forsythe, T. A. Keenan, and W. Stenberg, was an immediate success and was translated into five languages. *Programming Language Structures,* authored with Forsythe and R. P. Plummer, was distinctive in its application of comparative linguistic analysis to a wide range of then-current programming languages.

As noted in Lee's book, when Organick was asked how he created so many outstanding texts, Organick replied: "I am such a slow learner that once I understand something, I might as well write it down!"

Organick was deeply committed to education and professional service, which led him to take on a variety of leadership positions in the Association for Computing Machinery (ACM). He served six years on the ACM Education Committee and in 1968 was instrumental in founding the Special Interest Group on Computer Science Education (SIGCSE). He was editor of the education section of the *Communications* of the ACM for two years, and was editor-in-chief of *Computing Surveys* during its first six years, building its circulation to more than 30,000. In 1985 he received the SIGCSE annual award for Outstanding Contributions to Computer Science Education. Organick died of leukemia in Shreveport, Louisiana, on December 21, 1985.

▶ *See also* **Computer Assisted Instruction • Kemeny, John G. • Logo • Mathematics**

Resources

Books

Lee, John A. N. *International Biographical Dictionary of Computer Pioneers.* Chicago: Fitzroy Dearborn, 1995.

Periodical

Lindstrom, Gary. "Elliot Organick." *Communications of the ACM* 29, no. 3 (1986): 231.

PR

Péter, Rózsa
Hungarian Mathematician
1905–1977

A pioneering theorist of a mathematical discipline with important applications in computer science, Rózsa Politzer was born February 17, 1905, in Budapest, Hungary. Although she never married, Politzer changed her name to Rózsa Péter in 1930. Initially, Péter intended to fulfill her father's wish for her to become a chemist, but lectures by mathematicians enticed her to a course that would change her life as well as the field of mathematics. Through lectures and papers in the 1930s, she promoted the study of recursive functions as a distinct field of mathematics. This aspect of number theory considers functions that are used to study the structure of number classes or functions in terms of the complexity of the calculations required to determine them. Since theories of relay contact systems*, cybernetics*, and computer programming are dependent on recursive functions, Péter's work is indispensable to computer science.

After attending the Mária Terézia Girls' School in Budapest, Péter enrolled at Eötvös Loránd University in 1922 to pursue a career in chemistry. Soon after starting, however, she decided to change her field of study to mathematics. Also while in school, she met László Kalmár, with whom she maintained a close, lifelong professional friendship. Kalmár, who became a famous mathematics pioneer in his own right, was the person who later introduced her to recursive functions.

In 1932 Péter wrote a paper on recursive functions. She lectured on the subject at the International Congress of Mathematicians in Zurich in 1932 and again in 1936. At this conference, she was the first to formally suggest recursive mathematics as a field unto itself. In 1935, she received her Ph.D. summa cum laude from Eötvös Loránd University. After publishing several papers on recursive functions, she was invited to join the editorial boards of several international mathematical journals, including, in 1937, the *Journal of Symbolic Logic*.

In 1943 Péter wrote *Playing with Infinity: Mathematical Explorations and Excursions* (not released until 1945 because of World War II), a work intended for the general public. It discussed number theory, geometry, calculus, logic, and Gödel's undecidability theory, all in a manner accessible to nonspecialists. This book successfully attempted to bridge the gap between mathematics and science and the humanities. Péter's work has since been translated into forty languages.

* **relay contact systems** systems constructed to carry out logic functions, implemented in relays (electromechanical switches) rather than semiconductor devices

* **cybernetics** a unified approach to understanding the behavior of machines and animals developed by Norbert Wiener (1894–1964)

Péter's Perseverance

Péter held no permanent job for eighteen years after graduating from college because, Hungary, as an ally of Nazi Germany, engaged in academic purges aimed at eliminating Jews and others whom the Nazis considered "enemies" from serving on school faculties. Instead, she tutored students and took temporary teaching assignments for financial support. But her lack of employment did not prevent her from establishing herself as a world leader in mathematical logic.

* **ALGOL** a language developed by the ALGOL committee for scientific applications—acronym for ALGOrithmic Language

After Germany's 1945 defeat in World War II, Péter enjoyed teaching at Pedagógiai Förskola, a teacher's college in Budapest, for the next ten years. In 1951 she published *Recursive Functions,* the first book on recursive functions. This book was also translated into numerous other languages and became a standard reference. In 1955 the teacher's college was shut down. Péter became a professor of mathematics at Eötvös Loránd University in Budapest. Her interests turned to the use of recursive functions and their relevance to computers. Her first paper on this subject addressed primitive recursive functions and ALGOL*. After her retirement, she continued her research into recursive functions and their relationship to computer program languages. She published her last book, *Recursive Functions in Computer Theory,* in 1976.

Péter was awarded the Kossuth Prize in 1951 by the state of Hungary for her achievements. She also received the State Award, Silver Degree, in 1970, and the State Award, Gold Degree, in 1973. That same year, she became a corresponding member and the first female member of the Hungarian Academy of Sciences. She was made an honorary president of the János Bolyai Mathematical Association in 1975.

In addition to the study of recursive mathematics, Péter was very active in mathematics education, writing textbooks and teaching both children and mathematics teachers. Péter challenged society, and particularly children, to see mathematics and the sciences as entertaining, joyful, adventurous, and ultimately more than dry, intellectual exercises. She believed mathematics to be an indispensable part of science, and science to be an indispensable part of humanity.

Péter's interests extended beyond mathematics; she enjoyed art and cooking and also wrote theater reviews. She enjoyed literature as well and translated poetry into Hungarian. However, mathematics remained her first love, and in *Playing with Infinity,* she wrote: "I love mathematics not only for its technical applications, but principally because it is beautiful: because man has breathed his spirit of play into it, and because it has given him his greatest game—the encompassing of the infinite." Péter died of cancer on February 17, 1977.

 See also **King, Ada Byron • Mathematics • Procedural Languages**

Resources

Books

Grinstein, Louise S., and Paul J. Campbell, eds. *Women of Mathematics: A Bibliographic Sourcebook.* New York: Greenwood Press, 1987.

Péter, Rózsa. *Recursive Functions.* New York: Academic Press, 1967.

Periodical

Morris, Edie, and Leon Harkleroad. "Rózsa Péter: Recursive Function Theory's Founding Mother." *Mathematical Intelligencer* 12, no. 1 (1990): 59–61.

Physics

In some ways there would not be computers today were it not for physics. Furthermore, the needs of physics have stimulated computer development at every step. This all started due to one man's desire to eliminate needless work by transferring it to a machine.

Charles Babbage (1791–1871) was a well-to-do Englishman attending Cambridge University in the early 1800s. One day he was nodding off over a book containing tables of astronomical phenomena. He fancied that he would become an astronomical mathematician. The motion of heavenly bodies is, of course, governed by the laws of physics. For a moment, he thought of having the tables calculated automatically. This idea came up several times in succeeding years until he finally designed a calculator, the Difference Engine that could figure the numbers and print the tables. A version of the Difference Engine made by someone else found its way to the Dudley Observatory in Albany, New York, where it merrily cranked out numbers until the 1920s. Babbage followed this machine with a programmable version, the Analytical Engine, which was never built. The Analytical Engine, planned as a more robust successor to the Difference Engine, is considered by many to be the first example of a modern computer.

In the late 1800s, mathematician and scientist Lord Kelvin (William Thomson) (1824–1907) tried to understand wave phenomena by building a mechanical analog* computer that modeled the waves on beaches in England. This was a continuation of the thread of mechanical computation applied to understand physical phenomena in the 1800s.

In the 1920s, physicist Vannevar Bush (1890–1974) of the Massachusetts Institute of Technology built a Differential Analyzer that used a combination of mechanical and electrical parts to create an analog computer useful for many problems. The Differential Analyzer was especially suited for physics calculations, as its output was a smooth curve showing the results of mathematical modeling. This curve was very accurate, more so than the slide rule*s that were the ubiquitous* calculators in physics and engineering in the first seven decades of the twentieth century.

Beginning during World War II (1938–1945) and finishing just after the war ended, the Moore School of the University of Pennsylvania built an electronic digital* computer for the U.S. Army. One of the first problems run on it was a model of a nuclear explosion. The advent of computers opened up whole new realms of research for physicists.

* **analog** a quantity (often an electrical signal) that is continuous in time and amplitude

* **slide rule** based on work by Scotsman John Napier (1550–1617), it permits the mechanical automation of calculations using logarithms

* **ubiquitous** to be commonly available everywhere

* **digital** a quantity that can exist only at distinct levels, not having values in between these levels (for example, binary)

* **visualization** a technique whereby complex systems are portrayed in a meaningful way using sophisticated computer graphics systems; e.g., chemical molecules

Physicists like digital computers because they are fast. Thus, big problems can be figured out, and calculations that are boring and repetitive by hand can be transferred to computers. Some of the first subroutines, which are blocks of computer code executed many times during the run of a program, were inspired by the needs of physics.

Even though digital computers were fast with repetitious tasks, the use of approximation and visualization* has the largest effect on physicists using electronic computers. Analog machines, both mechanical and electronic, have output that models real world curves and other shapes representing certain kinds of mathematics. To calculate the mathematical solution of physical problems on digital computers meant the use of approximation. For example, the area under a curve (the integral) is approximated by dividing the space below the curve into rectangles, figuring out their area, and adding the small areas to find the one big area. As computers got faster, such approximations were made up of an ever-increasing number of smaller rectangles.

Visualization is probably the physicist's task most aided by computers. The outputs of Lord Kelvin's machine and the Differential Analyzer were drawn by pens connected to the computational components of the machine.

The early digital computers could print rough curves, supplemented by cleaner curves done on a larger scale by big plotters. Interestingly, the plotters drew what appeared to be smooth lines by drawing numerous tiny straight lines, just like a newspaper photograph is really a large number of gray points with different shades. Even these primitive drawing tools represented a significant advance. They permitted physicists to see much more than could be calculated by hand.

In the 1960s, physicists took millions of photographs of sub-atomic particle collisions. These were then processed with human intervention. A "scanner" (usually a student) using a special machine would have the photographs of the collisions brought up one by one. The scanner would use a trackball to place a cursor over a sub-atomic particle track. At each point, the scanner would press a button, which then allowed the machine to punch the coordinates on a card. These thousands upon thousands of cards were processed to calculate the mass and velocity of the various known and newly discovered particles. These were such big jobs that they were often run on a computer overnight. Physicists could use the printed output of batch-type computer systems to visualize mentally what was really happening. This is one of the first examples of truly large-scale computing. In fact, most of the big calculations done over the first decades of electronic digital computing had some relationship to physics, including atomic bomb models, satellite orbits, and cyclotron experiments.

The advent of powerful workstations and desktop systems with color displays ended the crude graphical representations of early forms of visualization. Today, many invisible phenomena, such as fields, waves, and quantum mechanical systems, can be modeled accurately in full color.

This is helping to eliminate erroneous ideas inspired by the poor visualizations of years past. Also, these computer game–quality images can be used to train the next generation of physics students and their counterparts in chemistry and biology classes, making tangible what was invisible before.

Computational Physics

The extensive use of computer processing capabilities has become an integral part of many disciplines within physics. Computers are used in many branches of physics (such as particle physics and astronomy) in order to sort through massive amounts of data. Additionally, the use of computers to numerically solve problems in physics is so important that the field of computational physics became recognized. Computational physics entails the numerical solution of algorithms that are used to represent particular physics problems, as long as those problems can be described by a precise, quantitative theory.

Numerical computation has become essential to a variety of disciplines in physics. For instance, large particle colliders are used to reveal previously unknown fundamental particles in nature, or to confirm the existence of elementary particles predicted by mainstream theory. Indeed, the search for the fundamental Higgs boson was completed in summer 2012 at both Fermilab's large Tevatron particle collider in the United States, and at the world's largest particle collider, CERN's Large Hadron Collider, located in Europe. Without the massive computational capabilities of modern computer systems, sorting through (and making sense of) the billions of collisions that are recorded by detectors at such large particle collider facilities would not be feasible.

The Inspiration For The World Wide Web

Perhaps most pervasive of physics-inspired computer developments is the World Wide Web. It was first developed as a way of easily sharing data, including graphics, among researchers in the European cyclotron community and also for those outside of it with appropriate interests. So whenever a browser is launched, 200 years of physics-driving computer development is commemorated.

▶ *See also* **Astronomy • Data Visualization • Mathematics • Navigation**

Resources

Books

Harrison, P. *Quantum Wells, Wires and Dots: Theoretical and Computational Physics*. 3rd ed. West Sussex, UK: Wiley, 2009.

Kaku, Michio. *Physics of the Future: How Science Will Shape Human Destiny and Our Daily Lives by the Year 2100*. New York: Doubleday, 2011.

It Bears Repeating

Physics calculations are often large, but repetitious. As such, they are perfect motivators for the development of computers, which handle such calculations extremely well.

Klein, Andi. *Introductory Computational Physics.* Cambridge, UK, and New York: Cambridge University Press, 2010.

Landau, Rubin H., Manuel Jose Paez Mejia, and Cristian C. Bordeianu. *Computational Physics: Problem Solving with Computers.* 2nd ed. Weinheim, Germany: Wiley-VCH, 2007.

Morsch, Oliver. *Quantum Bits and Quantum Secrets: How Quantum Physics Is Revolutionizing Codes and Computers.* Weinheim, Germany: Wiley-VCH, 2008.

Nahin, Paul J. *Number-Crunching: Taming Unruly Computational Problems from Mathematical Physics to Science Fiction.* Princeton, NJ: Princeton University Press, 2011.

Thijssen, Joseph Marie. *Computational Physics.* Cambridge, UK: Cambridge University Press, 2007, reprint. 2010.

Web Sites

CERN. "The Large Hadron Collider." http://lhc.web.cern.ch/lhc/ (accessed October 28, 2011).

Process Control

Process control is a discipline that deals with engineering and statistics. Specifically, it involves algorithms, architectures, and mechanisms needed for the proper and accurate output of tasks within a stated range. As such, process control encompasses the means by which tasks are accomplished by industries, machines, or organisms. Process control mechanisms are found in all complex systems, whether they are mechanical, electrical, or

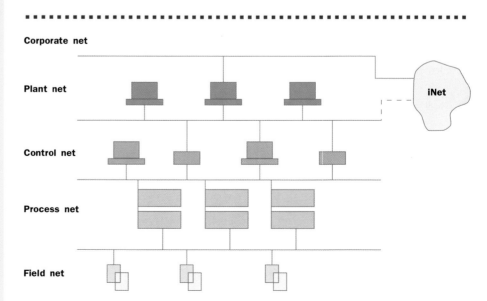

Figure 1: A generic control system architecture. *Reproduced by permission of Gale, a part of Cengage Learning.*

biological—human-made or natural. Major applications of process control are found in such continuous production industries as energy, oil refining, pulp and paper, and steel, and in such complex machines as cars, aircraft, computers, and robots.

In the context of computer science, process control is defined as the use of a computer system to automate and regulate the operations or processes of a system. One of the challenges in the industry regards the fact that processes often proliferate faster than they can be identified, defined, and managed using high-quality, reliable standards. Because of this, process control has increasingly come to include the coordination and accumulation of human expertise (organizational memory) as well as the use of machines and computerized control mechanisms.

Process control is generally a continuous (24/7, meaning 24 hours per day, 7 days per week) working effort; people responsible for process control are organized into round-the-clock staff shifts. Continuous process control is typical of the energy industries. It is also standard in crisis management, air and train control, military forces, hospitals, police and rescue services, and communications. The global economic value of these sectors is huge. All are centrally interested in avoiding operational interruptions while simultaneously improving their processes. All express the need to include, as part of process control, the sharing of information between shifts, the coordination of work processes, and the development of expertise and learning. Business culture issues, the need for high standards of quality and reliability, and time- and safety-critical concerns can prevent easy adoption of new or experimental tools, however.

Process Control Structures

An understanding of information technology (IT) architectures is necessary to comprehend the available variety of control mechanisms and processes, the ways in which they are embedded, and how they need to interrelate. Process control consists of numbers of different information systems. There are multiple ways to categorize them because different concepts are interpreted liberally. Usage varies according to vendor, user, product, or even continent. The semantics can be confusing. Most traditional ways of defining plant system architecture divide it into technical layers, as in Figure 1.

Figure 1 is an illustration of a generic system architecture. Information systems for immediate process control are contained in the bottom three layers, which are the field net, the process net, and the control net. The field net manages input and output equipment. The process net defines Proportional-Integral-Derivative (PID) controllers, motor controls, interlocking and basic logic, and calculations. It usually contains advanced features such as sequences, batches, and optimizing. The control net is where section- or department-wide control is implemented. The various functions of process control are the responsibility of different departments of an organization. Areas of process-control responsibility can usually

Shifting Focus

Process control of continuous production is being revolutionized. The energy, oil refining, pulp and paper, steel, car, and computer industries used to concentrate on automated control of complex physical machines. This is now just one layer, and the focus has moved to supporting human activity and organizational memory.

* **fuzzy logic** models human reasoning by permitting elements to have partial membership to a set; derived from fuzzy set theory

* **neural networks** pattern recognition systems whose structure and operation are loosely inspired by analogy to neurons in the human brain

be divided into production management, automation/process control, maintenance, quality, laboratory, repair, service, spare parts, raw material, stock, and materials.

Interconnectivity of Process Control

Each department is responsible for a variety of actions, each of which has its own information needs and handling mechanisms, but these are also interconnected. Interconnection is usually expedited by different systems. These include general purpose systems, process information systems, automation systems, logic systems, and special purpose systems (e.g., machine condition monitoring and diagnosis systems). These systems are responsible for a variety of activities including process monitoring, predefined tasks, disturbance control, information exchange, knowledge management, continuous development, and learning. Hardware and information systems have to span information needs at the field, process, control, plant, and corporate levels. Furthermore, these systems need to be interconnected in a user-friendly way. A challenge for IT personnel is to maintain system architectures and prevent them from becoming too complex for end-users.

The work of operating crew personnel can be illustrated on the control-net layer. They routinely monitor processes and perform predefined tasks such as starting batches or accomplishing sequences. When a disturbance occurs, operators concentrate on recovering a normal state as soon as possible. A large amount of information is handled, usually, in a short time. Sometimes process interruptions may last for weeks, and much expertise and information exchange is needed. When a solution is found, staff members have usually learned something; ideally, they share this experience with others. Based on accumulated expertise, the process continuously evolves. The development of higher levels of process control in this field of organizational memory is still in its infancy.

Organizational Memory and Process Control

The nature of automation has changed radically. Whereas earlier systems mainly followed process developments, new methods are now revolutionizing process management. Open information systems architecture has become an essential part of automation. Advanced control methods, such as fuzzy logic* and neural networks*, are combined with information and knowledge tools, memos, and reports. The so-called knowledge network is a new dimension that plays a vital role in increasing production line efficiency. When combined with history and real-time process data, it is a powerful decision-making asset for those responsible for handling disturbance management or production optimization.

The challenge is to be able to select, save, and distribute the right information to the right person at the right time with a process control system that uses standardized user interfaces and tools for collecting and storing process data. It also makes the collected data available to other systems through standard database interfaces within an overall architecture.

See also **CAC/CAM, CA Engineering** • **Embedded Technology (Ubiquitous Computing)** • **Ergonomics** • **User Interfaces**

Resources

Books

Ashby, William Ross. *An Introduction to Cybernetics.* London: Chapman & Hall, 1956.

Bao, Jie, and Peter L. Lee. *Process Control: The Passive Systems Approach.* London: Springer, 2007.

Bertalanffy, Ludwig von. *General System Theory.* New York: George Braziller, 1969.

Smith, Cecil L. *Practical Process Control: Tuning and Troubleshooting.* Hoboken, NJ: Wiley, 2009.

Wiener, Norbert. *Cybernetics: Or, Control and Communication in the Animal and the Machine.* Cambridge, MA: MIT Press, 1965.

Web Sites

McMaster University. "Welcome to the Process Control Education Web Site." http://www.pc-education.mcmaster.ca/ (accessed October 18, 2012).

Sun Microsystems delivers Staroffice 7 software. © *AP Images/PR NEWSWIRE.*

Productivity Software

Computer software consists of programs that control computer hardware (systems software) and programs that help users solve problems (application software). System software consists of operating systems (e.g., Google's Android, IBM's z/OS, Apple's iOS, Linux, and Microsoft's Windows), device drivers, utilities, and programming languages. Application software consists of a variety of programs that help individuals or groups perform tasks effectively. Application software is divided into different categories based on how it is used. These categories include word processing, spreadsheet software, data management, entertainment, education, and many others. One of the ways to categorize application software is to group word processing, spreadsheets, data management software, and presentation software into a category termed *productivity software*.

Word Processing Software

Word processing software has replaced the typewriter to manipulate text. It can be used to produce documents, such as letters, reports, papers, and manuscripts. Word processing software is the most widely used type of software. Word processing software is used by students to write reports and papers, by business people to produce memorandums and reports, and by scientists to write research papers and grants. Modern word processing software is termed WYSIWYG, or What You See Is What You Get editors. This stems from the fact that how a document appears on screen is how it will appear in print. This is in contrast to older word processing software that used markup and codes to denote formatting changes and often had little visual similarities between how a document looked on-screen versus how it looked when printed.

Word processing software enables users to edit, revise, store, format, and print documents. With word processing software, a user easily can delete, insert, and replace text; use the search-and-replace feature to make global changes to a document; and highlight areas of text (block) on which to perform actions such as move or copy. The user can create informative tables, and may incorporate images from clip art files or other sources to add clarity or drama to a document. Once the content of a document is set, the user can change the layout and style of the printed page using formatting features of the software such as margins, page orientation (landscape/portrait), justification, and line spacing. Spelling and grammar checkers allow the document to be checked for misspellings and grammatical errors. A useful feature of word processing systems is the ability to track changes (e.g., deleted text, re-worded text) made to a document, making it possible for more than one person to edit a document and see changes made by another editor. A thesaurus helps the user pick alternate words, and the word count feature provides a quick way to know how many words a document contains. Many word processing programs contain mail-merge options to print customized form letters and have formatting options for printing envelopes and labels. Common word processing software includes Microsoft Word, Corel WordPerfect, and IBM (International Business Machines Corporation) Lotus Word Pro.

Spreadsheet Software

Spreadsheet software applications, sometimes referred to as electronic spreadsheets, perform calculations based on numbers and formulas entered by users. The data can be presented in a traditional accounting format or transformed into graphics such as pie charts, bar graphs, and other visual representations of the information.

Traditional, non-electronic spreadsheets consisted of grids of rows and columns printed on special green paper used by accountants to produce financial projections and reports. In 1978, American computer scientist Daniel Bricklin (1951–), a student at Harvard Business School (Harvard University), created the first electronic spreadsheet (Visi-Calc). It allowed users to create tables and financial information by entering data into rows and columns arranged as a grid on a computer screen. Spreadsheet software like VisiCalc and its successors, which automated many functions of financial record keeping and data analysis, helped build the popularity of microcomputers as business tools. Electronic spreadsheets also are used by individuals to track household budgets and balance checkbooks, by business people to create budgets, and by educators to track student grades.

To use an electronic spreadsheet, numbers are entered in cells (the intersection of a row and a column). Cells are given a name consisting of the column letter (such as A–Z) and the row number (such as 1–100). The user indicates how these numbers are to be manipulated using formulas or functions. For example, on a household budget spreadsheet, a formula can be created to add the household monthly expenses and store the results in cell B20. The formula, =SUM (B1:B19), would sum the values stored in the range of cells starting in B1 and through cell B19. Another formula, =B21–B20, could be created to subtract the expenses (in cell B20) from the income (in cell B21) on a household budget spreadsheet. Most spreadsheets also offer a variety of pre-defined formulas termed functions that provide powerful mathematical calculations. Typically, these functions are divided into a variety of categories including financial functions (e.g., depreciation, future value, net present value), date and time functions, mathematical and trigonometric functions (e.g., absolute value, sine, cosine, pi), statistical functions (e.g., average, median, variance, standard deviation), and database functions (e.g., average or count the values in a column), to name a few. In 2012, some of the most popular spreadsheet software packages included IBM's Lotus 1-2-3, Microsoft's Excel, Intuit's Quicken, and Corel's Quattro Pro.

Both word processing and spreadsheet software is progressing towards online distribution. Google developed Google Docs, which is a Web-based office productivity suite that includes a word processor, presentation, and spreadsheet programs. This type of Web-based system allows users to create and work on their files in real-time for sharing and multiple user editing purposes. As of April 2012, Google Docs is offered through the Google Drive cloud storage system.

Database Software

Database software provides a flexible way to join and summarize information from more than one file. Databases are designed, built, and populated with data for a specific purpose and for an intended group of users. Databases help people keep track of things. For example, a high school has a database with information about its students—names, identification numbers, addresses, years in school, grade point averages, and so on. These data are used by the school administration to know how many students are enrolled in the school and determine what kinds of classes are needed for these students. Databases are designed, built, maintained, and queried using a set of tools termed a database management system (DBMS). Some common database software packages include Microsoft Access, Oracle Database, FileMaker Pro (by FileMaker), and Microsoft SQL Server.

Desktop Publishing, Graphics, and Presentation Software

Desktop publishing software expands the capabilities of word processing software by incorporating graphic design techniques. These techniques enhance the format and appearance of a document to produce professional-quality newspapers, newsletters, brochures, books, and magazines. Common desktop publishing software includes Adobe PageMaker, Microsoft Publisher, Quark Xpress (by Quark Software), and Corel Ventura.

Graphics software helps users to create, edit, and manipulate images. Graphics software can be classified into two major types: (1) presentation graphics used to communicate or make a presentation of data to others, and (2) analytical graphics used to make numeric data easier to analyze (e.g., bar charts, line graphs, pie charts). Common graphics software packages include Adobe Illustrator, Serif Harvard Graphics, Crystal Graphics PowerPlugs, Adobe Flash, CorelDraw, and Corel Painter. Many graphics packages specialize in manipulating photographs (e.g., Adobe Photoshop, Microsoft Picture It, or Corel Photo-Paint) or business charts and graphs, such as flowcharts (e.g., Microsoft Visio, Smart Draw). Many graphics packages allow the creation of three-dimensional (3-D) graphics and wireframe models or images that resemble paintings or sketches.

Presentation software provides the tools that users need to combine text, graphics, animations, and sound into a series of electronic slides. Many executives or public speakers rely on presentation software such as Microsoft PowerPoint, Apple Keynote, or IBM Lotus Freelance Graphics to create interesting and informative speeches. Educators use this software in the classroom. Researchers use electronic slides to present their research results at conferences. Business people use slides to make reports or give sales presentations. Both PowerPoint and Freelance contain collections of images and sounds to enhance presentations and provide features to animate both text and graphics. Once a set of slides has been created, it can be viewed as a computer slide show or printed as overhead transparencies, paper copies, or 35 millimeter (mm) slides.

Integrated Productivity Software

Integrated productivity software packages combine features of several applications programs into one software package that is sold as a unit. Popular integrated packages in 2012 include Microsoft Office and Apache OpenOffice. The benefit of using an integrated package is that the individual applications are designed to work well together, and a user can easily exchange files created in different parts of the integrated package. In addition, the user interface of the package has been integrated so that the user does not need to learn different ways of interfacing with each individual application. Software suites also integrate different applications into one software package. However, the amount of cohesiveness among the applications in a software suite may not be as complete as in an integrated package. OpenOffice is a free, open source software suite that is available for various platforms and allows users to format files as Microsoft Office files for file sharing.

Groupware

Another type of application software program that is growing in popularity is groupware, also known as collaboration software. This software provides a way for more than one person to collaborate on a project by maintaining a pool of data that can be shared by members of a workgroup. Typically, groupware software combines single-user applications such as calendars, word processors, and databases into a multi-user application along with an electronic meeting system (EMS). The scheduling component of the groupware system helps to coordinate coworkers' electronic date books or appointment calendars. Groupware can also contain workflow software that helps workers understand and redesign the steps that compose a particular process. In general, groupware is thought to improve productivity by keeping members of a group in contact with one another via calendars and documents. One groupware system, IBM Lotus Notes, uses a very large database containing work records, memos, and notations, and combines it with a multi-function messaging system. The most popular groupware system in use today is Microsoft Exchange Server, used to manage e-mail and schedules for corporations, governments, and other medium to large organizations. Microsoft Outlook is the traditional client used to interact with Exchange as well as a provided Web-based e-mail client. Microsoft SharePoint has also recently been developed to help provide content creation and sharing capabilities.

Other Productivity Software

A few companies have developed tax preparation software for filing federal and state income tax returns. An individual or a business can use these programs to calculate owed tax and itemize deductions. The returns can either be submitted online or printed for mailing and for keeping records. The preparation of tax returns through these software packages is a step-by-step process. The software must be purchased annually for tax preparation, but enables individuals to file their own tax returns rather than paying a tax professional for this service. Examples of such software are Intuit's TurboTax and H&R Block's TaxCut.

Ironically, whether these productivity tools actually make their users more productive is questionable. While many researchers believe that these software applications actually decrease productivity, others are convinced that people are more productive when using productivity software.

 See also **Database Management Systems • Hollerith, Herman • Office Automation Systems**

Resources

Books

Andresen, Katheryn A. *The Law and Business of Computer Software.* 10th ed. Eagan, MN: Thomson/West, 2010.

Parsons, June Jamrich, and Dan Oja. *Computer Concepts.* 8th ed. Boston: Course Technology Cengage Learning, 2011.

What If Analysis

In addition to providing standard calculating formulas and functions, electronic spreadsheets provide modeling capabilities that allow users to describe real-world situations and then test a variety of possible outcomes using different numbers. This ability to perform a what-if analysis is a useful tool. Users can investigate what would happen if sales increase by 10 percent or decrease by 5 percent, or students can determine the semester grade implications of earning an A grade on the next examination— or a B or C.

Web Sites

How Stuff Works. "What Is So Productive about Productivity Software?" http://computer.howstuffworks.com/productivity-software.htm (accessed October 18, 2012).

PC World. "Productivity Software: Best of 2010." http://www.pcworld.com/article/208136/software_services_pcworld_100.html (accessed October 18, 2012).

Project Management

To understand project management, it is necessary to have a clear understanding of what a project is. A project exists to achieve some goal and once that goal has been achieved, the project is finished. Projects do not carry on indefinitely; they have a start, a lifetime, and an end. Projects can range from such challenging undertakings as sending a person to the Moon to more everyday tasks such as building a house. A complex project may involve thousands of people working over a number of years to achieve a goal; a simple project may involve only a single person working for a short time.

Project management involves organizing the actions needed to achieve the project goal. The two primary aspects of project management are project planning and project tracking. Project planning involves defining how you will achieve the goal, including listing the specific tasks required. Project tracking means looking at how the project is progressing and comparing that to the plan that describes how you expected things to happen.

Project Planning

The first step in project planning is to define very clearly what the goal of the project is. A clear goal is necessary so that everybody involved can agree on what constitutes a finished project. For example, the goal of a project to build a house could be that the house has everything necessary for living in it except for the furniture. This implies that the house includes plumbing, electricity, and decorations. Exactly what is required to meet the goal must then be spelled out in detail.

▶

Figure 1: PERT chart showing dependencies between tasks. *Reproduced by permission of Gale, a part of Cengage Learning.*

Figure 2. Gantt chart showing project schedule. *Reproduced by permission of Gale, a part of Cengage Learning.*

◀

Once the project has a clear goal, the next step in project planning is to define the tasks that need to be completed to achieve this goal. For example, the project to build a house includes the following general tasks:

1. Lay the foundation
2. Build the structure (walls, floors etc.)
3. Install the roof
4. Install plumbing
5. Install electricity
6. Decorate the house.

Ideally, a project plan would include these general categories, plus the sub-tasks that must be accomplished within each category to constitute a finished task. Without a detailed list of the necessary tasks and sub-tasks, it is very difficult to plan a project accurately.

Once tasks are identified, they must be organized to reflect the dependencies between them. Some tasks depend on the output of others. For example, decorating the house cannot be started until the structure has been built and the roof has been installed. In our example, we have defined six tasks but a complex project may have hundreds of interdependent tasks. To help manage this complexity, a technique termed Program Evaluation and Revue Technique (PERT) was developed by the U.S. Navy for its Polaris missile project. Project planning using PERT involves drawing a diagram, termed a PERT chart, to show the dependencies between the tasks. On a PERT chart, the tasks are represented as arrows and events are represented as circles. One event that will appear on all PERT charts is the end of the project. The time order of the tasks on a PERT chart is from left to right, so the end of the project event will be the rightmost, however, the PERT chart does not say anything about the actual duration of the tasks. Figure 1 shows a PERT chart for our build-a-house project. Event A is the start of the project and event E is the end of the project. This PERT chart shows the dependencies between the six general tasks we have defined.

As well as identifying the tasks to be performed, it is necessary to estimate how much work it will take to complete the task. Table 1 shows estimates for how long each of the house building tasks will take.

Based on the time estimates for the tasks and the list of dependencies between tasks, a schedule can be created. The schedule maps the project

Table 1. Chart showing estimated time needed for each task. *Reproduced by permission of Gale, a part of Cengage Learning.*

Task Number	Task Name	Estimate (in weeks)
1	Lay the foundation	8 weeks
2	Build the structure (walls, floors etc.)	6 weeks
3	Put on the roof	3 weeks
4	Install plumbing	2 weeks
5	Install electricity	4 weeks
6	Decorate the house	3 weeks

tasks to time, indicating when individual tasks will be completed and ultimately when the complete project will be finished. Just as the PERT chart is a good way to identify and track dependencies between tasks, Gantt charts are useful for representing project schedules in a graphic format. The Gantt chart displays a list of tasks. For each task, it shows when in time it will be performed. Figure 2 shows a Gantt chart for the build-a-house project. As shown on the PERT chart, tasks 1, 2, and 3 are scheduled sequentially, due to dependencies among them, while tasks 4, 5, and 6 are scheduled simultaneously, because there are no dependencies between them.

Project Tracking

While the project is underway, the project manager must focus on tracking the progress of the project. Project tracking involves comparing the actual progress of the project against the plan for the project. While the project is running, the project manager may modify the plan to take account of unexpected events that happen during the project.

Planning and Tracking Tools

Many software tools are available to support project management. These tools typically support a number of graphical descriptions of the project including PERT and Gantt charts. The software tools will check that the various representations of the project are consistent, highlighting any inconsistencies. Although software tools can be very helpful in managing a project, it is important to remember that the software will not manage the project for you. The project manager must do the project planning and tracking; the software is only a tool to support the project manager.

Project management for software development efforts often becomes an exercise in tracking and managing the resolution of bugs. Software programmers can use bug-tracking software to keep a record of bugs, or errors, reported for a particular project. This software may allow users to report a bug for a piece of software or the program may be intended for internal tracking of progress within a software development company. Generally, details about the bug such as time of occurrence, specific error information, and method of reproducing the bug are included in reporting. As a bug is fixed, developers can add additional information about what caused the bug and what action was taken to correct the issue. Information about which version of the software will contain the bug fix is critical to allow end-users to decide when they need to update to a new version. Bugzilla, initially developed for Mozilla and licensed under the

Mozilla Public License, is a web-based bug-tracking and testing tool that was released as open source software in 1998.

Project management is about organizing actions to achieve some goal. The principles of project management are the same no matter what the goal of the project is. The example we have used is of building a house but the same principles apply to other types of projects including the development of computer hardware and software.

▶ *See also* **Decision Support Systems • Information Systems • Office Automation Systems**

Resources

Books

Burke, Rory. *Fundamentals of Product Management; Tools and Techniques.* Ringwood, NJ: Burke Publishing, 2010.

Hughes, Bob, and Mike Cotterell. *Software Project Management.* 5th ed. London: McGraw-Hill Higher Education, 2009.

Marchewka, Jack T. *Information Technology Project Management: Providing Measurable Organizational Value.* 4th ed. Hoboken, NJ: Wiley, 2012.

Rothman, Johanna. *Manage It!: Your Guide to Modern, Pragmatic Project Management.* The pragmatic programmers. Raleigh, NC: Pragmatic Bookshelf, 2007.

Web Sites

Bugzilla. "Home" http://www.bugzilla.org/ (accessed October 31, 2012).

Railroad Applications

To increase the safety and reliability of its trains and railways, railroads have integrated computer controlled, GPS-enabled information management systems. The railroads, however, struggle with the inherent difficulties of integrating cutting-edge technologies with decades-old infrastructure*. The railroad company must monitor each locomotive, car, maintenance crew member, train crew member, passenger, railway switch, crossroad signal, and piece of cargo for maximum efficiency. It even needs to monitor bad weather.

From Telegraphs to Satellites

In 1851, the railroads discovered that the newly invented telegraph* gave engineers and train station operators a new ability to communicate among themselves. For the first time, the arrival and departure of trains

* **infrastructure** the foundation or permanent installation necessary for a structure or system to operate

* **telegraph** a communication channel that uses cables to convey encoded low bandwidth electrical signals

Engineers analyze data during train inspection. © *AP Images/Stewart Cairns.*

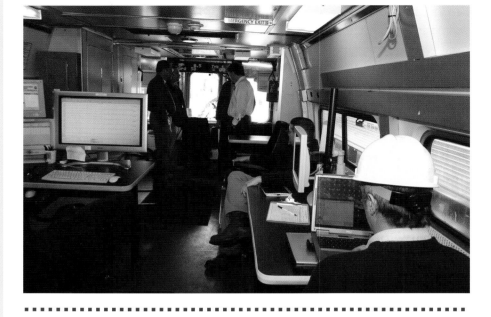

* **minicomputers** computers midway in size between a desktop computer and a mainframe computer; most modern desktops are much more powerful than the older minicomputers

could be coordinated safely, which was especially important when multiple trains shared a single track. Later, when the telephone was invented, train management again improved.

In the 1970s, the first modern computers bought by the railroads were minicomputers* that recorded and stored critical information in databases. Although the databases represented a significant improvement over paper records, they worked independently of each other: one was for scheduling crews, one for planning cargo shipments, one for moving locomotives, and so on. The databases could not communicate with each other, and most were updated only on a nightly or sometimes weekly basis.

In the 1980s, companies adopted a new train-tracking system using bar codes painted on the sides of rail cars. As the trains passed by, the bar codes were scanned and the data was sent to the local computer. In actual operations, however, the bar codes got dirty or the paint wore off so scanners could not read them all at high speeds.

Credit-card-sized electronic tags, called transponders, replaced the bar codes. Each one sent out a radio signal that could be read as the train passed by a reader placed along the railway. The technology worked successfully at speeds exceeding 130 kilometers (80 miles) per hour, but the data were collected in local databases, which were not networked together.

In the mid-1990s, railroad companies began linking their databases. The trackside readers became part of an electronic data interchange network that collected data in a worldwide database for the entire rail industry. With these new tools, analysts could spot trends and plan solutions for improved service.

Some railroads consolidated their trackers and analysts in a central operations room, from which they could control almost every aspect of the entire railway quickly. With the aid of these computerized systems, the operators had fast access to every locomotive, train, signal, and switch on the system.

Some railroad companies adopted satellite tracking in 2000. For example, the CXS Railroad equipped 3,000 locomotives with) global positioning system (GPS)* technology so the company could track the fuel data and location of each car to within 100 meters (110 yards).

Conversion Challenges

Operating a railroad is so complex that when something goes wrong, the effects ripple throughout the company and the communities it serves. For example, in June 1999 Norfolk Southern Railroad attempted to create a single combined computer system to replace its primary train control system and that of the newly acquired part of Conrail, the Consolidated Rail Corporation. The switch from the old systems to new ones—called a *conversion*—took place on a single day, but the difficulties lasted for many months.

The first problem became evident immediately when, on conversion day, the wrong magnetic storage tape was loaded onto the new system. The tape held old data ("test data") instead of real information, which tracked real-life trains, crews, and shipments.

The system began creating incorrect waybills, or instructions, which sent trains and cars to the wrong destinations. In some cases, trains filled with cargo sat idle in train yards waiting for crews that never arrived. Several cars held loads that were never emptied as the cars moved undetected back and forth between terminals. Other trains traveled successfully to their intended destination but were empty of cargo. Crews worked overtime and certain crew members, who by law cannot work overtime, had to wait for fresh replacements.

Average train speed dropped from 32 kilometers (20 miles) per hour to 26.9 kilometers (16.7 miles) per hour causing widespread congestion and even slower shipments. Extra trains were added for extraordinarily important shipments, which added to the delays. In Ohio, rail cars blocked a traffic intersection causing emergency vehicles to take a 34-kilometer (21-mile) detour around them.

As the delays increased, shippers pulled their cargo from the railroad, choosing instead to send shipments by truck. Even the Norfolk Southern Railroad was forced to spend millions of dollars ($29 million in June of 1999 alone) to ship cargo for its best customers by alternative means.

In time, the problems receded. Six months after the conversion, the new computer system was operational and experiencing only a few glitches.

Increasing vehicle fuel costs again have made trains a popular and increasingly economical means of transporting both cargo and commuters. In 2007, the average cargo efficiency for U.S. trains was the movement of about 435.8 tons of cargo one mile on one gallon of fuel. Freight rail traffic in the United States is expected to increase by 80 to 100 percent by 2050. Such increases require a substantial investment in

* **Global Positioning System (GPS)** a method of locating a point on the Earth's surface that uses received signals transmitted from satellites to calculate position accurately

Bullet Trains

Japan's *Shinkansen* or bullet trains, inaugurated in 1964, were the world's first high-speed trains. Today, they can reach speeds of 300 kilometers per hour and are enormously popular. On average, more than 16 million passengers per day use the bullet trains in the eastern Honshu and Tokyo areas alone.

AI Software for the Dutch Railways

The many possible combinations of crew tasks, inconsistent train schedules, and constantly changing crew data make scheduling railway crew members a complex task. The Dutch Railways, Nederlandse Spoorwegen (NS), found that moving to computerized schedules was not easy, either. Tests of software that created the schedules on its own were disappointing because the software could not adapt easily to changing circumstances or manage the vast number of possible crew combinations. The human planners also found they could not tinker with the software's variables in mid- process to try alternatives.

Since 1996, the railroad has used software that relies heavily on artificial intelligence (AI) technology. The combination of human intervention and computer assistance is powerful. Without computers, twenty-four planners working full-time for six to twelve months were needed to schedule 5,000 engineers and train guards. With the AI software, the same task can be accomplished by five people in about two weeks.

the technological infrastructure of railroads to make them run at peak efficiency with optimal safety.

Positive Train Control

The Positive Train Control (PTC) project, run by the U.S. Department of Transportation's Federal Railroad Administration (FRA), promotes the use of GPS-enabled computerized technology to manage and control all railroad and rail yard operations in the United States and Canada.

The project's primary goal is to reduce the probability of collisions and promote lineworker and public safety. In addition, project planners hope to reduce train delays, increase running-time reliability, increase track capacity, and improve the use of crews and equipment. The project began with a series of program tests conducted in cooperation with railroad companies. The Rail Safety Improvement Act of 2008 sets 2015 as a deadline for full implementation of PTC technology.

 See also **Aircraft Flight Control • Astronomy • Display Devices • Navigation**

Resources

Web Sites

American Association of Railroads. http://www.aar.org (accessed November 2, 2012).

Federal Railroad Administration. "Positive Train Control." http://www.fra.dot.gov/Pages/784.shtml (accessed November 2, 2012).

S

Scientific Visualization

The term visualization for scientific computing, shortened to scientific visualization, refers to the methodology of quickly and effectively displaying scientific data. Once a computer experiment has been performed, the results must be interpreted. As the volume of data accumulated from computations or from recorded measurements increases, it becomes more important to analyze data quickly. It is also important to design future experiments focused on examining interesting relationships. While looking at statistics can provide insights, it is difficult for the human mind to comprehend large volumes of numbers. Visualization techniques are another approach for interpreting large data sets, providing insights that might be missed by statistical methods.

Scientific visualization is the process of representing raw data output as images that can aid in understanding the meaning of the computer experiment results. However, the purpose of scientific visualization is insight. The pictures provide a vehicle for thinking about the data. Scientific visualization is an external aid to enhance human cognitive abilities for discovery, decision-making, and exploration. Emphasizing parameters of interest using color and highlighting may be necessary to draw attention to particular features. Animation can draw out features dependent on time and help clarify the size and relative position of features.

This technique of converting data into static graphical pictures or dynamic animations works because human beings are inherently better at analyzing information if it is in visual form. The two sides of the human brain function differently. The left side of the brain helps with analytical calculations, verbal communications, and abstract symbols. In contrast, the right side of the brain emphasizes spatial, intuitive, or holistic thinking. Graphical representations of data stimulate this part of the brain. Representing a data set visually allows the scientist to view an entire complex situation. Using this approach, a scientist is able to get an overall picture of the data. Later a scientist may use a more analytical method to examine certain anomalies or patterns in the data.

Applications

The main reasons for using scientific visualization are the following: it compresses large volumes of data into a limited number of pictures; it can reveal the correlation between different quantities both in space and time; it can furnish new space-like structures beside the ones which are already known from previous calculations; and it opens up the possibility

A composite image of Earth created using data from Defense Meteorological Satellite Program (DMSP) Operational Linescan System. © *AP Images/NASA Goddard Space Flight Center - Scientific Visualization Studio, Craig Mayhew and Robert Simmon*

* **central processing unit (CPU)** the part of a computer that performs computations and controls and coordinates other parts of the computer

* **tomography** the process of capturing and analyzing three-dimensional (3-D) X-ray images

to view the data selectively and interactively in real time. By following the motions of structures in time, one can gain insight into complicated dynamics. It is also very useful to have the possibility to change parameters interactively and to immediately see the effect of this change. This process is called computational steering. It increases the effective use of central processing unit (CPU)* time.

Scientific visualization is used in business to organize, identify, and communicate trends in market and customer data that are obscured or too small to see without amplification. Scientific visualization is used in astronomy to visualize objects known to exist but not directly observed such as black holes, gravitational waves, and collisions of neutron stars. Scientific visualization is used in medicine to visualize cell growth, assist in medical diagnosis, and prepare surgeons for operations. A common example of scientific visualization is the combination of atmospheric data with color, placement, illumination, and texture for use in television weather programs. Two notable scientific visualizations are the visualization of ash plumes from volcanic eruptions, and the visualization of the Visible Human (a part of the Visible Human Project by the U.S. National Library of Medicine) from microtomed traversal and computed tomography* scans.

Related Domains and Techniques

Scientific visualization uses techniques from the fields of computer animation, computer graphics, image processing, computer vision, computer-aided design, human-computer interaction, and signal processing. Scientific visualization is closely related to the new field of data mining*. While scientific visualization seeks to illuminate known relationships within data, seeks to uncover previously unknown relationships within data.

Software Tools

Images have long been a part of science. In the Renaissance period, Italian astronomer Galileo (1564–1642) interspersed his writings with drawings of the moons of Jupiter and anatomical sketches. Today, more powerful computers and new graphic tools are creating opportunities to visualize events previously too small, too far, or too obscure for a human to see.

Scientific visualization tools range from custom software built specifically for handling certain classes of algorithm*s, to general-purpose visualization systems that support a variety of techniques and handle a wide variety and range of data types. Graphical software tools used in scientific visualization include self-organizing maps, charts, graphs, scatterplots, zoom, sort, overview/detail, fly-throughs, and hierarchies.

It is important to differentiate between scientific visualization and presentation graphics. Not all computer graphics packages qualify as visualization systems. Presentation graphics are primarily concerned with the communication of information and results in ways that are easily understood. In scientific visualization, one seeks to better understand the data. However, the two methods are often intertwined. The two most common underlying approaches to transforming data into visual representations are graphical primitives and data sampling. Graphical primitives involve filtering data to extract information and map these data using geometric primitives such as points, lines, or polygons. Data sampling involves moving data into structured grid fields of different types (uniform, rectilinear, irregular) using interpolation and extrapolation.

Availability

There are many companies that produce and sell visualization software. Non-profit organizations, such as government and academia, also create and distribute scientific visualization software, often for free. The National Science Foundation (NSF) sponsors research in a variety of scientific and engineering fields, including scientific visualization. An example of collaboration between government and academia is the creation of the software package VisTrails. The software was developed at the Scientific Computing and Imaging Institute located at the University of Utah, with funding provided by the NSF. VisTrails is an advanced visualization software package designed with large data sets and intricate visualizations in mind. First released as version 1.0 in 2007, version 1.4 was available for download in early 2010. In 2011, version 1.7 of VisTrails was formally released. While VisTrails itself is available for users free of charge, additional support and specialized features are available for a fee from VisTrails, Inc., which is a spin-off company formed by the program's creators and the University of Utah.

Galileo

Galileo Galilei (often referred to simply as Galileo) was a seventeenth-century astronomer and mathematician who discovered the moons of Jupiter. Using a telescope that he developed, Galileo observed four moons orbiting the planet. This discovery was not well received by the scientific and religious communities, as most believed that all objects in the heavens revolved around earth. Galileo also plotted the phases of Venus and observed sunspots.

* **data mining** a technique of automatically obtaining information from databases that is normally hidden or not obvious

* **algorithm** a rule or procedure used to solve a mathematical problem—most often described as a sequence of steps

* **pixel** a single picture element on a video screen; one of the individual dots making up a picture on a video screen or digital image

Research on New Uses

Scientific visualization has already had a great impact on scientific work by making the evaluation of computer experiments easier and helping the scientist to gain more insight into unknown aspects of scientific problems. Datasets are growing at a substantial rate as researchers explore science in greater detail. Effectively visualizing volumes of data using only one million pixel*s in the average computer display requires new methods of visualization. Current scientific visualization research focuses on combining data from multiple sources in the same visualization, developing new tools to help users find what they are looking for using visual search engines, and providing collaborative visualization between geographically remote sites.

Laboratories performing research in the field of scientific visualization include the Electronic Visualization Laboratory (EVL, http://www.evl.uic.edu/), at the University of Illinois in Chicago, and the NASA Goddard Scientific Visualization Studio (SVS, http://svs.gsfc.nasa.gov/) in Greenbelt, Maryland. The NASA facility states that its mission "is to facilitate scientific inquiry and outreach within NASA programs through visualization. To that end, the SVS works closely with scientists in the creation of visualization products, systems, and processes in order to promote a greater understanding of Earth and Space Science research activities at Goddard Space Flight Center and within the NASA research community."

 See also **Data Visualization • Pattern Recognition • Physics**

Resources

Books

Mazza, Riccardo. *Introduction to Information Visualization*. London: Springer, 2009.

Wright, Helen. *Introduction to Scientific Visualization*. New York: Springer, 2006.

Web Sites

Georgia Tech College of Computing. "Scientific Visualization Tutorials." http://www.cc.gatech.edu/scivis/tutorial/tutorial.html (accessed October 18, 2012).

NASA Goddard Space Flight Center. "Scientific Visualization Studio." http://svs.gsfc.nasa.gov/ (accessed October 22, 2012).

ScienceDaily.com. "Scientific Visualization." http://www.sciencedaily.com/articles/s/scientific_visualization.htm (accessed October 18, 2012).

University of Illinois. "Electronic Visualization Laboratory." http://www.evl.uic.edu/ (accessed October 22, 2012).

Security Applications

Security applications programs are designed to protect computer files, operating systems, and program software, particularly on computers that are connected to networks or are otherwise subject to attack from outside locations. Security programs may be designed to detect the effects of intrusive activity, identify intrusive activity while it is occurring, look for vulnerabilities that might be exploited by an intruder, or help prevent intrusive activity.

Intrusive activity can take place directly, as in the case of an unauthorized user sitting down at an unattended computer and taking some action that affects the data, system, or program software in some way. More commonly, however, computer intruders gain unauthorized access through network or online connections. An intruder may alter programs or data contained in the computer, either as an end in itself or to allow future break-ins. An intruder may also install processes on the attacked machine to use in attacking other computers. Distributed Denial of Service (DDoS)* tools that flood a victim with large amounts of network traffic are an example of the latter.

A well-known tool for detecting modified program or data files is Tripwire. An open-source security and data integrity software package, Tripwire computes a cryptographic checksum* for each file that is to be protected and stores this information in a safe place, preferably on write-protected removable media. Periodically, and especially when an intrusion is detected, Tripwire is used to recalculate the file checksums. A change in the indicates a change in the file. If an intrusion has occurred, it may be necessary to examine disks and run Tripwire from a clean copy of the operating system because clever intruders can replace programs, including Tripwire, with versions that have been designed to hide their tracks.

Intrusion detection systems are programs that examine a network or a computer for signs of intrusive activity. Signature-based systems have a built-in model of intrusive activity; they attempt to detect activity known to be intrusive. Anomaly-based systems, by comparison, use a model of normal activity; abnormal activities then become a trigger for suspecting an intrusion. Either form of intrusion detection system (IDS) may rely on a variety of sources of information.

Network-based IDSs examine the packets* that flow over a segment of a local network. Host-based IDSs get their information from system logs or from information supplied by individual applications. Each approach has strengths and weaknesses. Network-based systems cannot see inside encrypted such as those used by Secure Sockets Layer (SSL)* or Virtual Private Networks (VPNs)*. In addition, network-based systems have difficulty in keeping up with the high speed (100 base T and gigabit) networks that are becoming common.

Host-based systems cannot easily detect activities such as probes that attempt to discover which hosts are on the network and which ports they support. Signature-based systems can, in general, only detect attacks that

* **distributed denial of service (DDoS)** an attack in which large numbers of messages are directed to send network traffic to a target computer, overloading it or its network connection; typically, the attacking computers have been subverted

* **checksum** a number that is derived from adding together parts of an electronic message before it is dispatched; it can be used at the receiver to check against message corruption

* **packets** collections of digital data elements that are part of a complete message or signal; packets contain their destination addresses to enable reassembly of the message or signal

* **Secure Sockets Layer (SSL)** a technology that supports encryption, authentication, and other facilities and is built into standard UNIX communication protocols (sockets over TCP/IP)

* **Virtual Private Networks (VPNs)** a commercial approach to network management where privately owned voice and data networks are set up on public network infrastructure

* **UNIX** operating system that
was originally developed at Bell
Laboratories in the early 1970s

* **subnet** a logical section of a
large network that simplifies
the management of machine
addresses

are both known and encoded into the program's model of intrusive activity. Anomaly-based systems can only report unusual activity, but there is no assurance that unusual means intrusive. False alarms and missed attacks are problems for both kinds of programs. Too general of signatures will trigger alarms for non-intrusive activities, whereas too specific ones will miss minor variations on known attacks. Similarly, an inadequate characterization of *normal* may lead to excessive false alarms, missed intrusions, or both. In addition, intrusion detection programs may be attacked, causing them to miss attacks or issue false alarms.

Virus detection programs are another form of security application that detects intrusive activity. The original virus detection programs looked for the artifacts of infections, examining files for the signatures of known viruses. Modern virus detection programs retain this functionality but also act like host-based intrusion detection systems, checking newly imported files, including e-mail attachments, for known viruses and removing them before they can be executed and do damage.

There are a number of security applications that examine a system for vulnerabilities that might be exploited by an attacker. One of the first was the program COPS (also called Cops Security Checker System), developed at Purdue University. COPS is a suite of security applications that checks a UNIX* system for common security vulnerabilities. Most of these involve inappropriate permission settings on system files that might allow an ordinary user to obtain root or superuser privileges. Other vulnerabilities detected include poorly formatted group and password files, individual login scripts that could be modified by others, and weak passwords.

Good systems administrators regularly run tools such as COPS and CRACK (Computer Oracle and Password System) against their systems to detect security problems and patch them; however, such tools are two-edged swords since they could help a potential intruder find system weaknesses. Whereas COPS and CRACK are host-specific, security applications such as SATAN (Security Administrator Tool for Analyzing Networks) and NMAP (Network Mapper) are intended to discover vulnerabilities in machines that are connected to the network. SATAN looks for a set of known problems and offers suggestions for fixing them. NMAP is capable of exploring a subnet* and reporting on the computers that are present. It will attempt to identify the operating system and services offered by each computer. Both SATAN and NMAP are useful to systems administrators but may be even more useful to potential attackers since the information provided may identify an attack that is likely to succeed. As a result, considerable controversy has surrounded their public release, and their developers have been both praised and criticized for their actions. According to SecTools.org, the top ten network security tools in 2011 are (in order of popularity): Wireshark, Metasploit, Nessus, Aircrack, Snort, Cain and Abel, BackTrack, Netcat, tcpdump, and John the Ripper.

Firewall programs are examples of protective security applications. Firewalls restrict the network traffic that can pass between a computer and the network by limiting the addresses with which the computer can communicate and by identifying the protocols that can be used for communication. Firewalls can be implemented on their own hardware platforms (typically the case when an enterprise is being protected), made part of a network interface component such as a cable or DSL modem, or deployed directly on the protected computer. Personal firewalls of the latter sort are sold as a component of security packages that include virus protection. Some of the more popular firewall programs in the early 2010s are Comodo Internet Security, PC Tools Firewall Plus, ZoneAlarm Pro Firewall, BitDefender Internet Security, Kaspersky Internet Security, and Online Armor.

 See also **Internet • Security Hardware • Security Software**

Resources

Books

Tambe, Milind. *Security and Game Theory: Algorithms, Deployed Systems, Lessons Learned.* Cambridge, UK, and New York: Cambridge University Press, 2012

Zalewski, Michal. *The Tangled Web: A Guide to Securing Modern Web Applications.* San Francisco: No Starch Press, 2012

Periodicals

Farmer, Daniel, and Eugene H. Spafford. *The COPS Security Checker System.* Purdue University, Report Number 90–993, 1990.

Kim, Gene, and E. H. Spafford. *Monitoring File System Integrity on Unix Platforms.* Purdue University, Technical Report Coast TR 93–02, July 1993.

Web Sites

LinuxSecurity.com. "Computer Oracle and Password System (COPS)." http://www.linuxsecurity.com/content/view/124223/161/ (accessed October 22, 2012).

NMAP.org. "NMAP." http://nmap.org/ (accessed October 22, 2012).

Porcupine.org, Dan Farmer and Wietse Venema. "Improving the Security of Your Site by Breaking Into It." http://www.porcupine. org/satan/demo/docs/admin_guide_to_cracking.html (accessed October 22, 2012).

SecTools.org. "SecTools.Org: Top 125 Network Security Tools." http:// sectools.org/ (accessed October 22, 2012).

Take a CRACK at It

CRACK, a UNIX utility developed by Alec Muffett, efficiently compares a password file containing encrypted passwords with large dictionaries (encrypted lists of words that might be used as passwords). It is fairly easy to add new dictionaries, so choosing a password from, for example, the Klingon dictionary, does not provide security.

Social Media

Social media allows users to connect, communicate, and share multimedia via Web-based or mobile technology. This interaction is usually achieved through social networking sites and applications for mobile devices such as smartphones and tablets. According to Nielsen Ratings, the polling company, as of 2012, in a survey of ten different countries Internet usage, social media has reached about three quarters of all active Internet users. Almost 80 percent of American Internet users visit social media sites and it is the main source of their time online, making four out of five active Internet users involved in social media.

Historical Development

Social media got its start early on in computing history with the creation of in 1969 with CompuServe which allowed the public to connect via the Internet. In 1971 email was used for the first time. In 1978 two computer hobbyists in Chicago invented the first message board which they called a bulletin board system (BBS). After this, in 1979 Usenet was created to connect the University of North Carolina and Duke University. A true breakthrough in social networking sites came with the creation of Prodigy in 1984. By 1990 Prodigy was the second largest online service provider. It had 465,000 subscribers. Prodigy allowed the public to access web hosting to publish Web sites. In 1993 the European Organization for Nuclear Research in Switzerland donated its World Wide Web technology to the public, effectively opening the use of the Internet up to the world. With the Internet now something accessible to the public, sites started to pop up around the Internet that allowed people to interact and connect with one another. Sites like GeoCities and Tripod allowed people to make their own Web sites and interact with one another. America Online allowed people to message one another in real time. Blogs, or online journals, such as LiveJournal, Xanga, and Blogger allowed people to post their thoughts and feelings in a open forum which attracted other users.

When MySpace launched in 2003 it was primarily a tool for bands to reach their fans, and vice versa. Sharing photos, music, announcements and more MySpace soon attracted teenagers and young adults in droves. Word of mouth increased user sign up. Users could customize their pages with HTML and other codes, and add whomever they pleased as friends and contacts.

The social media world was turned on its head with Facebook, created by Harvard student Mark Zuckerberg. It started in 2004 as a Harvard University network. Facebook slowly added more schools to the network. In 2005 it began to expand its inclusion of people. Facebook allowed people to create profiles, use different applications, and eventually share a plethora of media types. In 2011, U.S. users spent more time on Facebook than any other Web site on the Internet, and the site had 140 million visitors.

Sharing of photos and videos became very important as well. YouTube began sharing and streaming videos in 2005. By 2011 it had 2 billion video views every day.

In 2006 Biz Stone and Evan Williams and Jack Dorsey created Twitter, which allowed people to post real-time status updates and share it with their own community of users. At first Twitter was derided as un-useful, but eventually Twitter revealed itself to be an influential journalistic tool when people started to break stories in real time with it. In 2009 protestors in Iran were able to use Twitter to reveal to one another and the outside world what was happening once the government suppressed them. The use of hashtags, an archiving tool that uses a # symbol and allows other users to search for all topics with that tag, allowed protestors to communicate what was happening in real time.

Current Application

Most social networking sites have specific facets in common. When a user joins a social media and network site they are asked to find other users in the system to create a relationship. Some of these sites promote meeting people they do not know but have common interests with, some sites ask them to find people they already know in real life. These become "friends" or "contacts." An important function of social media is the ability to display social connections. This means that users can look through their friends' contact list and see if there is anyone there they know or would like to know. Many of these sites allow sharing of photos and videos. Some allow private messaging, comments. Some are only widely available over mobile devices. Many social networking sites have a "feed," or a constantly updating front page that has all of the updates from a user's contact or friends list.

Users use mobile devices to heavily engage in social media in a variety of activities such as social networking, playing games, to check into locations where they may be at the moment, and to make mobile payments. Applications, or "apps," play a major part of mobile social media. These allow users to easily use and load their favorite social media sites. In the United States 60 percent of app usage is dedicated to social networking. According to a 2012 Nielsen/McKinsey survey of social media in the United States, 2 out of 5 social media users access their social networks and media through the use of mobile phones. This included a large number of people over the age of 55.

Another 2012 Nielsen study of social media use in the United States found that the most active users of social media are 18 to 34-year-olds. Women edge out men only slightly, with Asians as the highest race and ethnicity demographic.

The emergence of social media created a whole new way for companies, newspapers, artists, and more to look at marketing. Now there was a need to create viral content which users felt the urge to share and create interactive and candid profiles on social networking sites. Interaction with users and demographics became very popular.

Many of these networking sites began to keep extensive behavioral data. From this emerged the practice of network analysis and data mining. Using data from what users post on their profile, what they link, what they search for, and interests, many analysts are able to target and tailor products to specific user or even determine if there is someone who may be a terror suspect. In 2003 the capture of Saddam Hussein was partially possible because detectives mined the data of chauffeurs rural links, and were able to track him to a farm in the town of Tikrit. Because of data mining, analysts have been able to study what causes information and ideas to be spread, trends, and more. Because of concerns over privacy as of 2012, data-mining is still an issue of contention. In 2012 the European Union warned Google, saying that this use of data-mining needed to be voluntary or it would face drastic penalties.

Social media is transforming the way the world connects and dispenses information. Media of all types, text, video, photos, commentary, editorial, is shared by users who are managing their own circles of influence.

Micro-communities

Social media also creates online micro-communities, limited groups of people with common interests. Micro-communities have had a wide-ranging impact. Advertisers have discovered that micro-communities have singled themselves out as being interested in certain topics, and marketers constantly work on finding new ways of targeting specific micro-communities with advertisements for products related to their interest. In fact, many forum hosts and bloggers are able to earn income by selling advertising space on their Web sites. For example, if one were to visit a popular cooking forum, most likely there would be ads on the side of the page for cookbooks or kitchen tools. In addition, some micro-communities allow for certain small businesses to operate. As an example, there are several independent street-food vendors in New York City that are run by a single owner-operator, and have only one truck from which they can sell their food. Fans of these vendors sign up to follow the vendor's Twitter feed, and every day the vendor posts on the website where he or she will be operating that day. Those who have signed up will receive the message on their phones or computers, so they will know where to go to find the street vendor's truck.

Social Media in Action

Social media is now the most used medium for consumer input and reviews of services. For example, traditionally a restaurant would receive a review from a local newspaper, and that review would stand until the newspaper decided to review the restaurant again. On the Internet there are many different Web sites that review restaurants, and many of them are simply a collection of reviews written by users of the site. This again encounters the issue of the veracity of information on the Internet. Anyone can post a review, whether they have eaten at a restaurant or not. Sometimes false negative or false positive reviews will be posted for myriad different reasons. However, if a Web site is popular enough to have a large number of reviews, one can get a picture of average public opinion of the restaurant. Some review sites, such as the user reviews on Google Maps, Yelp!, and OpenTable (which also serves as a means of reserving a table at a restaurant via the Internet) are so popular that they are becoming more trusted than the reviews given by traditional media. This has opened up the market for restaurants that serve simple day-to-day fare, because it avoids the bias in traditional media towards favoring sophisticated cuisine. If a restaurant is reviewed and given no stars, but the reviews online have multiple comments along the lines of "simple food but well cooked," the online reviews may attract customers who, prior to the Internet, would have overlooked the restaurant due to its low rating.

While the Internet allows access to a wide variety of information and opinions, anyone with access to a computer may post opinions and ideas online. The absence of any kind of review or fact checking process means that there is a great deal of information on the Internet that is false or simply incorrect. The concept of legislating the Internet, however, is a difficult and controversial topic.

Arab Spring Facebook and Twitter were credited with helping to galvanize support for mass demonstrations aimed at overthrowing the governments in Tunisia, Egypt, Bahrain, and Libya in early 2011. Smaller-scale, pro-reform demonstrations also occurred in Algeria, Jordan, Morocco, Syria, Yemen, and elsewhere.

In Tunisia, the public self-immolation of Mohamed Bouazizi, a young Tunisian protesting the closure and seizure of his unlicensed fruit-and-vegetable stand, spurred social network coordinated massive demonstrations that ultimately brought down the government. Analysts contended that Tunisian citizens were already angry over allegations of corruption within the Tunisian government in the wake of earlier Wikileaks revelations and that Bouazizi's protest and death created a social tipping point. (Bouazizi died on January 4, 2011, after setting himself on fire in front of a government building on December 17, 2010.)

Bouazizi was embraced as a revolutionary martyr, especially by young people. In Tunisia, unemployment rates for young people are high and Bouazizi's protest resonated across class and generational lines to force former Tunisian dictator Zine el-Abidine Ben Ali to flee to Saudi Arabia. Analysts specifically credited highly negative "live commenting" via online and social networks during a speech made by the former leader (in which he promised to lower bread prices) as critical to the collapse of the government. Former online activists took places in the interim Tunisian government and the new minister for youth affairs made a public effort to send Twitter messages from cabinet meetings concerning the transition of power.

In late January 2011, massive demonstrations in Egypt turned deadly. After days of escalating protest, Egyptian authorities more broadly blocked Internet access. According to Internet analytics experts, Egypt effectively blocked commonly used Internet connections by requiring four major Egyptian service providers to sever international connections. The action was unprecedented in Internet history. The move appeared specifically targeted at popular content connections and portals. Major infrastructure connections used by the military services, including the European-Asian fiber-optic routes, remained connected. In addition, the Egyptian Stock Exchange and major credit markets initially remained connected.

After nearly a week of protests in Cairo and other major Egyptian cities, Egyptian authorities restored general Internet service. Social media sites burst into renewed activity, with critics claiming that during the outage, government authorities created online sites to help organize pro-government groups. Clashes in virtual social media space then spilled into street fighting between anti-government protesters and supporters of Egyptian President Hosni Mubarak. The riots, largely unchecked by the Egyptian military and the absent police forces, escalated from rock throwing-clashes in the streets of Cairo centered on Tahrir Square (Liberation Square) to more deadly organized battles using automatic weapons fire and Molotov cocktails (petrol bombs) thrown from rooftops into protesting crowds. During weeks of protests, journalists and social media activists were beaten and jailed.

Internet analysts said that the Egyptian government's blocking of the Internet was a far bolder action than previously attempted by other governments facing demonstrations buoyed by online activism. Recent attempts by the Tunisian government largely failed because only specific social networking sites were blocked, leaving demonstrators the capacity to open alternative sites. Attempts by Iran to suppress Internet traffic in 2009 centered on limiting the rate of transmission, essentially trying to functionally block large media transfers and the rapid communication applications favored by many social networking sites. Impositions of packet transmission speed restrictions imposed by several governments during the 2011 protests were also designed to impair and impede online activism. SMS (text-message) traffic and cell phone service was also disrupted.

Unrest that was driven and organized by social media sites continued to spread. Protests in Iran, Bahrain, Libya, Algeria, and Yemen were met with varying degrees of repression by their respective governments. Site-specific censorship targets that promoted anti-government protests were also subject to varying levels of government interference. In multiple countries, government officials ordered ISPs to block independent or pro-opposition Web sites.

At one point after a series of alternating concessions and crackdowns by the Egyptian government, the revolution appeared to lose momentum with regard to popular support. Released from police detention, Wael Ghonim, a Google employee and one of the key organizers of the anti-government "We Are all Khaled Said" Facebook page, re-energized crowds with an emotional televised and webcast interview. The protesters in Tahrir square established a "bloggers" corner. The Al Jazeera television network devoted special coverage to Facebook pages and videos to spread news of the revolution across the Middle East. After eighteen days of protests, Mubarak resigned, leaving a military council that promised reforms and democratic elections. Al Jazeera and other global media commentators gave substantial credit for the success of the revolution to online activist and social networking Web sites. When asked which government would fall next in response to public pressure, one Egyptian protester answered, "Ask Facebook."

Many of these same media sources, however, including Al Jazeera, cautioned that labeling the demonstrations as social media revolutions diminished their human aspects. Although social media was a key communication device for activists, the revolutions required a significant amount of direct action. Protesters had to physically occupy public spaces and establish working communities of protesters to supply aid, food, water, and other necessities. Demonstrators took large personal risks that jeopardized their employment, freedom, and in some cases their lives. Echoing criticisms of the emphasis on the role of social media in the revolutions, Jillian York, co-founder of Talk Morocco and a contributor to Al Jazeera English and the *Guardian* newspaper, reminded international observers that the violence against reformers had resulted in economic hardships, injuries, imprisonment, torture, and deaths. In the case of Libya, conflicts between protesters and government escalated into civil war.

The Arab Spring protests spread to the Libyan capital of Tripoli by February 2011. Muammar Gaddafi (also transliterated as Kadafi, Qaddafi, or many other ways), who had ruled Libya since the country's 1969 revolution, claimed that demonstrations could fragment and economically cripple the nation. Both Gaddafi and his son Saif al-Islam Muammar Al-Gaddafi also claimed that the demonstrators were backed by foreign interests ranging from Western nations, to Israel, to the al-Qaeda Islamist terrorist network, and that protesters were under the influence of drugs. The government used violence to crack down on the protests, but full-scale armed revolt took hold. Opposition leaders, based in the port city of Benghazi, formed the National Transitional Council (NTC) to oversee opposition-controlled areas and help coordinate diplomatic relations with foreign governments. In August 2011, NTC forces captured Tripoli, the Libyan capital. NTC forces took the Gaddafi stronghold city of Sirte in October 2011 and captured and killed Gaddafi on October 20, 2011.

Protests calling for reform erupted in Syria in March 2011. Although Syrian leader Bashar al-Assad (1965–) acknowledged the protests in other nations and called for reform, advocates for reform noted that Syria has governed under a set of rights-limiting emergency laws since 1962. Syria only recently permitted citizens to access popular social media sites, including Facebook and YouTube, but improvements in Internet access and a loosening in government Internet censorship enabled reform activists to mobilize online quickly. On March 15, demonstrations took place in several Syrian cities. Online calls for larger protests launched the "Day of Dignity" demonstrations on March 18, 2011. State security forces in several cities used violence to quell demonstrators. Demonstrators posted videos online of security forces arresting protesters and clashing with demonstrators before the Syrian government disrupted Internet access and attempted to block social media outlets. In 2012, Syria fell into civil war.

Scholars continue to debate the extent of the role played by social media in Arab Spring Iranian protests. Like criticism of the role of social media in June 2009 protests in Iran, critics of the assertion that the protests were largely dependent on social media contend that the role of online communications is exaggerated, a manifestation of the fact that many Western journalists could, in most cases, monitor events via English-language social media.

Social Media Protests Internet Regulation Web sites, online media providers, search engines, and individual bloggers in the United States participated in an online strike in January 2012 to protest proposed legislation that would expand Internet regulation. The two bills, the Stop Online Piracy Act (SOPA) and Protect IP Act (PIPA), are supported by the entertainment industry, which wants tougher laws to combat copyright violations on the Internet. Critics of the bills argue that such legislation would do little to stop the proliferation of pirated intellectual property and that its provisions are overreaching, violate due process rights, censor online channels for free speech, and hurt technology and Internet business development. They further assert that rights holders already have several legal means to have infringing or pirated works removed from the Internet. Web sites went dark (displaying only a black screen or blacking out their logo), took their content offline, or displayed only messages informing site visitors about SOPA and PIPA and urging people to contact their Congressional representatives about opposing the legislation. Popular participating sites and search engines, many with social media components, included Wikipedia (English), Google, Craigslist, *Wired* magazine, Mozilla Foxfire, Reddit, and WordPress, among others.

Monitoring and Censorship

In times of turmoil, or as part of ongoing censorship policy, governments move to Services such as Google, Facebook, and YouTube. China's Golden Shield Project, for example, monitors and censors social networking sites, and specifically blocks Facebook. Alternative social media sites based in China are also subject to tight government control.

Resources

Periodicals

Boyd, Danah M., and Nicole B. Ellison. "Social Network Sites: Definition, History, and Scholarship." *Journal of Computer-Mediated Communication* 13, no. 1 (October 2007): 210–230.

Grossman, Levi. "Iran Protests: Twitter, the Medium of the Movement." *Time*, June 17, 2009.

Pfanner, Eric, and Kevin J. O'Brien. "Europe Presses Google to Change Privacy Policy." *The New York Times*, October 16, 2012.

"Untangling the Social Web." *The Economist* 396, no. 8698 (September 4, 2010): Technology Quarterly Section, 16–17.

Web Sites

Kimbarovsky, Ross. "10 Small Business Social Media Marketing Tips." Mashable. http://mashable.com/2009/10/28/small-business-marketing/ (accessed November 7, 2012).

Nielsen. "State of the Media: Nielsen Social Media Report Q3 2011." http://blog.nielsen.com/nielsenwire/social/ (accessed November 5, 2012).

University of North Carolina at Pembroke. "The Brief History of Social Media." http://www.uncp.edu/home/acurtis/NewMedia/SocialMedia/SocialMediaHistory.html (accessed November 5, 2012).

Software Piracy

When someone buys a commercial piece of software, such as Microsoft Office, he or she is bound by a copyright license that specifies how many machines the buyer can load with the software. Thus, an end-user license agreement (EULA) for a single user allows the buyer to load the software onto one computer, and to make a back-up copy just in case something happens to the original disk or compact disc-read only memory (CD-ROM).

Business and Personal Concerns

Companies that want all of their employees to use a particular software must buy multiple licenses, or volume licenses. Often, a volume license allows the buyer to install the software onto multiple computers or install the software on a network server, so that each user can log on to the company network and access the program. Each user on a network is termed a client and the company must pay the volume license fee for each install of the software. For home use, many software companies sell software that allows a home user to load the software onto more than one computer. Such multi-license software is usually more expensive than single-license versions, but cheaper than buying multiple copies of the single-license version.

If a person with a single user license loads the software onto a friend's machine, or if a company loads a software package onto each employee's machine without buying a volume or multiple license, then both the single

Pirated movies and software discs are gathered in China. © *AP Images/ Eyepress, File.*

* **softlifting** the act of stealing software, usually for personal use (piracy)

* **OEM** the acronym for Original Equipment Manufacturer; a manufacturer of computer components

* **counterfeiting** the act of knowingly producing non-genuine objects

user and the company have broken the terms of the software license agreement and are therefore guilty of software piracy. Software piracy involves the unauthorized use, duplication, distribution, or sale of commercially available software.

Types of Piracy

Software piracy is often described as softlifting*, counterfeiting, Internet piracy, hard-disk loading, OEM* unbundling, and unauthorized renting.

Softlifting This involves installing software with a single-user license on multiple machines, and is the most common type of software piracy within companies. The Business Software Alliance (BSA), a consortium of software developers, reports that it has collected tens of millions of dollars in penalties and court settlements from companies that pirate software. In most cases, companies cited for copyright infringement attributed illegal downloading to insufficient management control over their employees.

Counterfeiting and Internet Piracy These are similar acts and involve the unauthorized duplication, distribution, or sale of commercial software. A person who makes copies of software and sells it to others is engaging in counterfeiting*. Internet piracy involves selling the counterfeit products online, often on Internet auction sites on on illegal download services.

Hard-disk Loading, OEM Unbundling, and Unauthorized Renting These are perhaps less well-known examples of software piracy because they can appear to be legitimate practices. Hard-disk loading involves loading software onto new computers when they are sold to a customer. OEM unbundling involves selling a component of a multi-application package as a stand-alone application against the software manufacturer's wishes.

Unauthorized renting involves hiring out software in violation of single-user licenses. Most buyers have purchased PCs with pre-loaded software; however, a person buying small component software, or renting items such as videos and even computer games, would have to know something about particular software licensing agreements to realize whether the software has been pirated.

Piracy Rates

The software piracy rate can be estimated by comparing the number of personal computers sold with the number of software packages sold. Based on the assumption that for each new PC, a standard set of software would also be sold, the software piracy rate is calculated as the percentage shortfall in software sales. The financial loss is then the cost of these missing software sales. Software auditors also conduct user surveys about the nature and extent of software piracy to assist them with their estimates.

Using these methods, the BSA estimates that the software industry lost $63.4 billion in revenue in 2012 due to software piracy. The BSA's report for 2012 also revealed that 57 percent of computer users have at least one pirated copy of software installed, which represents a 17 percent increase over 2011.

In 2012, the BSA reported that 42 percent of software used worldwide had been pirated. The world's highest software piracy rates were in Latin America and Central and Eastern Europe with a 64 percent piracy rate in each region. More than thirty countries had piracy rates of greater than 75 percent.

Because of the size of their respective software markets, however, the greatest financial losses occur in the United States, China, and Russia. In 2011, software manufacturers lost more than $9.7 billion to pirated software in the United States, despite the United States having the lowest piracy rate in the world at 19 percent. Software manufacturers lost $8.9 billion and $3.2 billion in revenue in China and Russia, respectively.

Countering Piracy

The Software and Information Industry Association (SIIA) suggests a three-pronged attack on software piracy—using legislation, effective enforcement, and public education. This approach is based on the conviction that buying and selling pirated software is essentially trafficking* in counterfeit goods. Indeed, most countries provide legal protection for software by extending copyright, patent, contract, and trade secret legislation. They also recognize software as intellectual property*, just like literary creations and works of art, which are all subject to intellectual property right (IPR) protection.

Legislation enacted by the United States to combat digital theft includes the 1998 Digital Millennium Copyright Act (DMCA). The DMCA incorporates a provision, modeled on the World Intellectual Property Organization (WIPO) Copyright Treaty, which prohibits individuals from circumventing security measures that control access to software or some other work.

In addition to legislative and educational efforts to combat piracy, many software vendors have taken technical measures in attempt to prevent pirates from successfully copying their software. This ranges from activation procedures, which cripple software functionality until activated, to complex anti-tamper measures designed to prevent reverse engineering of the underlying algorithms, which embody the software. Copies that are not properly activated experience reduced functionality and limited access to updates. In response to the spread of copy protection measures, groups of software pirates exist that identify the protection scheme and design methods of defeating it. Known as cracking, methods for bypassing software protection include key generators, which can generate keys for software activation, and protection removal, in which the code that enforces the protection scheme is removed from the compiled software, among others. Such efforts are illegal in the United States under the DMCA and in countries that have adopted the WIPO Copyright Treaty or similar measures.

* **trafficking** transporting and selling; especially with regard to illegal merchandise

* **intellectual property** the acknowledgement that an individual's creativity and innovation can be owned in the same way as physical property

Pirating Abounds

In some countries, more than ninety percent of the software in use is pirated. When legal copies of office suites or design programs cost hundreds or thousands of dollars while pirated versions cost less than $10, the economic motivation is clear. But pirated software currently costs the software industry more than $60 billion per year.

Software Pirates

Many studies have shown that software pirates are disproportionately young males. In November 1999, a twenty-two-year-old senior at the University of Oregon was the first person to be convicted under the No Internet Theft Act (NET Act). The student was sentenced to two years of probation for making copies of software available for download from a university Web site.

When asked why someone might pirate software, people often cite cost as the key reason. Software can be expensive. The highest piracy rates often occur in some of the poorest countries in the world (e.g., Vietnam, China). Given how easy it is to copy software, such theft will continue to be a major issue for software developers for decades to come.

▶ *See also* **E-Commerce** • **Privacy** • **Security**

Resources

Books

Britz, Marjie. *Computer Forensics and Cyber Crime: An Introduction.* 2nd ed. Upper Saddle River, NJ: Pearson Prentice Hall, 2009.

Johns, Adrian. *Piracy: The Intellectual Property Wars from Gutenberg to Gates.* Chicago: The University of Chicago Press, 2010.

Sinjela, Mpazi, ed. *Human Rights and Intellectual Property Rights: Tensions and Convergences.* Leiden, The Netherlands: Martinus Nijhoff Publishers, 2007.

Web Sites

BSA: The Software Alliance. "Anti-Piracy." http://www.bsa.org/country/Anti-Piracy.aspx (accessed November 3, 2012).

Software and Information Industry Association. "Anti-Piracy." http://www.siia.net/index.php?option=com_content&view=article&id=77&Itemid=7 (accessed November 3, 2012).

Space Travel and Exploration

Many people believe that the rapid increase in the capability of computers was due largely to the demands of the American Space Program. It is indeed true that the National Aeronautics and Space Administration (NASA) did pressure the computer industry for more speed and more memory in its ground based systems, but the computers in the Apollo spacecraft that traveled to the Moon and those flying in the later space shuttles are relics of a bygone era. This conservative attitude is the result of NASA's unwillingness to risk human lives: Old technologies have a known track

* **ballistics** the science and
engineering of the motion of
projectiles of various types,
including bullets, bombs, and
rockets

* **magnetic tape** a way of storing
programs and data from
computers; tapes are generally
slow and prone to deterioration
over time but are inexpensive

record whereas there is implicit risk in an untested technology. However, even the unpiloted spacecraft use mostly obsolete computers, though NASA has allowed chances to be taken with their memory technologies. Nevertheless, NASA has been a good customer of the computing industry, demanding new techniques even while using older hardware.

Early Piloted Spacecraft Computers

When American astronaut John Glenn (1921–) rode his *Mercury-Atlas* rocket into orbit and into history in February 1962, not a single computer rode with him. The Mercury spacecraft was a ballistic* object, like a warhead, just going fast enough for a few orbits of the Earth. It could not change its orbit, nor could it maneuver in any way except to fire its retro-rockets to return to Earth. In essence, it did not need a computer.

The Apollo Program was a piloted American space flight effort designed to fulfill U.S. President John F. Kennedy's (1917–1963) 1961 promise to go to the Moon and back by the end of that decade. To help develop technologies for the piloted Apollo spacecraft, there were several programs involving unpiloted lunar spacecraft. One of them, the Ranger series of lunar impact probes, was ground-commanded. The probes were designed only to hit the Moon, taking pictures all the way down. The command to start the camera going was the last command that spacecraft received.

The Apollo spacecraft, designed to make a soft landing, was an entirely different matter. The soft landing could not be commanded from the Earth, owing to the fact that radio waves take about three seconds to make a round trip. This is why an on-board computer was necessary. The later decision to use a two-part spacecraft, one part landing and one part staying in orbit around the Moon, and the realization that making a re-entry to Earth at 25,000miles (40,230 kilometers) per hour would be very difficult with a tired crew, sealed the decision. Several years before the Apollo spacecraft flew, the interim Gemini Program, using a Mercury spacecraft widened to accommodate a crew of two, had a computer put on board to practice rendezvous and computer-controlled descents that would later be used on the Moon mission.

This computer, designed and built by International Business Machines (IBM), was a small, custom-made machine with only four thousand words of memory. More storage was provided by a magnetic tape* similar to the ones especially made for the Orbiting Astronomical Observatory flight series. This computer hardly stretched the state of the art, but performed flawlessly.

Nevertheless, if there were any problems, a Gemini spacecraft could land in minutes. An Apollo spacecraft could take days to get back. NASA was worried about reliability. The easiest way to assure reliability was to carry multiple copies of the same computer, so there is always a spare if one computer fails. However, as in all of aeronautics and astronautics, the biggest considerations are size, power, and weight. A redundant system would negatively affect all three, adding the problems of redundancy

* **integrated circuit** a circuit with the transistors, resistors, and other circuit elements etched into the surface of a single chip of semiconducting material, usually silicon

management as well. NASA therefore decided to use only one full-sized computer in each part of the spacecraft. One part would always be in touch with the Earth (except when its orbit passed the far side of the Moon). Using the near constant communication with Earth, redundancy could be achieved with big IBM-built ground computers, which could replicate the function of the computers aboard the spacecraft. Because it could not be commanded from the ground, the lander would carry a tiny computer as a backup that could only put the lander in a parking orbit. The command module would then have to rendezvous and save the crew.

NASA got away with using one computer by extensive testing and knowledge of the history of the various parts. Early in the program, when the requirements for lunar rendezvous and other maneuvers were established, the Massachusetts Institute of Technology's (MIT) Instrumentation Lab, the designers, asked NASA if the lab could make the machine more capable by using the first mass-produced integrated circuit* in its construction. This was a four-logic-gate chip. Initially, NASA balked because this represented new technology, but it relented after assurances by MIT that the actual use of this technology was still years away. There were no in-flight failures of the Apollo computer.

The Space Shuttle

The huge size of the orbiter part of the space transportation system suggested the idea that considerable weight could be saved if digital flight controls were used instead of mechanical linkages. Because this system would be used for active flight control, more than one computer was needed. The failure of the single computer would cause the loss of an expensive spacecraft and its crew. Two computers were not enough either, as it would be difficult to tell, in case of malfunction, which one of the two had failed. Both machines would be indicating that the other one was at fault! Similarly, three machines would devolve to that standoff if one failed. So four computers became the minimum, with a fifth machine added and a sixth carried in a locker as a spare unconnected to anything else.

In the 1970s, after the shuttle design was frozen, an airborne computer termed the IBM AP–101 was procured for it. This machine is also used in the B–52, B–1, and FB–111 bombers as a navigation and weapons delivery computer. The AP–101 originally had 106,000 words of memory and ran at one million instructions per second, which is considerably less capability than a typical desktop computer of the 2010s.

After the loss of the shuttle *Challenger*, the memory was increased to 256K of CMOS (complimentary metal-oxide semiconductor), and the processor was shrunk to fit on one chip. Shrinking the processor provided savings in both less power consumed and a smaller and lighter package. By continuing to use the same processor instead of upgrading to a newer design, NASA avoided a prohibitively expensive rewrite of the software. These changes were being developed before the disaster, but were delayed by safety considerations.

In July 2011, the successful launch and return of the space shuttle *Atlantis* marked the 135th and final flight of the U.S. shuttle program. The International Space Station (ISS) will be serviced by a combination of launches of Russian-launched Soyuz capsules and private U.S. companies such as Space Exploration Technologies (SpaceX), which have taken over piloted low-orbital service missions.

The Future of Space Exploration

Many questions surround the future of space exploration. Although space programs led directly to advances in computers, miniature equipment, and other technologies, the immediate commercial benefits of space exploration seem minimal; also, critics argue that these same technologies could have been developed far more cheaply by direct investment, rather than funding Moon flights that produced them as spin-offs. Russian rockets continue to make regular trips to orbit, but in the United States there is concern about a gap between the retirement of the space shuttle program in 2011 and flight-readiness of a successor program. Further doubt about the length of the gap in crewed spaceflight capacity followed cancellation of the Constellation program in January 2010.

The United States and Russia are no longer the only nations seriously involved in space exploration. Although the two rivals never had a monopoly on space, the cost of space missions is so great that few other nations attempted them on a large scale. France launched its own satellite in the mid–1960s, and other countries had satellites placed in orbit aboard U.S. and Soviet rockets. But only recently have other nations begun to take a leading role in space exploration.

In 1975, fourteen European nations pooled their resources to form the European Space Agency (ESA). By 1984, ESA had developed its own rocket, the Ariane, capable of lifting satellites into orbit. Many smaller nations as well as private businesses have used the Ariane to launch their satellites. The ESA also developed satellites for other nations including the United States, and it oversaw the design and development of Spacelab, a research unit flown aboard the space shuttle. In 1986, ESA launched its first space probe, *Giotto*, which made a close approach to Halley's Comet to study its atmosphere and magnetic field. In 2003, the ESA successfully orbited the *Mars Express* satellite. By 2011, budget cutbacks in the United States threatened a joint NASA/ESA Mars exploration program. Although the ExoMars European vehicles are designed and ready for construction, funding shortfalls on the U.S. side put NASA behind schedule in contributing to the agreement to send two rovers to Mars in 2018. NASA was slated to provide the launch facilities and command support to the European-led mission, but the agency has indicated that it is open to alternative Mars exploration projects if the United States pulls out of ExoMars and may even prefer to focus on smaller probe projects that scout for signs of life on the planet.

Japan entered the field of space exploration, sending its own probes to study Halley's Comet in coordination with ESA's *Giotto*. In recent years, the Japanese have launched many satellites and space probes to study the Sun, Moon, and space near Earth.

China has also made great strides in developing its space program, launching the county's own communications satellites and orbiting its first astronaut in 2003 with claims of plans for a moon landing in 2024. In June 2012, China announced plans to launch its *Shenzhou 9* spacecraft aboard a rocket for a mission to its *Tiangong 1* space station. The mission is the country's fourth crewed space flight. China had last carried out a human space mission in 2008.

A number of other nations, such as Israel and India, have varying launch capabilities. In October 2008, India launched its first robotic lunar exploration mission and plans a crewed space mission in 2016.

Private companies have designed and are currently testing several sub-orbital and low Earth orbital craft. Virgin Galactic's ship, *SpaceShipTwo*, which is also known as the VSS *Enterprise*, completed fifteen test flights while attached to mothership WhiteKnightTwo and sixteen glide tests by February 2012. The spaceship is undergoing testing by designer and manufacturer Scaled Composites of Mojave, California. Virgin Galactic plans to base operations out of a developing commercial spaceport located north of Las Cruces, New Mexico. The company announced it expects its first flights with paying customers in 2013.

In December 2010, SpaceX launched its Dragon capsule into orbit from Florida using a *Falcon 9* booster rocket. NASA is funding new initiatives by private companies to perform low orbital missions, including servicing the International Space Station (ISS). Prior to the SpaceX launch, private companies had succeeded in suborbital flight tests, but the Dragon capsule was the first to achieve orbital velocity and then and reenter the atmosphere, splashing down in the Pacific Ocean approximately 500 miles (approximately 800 km) off the coast of Mexico. The Dragon capsule reached an altitude of approximately 186 miles (300 kilometers) and completed two-thirds of an orbit before a planned deceleration terminated the mission. NASA has a contract with SpaceX for twelve re-supply missions to the ISS. Other companies have similar contracts through NASA's Commercial Orbital Transportation Services (COTS) program.

In May 2012, SpaceX became the first commercial venture to launch a spacecraft intended to dock with the International Space Station (ISS). The company launched a SpaceX *Falcon 9* rocket, with the unmanned Dragon vehicle aboard, from NASA's Cape Canaveral facilities on May 22, 2012, for a docking with the ISS three days later to deliver supplies and cargo.

Mars remains a particular focus because it lies within the zone of the solar system in which life is possible. The confirmation of water (in the form of ice crystals) found in 2008 outside of the Martian polar region fuels additional speculation that life may once have developed on Mars and perhaps still exists in special environments, although there is not yet any evidence that this is the case. For the near future, however, scientists and engineers will use remotely-operated probes and vehicles to exert more direct control over experiments conducted on Mars or elsewhere. Meanwhile, continued operation of the ISS enables astronauts to gain experience in extended space flight that they can apply to long missions to Mars or other planets, if such missions ever prove practical. In 2010, a study suggested that Mars colonization could begin with a series of "one-way" trips by more experienced astronauts who could establish outposts; those would grow and be resupplied by other "one-way" missions until technology advanced sufficiently to make regular return trips practical.

In August 2011, NASA created a new department, the Human Exploration and Operations Mission Directorate, to plan for post-shuttle human spaceflight, including a potential return to the Moon, and possible exploration of Mars, asteroids, and deep space. The following month, NASA announced plans to construct and launch Space Launch System (SLS) rockets. The proposed $18 billion program would center on the construction of a 320-foot-tall rocket that would be the most powerful since the multi-stage Saturn V rockets that launched astronauts to the Moon in the 1960s and 1970s. With modifications, the new generation of rockets also could be used in some deeper space explorations of Mars. If funded, NASA hopes to schedule an unmanned test in 2017.

Unpiloted Spacecraft

The number of robotic space missions launched since 1957 has far exceeded the number of crewed missions. Thousands of satellites have been sent into Earth's orbit, and more than 100 spacecraft have left Earth to explore other bodies in the solar system. Most of the earliest probes were sent to study the Moon, Earth's nearest neighbor. By the time the first Apollo astronauts set foot on the Moon, many probes had orbited, crash-landed, and soft-landed on the Moon, returning great quantities of photographic and other information. Much of this experience was used in creating the flight plans for the Apollo missions.

The use of CMOS memories, despite their low power consumption, was a breakthrough in piloted spacecraft, which were limited to the fifty-year-old technology of core memories until late in the 1990s. Meantime, the Jet Propulsion Laboratory (JPL), operated by the California Institute of Technology and funded by NASA, had been using CMOS memories since the *Voyager* interplanetary probe, launched in 1977.

Traditionally, NASA had always been more comfortable using innovative computer technology in unpiloted probes rather than in piloted spacecraft. Unpiloted spacecraft were operated by computers, mostly in pairs. The first time real general-purpose computers were used in a probe was the *Viking* lander on Mars in 1976. It contained two command computers and two lander computers. *Voyager* had three pairs of computers: command, attitude, and data formatting. The command computers, with four thousand words of memory, were a design similar to those on *Viking*. The attitude control computers, also with four thousand words, were a

Tourists in Space

Technological advances have made space travel safer. So safe, in fact, that the Russian space program has allowed one civilian, U.S. businessman Dennis Tito (1940–), to travel into space with its cosmonauts. Tito paid approximately $20 million in 2001 for his chance to get a better look at the stars. Internet entrepreneur Mark Shuttleworth (1973–) of South Africa was the second civilian in space, paying $20 million to spend eight days in space in 2002. Since 2002, several other space tourists have paid for trips into space costing as much as $35 million. Space tourists were barred from visits to the International Space Station (ISS) after 2010 as ISS crew sizes expanded after the station's completion.

little faster, but many orders of magnitude slower than computers today. The data formatting computers, which take experiment and camera data and prepare it for transmission to Earth, were designed by a JPL engineer as part of his graduate work in electrical engineering.

Beginning with the *Galileo* Jupiter probe, JPL has gone to distributed systems of processors and larger memories; however, they are usually obsolete by launch time.

The next generation of robotic probes was aimed at studying the sun and the planets of the inner solar system: Mercury, Venus, and Mars. From the mid–1960s to the mid–1970s, the Soviet Union's Venera series of probes enjoyed particular success in studying Venus. The Venera probes were the first spacecraft to land on another planet and send back information from its surface. The U.S. Mariner program, operating during the same period, made great progress in studying and photographing Mars. It was followed by the Viking pair of probes that landed on the Martian surface and provided scientists with data for years before losing power. Although crewed missions were more dramatic, robotic probes actually have gathered most of the scientific information gained during the space race.

The third generation of space probes extended human knowledge to the outer solar system and even somewhat beyond. The U.S. Voyager probes, launched in 1977, returned excellent photos of Jupiter, Saturn, Uranus, and Neptune and provided startling insights into these planets and their satellites. For example, they discovered that rings surround not only Saturn, but also the other so-called gas giants.

On May 25, 2008, the robotic probe *Phoenix* made a soft landing near the north pole of Mars. It was the first spacecraft since the twin Viking landers of 1976 to make a safe landing on Mars using rockets, rather than bouncing across the landscape protected by airbags. The probe, mostly built in the United States and launched by NASA, included many components recycled from the unsuccessful Mars Polar Lander mission, which crashed near Mars's south pole in 2001. The main goal of *Phoenix* was to search for signs of life. Using a robotic arm, the probe was scheduled to dig up samples of Martian soil and ice and to analyze the samples in an on-board laboratory. Several weeks after landing, *Phoenix*'s digging arm exposed water ice.

The most recent U.S. probes, which can be seen as a fourth generation, include *Galileo* and *Cassini-Huygens*, which were sent to study Jupiter and Saturn, respectively. *Huygens* landed on the surface of Saturn's moon Triton. Since the late 1990s, successful missions to Mars include *Mars Pathfinder*; the Mars Exploration Rovers *Spirit* and *Opportunity*; and the Mars Science Laboratory's rover, *Curiosity*, all of which have explored the Martian surface. Orbital missions to Mars included *Mars Odyssey* and *Mars Reconnaissance Orbiter*, among others, which have obtained Mars surface data from orbit. The last communication with the Spirit rover took place on March 22, 2010. In May 2011, NASA officially ended the Spirit rover mission and transitioned single-rover operations supporting the Opportunity rover. During its vastly extended operational lifetime, the Spirit rover covered 4.8 miles (7.73 kilometers) of the Martian surface, returning more than 124,000 images while conducting tests with its spectrometers and microscopic imaging equipment. As of 2012, there are also three active satellites orbiting Mars and collecting data.

▶ *See also* **National Aeronautics and Space Administration (NASA)**

Resources

Books

Dick, Steven J. *America in Space: NASA's First Fifty Years*. New York: Abrams, 2007.

Web Sites

National Aeronautics and Space Administration (NASA). "Apollo." http://www.nasa.gov/mission_pages/apollo/index.html (accessed June 21, 2012).

National Aeronautics and Space Administration (NASA). "Gemini." http://www.nasa.gov/mission_pages/gemini/index.html (accessed June 21, 2012).

National Aeronautics and Space Administration (NASA). "Mars Science Laboratory." http://www.nasa.gov/mission_pages/msl/index.html (accessed November 3, 2012).

Space Exploration Technologies (SpaceX). "Dragon Spacecraft Returns to Earth in First Official Cargo Resupply Mission to Space Station." http://www.spacex.com/press.php?page=20121028 (accessed November 3, 2012).

Speech Recognition

Speech recognition (SR), also called by such terms as automatic speech recognition (ASR) and speech to text (STT), is a process that enables people to speak naturally to a computer on any topic and to be understood accurately. Speech is a form of communication humans learn early and practice often, so the use of speech recognition software can simplify computer interface*s and make computers accessible to users unable to key text using a standard keyboard. However, computer-based speech recognition is more difficult to achieve than one might at first assume.

The speech recognition process is statistical in nature and is based on Hidden Markov Models (HMMs). An HMM is a finite set of states, each of which is associated with a probability distribution. Transitions among the states are governed by a set of probabilities called transition

▲

Michael Callahan wearing his invention, the AUDEO, a voice synthesizer. © *John B. Carnett/Popular Science/ via Getty Images.*

probabilities. The HMM is first trained using speech data for which the associated text is known. Subsequently, the trained HMM is used to decode new speech data into text.

The recognition vocabulary and vocabulary size play a key role in determining the accuracy of a system. A vocabulary defines the set of words that can be recognized by a speech recognition system. In addition, a language model is used to estimate the probability of a sequence of words in a particular domain. The language model assists the speech engine in recognizing speech by biasing the output toward high-probability word sequences. Together, vocabularies and language models are used in the selection of the best match for a word by the speech recognition engine. Therefore, speech systems can only recognize (hear) words that are present in the vocabulary; a word that is not in the vocabulary will be misinterpreted as a similar sounding word that is present in the vocabulary.

Since speech recognition is probabilistic, the most probable decoding of the audio signal is output as the recognized text, but multiple hypotheses are considered during the process. Recognition systems generally have no means to distinguish between correctly and incorrectly recognized words. Therefore, during recognition, a word lattice representation is often used to consider all hypothesized word sequences. A word lattice representation is an acyclic directed graph that consists of nodes and arcs used to represent the multiple hypotheses considered during recognition. The nodes represent points in time, and the arcs represent the hypothesized word. The path with the highest probability is generally output as the final recognized text. Often, the multiple hypotheses (for example phrases such as be quite and beak white) sound the same and may only be distinguished by higher level semantic knowledge provided by the language model.

Speech Recognition Applications

Speech recognition applications may be classified into three categories: dictation systems, navigational or transactional systems, and multimedia indexing systems. Each category of applications has a different tolerance for speech recognition errors. Advances in technology are making significant progress toward the goal of any individual being able to speak naturally to a computer on any topic and to be understood accurately.

Dictation Applications Such applications are those in which the words spoken by a user are transcribed directly into written text. Such applications are used to create text such as personal letters, business correspondence, or e-mail messages. Usually, the user has to be very explicit, specifying all punctuation and capitalization in the dictation. Dictation applications often combine mouse and keyboard input with spoken input. Using speech to create text can still be a challenging experience since users have a hard time getting used to the process of dictating. Best results are achieved when the user speaks clearly, enunciates each syllable properly, and has organized the content mentally before starting.

As the user speaks, the text appears on the screen and is available for correction. Correction can take place either with traditional methods such as a mouse and keyboard, or with speech.

* **keywords** words that are significant in some context or topic (often used in searching)

Transactional Applications   Speech is used in transactional applications to navigate around the application or to conduct a transaction. For example, speech can be used to purchase stock, reserve an airline itinerary, or transfer bank account balances. It can also be used to follow links on the Web or move from application to application on one's computer screen. Most often, but not exclusively, this category of speech applications involves the use of a telephone. The user speaks into a phone, the signal is interpreted by a computer (not the phone), and an appropriate response is produced. A custom, application-specific vocabulary is usually used; this means that the system can only hear the words in the vocabulary. This implies that the user can only speak what the system can hear. These applications require careful attention to what the system says to the user since these prompts are the only way to cue the user as to which words can be used for a successful outcome.

Multimedia Indexing Applications   In multimedia indexing applications, speech is used to transcribe words from an audio file into text. The audio may be part of a video. Subsequently, information retrieval techniques are applied on the transcript to create an index with time offsets into the audio. This enables a user to search a collection of audio/video documents using text keywords*. Retrieval of unstructured multimedia documents is a challenge; retrieval using keyword search based on speech recognition is a big step toward addressing this challenge. It is important to have realistic expectations with respect to retrieval performance when speech recognition is used. The user interface design is typically guided by the *search the speech, browse the video* metaphor where the primary search interface is through textual, and browsing of the video is through video segmentation techniques. In general, it has been observed that the accuracy of the top-ranking search results is more important than finding every relevant match in the audio. So, speech indexing systems often bias their ranking to reflect this. Since the user does not directly interact with the indexing system using speech input, standard search engine user interfaces are seamlessly applicable to speech indexing interfaces.

Conclusion

Advances in speech recognition technology have progressed to a point that it is practical to consider speech input in applications. Speech recognition is used in such fields as aerospace, healthcare, home automation, mobile telephony, robotics, telematics (vehicle navigational systems), and video gaming. For instance, the U.S. military has performed research and development for speech recognition within its fighter jets. Speech recognition is also gaining acceptance as a means of creating searchable text from audio streams. Dictation applications have the highest

algorithm a rule or procedure used to solve a mathematical problem—most often described as a sequence of steps

accuracy requirements and must be designed for efficient error correction. Transactional applications are more tolerant to speech errors but require careful designing of the constrained vocabulary and cueing of the user. Multimedia indexing applications are also tolerant to speech errors since the search algorithm* can be adapted to meet the requirements of the application. As of 2012, Dragon NaturallySpeaking 12 Premium and WordQ v.3 are two of the more popular speech recognition computer programs, according to PC Magazine.

 See also **Input Devices • Neural Networks • Pattern Recognition**

Resources

Books

Indurkhya, Nitin, and Fred J. Damerau, eds. *Handbook of Natural Language Processing.* Boca Raton, FL: Chapman & Hall, 2010.

McCarthy, Philip M., and Chutima Boonthum-Denecke, eds. *Applied Natural Language Processing: Identification, Investigation, and Resolution.* Hershey, PA: IGI Global, 2011.

Suendermann, David. *Advances in Commercial Deployment of Spoken Dialog Systems.* New York: Springer, 2011.

Web Sites

HowStuffWorks.com, and Ed Grabianowski. "How Speech Recognition Works." http://electronics.howstuffworks.com/gadgets/high-tech-gadgets/speech-recognition.htm (accessed October 23, 2012).

PC Magazine. "Speech Recogniton." http://www.pcmag.com/category2/0,2806,4830,00.asp (accessed October 23, 2012).

Spreadsheets

Traditionally, accountants use a grid of rows and columns printed on special green paper to produce financial projects and reports. An electronic spreadsheet is software that simulates this accountant's paper pad or worksheet. Using spreadsheet software, a worksheet appears on the computer screen as a grid of rows and columns. The software performs calculations based on the numbers and mathematical formulas that users enter into this grid. While the terms *worksheet* and *spreadsheet* are used interchangeably, they really refer to different things. The spreadsheet actually refers to the software itself, whereas a worksheet denotes the actual numbers and formulas that underlie a particular task.

The intersection of a row and a column on the worksheet grid is called a cell. Cells are identified by a name that consists of a column letter (A–Z, AA–ZZ, and so on) and a row number. For example, D10 refers

▲

Japanese electronics giant Sharp's employee displays 22-inch sized high-definition LCD television which has spreadsheet as a PC monitor. © *YOSHIKAZU TSUNO/AFP/ Getty Images.*

to the cell in the fourth column (D is the fourth letter of the alphabet) and the tenth (10) row down on the worksheet, and AB45 refers to the twenty-eighth column (the alphabet consists of the first 26 columns, with AA column 27 and AB column 28) and forty-fifth (45) row down on the worksheet. Because a worksheet can have thousands of cells, the software allows the user to scroll through the worksheet horizontally or vertically to view the cells.

Cells on a worksheet can be filled with one of four things:

1. nothing (which means that the cell is blank)
2. labels
3. numeric values
4. formulas.

A label in a cell is a descriptive text. Examples of labels include: Units Sold, Revenue, Total Cost, Name, Address, or City. The labels are used to help organize the worksheet. Numeric values refer to the actual numeric

Figure 1. Spreadsheet showing cells. *Reproduced by permission of Gale, a part of Cengage Learning.*

	A	B	C	D	E	F
1		INCOME STATEMENT				
2						
3	Units Sold	0	114	228	342	456
4						
5	Revenue	$0.00	$11,395.35	$22,790.70	$34,186.05	$45,581.40
6						
7	Fixed Cost	$9,800.00	$9,800.00	$9,800.00	$9,800.00	$9,800.00
8						
9	Variable Cost	$0.00	$6,495.35	$12,990.70	$19,486.05	$25,981.40
10						
11	Total Cost	$9,800.00	$16,295.35	$22,790.70	$29,286.05	$35,781.40
12						
13	Profit/Loss	($9,800.00)	($4,900.00)	$0.00	$4,900.00	$9,800.00
14						

data that are used on the worksheet in calculations. Numeric data can take the form of positive or negative numbers, integer numbers, decimal numbers, fractions, or scientific notations.

Formulas are used to indicate how the numeric values are to be manipulated. For example, on a household budget spreadsheet, a formula can be created to add the household monthly expenses and store the results in cell B20. The formula, =SUM (B1:B19), would add the values stored in the range of cells from B1 through cell B19. Another formula, =B21 − B20, could be created to subtract the expenses (in cell B20) from the income (in cell B21) on a household budget spreadsheet. Most spreadsheets also offer a variety of pre-defined formulas, called functions, which effect powerful mathematical calculations. Typically, these functions are divided into a variety of categories, such as financial functions (e.g., depreciation, future value, net present value), date and time functions, mathematical and trigonometry functions (e.g., absolute value, sine, cosine, pi), statistical functions (e.g., average, median, variance, standard deviation), and database functions (e.g., average or count the values in a column).

In addition to these formulas and functions, spreadsheets provide modeling capabilities that allow users to describe real-world situations and then experiment with different numbers. This ability to change numbers involved in calculations and see the immediate results is called What If analysis. What-if analysis is a very powerful and useful tool and it is what makes spreadsheet software indispensable. Users can investigate what would happen if sales increase by 10 percent or decrease by 5 percent. Students could examine the implications of an A grade on their next examination or a B grade. If done manually, each change would require erasing the contents of every cell involved in a formula, changing their numeric data, and then recalculating!

Spreadsheet software also has the capability of charting or plotting data, providing database querying and extracting, and macro building. Spreadsheet software can chart data in many different ways including area, bar, column, pie, and XY charts. By visually presenting the data in chart format, the data can be readily analyzed and trends spotted. Spreadsheet software also typically incorporates elementary database

BREAKEVEN ANALYSIS

Figure 2. Analysis shown by plotting data. *Reproduced by permission of Gale, a part of Cengage Learning.*

functions. Specific rows or columns of the worksheet can be selected for report production or advanced analysis. A macro is a collection of commands that the spreadsheet software can execute. These commands are written by the user and stored with a particular worksheet. Macros are used to perform repetitive tasks on a worksheet, such as extracting all rows that have an overdue balance and producing a report about it.

History

In 1978, American engineer and computer scientist Daniel Bricklin (1951–), a student at the Harvard Business School (Harvard University), came up with the idea for a computerized interactive visible calculator. Bricklin often is considered the Father of the Spreadsheet. Bricklin and Robert Frankston (1949–) created the first electronic spreadsheet software named VisiCalc, short for visible calculator. VisiCalc and electronic spreadsheets might never have gained acceptance if it were not for a Massachusetts Institute of Technology (MIT) graduate named Daniel Fylstra. He suggested that VisiCalc should be run on an Apple microcomputer. Bricklin and Frankston programmed the software for Apple microcomputers and Fylstra and his firm, Personal Software, began marketing VisiCalc by placing an ad in *Byte* Magazine. VisiCalc became an almost instant success in the business community.

In the early 1980s, International Business Machines Corporation (IBM) introduced a microcomputer (IBM-PC) that used an Intel microprocessor. However, due to legal problems, Bricklin and Frankston did not develop VisiCalc for this new microcomputer. Rather, Mitchell Kapor (1950–) developed another electronic spreadsheet named Lotus 1-2-3 that could be used on IBM's new computer. Kapor's Lotus 1-2-3 spreadsheet quickly replaced VisiCalc as the new industry standard. Lotus 1-2-3 was easier to use than VisiCalc and added charting, plotting, and database capabilities to the software. Lotus 1-2-3 was also the first spreadsheet to introduce naming of cells, cell ranges, and spreadsheet macros.

During the 1980s, many companies introduced new microcomputers, while others created new spreadsheet software. In 1984, Apple Computer introduced the Macintosh. The Excel spreadsheet from Microsoft Corporation was written for the Macintosh computer. Excel used a

Core Apple Product

The VisiCalc computer spreadsheet software became popular among business and personal computer users, driving the sales of Apple Computers higher. For many, VisiCalc revolutionized how financial data were stored, recorded, and presented.

* **graphical user interface (GUI)** an interface that allows computers to be operated through pictures (icons) and mouse-clicks, rather than through text and typing

graphical user interface (GUI)* and the mouse. This interface proved very easy to use, much easier than the command-line interface used by Lotus 1-2-3. In 1987, Microsoft introduced a new operating system for the IBM-PC. This operating system, called Windows, incorporated a graphical user interface. Excel was one of the first software products that ran under Windows. By 1989, when Windows had gained wide acceptance in the microcomputer market, the spreadsheet program Excel began to dominate the market and continues to do so in the 2010s.

In the late spring of 1995, IBM purchased Lotus Development Corporation. Around the turn of the century, Microsoft Excel became the market leader in spreadsheets. The Excel spreadsheet program is bundled with other application programs as part of Microsoft Office. In 2010, the latest release of Excel was contained in Microsoft Office 2010 for the Windows operating system.

 See also **Decision Support Systems • Information Systems • Productivity Software**

Resources

Books

Hayden, Yvonne. *So You Need to Make a Spreadsheet.* Chandler, Arizona: Copadego Publishing, 2006.

Nash Tyler, et al. *Don't Fear the Spreadsheet.* Uniontown, Ohio: Holy Macro! Books, 2012.

Shelly, Gary B., et al. *Microsoft Excel 2010: Comprehensive.* Boston: Course Technology/Cengage Learning, 2012.

Web Sites

Bricklin, Daniel. "VisiCalc: Information from its Creators, Dan Bricklin and Bob Frankston." http://www.bricklin.com/visicalc.htm (accessed October 23, 2012).

Harvard Business School, Harvard University. "Entrepreneur Daniel S. Bricklin: A Class Act." http://www.alumni.hbs.edu/bulletin/1999/october/profile.html (accessed October 23, 2012).

Microsoft. "Excel 2010." http://office.microsoft.com/en-us/excel/ (accessed October 23, 2012).

TU

Technology of Desktop Publishing

The technology of desktop publishing (DTP) relies on two primary hardware components: 1) a computer, supplemented by various input devices including scanners and cameras, and 2) a printer that can produce high quality typographical and pictorial output. The technical process of on-screen DTP page composition is made possible by WYSIWYG (what you see is what you get) page layout software for personal computer use, and page description languages, programming that bridges the gap between the page layout software and the printers that produce pages that match what the user sees on the computer screen.

The DTP Computer

The two key technological features of a DTP computer are an inexpensive personal computer with a graphical user interface (GUI*) based on windows, icons, menus, and point-and-click actions, and WYSIWYG page layout software.

The personal computer is at the heart of the DTP process. The development of inexpensive, powerful Macintosh computers with easy-to-use graphical user interfaces, based on windows, icons, menus, and pointing (WIMP) provided the driving force behind the development and rapid implementation of DTP applications throughout the 1980s. The key feature of this technology was the graphics (bit-mapped) display that allowed a user to manipulate text and graphics on an electronic page, using a combination of the mouse and the keyboard as input tools, and to see an accurate representation of the page on the computer screen as the layout work progressed.

WYSIWYG Software Composing text on a page has always been a complicated process. Computer software, running on mainframe computers*, made this somewhat easier, but early programs did not provide for the use of variable width type, specialized formatting, or artwork, or the ability for the user to see a reasonable image of what the page would look like when printed. As specialized systems for publishing were developed, these concerns were addressed, but the programs were complicated to use, requiring mastery of complex formatting instruction language. In addition, the specialized machines were expensive and beyond the means of any but the largest printing enterprises.

Word processing software running on personal computers in the early 1980s was easier to use, and provided some previewing capabilities, but it

* **graphical user interface (GUI)** an interface that allows computers to be operated through pictures (icons) and mouse-clicks, rather than through text and typing

* **mainframe computers** large computers used by businesses and government agencies to process massive amounts of data; generally faster and more powerful than desktop computers but usually requiring specialized software

did not have the functionality required for typesetting, and, without the availability of bit-mapped screens, it could not represent typefaces, exact placement, or art work.

Before long, however, word processors were able to compose variable typefaces and take advantage of emerging powerful graphical user interfaces for previewing and manipulating page layout. The first commercially significant software application for page layout that exploited the graphical user interface and included powerful layout capabilities for arranging and paginating content, was Aldus PageMaker, which was first available for use on the Macintosh computer. Today, other important DTP page layout systems include Adobe FrameMaker, Adobe HomePublisher, Adobe PageMaker, Corel Ventura, Fatpaint, iStudio Publisher, Microsoft Office Publisher, Ready,Set,Go, QuarkXpress, and Serif PagePlus.

The DTP Printer

The two key technological features of a DTP printer are a high resolution, all-points-addressable, matrix marking engine, and a high-function page description language.

High Resolution Printing   The products of late nineteenth- and early twentieth-century printing were aesthetically satisfying, but awkward and time-consuming to produce. The process was based on the use of metal type counters for type and engraving techniques for diagrams and art. Phototypesetting, which emerged later in the twentieth century, used optical and chemical techniques for typesetting, which improved functionality and maintained high-quality results, but still required very expensive equipment and highly trained operators.

Early computer printing reverted to solid type counters and mechanical inking techniques; these printers were fast, but they had a limited range of typically fixed-width typefaces that resembled typewriter output. Furthermore, they limited the user's ability to place type on the page and so were far below the functionality and quality needed for publishing. Mechanical matrix printers that used a matrix of striking pins—commonly called dot-matrix printers—could more easily create variable-width typefaces and even crude artwork, but the low resolution of the mechanical matrix and the limitation of the mechanism meant that the results, although adequate for office documents and business communications, were still well below traditional typesetting requirements.

DTP printers, on the other hand, use laser and ink-jet technologies and rely on marking techniques that organize the entire page into a very fine-grained matrix with more definition than is possible with a matrix of mechanical pins. This allows for the high resolution imaging of different typestyles and of both line and gray-scale bit-map graphics.

The first computer printer to use this technique was the Xerox 9700, a 300 dpi (dots per inch) laser printer released in 1979. The impact of this first commercial laser printer was limited in part by a lack of software that could take advantage of its functionality. In 1979, computer composition was based on batch processing*, with little support for graphics or printing preview. The 9700's internal software for operating it in all-points-addressable mode* could not be accessed by most existing composition or text processing software. Finally, the 9700, with a 120-page per minute printing engine and a price of around $350,000, was too expensive to have much impact beyond its intended market of high-volume printing firms.

In the early 1980s, another high-resolution matrix technology appeared commercially as part of a Hewlett-Packard ink-jet printer. Its price was about $6,000. However, it was the Apple Laserwriter, a 300 dpi laser printer designed for the Macintosh computer, that ultimately inaugurated the DTP era in 1985. The Laserwriter's incorporation of the Postscript page description language gave it extraordinary functionality that fully exploited the capabilities of the high-resolution matrix engine.

In the early days of DTP, 300 dpi resolution was arguably still well below the visual quality available from traditional typographic printing services. As a result, the expression *near typeset quality* became common to describe output produced by these printers. However, when the resolution rose to 600 dpi, and font designs and page description languages improved, many purchasers of typesetting services began to feel that the difference in quality between traditionally printed and DTP-produced pages was slight, and not worth the cost of selecting the more expensive traditional option.

Page Description Languages   Early computer printing typically involved machinery such as physical type counters, each of the same width, which made an ink impression on paper by striking an intervening ribbon. Although the software that composed lines and pages did not need to be as sophisticated as it is now because characters were the same width and relatively few specialized layout features were used, the software that actually operated the printers was even simpler. But while such printing was adequate for data or internal office communications, it did not offer the functionality or quality required by general publishing.

With the development of laser and ink jet printers that could compose high resolution characters and images by placing tiny dots of ink or toner anywhere on the page, both the composition software and the printer software had to become much more sophisticated to utilize the capabilities of such printers more fully. At the same time, a proliferation of printers, each with its own physical requirements, required each word processing or page layout software application to output different kinds of data files for every kind of printer. It was complex and expensive to match user needs with exactly the right combination of computer and printer hardware and software programs that would lead to the desired printed product.

In the 1970s, American computer scientist John Warnock (1940–), working at Xerox's Palo Alto Research Center (PARC), developed

* **batch processing** an approach to computer utilization that queues noninteractive programs and runs them one after another

* **all-points-addressable mode** a technique for organizing graphics devices where all points (pixels) on the screen are individually accessible to a running program

Research and Development

The core technologies at the heart of desktop publishing—the personal computer, WYSIWYG text processing, page description languages, and high-resolution laser printing—were developed at the Xerox Palo Alto Research Center (PARC) in the 1970s. However, the first commercially successful application of desktop publishing hardware and software did not appear until the next decade, with the advent of the Apple Macintosh in 1985.

* **XML** the acronym for eXtensible Markup Language; a method of applying structure to data so that documents can be represented

Interpress, a language for the control of high-resolution matrix marking. Warnock became dissatisfied with Xerox's marketing of Interpress and he left the company to form Adobe Systems. In 1984, Adobe released a page description language, Postscript, designed to provide precise programmable and device independent control of page images. This precise programmable control could exploit high-resolution marking engines to produce scalable high-quality diagrams and artwork as well as aesthetically satisfying typography.

In addition, the possibility of single printer language interface for communication between printers and page layout software simplified the engineering of both. Today almost all publishing systems are Postscript based, with word processing or page layout software producing a Postscript data stream (representing the formatted text), which is then sent to Postscript-based printers, where it undergoes raster image processing (RIP), which converts the programming instructions to a bitmap page image.

Beyond the Printed Page

With the advent of electronic publications in CD-ROM (compact disc-read only memory) and World Wide Web (usually shortened to simply Web) formats, DTP page layout systems are now designed to import and export XML*-encoded content to be integrated with XML-based publishing. Material can be prepared simultaneously for dissemination in multiple formats. With continuing improvement in this area, DTP will continue to play an effective role in the emerging ecology of networked information.

 See also **Desktop Publishing • Document Processing • Integrated Software • Markup Languages**

Resources

Books

Clements, Alan. *Principles of Computer Hardware.* 4th ed. Oxford and New York: Oxford University Press, 2006.

Lake, Susan E. L. *Desktop Publishing.* 2nd ed. Mason, OH: Thomson/South-Western, 2006.

Marmel, Elaine. *PCs Simplified.* Indianapolis, IN: Wiley, 2011.

Rosen, Mitchell, and Noboru Ohta, eds. *Color Desktop Printer Technology.* Boca Raton, FL: CRC Press, 2006.

Shelly, Gary B., and Misty E. Vermaat. *Discovering Computers: Fundamentals*, 8th ed. Mason, OH: South-Western, 2011.

White, Ron, and Timothy Edward Downs. *How Computers Work*, 9th ed. Indianapolis, IN: Que Publishing, 2007.

Web Sites

About.com, and Jacci Howard Bear. "Desktop Publishing." http://desktoppub.about.com/ (accessed October 24, 2012).

Adobe. "Dr. John E. Warnock." http://www.adobe.com/aboutadobe/pressroom/executivebios/johnwarnock.html (accessed October 24, 2012).

* **synergistic** relating to synergism, which is the phenomenon whereby the action of a group of elements is greater than their individual actions

Telephony

Telephony is the electronic point-to-point communication of audio signals; in other words, the systems and technology involving the use of telephones. At the start of the third millennium, the world had approximately 750 million telephone lines, half of which were in the United States. Half the people in the world have never talked on a telephone! Every telephone homes on (goes to) a *switching office,* either by copper wire or wireless link. Transmission lines, typically fiber or microwave links carrying thousands of simultaneous conversations, connect these switching offices to each other. Starting with American scientist Alexander Graham Bell's (1847–1922) invention of the telephone in 1876, telephony has become a trillion-dollar-a-year worldwide industry. This industry consists of: (1) the carriers (in some countries, a government branch) that own the networks and provide telephone service and (2) the manufacturers of the switching and transmission equipment that the carriers use. Telephony and computing have had a synergistic* relationship for about fifty years as of 2012.

Computing Supports Telephony

In the United States, Bell's company grew into the Bell System, a telephone monopoly that was broken up in 1984. When the Bell System introduced area codes and automated long-distance calling in the 1950s, the cost of modifying the nation's 40,000 switching offices motivated a change from the *wired control* used in electromechanical technology to *program control.* The world's first computer-controlled switching office, now called the 1E, was developed by the Bell System and was installed in 1965. The 1E processor had a 1-megahertz (MHz) clock and no operating system. Now, almost every switching office in the United States, and many of the offices in the world, are program-controlled by huge programs that run on modern processors.

Complicated switching software recognizes off-hooks and on-hooks, processes calls, controls special features and services, implements the numbering plan, routes calls through the carriers' networks, maintains the switching office, manages the network, and communicates with software in other switching offices. Program control not only manages telephony's complexity, but it also enables new features—such as call forwarding,

* **packets** collections of digital data elements that are part of a complete message or signal; packets contain their destination addresses to enable reassembly of the message or signal

toll-free numbers, calling party identification, and mobility—which makes the programs even more complicated. Switching software has become so complicated, and changes so frequently, that only large companies, such as global giants French-based Alcatel-Lucent and German-based Siemens, can afford the thousands of programmers required to maintain and update the programs.

Computer-controlled switching equipment was common by the 1980s when the world's carriers started using Signaling System 7, a global data network by which switch processors send packets* to each other for call control and routing. Then, in a 1990s evolution called the Intelligent Network, the SS7 network added special processors and databases for special service control, translation, and network management. The operation of switching software, the SS7 network, and these IN processors is illustrated by the following three examples.

Long-distance Busy Tone Suppose Dave in Denver, Colorado, calls Alice in Atlanta, Georgia. Dave dials Alice's number into the CenturyLink switching office on which his telephone homes. This office in Denver sends a packet to the AT&T switching office on which Alice's telephone homes and requests Alice's busy/idle status. If Alice's telephone is idle, the Denver office determines Dave's default long-distance carrier (Verizon, for example), routes the call to Verizon's gateway office in Denver, and sends a packet containing the calling and called telephone numbers to this gateway. Then, Verizon routes the call through its national network to the AT&T office in Atlanta, which rings Alice's telephone. If Alice's telephone had been busy, rather than route the call to Atlanta, the CenturyLink office in Denver would connect Dave to a local busy tone.

800-call Suppose Dave dials 1-800-555-4567 into the CenturyLink switching office in Denver on which his telephone homes. This office sends a packet to a special database on the SS7 network, which returns a packet identifying AT&T, for example, as the carrier that leases this 800 number. Then, the CenturyLink office routes Dave's call to AT&T's gateway office in Denver and sends a packet containing the calling and called telephone numbers to this gateway. This office sends a packet to AT&T's 800-number translation database, which returns the actual telephone number that AT&T assigned to this 800 number. The call is then routed through AT&T's national network to this real telephone.

Cell Phone Roaming Suppose Dave is not home in Denver today; he is in Atlanta and he brought his cell phone. Every cellular carrier's switching office maintains a pair of databases, the *home location register* (HLR) and the *visitor location register* (VLR). Dave's cell phone is registered in his cellular carrier's HLR in Denver. When Dave turns on his cell phone in Atlanta, the telephone communicates with a cellular switching office in Atlanta. This office records Dave's phone number (and home office) in its VLR and sends a packet to Dave's home office in Denver, which records the Atlanta office's ID in Dave's HLR entry. If anyone tries to call Dave's cell phone, the Denver HLR enables the call to be routed to Atlanta. If Dave tries to place a call, the VLR in Atlanta sends billing information to Denver.

It should be apparent that these services, and hundreds of others, would be practically impossible without computers, software, and the SS7 network.

Telephony Supports Computing

The companies that manufacture switching equipment have a long history of innovation in computing. Most notable was Bell Labs, when it was the R&D (research and development) branch of the former Bell System. Bell Labs' scientists built a prototype* computer in the late 1930s using electromechanical technology, and they developed the UNIX operating system and the C programming language in the 1970s.

More recently, the Internet would be practically impossible without telephone industry resources. Besides using their networks of transmission lines for telephone calls, the carriers also lease channels, typically for use as enterprise private networks for voice and data. Such channels, leased from the various telephone carriers, interconnect the Internet's IP (short for Internet Protocol) routers, providing its global backbone network. In addition, most residential personal computers get access to Internet service providers by using a modem* (the word is an abbreviation of *modulator-demodulator*). The computer's makes a telephone call to a at the Internet service provider (ISP). The s convert computer data (in the PC and ISP) to audio signals, which transmit like voice over the telephone channel.

The relationship between telephony and computing may get even stronger—in fact, the two industries may merge—if Voice-over-IP (VoIP) becomes practical and universally used. In 2010, the number of VoIP subscribers was approximately 157 million worldwide, and the number is expected to grow to 264 million by 2015. VoIP providers such as Skype, which is owned by Microsoft, are joining with larger names such as Apple, Google, and Yahoo!. VoIP is entering the mainstream of telecommunications, especially mobile telecommunications, as it continues its steady growth in the 2010s.

▶ *See also* **Bell, Alexander Graham** • **Bell Labs** • **Internet** • **Satellite Technology** • **Telecommunications** • **Wireless Technology**

Resources

Books

Bartolacci, Michael R., and Steven R. Powell, eds. *Research, Practice, and Educational Advancements in Telecommunications and Networking.* Hershey, PA: Information Science Reference, 2012.

The First Switchboard

The first telephone switchboard was installed in New Haven, Connecticut, in 1878. Operated manually by teenage boys at first, the switchboards connected many telephones through one or two exchanges in large cities. Within a few years, women replaced the boys as operators, as they were considered to be more polite to the callers.

* **prototype** a working model or experimental investigation of proposed systems under development

* **modem** the contraction of MOdulator DEModulator; a device which converts digital signals into signals suitable for transmission over analog channels, like telephone lines

Computer Sciences, 2nd Edition

Boucadair, Mohamed, et al. *IP Telephony Interconnection Reference: Challenges, Models, and Engineering.* Boca Raton, FL: CRC Press, 2012.

Dodd, Annabel Z. *The Essential Guide to Telecommunications.* 5th ed. Upper Saddle River, NJ: Prentice Hall, 2012.

Flanagan, William A. *VoIP and Unified Communications: Internet Telephony and the Future Voice Network.* Hoboken, NJ: Wiley, 2012.

Iannone, Eugenio. *Telecommunication Networks.* Boca Raton, FL: CRC Press, 2012.

Web Sites

About.com, and Mary Bellis. "The History of the Telephone—Alexander Graham Bell." http://inventors.about.com/od/bstartinventors/a/telephone.htm (accessed October 25, 2012).

VOIP-News. "A Brief History of Telephony." http://www.voip-news.com/articles/voip-blog/a-brief-history-of-telephony-51977 (accessed October 25, 2012).

User Interfaces

How do computers communicate with humans? The first computers, developed in the 1940s, were no more than huge boxes filled with complex electronics. The computer operators used binary code and primitive

Intuitive user interface. © *AP Images/PRNewsFoto/1 EDI Source, Inc.*

peripheral devices, such as punched card readers, to communicate with them. The next generation of computers used the typewriter as an input/output device. Since the end of the 1960s, monitors and keyboards have become the standard way of communication between computers and humans. Other input devices, such as touch screen, mouse, joystick, scanner, and voice recognition modules, also became available to users. All these devices have made possible the development of interactive computer systems, which permit users to communicate with computers by entering data and control directions during program execution. A part of an interactive computer system that communicates with the user is known as a user interface.

How Computers and Humans Work Together

Interaction between humans and computers is a two-way communication. To interact effectively, users need appropriate tools that are designed specifically for human-to-computer and computer-to-human links. As in communication with each other, people have a natural desire to be able to use a combination of vision, movements, and speech to communicate with computers. Hence, visual, audio, and physical motion components of user interface are interconnected.

Two different visual interface methods, graphical- and character-based, utilize different kinds of actions. The character-based interface typically requires typing on a keyboard. A graphical interface incorporates the use of a mouse or joystick, which translates physical motion into motion of objects on a computer screen. In addition, visual information may be sent from scanners, digital cameras, and faxes, which are able to translate images into computer code.

Speech also may be used, through voice input devices, to deliver system commands and data directly into a system. It is a complex multi-stage process that involves digital sampling of the acoustic signal, recognition of the elements of speech, and even machine knowledge of the language.

All of these methods and devices can be categorized as human-to-computer communication elements. Prompts, messages, and light and sound signals are examples of computer-to-human interaction. A prompt is a signal on a screen indicating that the computer is waiting for a command or data. In response to users' usually brief commands, computers may provide them with reports, graphics, music, links to Internet Web sites, and other digitized information or entertainment resources.

Visual Components

The way information is presented on the screen determines what type of user interface is being used. It could be text for DOS (disk operating system) or UNIX (sometimes written as Unix) commands or a graphical user interface (GUI)* for a Window-based environment or Web-style browser.

For example, DOS is command-driven and requires a user to know more than fifty commands that the system will accept. All commands are entered at the computer prompt. Although it is a reliable operating

* **graphical user interface (GUI)** an interface that allows computers to be operated through pictures (icons) and mouse-clicks, rather than through text and typing

system, it is not user-friendly since it is not based on the more familiar concepts of graphics and visual cues, which have subsequently been incorporated into the GUI design of window-based user interfaces.

The names and functions of basic GUI elements, such as files, menus, folders, and wastebasket, were selected to correspond to their familiar counterparts in a physical office environment. GUI requires a mouse to move the pointer or cursor, without a keyboard, and uses a point and click sequence. For instance, to select a menu item, an operator uses a mouse or similar device to move the cursor on the screen and highlights the menu item. Then a click or two on a mouse button indicates and executes the selection. Another technique involves choosing an option by entering a letter or number or simple combination of two or three characters that activate the desired option.

Certain software packages use pictures or icons to speed up the selection process. The user can access the function related to each icon by selecting it with the mouse. In this way the user can create, send, file, or discard documents by simply pointing at the appropriate icon. Data entry of specific information may be executed by filling in the appropriate blank fields on a screen form.

Development of the window-based interface was obviously a step forward compared to DOS but its presentation capabilities are limited to the traditional GUI elements that correspond to the paper world of print and graphic design. The emergence of the Internet and World Wide Web (or simply, Web) brought multimedia—a combination of text, images, animation, audio, and video—into a format called a Web page. Navigation through various electronic environments and possible connections became a very important concept for Web users. While in a Windows software environment, all possible links are pre-defined and limited within each application, Web users have full control of navigation, and users can access many types of links for almost unlimited travel through virtual environments, interactive files, and interconnected sources of content.

Using Multimedia

As computers become more knowledge- and media-oriented, their input and output devices become more sophisticated. In addition to graphics, other forms of data presentation, such as voice, music, and video are also available to users.

In voice input devices, speech produced by an operator is used to enter data or system commands directly into a computer system. The consumer used to have to pay extra to obtain speech recognition software for installation onto their computer. But, over the years companies such as Microsoft have bundled speech recognition software with their operating system (OS). The Windows XP, Vista, Windows 7 (released for sale in 2009), and Windows 8 (released for sale in 2012) OS versions have all come with built-in speech recognition capabilities. However, many people who use voice recognition programs still prefer to use third-party software

* **virtual reality (VR)** the use of elaborate input/output devices to create the illusion that the user is in a different environment

* **ergonomic** being of suitable geometry and structure to permit effective or optimal human user interaction with machines

that they purchase, no doubt because they feel that those vendors have a voice-recognition product that is superior to the pre-packaged ones.

Computers may also have speech-generation devices to deliver oral messages in response to signals from a data processing or control system. Messages are created by assembling elements of real speech or by the synthesis of sound waves of certain frequency.

A computer-vision system allows the user to create, save, and reproduce video images. The system consists of a camera connected to a personal computer to create images and software that permits the user to experiment with image processing.

Virtual reality (VR)* environments project the user into a simulated three-dimensional space generated by a computer. The illusion of being surrounded by a world of computer-generated images, or a virtual environment, is created by linking the motion of a user's head with changes in the images presented in the visual display. The use of a data glove and head-mounted stereoscopic display allow users to point to and manipulate illusory objects that appear within their view.

Interfaces for Specialized Computers

Making computers widely accessible to people with varying physical abilities requires customization of interactive styles for different user communities. For example, users with fine motor disabilities may utilize alternative input devices, such as programmable keyboards, which permit them to operate computers with limited use of hands. They can enter letters, numbers, words, or even phrases by using functional keys. Another way to enter data into the computer is to operate an electronic pointing device, which allows a user to move the cursor on the screen using ultrasound or an infrared beam. Utilizing speech recognition software is another way to make computers accessible to users unable to use manually operated input devices.

A variety of interface systems are widely used by health care practitioners and scientists. Medical doctors are able to study body organs by manipulating three-dimensional digital images. Chemists may observe the progression of simulated chemical reaction in slow motion. Scientists can rotate and re-size objects in hypothetical models, and change their angle and point of view. Environmental scientists and geographers may compile, retrieve, and visualize various geographic data, including maps in a three-dimensional format.

Telecommunication devices enable users to transmit text, graphics, video, and voice over a distance using computers. These users send electronic- or voice-mail all over the world and can exchange ideas and news in chat rooms and via instant messaging software programs.

Computer interface designers are challenged by the goal of creating an interface that resembles human-to-human interaction as closely as possible. Design considerations should include not only technical aspects but ergonomic* factors as well. The ideal interface would allow one to

Voice Commands

Many software companies produce user interfaces for the seeing and hearing impaired. Using speech recognition technology, a user calls out a command to access a particular file or function, such as adding bold to text. Others generate voice instruction coming from the computer itself, allowing the user to know when the bold command is being used. Translators also convert words into sign language for use in teleconferencing.

concentrate on his or her work without even being aware of the presence of the interface itself.

As an example of an advanced form of user interface, Microsoft announced at the end of 2010 that it was developing a tactile touchscreen that would allow users to sense the displayed image physically, with all of its bumps, edges, points, textures, or other features. The shape-shifting technology involves the use of pixel-sized plastic cells that remember their shape from one time to the next.

 See also **Ergonomics • Interactive Systems • Window Interfaces**

Resources

Books

Miller, Michael. *Easy Computer Basics*. Indianapolis: Que Publishing, 2006.

Patterson, David A., and John L. Hennessy. *Computer Organization and Design: The Hardware/software Interface*. 4th ed. Waltham, MA: Morgan Kaufmann, 2012.

Shneiderman, Ben, Catherine Plaisant, Maxine Cohen, and Steven Jacobs. *Designing the User Interface: Strategies for Effective Human-Computer Interaction*. 5th ed. Boston: Addison Wesley, 2010.

Web Sites

Marks, Paul. "Microsoft Develops Shape-shifting Touchscreen." *New Scientist*, November 29, 2010. http://www.newscientist.com/article/dn19776-microsoft-develops-shapeshifting-touchscreen.html (accessed October 29, 2012).

WZ

Wang, An
Chinese-born American Inventor and Entrepreneur
1920–1990

An Wang is remembered for his contributions to the invention of core memory; the accomplishments of his company, Wang Laboratories; and his many inventions, including the world's first commercially successful logarithmic calculator and word processing system. Wang's invention of the memory core helped fuel the spread of mainframe computers for decades.

An Wang was born in Shanghai, China, on February 7, 1920, the eldest son of a school teacher. His quick intellect became evident at an early age when he finished sixth grade at the age of nine. He studied electrical engineering at Chiao Tung University in Shanghai, an institution comparable to the Massachusetts Institute of Technology (MIT) in the United States. He was ranked first in his class throughout his years at college, graduating as valedictorian in 1940.

In 1944 the Chinese government selected a small group of engineers, including Wang, to travel to the United States at state expense. Their assignment was to learn American technology so they could help rebuild China after the war with Japan, which had begun in 1937 and continued for many years.

Wang enrolled at Harvard University and completed his graduate work with amazing speed. He began his studies in 1946, completing the requirements for a master's degree in applied physics in only two semesters. Thirteen months after starting work on his doctorate, Wang was awarded his Ph.D. in applied physics although graduate students typically study for four or more years before earning similar advanced degrees.

In 1948, with his government funding running out, Wang was reluctant to return to war-torn China and sought employment at Harvard's Computation Laboratory. There Howard Aiken was building the first all-electronic computing machine to be fabricated at Harvard, the Mark IV.

Aiken's first assignment for Wang was for him to find a way to record and read magnetically stored information without any mechanical motion in the machine. Wang worked on the problem for several weeks before discovering the key—a tiny donut-shaped magnetic switch that could be turned on and off electrically in a few thousandths of a second. Wang found that by stringing these switches, called *cores,* in a line, the computer could write zeros and ones to memory and read them back

The Philanthropy of An Wang

An Wang gained fame for his generous contributions to colleges and universities, hospitals, and arts organizations. In 1983 Wang donated $4 million to rescue Boston's decaying Metropolitan Theatre, which closed when a ceiling collapsed. Today, the facility is known as the Wang Center for the Performing Arts. When asked to explain his philanthropic contributions, Wang said: "In countries or civilizations where one generation has benefited in knowledge, physical faculties, or whatever, it means that you have already profited from the benefits that previous generations lacked. So you should pay back the past and pass other benefits onto the next generation."

* **microcomputer** a computer that is small enough to be used and managed by one person alone; often called a personal computer

* **minicomputers** computers midway in size between a desktop computer and a mainframe computer; most modern desktops are much more powerful than the older minicomputers

* **local area network (LAN)** a high-speed computer network that is designed for users who are located near each other

on demand. His invention was stable, fast, and required no mechanical motion. (While Wang invented the fundamental element of core memory, a fellow researcher, Jay W. Forrester at MIT, completed its development by placing the cores in a grid to make memory access faster than ever.) Core memory became a fundamental component of mainframe computers. Wang's patent for the core was the first of forty patents that he would be awarded.

In 1951 Wang took the bold step of quitting Harvard. Using his savings of $600, Wang began his own company, Wang Laboratories, to manufacture and market memory devices and other electronic components. The company grew steadily by manufacturing products for other companies.

In 1964 Wang invented a desktop calculator, called LOCI, his company's first Wang-invented product. For the first time, scientists and engineers could perform mathematical calculations from their desks, without a mainframe computer. When LOCI went to market in 1965, it became a hugely popular tool and company revenues tripled. A series of successful calculators followed, but Wang made a bigger impact with his invention of the commercial word processing machine (1971). The Wang Word Processing System was a revolutionary desktop device with a monitor, computer, and keyboard that was designed to make word processing easy and fast. It was not a microcomputer*, but each machine had its own microprocessor, freeing it from minicomputers* or mainframes, a radical idea at the time. By incorporating network functionality in his word processors, Wang was among the first to sell a local area network (LAN)* that allowed users to share applications, documents, and printers.

When the Wang Word Processing System was introduced in 1976, it catapulted Wang Laboratories to fame, causing company revenues to triple over the next three years. By 1978 the company was the largest supplier of stand-alone word processors in the world; this was several years before IBM entered the market. Other Wang products, including the VS minicomputer and microcomputers, followed.

Wang made several strategic business miscalculations, however. One was not broadening his word processing design to take commercial advantage of a desktop computer until after IBM did so in the 1980s. Later he erred by not making his computers compatible with the newest industry standard—the IBM Personal Computer. In time the huge markets for Wang Laboratories evaporated, and the company tumbled into bankruptcy in 1992.

Wang died of cancer on March 24, 1990, in Boston, Massachusetts. In spite of his humble beginnings in Shanghai, by 1983 he had come to be regarded as the fifth richest man in the world before his company began its slide. A member of the National Inventors Hall of Fame, Wang is still remembered for his contributions to computer science and for the millions of dollars he gave to local arts and educational organizations.

 See also **Word Processors**

Resources

Books

Kenney, Charles C. *Riding the Runaway Horse: The Rise and Decline of Wang Laboratories.* Boston: Little, Brown and Company, 1992.

Wang, An. *Lessons: An Autobiography.* Reading, MA: Addison-Wesley, 1986.

Weather Forecasting

It was not long ago that television weather reports were presented by local personalities standing in front of a marker or chalkboard with a map of the United States drawn on it. To add some spice, small vinyl symbols of the sun and clouds were applied. The local personality was—and for the most part still is—the star. But during the 1980s, a transformation took place. Computers entered the modern television forecast office.

A television weather anchor uses the green screen in the studio. © *AP Images/ Carolyn Kaster.*

meteorologists people who have studied the science of weather and weather forecasting

Supercomputers very high performance computers, usually comprised of many processors and used for modeling and simulation of complex phenomena, like meteorology

This was the beginning of a new era in the forecasting and presentation of TV weather.

In big cities across America, TV weather has become big business. Broadcast meteorologists* have always known that the weather is one of the most important parts of a local newscast. Weather affects everybody, and reports help people answer important questions concerning attire and personal comfort on a daily basis. Television station managers believed that the more gadgets a TV forecaster had, the more people would watch their station and their forecaster. They were correct for the most part. Weather segments and the associated broadcaster are huge audience draws.

Forecast models and guidance are produced by National Weather Service (NWS) supercomputers* in various places around the United States. In the role of a local broadcast weather person, a local TV forecaster has no need or ability to crunch all of those numbers. The local weather person receives data in raw form and also obtains prepared forecasts to aid in creating the forecast for the newscasts of the day.

Up to this point, the NWS has done a lot of the work. Measurements, or *soundings*, as they are termed, are taken at various cities around the country. This data is sent to the NWS for analysis and forecast model production. The final products are then sent to various outlets for distribution. The NWS makes the data available to end users and to private data vendors like Weather Services International (WSI).

Prior to the invention of the computer, weather forecasting had to be done by hand and was as much an art as it was a science. The primary tools were barometric readings, current weather patterns, and the appearance of the sky. Historical patterns of what conditions occurred before notable weather events also influenced predictions of what weather was to occur. Until the invention of the telegraph, readings and weather patterns from outside the area could not be used to adjust the forecast. Since the invention of the computer, weather forecasting has continued to improve as more measurements can be taken and the complexity of calculations continues to rise.

From Data to Televised Weather Forecasts

Data supplied by the government (NWS) is sent to a vendor. That private company takes the data and sends the information, either untouched or reconfigured, to television stations via a satellite delivery system. A small dish is placed on the TV station roof to receive the data. The information is then transmitted into a Windows-based PC for further distribution at the television station. Many people think that this information and raw data are then analyzed by the local PC to produce an instant five-day forecast, but this is not the case. The data PC only receives and distributes data; it does not automatically prepare anything. The role of the local forecaster is to take these data, analyze the information, do a bit of math, and rely on one more element … instinct. This helps the forecaster adjust for local geography, which may influence the weather in the local area, but may not be accounted for in larger models. Only then is a forecast prepared and ready to be broadcasted to the public. To make this happen, more computers are necessary. The main PC sends data to one or more printers that create printouts of forecasts and raw data. Local weather bulletins and statements are also printed. The main PC also sends information to other important office-based computers, as well, where it is processed in different ways for several purposes.

Weather Warnings A Windows-based PC takes the data and makes weather bulletins, such as watches and warnings, and automatically creates informational maps and crawls* to alert viewers to dangerous or potentially dangerous weather conditions. First Warning is a commercial severe weather warning system designed for broadcast television systems created by American meteorologist Gary England (1939), who was at the time a meteorologist in Kansas City. First Warning not only creates the maps and but signals the forecast staff and others in the TV station that severe weather is upon the community and action must be taken. At this point, other TV station staffers, such as engineers in Master Control, can interface with the First Warning System remotely and get the prepared maps or on the air, even if no trained forecaster is on duty at the time. First Alert is an automated version of First Warning with the goal of automating the process of creating televised alerts based upon severe weather bulletins.

Weather Maps Data is also sent to another computer that handles the production of colorful graphics that can be displayed behind the on-camera weather person. This color graphics computer must be able to prepare and display satellite pictures and other visual aids. It must stand ready to be used as an artistic tool by the forecaster or weather producer. Such a system is rarely a Windows-based PC. Most are manufactured by Silicon Graphics to run various "supercharged" operating systems that can handle the graphic requirements of sophisticated programs quickly and with great detail.

Forecasters use rather dull informational maps behind the scenes. Making these maps look understandable and interesting to the viewer is the challenge of the color graphics system. This system must also monitor or create incoming satellite, radar, and temperature maps. It must present thumbnail shots of each individual map to allow the forecast staff to select easily the ones they want to use. This powerhouse of a graphics system not only acts as a producer but must then become a director as well. Various color graphics ready for broadcast can be displayed in time lapse mode* or be custom-produced as an animated movie. These animations might show various weather fronts and features moving across the TV screen behind the on-camera forecaster. The staff also chooses special effects to highlight the display of various graphics. Different wipes between frames or movies can add interest to a TV weather segment and make it stand out from the competition.

* **crawls** severe weather warnings that are broadcast on the bottom of TV screens

* **time lapse mode** to show a sequence of events occurring at a higher than natural speed so it looks like it is happening rapidly rather than in real time

Computer Sciences, 2nd Edition

Highs and Lows

A big H on a map indicates High Pressure. That means heavy, descending air. Air circulates around a High in a clockwise fashion (in the northern hemisphere). The barometer rises as the High approaches. It is usually difficult for clouds to form. Thus, a High usually brings fair weather. A big L on the map signifies Low Pressure. If the L is approaching, a storm is coming. Low Pressure means that air is rising. Rising air is unstable, so clouds form and eventually rain or snow may develop. Hurricanes are intense areas of Low Pressure. The barometer falls as the Low approaches. Fronts usually are connected to Lows. Air circulates counterclockwise around a Low (in the northern hemisphere).

Doppler Radar

The first weather radar units were taken from old aircraft and adapted for use in forecast offices across the United States. The old aviation radars were looking for other airplanes. The forecast offices were concerned with smaller targets: raindrops or snowflakes. Raindrops are perceived by radar when the energy from the radar travels through the air and hits a target. The energy then bounces back to the radar unit and displays where the moving target is located. Doppler Radar takes this one step further by perceiving the rain being blown toward or away from the radar unit. This wind turbulence is then displayed on screen, making it appear that Doppler Radar can observe and show us the wind.

Radar, Internet Access, and Communication Computers

A TV weather office often includes a PC-based control system for Doppler Radar. The radar system itself might be located miles away from the TV station. But a Windows-based PC acts as the command and control center to determine how many miles out the radar should scan. And the computer can determine which radar maps should be displayed.

Various other PC-based systems exist in most TV weather offices. They might include PCs used for news gathering and scriptwriting. Usually these systems serve many functions. Along with news gathering, they can usually access the Internet and intranet systems for various administrative tasks. These systems can provide backup support to the primary data computer, by acquiring data from the Internet. If the main data PC crashes or experiences a problem receiving signals from the satellite or dish, this backup system can be invaluable. This PC may also be used for sending and receiving e-mail and interoffice communications.

There are numerous other options for individuals to get weather forecasts. Numerous websites like weather.com or wunderground.com serve national and local forecasts over the Internet, allowing you to enter a zip code to see the weather forecast for a specific area. Multiple software applications retrieve weather forecasts directly to the desktop to alert users of changing weather conditions.

In summary, there is no question that computers now rule the local TV weather office. Surge protection and backup generators are used regularly at stations all across the country to safeguard the reliance on these systems. Although the days of markers and chalk bring back fond memories, the computer-based systems in a modern TV weather office offer tremendous data capabilities and provide the on-air weather people with a host of sources to display the very latest weather from down the block or around the world.

 See also **Agriculture • Aircraft Traffic Management • Display Devices • Supercomputers**

Resources

Books

Anderson, Katharine. *Predicting the Weather: Victorians and the Science of Meteorology*. Chicago: University of Chicago Press, 2005.

Douglas, Paul. *Restless Skies: The Ultimate Weather Book*, revised ed. New York: Sterling Publishing Company, 2007.

Henson, Robert. *Weather on the Air: A History of Broadcast Meteorology*. Boston: American Meteorological Society, 2010.

Lutgens, Frederick K., and Edward J. Tarbuck. *The Atmosphere: An Introduction to Meteorology*, 11th ed. New York: Prentice Hall, 2010.

Web Sites

National Geographic Society. "How's the Weather Out There? Forecasting the Chaos of Weather." http://environment.national-geographic.com/environment/natural-disasters/weather-forecasting.html (accessed October 25, 2012).

National Geographic Society. "Weather Forecasting." http://science.nationalgeographic.com/science/earth/earths-atmosphere/weather-forecasting-science.html (accessed October 25, 2012).

National Oceanic and Atmospheric Administration (NOAA). "National Weather Service." http://www.weather.gov/ (accessed October 25, 2012).

National Weather Service. "National Data." http://www.nws.noaa.gov/view/national.php?map=on (accessed October 21, 2012).

U.S. Government; science.gov. "Weather Forecasting." http://www.science.gov/browse/w_119A2.htm (accessed October 26, 2012).

Word Processors

Word processing encompasses the process and technology used to create and edit text documents mechanically or on a computer. For years typewriters were the devices for word processing, but with the advent of the personal computer, word processing applications replaced typewriters.

In the mid-1960s typewriters were plentiful. That was when IBM coined the term "word processing" to market their Magnetic Tape Selectric Typewriter (MTST). It was very different from other typewriters because it recorded words on magnetic tape and printed them on paper at the same time. Each tape could store many documents, making it possible to retrieve any of them for later printing, or for generating multiple copies of the same document. This was the first device to allow semi-automatic production of personalized letters: after the user typed the names and addresses, the machine took over and completed the task.

The MTST underwent many transformations, and in 1974 it used internal storage along with external storage on magnetic tapes or cards. However, fast typists could not reach their full potential because it was still a mechanical device. It was not until the introduction of CRT*-based word processing equipment in 1976, with the Wang Computer System, that operators were released from the constraints of mechanical printing devices.

By the mid-1970s customer demand provided the thrust for a new industry: special-purpose computers dedicated to word processing. New vendors of word processors, such as Wang Laboratories, surpassed IBM in sales and product innovation. Word processors have undergone many

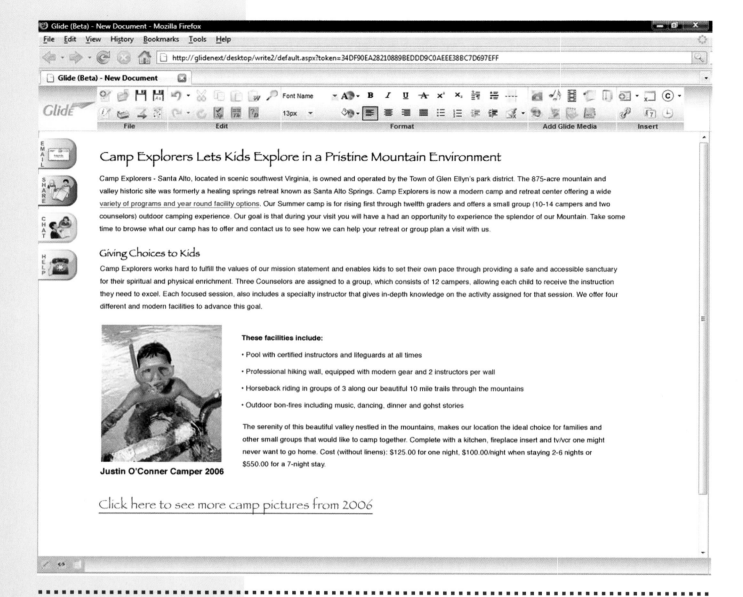

Camp Explorers Lets Kids Explore in a Pristine Mountain Environment

Camp Explorers - Santa Alto, located in scenic southwest Virginia, is owned and operated by the Town of Glen Ellyn's park district. The 875-acre mountain and valley historic site was formerly a healing springs retreat known as Santa Alto Springs. Camp Explorers is now a modern camp and retreat center offering a wide variety of programs and year round facility options. Our Summer camp is for rising first through twelfth graders and offers a small group (10-14 campers and two counselors) outdoor camping experience. Our goal is that during your visit you will have a had an opportunity to experience the splendor of our Mountain. Take some time to browse what our camp has to offer and contact us to see how we can help your retreat or group plan a visit with us.

Giving Choices to Kids

Camp Explorers works hard to fulfill the values of our mission statement and enables kids to set their own pace through providing a safe and accessible sanctuary for their spiritual and physical enrichment. Three Counselors are assigned to a group, which consists of 12 campers, allowing each child to receive the instruction they need to excel. Each focused session, also includes a specialty instructor that gives in-depth knowledge on the activity assigned for that session. We offer four different and modern facilities to advance this goal.

These facilities include:

- Pool with certified instructors and lifeguards at all times
- Professional hiking wall, equipped with modern gear and 2 instructors per wall
- Horseback riding in groups of 3 along our beautiful 10 mile trails through the mountains
- Outdoor bon-fires including music, dancing, dinner and gohst stories

The serenity of this beautiful valley nestled in the mountains, makes our location the ideal choice for families and other small groups that would like to camp together. Complete with a kitchen, fireplace insert and tv/vcr one might never want to go home. Cost (without linens): $125.00 for one night, $100.00/night when staying 2-6 nights or $550.00 for a 7-night stay.

Justin O'Conner Camper 2006

Click here to see more camp pictures from 2006

Transmedia Glide Write, a word processing program. © *AP Images/ PR NEWSWIRE.*

transformations while evolving from dedicated units to multi-purpose personal computers that can perform several functions, including word processing, database management, and accessing the Internet. "Word processor" now refers primarily to the software used to create and manipulate text documents, rather than to the hardware on which the software is run.

Functions of Word Processing Systems

Most word processing systems provide, in a single software package, all the necessary tools that users need to produce a finished document, from entering and editing text, to formatting and proofreading it, and finally to saving and printing it. Here are the steps one would follow to create a document using a word processing program.

Entering Text   A word processing document starts as an empty window on the computer screen with a flashing cursor bar that indicates your location in the document. As you type, the cursor moves to the right, and the characters are displayed on the screen and stored in the computer's memory. You can fix your typing mistakes at any time by pressing the Delete or Backspace keys. Word processors are equipped with the "word wrap" feature, which automatically moves a word to the next line once a line has reached its full capacity. Therefore, the only time you need to press the Return or Enter key is when you want to begin a new line, such as at the end of a paragraph. On typewriters, a typist had to press the return key to begin a new line of text.

Editing Text   Word processors make it easy for you to change and rearrange your work in many different ways. For example you can easily:

- Navigate to different parts of a document by scrolling;
- Search for and replace specific words or phrases throughout a document;
- Insert text at any point;
- Delete text from any section;
- Move text from one part of a document to another;
- Copy text from one part and duplicate it in another section of the same document or to another document.

Formatting Text   This refers to arranging a document so it will look the way you want it to once it is printed. All word processors allow you to format individual characters, lines, paragraphs, or whole documents. What You See Is What You Get (WYSIWYG) systems also give you a good view on screen of what the final product will look like.

Formatting characters affects the size of the characters (point size), their style (typeface, sometimes called font), and whether they are underlined, written in italic, or displayed in bold, heavy type. The formatting of lines and paragraphs determines the spacing between lines of text, the placement of indents or tabs, and the finished length and position of the lines of type on a page. Document formatting applies to margin settings, as well as headers and footers—blocks of text that appear at the top and bottom of every page.

Other text formatting features give you the ability to:

- Create documents with variable-width multiple columns;
- Perform automatic footnoting;
- Generate table-of-contents and indexing for books and other long works;
- Create and format multicolumn tables;
- Attach hidden text, pop-up notes, or audio notes that can be seen or heard by the user but do not show up in the final document;
- Incorporate graphics created with other applications.

An Wang, Innovator

In November 1971 An Wang (1920–1990) launched the Wang 1200, which by twenty-first century standards was an extremely primitive word processor. The Wang 1200's direct competition was IBM's MTST. In 1975, when Wang was well positioned in the word processing market, the Xerox 800 was introduced. It had a Diablo printer and was twice as fast as the Wang 1200. Wang ordered the design of a system that would offer features specifically requested by users—most of whom were women and secretaries. The result, introduced in June 1976 at the New York Syntopican trade show, was the Wang Computer System (WCS). Its price was $30,000. People came in droves to see text editing done on a screen for the first time. The success of the WCS led to a new division of the Wang company devoted exclusively to word processors.

---

* **social network site** a website that enables users to connect with others online and share ideas, interests, media, and more

Additional Tools Word processing does not end with editing and formatting. Most high-end word processors also include a built-in outliner, spell checker, grammar and style checker, thesaurus, mail merger, and indexer. As word processors become more powerful, they take on many features previously found only in desktop publishing (DTP) software such as merging graphics, tables, and text into one document. Many word processors are capable of producing professional-quality books and periodicals, so the line between word processors and DTP programs has faded with time.

Word Processor Programs

From the mid-1990s through the 2000s, the most popular word processing program worldwide was Microsoft's "Word." It is bundled with a variety of other applications as part of the Microsoft Office suite of programs. The latest version of Word (as of 2010) is Microsoft Word 2010 (for the Windows operating system). Another notable word processing program is Corel's "WordPerfect." WordPerfect was the most popular word processing program in the late 1980s, and continuing into the early 1990s. However, WordPerfect's market share decreased in the later part of the 1990s, while Microsoft Word's market share increased. In mid-2012, Corel released version X6 of WordPerfect. Many other word processing programs are available to consumers; for instance, Google Docs is a suite of web-based programs, including a word processor, which is offered for free to online users.

▶ *See also* **Office Automation Systems • Productivity Software • Wang, An**

Resources

Books

Wempen, Faithe. *Microsoft Word 2010 In Depth*. Indianapolis, IN: Que Publishing, 2010.

Web Sites

PC Magazine "WordPerfect Office X6" http://www.pcmag.com/article2/0,2817,2403590,00.asp (accessed October 21, 2012).

Zuckerberg, Mark

American Inventor

1984–

Mark Zuckerberg is one of the most influential young innovators of the twenty-first century. He created the world's most popular social network site* of all time and became one of the richest men on earth with a net worth of $9.4 billion dollars as of 2012.

Beginnings

Zuckerberg was born in 1984 in Dobb's Ferry, New York. He began dabbling in computer programming at an early age using the programming language BASIC. Zuckerberg created a messaging service similar to AOL Instant Messenger (which came out a year later) called ZuckNet. He used it in his father's practice to help announce new patients.

Zuckerberg soon transferred to the preparatory school, Philips Exeter Academy, in New Hampshire. There he began to develop an application called Synapse that could predict the music listening habits of users. This caught the attention of Microsoft and America Online; the latter attempted to hire him, but he declined.

In fall of 2002 he enrolled at Harvard University. There he began to write new applications. As a sophomore, he created CourseMatch, a program that helped student users decide which course to enroll in based on the courses co-students were choosing. He quickly moved on to FaceMash, an application that enabled students to vote on the attractiveness of fellow students. FaceMash was shut down quickly by university authorities.

This incident garnered Zuckerberg some attention from twins Cameron and Tyler Winklevoss (1981–), and Divya Narenda (1982–), who wanted Mark's help in creating a database for Harvard students called the Harvard Connection. Zuckerberg agreed to help, but eventually abandoned their project to work on his own network called The Facebook. The Facebook soon became so popular that Zuckerberg dropped out of Harvard in order to dedicate his time to the site.

Facebook

Facebook started as a way for students at Harvard to communicate with one another and network. The Facebook.com's mission statement is "to make the world more open and connected. People use Facebook to stay connected with friends and family, to discover what's going on in the world, and to share and express what matters to them." Soon it had expanded to hundreds of colleges around the United States. By 2005 it had spread to high schools; in 2006 it opened to the general public and had 12 million users. As of late 2012 it had one billion active monthly users worldwide, with about 81 percent of its monthly users from outside of the United States and Canada.

Its success was not without controversy, though. The Winklevoss Twins and Narenda filed a lawsuit against Zuckerberg and Facebook claiming that he had stolen their concept and prevented them from launching their own site. After six years in court a settlement finally was reached, purported to be approximately sixty-five million dollars. The Winklevosses and Narendra also filed another suit saying they were misled in regards to their stock shares.

In 2010 a Hollywood adaptation of the Facebook story, titled "The Social Network," received a great deal of critical praise and

Mark Zuckerberg. © *Justin Sullivan/ Getty Images. News/Getty Images.*

* initial public offering a company's first public stock offering on the stock market

recognition, although it portrayed Zuckerberg unflatteringly as an anti-hero who deliberately cheated the Winklevosses out of their idea and had a difficult time relating to people. At the same time the film was released, Zuckerberg donated $100 million dollars to the Newark, New Jersey, public school system, saying that he was worried that teaching was not properly compensated or respected in American society. Worried that it would look like a publicity stunt to distract from the film, he attempted to donate it anonymously, but Newark mayor Cory Booker (1969–) pleaded with Zuckerberg to donate it publicly. That winter Zuckerberg also pledged to give away half of his wealth during his lifetime.

The Road Ahead

In 2010, Facebook began experimenting with new features that would eventually redefine much of the way that users experienced the Internet. It created the "like" feature, which allowed users to, literally, give a thumbs-up to their friends' posts. This soon led to websites all around the Internet integrating their content with Facebook so that users could "like" articles, products, videos, and photos. Soon Facebook was omnipresent. According to Nielsen Ratings company, as of 2011 Internet users in the United States spent more time using Facebook than any other Web site.

In 2012 Facebook went public with an initial public offering* on the stock market. Unfortunately for the company, it lost $50 billion of market value because of too large an offering of shares on the market, at too high a price, with little information on how the company would lift the stock value.

On a personal note, the same week that the company went public, Zuckerberg married his girlfriend Priscilla Chan (1965–). The couple had been dating since they met at Harvard.

At a young age, Mark Zuckerberg reinvented the Internet, became one of the most intriguing innovators and billionaires in recent memory, and created a new way for the world to connect.

Resources

Books

Kirkpatrick, David. *The Facebook Effect: The Inside Story of the Company That Is Connecting the World.* New York: Simon & Schuster, 2010.

Periodicals

Grossman, Lev. "Person of the Year 2010: Mark Zuckerberg" *Time,* December 15, 2010.

Isaac, Mike. "Zuckerberg Pressured to Announce $100 Million Donation to Newark," *Forbes,* September 24, 2010.

Vargas, Jose Antonio. "The Face of Facebook" *The New Yorker,* September 20, 2010.

Web Sites

Facebook. "Key Facts" http://newsroom.fb.com/Key-Facts (accessed November 10, 2012).

Forbes. "Mark Zuckerberg" http://www.forbes.com/profile/mark-zuckerberg/ (accessed November 10, 2012).

Nielsen. "State of the Media: The Social Media Report Q3 2011" http://blog.nielsen.com/nielsenwire/social/ (accessed November 10, 2012).

Wohlsen, Marcus "Facebook's Mark Zuckerberg Marries Longtime Girlfriend, Priscilla Chan" http://www.msnbc.msn.com/id/47491836/ns/business/?gt1=54001 (accessed November 11, 2012).

Glossary

3D printing a manufacturing process in which machines lay down successive layers of materials to create three-dimensional products from digital information. Also known as additive manufacturing.

4G shorthand for fourth generation mobile communication and mobile Internet standards, including LTE and Mobile WiMAX networks.

abacus an ancient counting device that probably originated in Babylon around 2400 BCE.

acuity sharpness or keenness, especially when used to describe vision.

additive manufacturing an additive manufacturing process in which machines lay down successive layers of materials to create three-dimensional products from digital information. Also known as 3D printing.

address bus a collection of electrical signals used to transmit the address of a memory location or input/output port in a computer.

aerodynamics the science and engineering of systems that are capable of flight.

agents systems (software programs and/or computing machines) that can act on behalf of another, or on behalf of a human.

aggregate a numerical summation of multiple individual scores.

ailerons control surfaces on the trailing edges of the wings of an aircraft—used to manage roll control.

ALGOL a language developed by the ALGOL committee for scientific applications—acronym for ALGOrithmic Language.

algorithm a rule or procedure used to solve a mathematical problem—most often described as a sequence of steps.

all-points-addressable mode a technique for organizing graphics devices where all points (pixels) on the screen are individually accessible to a running program.

alpha beta pruning a technique that under certain conditions offers an optimal way to search through data structures called "trees."

alphanumeric a character set which is the union of the set of alphabetic characters and the set of single digit numbers.

ambient pertaining to the surrounding atmosphere or environment.

ambiguity the quality of doubtfulness or uncertainty; often subject to multiple interpretations.

amortized phasing out something in until it is gradually extinguished, like a mortgage loan.

amplitude the size or magnitude of an electrical signal.

analog a quantity (often an electrical signal) that is continuous in time and amplitude.

analogous a relationship of logical similarity between two or more objects.

analytic simulation modeling of systems by using mathematical equations (often differential equations) and programming a computer with them to simulate the behavior of the real system.

Analytical Engine Charles Babbage's vision of a programmable mechanical computer.

animatronics the animation (movement) of something by the use of electronic motors, drives, and controls.

anthropomorphic having human form, or generally resembling human appearance.

anti-aliasing introducing shades of gray or other intermediate shades around an image to make the edge appear to be smoother.

app short for application or application software, apps are software features designed to perform specific tasks or improve the user interface with Internet-based resources in a mobile operating system. Apps are common to smartphones, tablets, and other Internet-enabled portable devices.

applet a program component that requires extra support at run time from a browser or run-time environment in order to execute.

approximation an estimate.

arc tangent the circular trigonometric function that is the inverse of the tangent function; values range from $-\Pi/2$ to $\Pi/2$.

artificial intelligence (AI) a branch of computer science dealing with creating computer hardware and software to mimic the way people think and perform practical tasks.

ASCII an acronym that stands for American Standard Code for Information Interchange; assigns a unique 8-bit binary number to every letter of the alphabet, the digits (0 to 9), and most keyboard symbols.

assembler a program that translates human readable assembly language programs to machine readable instructions.

assembly language the natural language of a central processing unit (CPU); often classed as a low level language.

asynchronous events that have no systematic relationship to one another in time.

attenuation the reduction in magnitude (size or amplitude) of a signal that makes a signal weaker.

authentication the act of ensuring that an object or entity is what it is intended to be.

automata theory the analytical (mathematical) treatment and study of automated systems.

automaton an object or being that has a behavior that can be modeled or explained completely by using automata theory.

autonomous self-governing, or being able to exist independently.

autonomy the capability of acting in a self-governing manner; being able to exist independently or with some degree of independence.

axioms statements that are taken to be true, the foundation of a theory.

Bakelite an insulating material used in synthetic goods, including plastics and resins.

ballistics the science and engineering of the motion of projectiles of various types, including bullets, bombs, and rockets.

bandwidth a measure of the frequency component of a signal or the capacity of a communication channel to carry signals.

bar code a graphical number representation system where alphanumeric characters are represented by vertical black and white lines of varying width.

base-2 a number system in which each place represents a power of 2 larger than the place to its right (binary).

base-8 a number system in which each place represents a power of 8 larger than the place to its right (octal).

base-10 a number system in which each place represents a power of 10 larger than the place to its right (decimal).

base-16 a number system in which each place represents a power of 16 larger than the place to its right (hexadecimal).

batch processing an approach to computer utilization that queues non-interactive programs and runs them one after another.

Bayesian networks structures that describe systems in which there is a degree of uncertainty; used in automated decision making.

Bernoulli numbers the sums of powers of consecutive integers; named after Swiss mathematician Jacques Bernoulli (1654–1705).

binary existing in only two states, such as "on" or "off," "one" or "zero."

binary code a representation of information that permits only two states, such as "on" or "off," "one" or "zero."

binary coded decimal (BCD) an ANSI/ISO standard encoding of the digits 0 to 9 using 4 binary bits; the encoding only uses 10 of the available 16 4-bit combinations.

binary digit a single bit, 1 or 0.

binary number system a number system in which each place represents a power of 2 larger than the place on its right (base-2).

binary system a machine or abstraction that uses binary codes.

binomial theorem a theorem giving the procedure by which a binomial expression may be raised to any power without using successive multiplications.

bit a single binary digit, 1 or 0—a contraction of Binary digIT; the smallest unit for storing data in a computer.

bit mapped display a computer display that uses a table of binary bits in memory to represent the image that is projected onto the screen.

bit maps images comprised of bit descriptions of the image, in black and white or color, such that the colors can be represented by the two values of a binary bit.

bit rate the rate at which binary bits can be processed or transferred per unit time, in a system (often a computer communications system).

bit serial mode a method of transferring binary bits one after another in a sequence or serial stream.

bitstream a serialized collection of bits; usually used in transfer of bits from one system to another.

Boolean algebra a system developed by George Boole that deals with the theorems of undefined symbols and axioms concerning those symbols.

Boolean logic a system, developed by George Boole, which treats abstract objects (such as sets or classes) as algebraic quantities; Boole applied his mathematical system to the study of classical logic.

Boolean operators fundamental logical operations (for example "and" and "or") expressed in a mathematical form.

broadband access a term given to denote high bandwidth services.

browsers programs that permit a user to view and navigate through documents, most often hypertext documents.

bugs errors in program source code.

bus a group of related signals that form an interconnecting pathway between two or more electronic devices.

bus topology a particular arrangement of buses that constitutes a designed set of pathways for information transfer within a computer.

byte a group of eight binary digits; represents a single character of text.

C   a programming language developed for the UNIX operating system; it is designed to run on most machines and with most operating systems.

cache   a small sample of a larger set of objects, stored in a way that makes them accessible.

calculus   a method of dealing mathematically with variables that may be changing continuously with respect to each other.

Callback modems   security techniques that collect telephone numbers from authorized users on calls and then dial the users to establish the connections.

capacitates   fundamental electrical components used for storing electrical charges.

capacitive touch   one of the two primary types of touch screen technology, it detects touches utilizing the conductive electrical properties of human skin. This systems, common on many popular smartphones, allows for user control of the device with very light touches.

capacitor   a fundamental electrical component used for storing electrical charge.

carpal tunnel syndrome   a repetitive stress injury that can lead to pain, numbness, tingling, and loss of muscle control in the hands and wrists.

cartography   map-making.

cathode ray tube (CRT)   a glass enclosure that projects images by directing a beam of electrons onto the back of a screen.

cellular automata   a collection or array of objects that are programmed identically to interact with one another.

cellular neural networks (CNN)   a neural network topology that uses multidimensional array structures comprised of cells that work together in localized groups.

central processing unit (CPU)   the part of a computer that performs computations and controls and coordinates other parts of the computer.

certificate   a unique electronic document that is used to assist authentication.

chaos theory   a branch of mathematics dealing with differential equations having solutions which are very sensitive to initial conditions.

checksum   a number that is derived from adding together parts of an electronic message before it is dispatched; it can be used at the receiver to check against message corruption.

chromatic dispersion   the natural distortion of pulses of light as they move through an optical network; it results in data corruption.

cipher   a code or encryption method.

client   a program or computer often managed by a human user, that makes requests to another computer for information.

client/server technology   computer systems that are structured using clients (usually human-driven computers) to access information stored (often remotely) on other computers known as servers.

cloud computing   the use over a network of remote hardware and software computing resources.

cloud storage   a remote network of computing resources accessible over the Internet that hosts user files. Also called a cyberlocker or file hosting service and popular as a location for remote computer back-ups or storing media, cloud storage allows users to access files stored "in the cloud" from other computers, tablets, or smartphones.

coaxial cable   a cable with an inner conducting core, a dielectric material and an outer sheath that is designed for high frequency signal transmission.

cognitive   pertaining to the concepts of knowing or perceiving.

collocation   the act of placing elements or objects in a specific order.

commodity   raw material or service marketed prior to being used.

compiled   a program that is translated from human-readable code to binary code that a central processing unit (CPU) can understand.

compiled executable code   the binary code that a central processing unit (CPU) can understand; the product of the compilation process.

compilers   programs that translate human-readable high-level computer languages to machine-readable code.

computer-aided design (CAD)   the use of computers to replace traditional drawing instruments and tools for engineering or architectural design.

computer-assisted tomography   the use of computers in assisting with the management of X-ray images.

computer peripheral   a device that is connected to a computer to support its operation; for example, a keyboard or a disk drive unit.

concatenates   the joining together of two elements or objects; for example, words are formed by concatenating letters.

concentric circles   circles that have coincident centers.

conceptualization   a creative process that is directed at envisaging a structure or collection of relationships within components of a complex system.

concurrency control   the management and coordination of several actions that occur simultaneously; for example, several computer programs running at once.

concurrent   pertaining to simultaneous activities, for example simultaneous execution of many computer programs.

configuration files   special disk files containing information that can be used to tell running programs about system settings.

cookie   a small text file that a Web site can place on a computer's hard drive to collect information about a user's browsing activities or to activate an online shopping cart to keep track of purchases.

copyrights   the legal rules and regulations concerning the copying and redistribution of documents.

cord cutting   a term that refers to forging traditional cable and satellite-based television subscription services in favor of online streaming media.

cosine   a trigonometric function of an angle, defined as the ratio of the length of the adjacent side of a right-angled triangle divided by the length of its hypotenuse.

counterfeiting   the act of knowingly producing non-genuine objects, especially in relation to currency.

crawls   severe weather warnings that are broadcast on the bottom of TV screens.

creative commons licensing   a free, easy-to-understand, rights management scheme that allows creators to reserve or waive some of their intellectual property rights in the interest of sharing and using works in public forums such as the Internet.

cross-platform   pertaining to a program that can run on many different computer types (often called hardware platforms).

CRT   the acronym for cathode ray tube, which is a glass enclosure that projects images by directing a beam of electrons onto the back of a screen.

cryptanalysis   the act of attempting to discover the algorithm used to encrypt a message.

cryptanalyst a person or agent who attempts to discover the algorithm used to encrypt a message.

cryptography the science of understanding codes and ciphers and their application.

cryptosystem a system or mechanism that is used to automate the processes of encryption and decryption.

cuneiform in the shape of a wedge.

cybercafe a shop, cafe, or meeting place where users can rent a computer for a short time to access the Internet.

cybernetics a unified approach to understanding the behavior of machines and animals developed by Norbert Wiener (1894–1964).

cycloids pertaining to circles, in either a static way or in a way that involves movement.

dark fiber a fiber optic network that exists but is not actively in service, hence the darkness.

data mining a technique of automatically obtaining information from databases that is normally hidden or not obvious.

data partitioning a technique applied to databases (but not restricted to them) which organizes data objects into related groups.

data reduction technique an approach to simplifying data, e.g. summarization.

data warehousing to implement an informational database used to store shared data.

de facto as is.

de jure strictly according to the law.

debug the act of trying to trace, identify, and then remove errors in program source code.

decimal system a number system in which each place represents a power of 10 larger than the place to its right (base-10).

decision trees classifiers in which a sequence of tests are made to decide the class label to assign to an unknown data item; the sequence of.

deformations mechanical systems where a structure is physically misshapen, e.g., dented.

degrade to reduce quality or performance of a system.

delimiters special symbols that mark the beginnings and/or endings of other groups of symbols (for example to mark out comments in program source code).

demographics the study of the statistical data pertaining to a population.

densities measures of the density of a material; defined as the mass of a sample of material, divided by its volume.

deregulation the lowering of restrictions, rules, or regulations pertaining to an activity or operation (often commercial).

die the silicon chip that is the heart of integrated circuit fabrication; the die is encased in a ceramic or plastic package to make the completed integrated circuit (IC).

dielectric a material that exhibits insulating properties, as opposed to conducting properties.

Difference Engine a mechanical calculator designed by Charles Babbage that automated the production of mathematical tables by using the method of differences.

differential analyzer a computer constructed in the early 1930s by Vannevar Bush at Massachusetts Institute of Technology (MIT); it solved differential equations by mechanical integration.

digital a quantity that can exist only at distinct levels, not having values in between these levels (for example, binary).

digital certificates   certificates used in authentication that contain encrypted digital identification information.

digital divide   imaginary line separating those who can access digital information from those who cannot.

digital library   distributed access to collections of digital information.

digital media receiver   any device that connects to a network to locate, download, or stream digital media files from a server so that users can broadcast them to their television. They are also known as media streaming devices or digital media hubs.

digital signature   identifier used to authenticate the sender of an electronic message or the signer of an electronic document.

digital subscriber line (DSL)   a technology that permits high speed voice and data communications over public telephone networks; it requires the use of a DSL modem.

digital subscriber loop (DSL)   the enabling of high-speed digital data transfer over standard telephone cables and systems in conjunction with normal telephone speech data.

digital watermarks   special data structures permanently embedded into a program or other file type, which contain information about the author and the program.

digitizes   converts analog information into a digital form for processing by a computer.

diode   a semiconductor device that forces current flow in a conductor to be in one direction only, also known as a rectifier.

diode tube   an obsolete form of diode that was made of metal elements in a sealed and evacuated glass tube.

direction buttons   buttons on a program with a graphical user interface that provide

a way of navigating through information or documents.

discrete   composed of distinct elements.

disintermediation   a change in business practice whereby consumers elect to cut out intermediary agencies and deal directly with a provider or vendor.

distance learning   the form of education where the instructor and students are separated by either location or time (or both), usually mediated by some electronic communication mechanism.

distributed denial of service (DDoS)   an attack in which large numbers of messages are directed to send network traffic to a target computer, overloading it or its network connection; typically, the attacking computers have been subverted.

distributed systems   computer systems comprising many individual computers that are interconnected and act in concert to complete operations.

documentation   literature in a human readable form that is referred to in support of using a computer or computer system.

domain   a region in which a particular element or object exists or has influence; (math) the inputs to a function or relation.

doping   a step used in the production of semiconductor materials where charged particles are embedded into the device so as to tailor its operational characteristics.

dot.com   a common term used to describe an Internet-based commercial company or organization.

dragged   to have been moved by the application of an external pulling force; quite often occurring in graphical user interfaces when objects are moved with a mouse.

DRAM the acronym for Dynamic Random Access Memory; high density, low cost and low speed memory devices used in most computer systems.

driver a special program that manages the sequential execution of several other programs; a part of an operating system that handles input/output devices.

drop-down menu a menu on a program with a graphical user interface that produces a vertical list of items when activated.

dumb terminal a keyboard and screen connected to a distant computer without any processing capability.

duplex simultaneous two-directional communication over a single communication channel.

dynamic changing; possessing volatility.

dynamic links logical connections between two objects that can be modified if the objects themselves move or change state.

EBCDIC the acronym for Extended Binary Coded Decimal Interchange Code, which assigns a unique 8-bit binary number to every letter of the alphabet, the digits (0-9), and most keyboard symbols.

e-books short for electronic books; books available for downloading onto an e-book reader.

e-reader an electronic device that displays and stores books and other texts.

egress to move out of an object, system, or environment.

electromagnetic a piece of metal that becomes magnetic only when electricity is applied to it; in general, the more electricity applied to metal, the stronger its magnetism.

electromagnetic relays switches that have a high current carrying capacity, which are opened and closed by an electromagnet.

electromagnetic spectrum a range of frequencies over which electromagnetic radiation can be generated, transmitted, and received.

embedded computers computers that do not have human user orientated I/O devices; they are directly contained within other machines.

embedded systems another term for "embedded computers"; computers that do not have human user orientated input/output devices; they are directly contained within other machines.

emoticons symbols or key combinations used in electronic correspondence to convey emotions.

enciphered encrypted or encoded; a mathematical process that disguises the content of messages transmitted.

encryption also known as encoding; a mathematical process that disguises the content of messages transmitted.

end-effector the end piece of a robotic arm that can receive various types of grippers and tools.

end users computer users.

enterprise information system a system of client and server computers that can be used to manage all of the tasks required to manage and run a large organization.

entropy a measure of the state of disorder or randomness in a system.

ephemeris a record showing positions of astronomical objects and artificial satellites in a time-ordered sequence.

ergonomic being of suitable geometry and structure to permit effective or optimal human user interaction with machines.

esoteric relating to a specialized field of endeavor that is characterized by its restricted size.

ether a highly volatile liquid solvent; also, the far regions of outer space.

ethernets a networking technology for mini and microcomputer systems consisting of network interface cards and interconnecting coaxial cables; invented in the 1970s by Xerox corporation.

Euclidean geometry the study of points, lines, angles, polygons, and curves confined to a plane.

expert system a computer system that uses a collection of rules to exhibit behavior which mimics the behavior of a human expert in some area.

fiber optics transmission technology using long, thin strands of glass fiber; internal reflections in the fiber assure that light entering one end is transmitted to the other end with only small losses in intensity; used widely in transmitting digital information.

field searching a strategy in which a search is limited to a particular field; in a search engine, a search may be limited to a particular domain name or date, narrowing the scope of searchable items and helping to eliminate the chance of retrieving irrelevant data.

file transfer protocol (FTP) a communications protocol used to transfer files.

filter queries queries used to select subsets from a data collection, e.g., all documents with a creation date later than 01/01/2013.

firewall a special purpose network computer or software that is used to ensure that no access is permitted to a sub-network unless authenticated and authorized.

firing tables precalculated tables that can give an artillery gunner the correct allowances for wind conditions and distance by dictating the elevation and deflection of a gun.

flashdrive a small, typically portable, solid state drive (SSD) utilizing flash memory for storing or transferring computer data.

floating point operations numerical operations involving real numbers where in achieving a result, the number of digits to the left or right of the decimal point can change.

flowcharts techniques for graphically describing the sequencing and structure of program source code.

fluid dynamics the science and engineering of the motion of gases and liquids.

Freedom of Information Act (FOIA) permits individuals to gain access to records and documents that are in the possession of the government.

freon hydrocarbon based gases used as refrigerants and as pressurants in aerosols.

frequency bands ranges of signal frequencies that are of particular interest in a given application.

frequency modulation a technique whereby a signal is transformed so that it is represented by another signal with a frequency that varies in a way related to the original signal.

full-text indexing a search engine feature in which every word in a document, significant or insignificant, is indexed and retrievable through a search.

fuzzy logic models human reasoning by permitting elements to have partial membership to a set; derived from fuzzy set theory.

gallium arsenide a chemical used in the production of semiconductor devices; chemical symbol GaAs.

gates fundamental building blocks of digital and computer based electric circuits that perform logical operations; for example logical AND, logical OR.

Gaussian classifiers classifiers constructed on the assumption that the feature values of data will follow a Gaussian distribution.

gbps acronym for gigabits per second; a binary data transfer rate that corresponds to a thousand million (billion, or 109) bits per second.

Geographic Information Systems (GIS) computing systems that capture, compare, create, analyze, organize, and display geographical data in a searchable and visually useful ways.

geometric relating to the principles of geometry, a branch of mathematics related to the properties and relationships of points, lines, angles, surfaces, planes, and solids.

germanium a chemical often used as a high performance semiconductor material; chemical symbol Ge.

gestural interface technologies designed to use mathematical algorithms to interpret or respond to human gestures.

GIF animation a technique using Graphic Interchange Format where many images are overlaid on one another and cycled through a sequence to produce an animation.

GIF image the acronym for Graphic Interchange Format where a static image is represented by binary bits in a data file.

gigabit networking the construction and use of a computer network that is capable of transferring information at rates in the gigahertz range.

gigabytes units of measure equivalent to a thousand million (billion, or 109) bytes.

gigahertz (GHz) a unit or measure of frequency, equivalent to a thousand million (billion, or 109) hertz, or cycles per second.

Global Positioning System (GPS) a method of locating a point on the Earth's surface that uses received signals transmitted from satellites to accurately calculate position.

granularity a description of the level of precision that can be achieved in making measurements of a quantity; for example coarse granularity means inexpensive but imprecise measurements.

graphical user interface (GUI) an interface that allows computers to be operated through pictures (icons) and mouse-clicks, rather than through text and typing.

groupware a software technology common in client/server systems whereby many users can access and process data at the same time.

gyros a contraction of gyroscopes; a mechanical device that uses one or more spinning discs which resist changes to their position in space.

half tones black and white dots of certain sizes, which provide a perception of shades of gray.

ham radio a legal (or licensed) amateur radio.

haptic pertaining to the sense of touch.

Harvard Cyclotron a specialized machine (cyclotron) developed in 1948 at Harvard University; it is used to carry out experiments in sub-atomic physics and medicine.

head-mounted displays (HMD) helmets worn by a virtual reality (VR) participant that include speakers and screens for each eye, which display three-dimensional images.

hertz (Hz) a unit of measurement of frequency, equal to one cycle per second; named in honor of German physicist Heinrich Hertz.

heuristic a procedure that serves to guide investigation but that has not been proven.

hexadecimal a number system in which each place represents a power of 16 larger than the place to its right (base-16).

high-bandwidth a communication channel that permits many signals of differing frequencies to be transmitted simultaneously.

high precision/high recall a phenomenon that occurs during a search when all the relevant documents are retrieved with no unwanted ones.

high precision/low recall a phenomenon that occurs when a search yields a small set of hits; although each one may be highly relevant to the search topic, some relevant documents are missed.

high-speed data links digital communications systems that permit digital data to be reliably transferred at high speed.

hoaxes false claims or assertions, sometimes made unlawfully in order to extort money.

holistic looking at the entire system, rather than just its parts.

hydraulic motion being powered by a pressurized liquid (such as water or oil), supplied through tubes or pipes.

hydrologic relating to water.

hyperlinks connections between electronic documents that permit automatic browsing transfer at the point of the link.

Hypertext Markup Language (HTML) an encoding scheme for text data that uses special tags in the text to signify properties to the viewing program (browser) like links to other documents or document parts.

Hypertext Transfer Protocol (HTTP) a simple connectionless communications protocol developed for the electronic transfer (serving) of HTML documents.

I/O the acronym for input/output; used to describe devices that can accept input data to a computer and to other devices that can produce output.

I/O devices devices that can accept "input" data to a computer and to other devices that can produce "output."

icon a small image that is used to signify a program or operation to a user.

illiquid lacking in liquid assets; or something that is not easily transferable into currency.

ImmersaDesks large 4 x 5 foot screens that allow for stereoscopic visualization; the 3-D computer graphics create the illusion of a virtual environment.

ImmersaWalls large-scale, flat screen visualization environments that include passive and active multi-projector displays of 3-D images.

immersive involved in something totally.

in-band pertaining to elements or objects that are within the limits of a certain Local Area Network (LAN).

inference a suggestion or implication of something based on other known related facts and conclusions.

information theory a branch of mathematics and engineering that deals with the encoding, transmission, reception, and decoding of information.

infrared (IR) waves radiation in a band of the electromagnetic spectrum within the infrared range.

infrastructure the foundation or permanent installation necessary for a structure or system to operate.

ingot a formed block of metal (often cast) used to facilitate bulk handling and transportation.

ingress the act of entering a system or object.

init method a special function in an object oriented program that is automatically called to initialize the elements of an object when it is created.

input/output (I/O) used to describe devices that can accept input data to a computer and to other devices that can produce output.

Inquisition the establishment of a religious court (1478–1834) where Christians as well as non-Christians were prosecuted for heresy.

intangible a concept to which it is difficult to apply any form of analysis; something which is not perceived by the sense of touch.

integrated circuit a circuit with the transistors, resistors, and other circuit elements etched into the surface of a single chip of semiconducting material, usually silicon.

integrated modem a modem device that is built into a computer, rather than being attached as a separate peripheral.

intellectual property the acknowledgement that an individual's creativity and innovation can be owned in the same way as physical property.

interconnectivity the ability of more than one physical computer to operate with one or more other physical computers; interconnectivity is usually accomplished by means of network wiring, cable, or telephone lines.

interface a boundary or border between two or more objects or systems; also a point of access.

Internet Protocol (IP) a method of organizing information transfer between computers; the IP was specifically designed to offer low-level support to Transmission Control Protocol (TCP).

Internet Service Provider (ISP) a commercial enterprise which offers paying subscribers access to the Internet (usually via modem) for a fee.

interpolation estimating data values between known points but the values in between are not and are therefore estimated.

intranet an interconnected network of computers that operates like the Internet, but is restricted in size to a company or organization.

ionosphere a region of the upper atmosphere (above about 60,000 meters or 196,850 feet) where the air molecules are affected by the sun's radiation and influence electromagnetic wave propagation.

isosceles triangle a triangle that has two sides of equivalent length (and therefore two angles of the same size).

iterative a procedure that involves repetitive operations before being completed.

Jacquard's Loom a weaving loom, developed by Joseph-Marie Jacquard ((1752–1834), controlled by punched cards; identified as one of the earliest examples of programming automation.

Java applets applets written in the Java programming language and executed with the support of a Java Virtual Machine (JVM) or a Java enabled browser.

joysticks the main controlling levers of small aircraft; models of these can be connected to computers to facilitate playing interactive games.

JPEG (Joint Photographic Experts Group) organization that developed a standard for encoding image data in a compressed format to save space.

k-nearest neighbors a classifier that assigns a class label for an unknown data item by looking at the class labels of the nearest items in the training data.

Kbps a measure of digital data transfer per unit time—one thousand (kilo, K) bits per second.

keywords words that are significant in some context or topic (often used in searching).

kilohertz (kHz) a unit or measure of frequency, equivalent to a thousand (or 103) hertz, or cycles per second.

kinematics a branch of physics and mechanical engineering that involves the study of moving bodies and particles.

kinetics a branch of physics or chemistry concerned with the rate of change in chemical or physical systems.

labeled data a data item whose class assignment is known independent of the classifier being constructed.

lambda calculus important in the development of programming languages, a specialized logic using substitutions that was developed by Alonzo Church (1903–1995).

LEDs the acronym for Light Emitting Diode; a diode that emits light when passing a current and used as an indicating lamp.

lexical analyzer a portion of a compiler that is responsible for checking the program source code produced by a programmer for proper words and symbols.

Library of Congress Classification the scheme by which the Library of Congress organizes classes of books and documents.

light-emitting diode (LED) a discrete electronic component that emits visible light when permitting current to flow in a certain direction; often used as an indicating lamp.

linear pertaining to a type of system that has a relationship between its outputs and its inputs that can be graphed as a straight line.

Linux operating system an open source UNIX operating system that was originally created by Linus Torvalds in the early 1990s.

liquid crystal display (LCD) a type of crystal that changes its level of transparency when subjected to an electric current; used as an output device on a computer.

local area network (LAN) a high-speed computer network that is designed for users who are located near each other.

logarithm the power to which a certain number called the base is to be raised to produce a particular number.

logic a branch of philosophy and mathematics that uses provable rules to apply deductive reasoning.

lossy a nonreversible way of compressing digital images; making images take up less space

by permanently removing parts that cannot be easily seen anyway.

low precision/high recall a phenomenon that occurs during a search when a large set of results are retrieved, including many relevant and irrelevant documents.

lumens a unit of measure of light intensity.

magnetic tape a way of storing programs and data from computers; tapes are generally slow and prone to deterioration over time but are inexpensive.

mainframe large computer used by businesses and government agencies to process massive amounts of data; generally faster and more powerful than desktop computers but usually requiring specialized software.

malicious code program instructions that are intended to carry out malicious or hostile actions; e.g., deleting a user's files.

mammogram an X-ray image of the breast, used to detect signs of possible cancer.

Manhattan Project the U.S. project designed to create the world's first atomic bomb.

mass spectrometers instruments that can identify elemental particles in a sample by examining the frequencies of the particles that comprise the sample.

mass spectrometry the process of identifying the compounds or elemental particles within a substance.

media streaming device a device that enables users to connect to a network or server and view digital media files on their television; also known as a digital media receiver or digital media hub.

megahertz (MHz) a unit or measure of frequency, equivalent to a million (or 106) hertz, or cycles per second.

memex a device that can be used to store personal information, notes, and records that permits managed access at high speed; a hypothetical creation of Vannevar Bush.

menu label the text or icon on a menu item in a program with a graphical user interface.

metadata data about data, such as the date and time created.

meteorologists people who have studied the science of weather and weather forecasting.

metropolitan area network (MAN) a high-speed interconnected network of computers spanning entire cities.

microampere a unit of measure of electrical current that is one-millionth (10^{-6}) amperes.

microchip a common term for a semiconductor integrated circuit device.

microcomputer a computer that is small enough to be used and managed by one person alone; often called a personal computer.

microprocessor the principle element in a computer; the component that understands how to carry out operations under the direction of the running program (CPU).

millisecond a time measurement indicating one-thousandth (or 10^{-3}) of a second.

milliwatt a power measurement indicating one-thousandth (or 10^{-3}) of a watt.

minicomputers computers midway in size between a desktop computer and a mainframe computer; most modern desktops are much more powerful than the older minicomputers.

minimax algorithm an approach to developing an optimal solution to a game or contest where two opposing systems are aiming at mutually exclusive goals.

Minitel network used in France that preceded the Internet, connecting most French homes, businesses, cultural organizations, and government offices.

mnemonic a device or process that aids one's memory.

Mobile device management (MDM) software that aids in standardizing settings, managing programs, protecting confidential information, and securing mobile devices.

mobile operating system (MOS) the software that allows smartphones, tablets, other portable devices to run programs and apps.

modalities classifications of the truth of a logical proposition or statement, or characteristics of an object or entity.

modem the contraction of MOdulator DEModulator; a device which converts digital signals into signals suitable for transmission over analog channels, like telephone lines.

modulation a technique whereby signals are translated to analog so that the resultant signal can be more easily transmitted and received by other elements in a communication system.

modules a generic term that is applied to small elements or components that can be used in combination to build an operational system.

molecular modeling a technique that uses high performance computer graphics to represent the structure of chemical compounds.

motherboard the part of the computer that holds vital hardware, such as the processors, memory, expansion slots, and circuitry.

MPEG (Motion Picture Coding Experts Group) an encoding scheme for data files that contain motion pictures—it is lossy in the same way as JPEG (Joint Photographic Experts Group) encoding.

multiplexes operations in ATM communications whereby data cells are blended into one continuous stream at the transmitter and then separated again at the receiver.

multiplexor a complex device that acts as a multi-way switch for analog or digital signals.

multitasking the ability of a computer system to execute more than one program at the same time; also known as multiprogramming.

mylar a synthetic film, invented by the DuPont corporation, used in photographic printing and production processes, as well as disks and tapes.

nanocomputing the science and engineering of building mechanical machines at the atomic level.

nanometers one-thousand-millionth (one billionth, or 10^{-9}) of a meter.

nanosecond one-thousand-millionth (one billionth, or 10^{-9}) of a second.

nanotechnology the design and construction of machines at the atomic or molecular level.

narrowband a general term in communication systems pertaining to a signal that has a small collection of differing frequency components (as opposed to broadband which has many frequency components).

National Computer Security Center (NCSC) a branch of the National Security Agency responsible for evaluating secure computing systems; the Trusted Computer Systems Evaluation Criteria (TCSEC) were developed by the NCSC.

Network Control Protocol (NCP) a host-to-host protocol originally developed in the early 1970s to support the Internet, which was then a research project.

network packet switching the act of routing and transferring packets (or small sections) of a carrier signal that conveys digital information.

neural modeling the mathematical study and the construction of elements that mimic the behavior of the brain cell (neuron).

neural networks pattern recognition systems whose structure and operation are loosely inspired by analogy to neurons in the human brain.

Newtonian view an approach to the study of mechanics that obeys the rules of Newtonian physics, as opposed to relativistic mechanics; named after Sir Isaac Newton (1643–1727).

nonlinear a system that has relationships between outputs and inputs which cannot be expressed in the form of a straight line.

O-rings 37-foot (11-meter) rubber circles (rings) that seal the joints between the space shuttle's rocket booster segments.

OEM the acronym for Original Equipment Manufacturer; a manufacturer of computer components.

offline the mode of operation of a computer that applies when it is completely disconnected from other computers and peripherals (like printers).

Open Systems Interconnections (OSI) a communications standard developed by the International Organization for Standardization (ISO) to facilitate compatible network systems.

operands when a computer is executing instructions in a program, the elements on which it performs the instructions are known as the.

operating system a set of programs which control all the hardware of a computer and provide user and device input/output functions.

optical character recognition the science and engineering of creating programs that can recognize and interpret printed characters.

optical computing a proposed computing technology which would operate on particles of light, rather than electric currents.

optophone a system that uses artificial intelligence techniques to convert images of text into audible sound.

orthogonal elements or objects that are perpendicular to one another; in a logical sense this means that changes in one have no effect on the other.

oscillator an electronic component that produces a precise waveform of a fixed known frequency; this can be used as a time base (clock) signal to other devices.

oscilloscopes measuring instruments for electrical circuitry; connected to circuits under test using probes on leads and having small screens that display the signal waveforms.

out-of-band pertaining to elements or objects that are external to the limits of a certain local area network (LAN).

overhead the expense or cost involved in carrying out a particular operation.

packet-switched network a network based on digital communications systems whereby packets of data are dispatched to receivers based on addresses that they contain.

packet-switching an operation used in digital communications systems whereby packets (collections) of data are dispatched to receivers based on addresses contained in the packets.

packets collections of digital data elements that are part of a complete message or signal; packets contain their destination addresses to enable reassembly of the message or signal.

paradigm an example, pattern, or way of thinking.

parallel debugging specialized approaches to locating and correcting errors in computer programs that are to be executed on parallel computing machine architectures.

parallel processing the presence of more than one central processing unit (CPU) in a computer, which enables the true execution of more than one program.

parametric modeling a system using variables or parameters that can be observed to change as the system operates.

parity a method of introducing error checking on binary data by adding a redundant bit and using that to enable consistency checks.

pattern recognition a process used by some artificial-intelligence systems to identify a variety of patterns, including visual patterns, information patterns buried in a noisy signal, and word patterns imbedded in text.

PDF the acronym for Portable Document Format, developed by Adobe Corporation to facilitate the storage and transfer of electronic documents.

peer-to-peer services the ways in which computers on the same logical level can interoperate in a structured network hierarchy.

permutations significant changes or rearrangement.

personal area networking the interconnectivity of personal productivity devices such as computers, mobile telephones, and personal organizers.

personal digital assistants (PDA) small-scale hand-held computers that can be used in place of diaries and appointment books.

phosphor a coating applied to the back of a glass screen on a cathode ray tube (CRT) that emits light when a beam of electrons strikes its surface.

photolithography the process of transferring an image from a film to a metal surface for etching, often used in the production of printed circuit boards.

photonic switching the technology that is centered on routing and managing optical packets of digital data.

photons the smallest fundamental units of electromagnetic radiation in the visible spectrum—light.

photosensitive describes any material that will change its properties in some way if subjected to visible light, such as photographic film.

picoseconds one-millionth of a millionth of a second (one-trillionth, or 10^{12}).

piezoelectric crystal an electronic component that when subjected to a current will produce a waveform signal at a precise rate, which can then be used as a clock signal in a computer.

PIN (personal identification number) a password, usually numeric, used in conjunction with a cryptographic token, smart card, or bank card, to ensure that only an authorized user can activate an account governed by the token or card.

ping sweeps technique that identifies properties belonging to a server computer, by sending it collections of "ping" packets and examining the responses from the server.

piracy the unlawful copying and redistribution of computer software, ignoring the copyright and ownership rights of the publisher.

pixel a single picture element on a video screen; one of the individual dots making up a picture on a video screen or digital image.

pixilation the process of generating animation, frame by frame.

plug-in a term used to describe the way that hardware and software modules can be added to a computer system, if they possess interfaces that have been built to a documented standard.

pneumatic powered by pressurized air, supplied through tubes or pipes.

polarity the positive (+) or negative (–) state of an object, which dictates how it will react to forces such as magnetism or electricity.

polarizer a translucent sheet that permits only plane-polarized light to pass through, blocking all other light.

polygon a many-sided, closed, geometrical figure.

polynomial an expression with more than one term.

polypeptide the product of many amino acid molecules bonded together.

population inversion used in quantum mechanics to describe when the number of atoms at higher energy levels is greater than the number at lower energy levels—a condition needed for photons (light) to be emitted.

port logical input/output points on computers that exist in a network.

port scans operations whereby ports are probed so that information about their status can be collected.

potentiometer an element in an electrical circuit that resists current flow (a resistor) but the value of the resistance can be mechanically adjusted (a variable resistor).

predicate calculus a branch of logic that uses individuals and predicates, or elements and classes, and the existential and universal quantifiers, all and some, to represent statements.

privatized to convert a service traditionally offered by a government or public agency into a service provided by a private corporation or other private entity.

progenitor the direct parent of something or someone.

propositional calculus a branch of logic that uses expressions such as "If … then …" to make statements and deductions.

proprietary a process or technology developed and owned by an individual or company, and not published openly.

proprietary software software created by an individual or company that is sold under a license that dictates use and distribution.

protocol an agreed understanding for the sub-operations that make up a transaction, usually found in the specification of inter-computer communications.

prototype a working model or experimental investigation of proposed systems under development.

proxy server a server, system, or application in a computer network that acts as an intermediary for clients needing to mask a computer's location or identity on the network, get around network access restrictions, or that otherwise cannot access information on other servers directly.

pseudocode a language-neutral, structural description of the algorithms that are to be used in a program.

public key information certain status and identification information that pertains to a particular public key (i.e., a key available for public use in encryption).

public key infrastructure (PKI) the supporting programs and protocols that act together to enable public key encryption/decryption.

punched card a paper card with punched holes which give instructions to a computer in order to encode program instructions and data.

quadtrees data structures resembling trees, which have four branches at every node (rather than two as with a binary tree); used in the construction of complex databases.

quality-of-service (QoS) a set of performance criteria that a system is designed to guarantee and support as a minimum.

quantification to quantify (or measure) something.

quantum-dot cellular automata (QCA) the theory of automata as applied to quantum dot architectures, which are a proposed approach for the development of computers at nano-technology scales.

quantum mechanical something influenced by the set of rules that govern the energy and wave behavior of subatomic particles on the scale of sizes that are comparable to the particles themselves.

queue the ordering of elements or objects such that they are processed in turn; first-in, first-out.

radar the acronym for RAdio Direction And Ranging; a technique developed in the 1930s that uses frequency shifts in reflected radio waves to measure distance and speed of a target.

radio telescopes telescopes used for astronomical observation that operate on collecting electromagnetic radiation in frequency bands above the visible spectrum.

random access memory (RAM) a type of memory device that supports the nonpermanent storage of programs and data; so called because various locations can be accessed in any order (as if at random), rather than in a sequence (like a tape memory device).

raster a line traced out by a beam of electrons as they strike a cathode ray tube (CRT).

raster scan pattern a sequence of raster lines drawn on a cathode ray tube such that an image or text can be made to appear.

read-only memory (ROM) a type of memory device that supports permanent storage of programs.

real-time a system, often computer based, that ensures the rates at which it inputs, processes, and outputs information meet the timing requirements of another system.

recursive operations expressed and implemented in a way that requires them to invoke themselves.

recursive functions functions expressed and implemented in a way that requires them to call themselves.

relational database a collection of records that permits logical and business relationships to be developed between themselves and their contents.

relay contact systems systems constructed to carry out logic functions, implemented in relays (electromechanical switches) rather than semiconductor devices.

resistive touch one of the two primary types of touch screen technology, it detects variously applied pressure as device-controlling touches.

resistors electrical components that slow the flow of current.

retinal scan a scan of the retina of the eye, which contains a unique pattern for each individual, in order to identify (or authenticate) someone.

robotics the science and engineering of building electromechanical machines that aim to serve as replacements for human laborers.

routers network devices that direct packets to the next network device or to the final destination.

routing the operation that involves collecting and forwarding packets of information by way of address.

satellite an object that orbits a planet.

scalar a quantity that has magnitude (size) only; there is no associated direction or bearing.

scalar processor a processor designed for high-speed computation of scalar values.

schematic a diagrammatic representation of a system, showing logical structure without regard to physical constraints.

scripting languages modern high level programming languages that are interpreted rather than compiled; they are usually cross-platform and support rapid application development.

search engine optimization (SEO) takes advantage of the way search engines crawl and index the Internet to increase visibility and prominence of a Web site among search engine results.

Secure Sockets Layer (SSL) a technology that supports encryption, authentication, and other facilities and is built into standard UNIX communication protocols (sockets over TCP/IP).

semantics the study of how words acquire meaning and how those meanings change over time.

semiconductor solid material that possesses electrical conductivity characteristics that are similar to those of metals under certain conditions, but can also exhibit insulating qualities under other conditions.

semiconductor diode laser a diode that emits electromagnetic radiation at wavelengths above about 630 nanometers, creating a laser beam for industrial applications.

sensors devices that can record and transmit data regarding the altitude, flight path, attitude, etc., so that they can enter into the system's calculations.

sequentially operations occurring in order, one after another.

server a computer that does not deal directly with human users, but instead handles requests from other computers for services to be performed.

SGML the acronym for Standard Generalized Markup Language, an international standard for structuring electronic documents.

shadow mask a metal sheet behind the glass screen of a cathode ray tube (CRT) that ensures the correct color phosphor elements are struck by the electron beams.

shareware a software distribution technique, whereby the author shares copies of his programs at no cost, in the expectation that users will later pay a fee of some sort.

Sherman Antitrust Act the act of the U.S. Congress in 1890 that is the foundation for all American anti-monopoly laws.

signaling protocols protocols used in the management of integrated data networks that convey a mix of audio, video, and data packets.

SIGs short for "Special Interest Group," SIGs concentrate their energies on specific categories of computer science, such as programming languages or computer architecture.

silica silicon oxide; found in sand and some forms of rock.

silicon a chemical element with symbol Si; the most abundant element in the Earth's crust and the most commonly used semiconductor material.

silicon chip a common term for a semiconductor integrated circuit device.

Silicon Valley an area in California near San Francisco, which has been the home location of many of the most significant information technology-related companies and universities.

silver halide a photosensitive product that has been used in traditional cameras to record an image.

simplex uni-directional communication over a single communication channel.

simputers simple to use computers that take on the functionality of personal computers, but are mobile and act as personal assistants and information organizers.

sine wave a wave traced by a point on the circumference of a circle when the point starts at height zero (amplitude zero) and goes through one full revolution.

single-chip a computer system that is constructed so that it contains just one integrated circuit device.

slide rule invented by Scotsman John Napier (1550–1617), it permits the mechanical automation of calculations using logarithms.

smart card a credit-card style card that has a microcomputer embedded within it; it carries more information to assist the owner or user.

smart devices devices and appliances that host an embedded computer system that offers greater control and flexibility.

smart matter materials, machines, and systems whose physical properties depend on the computing that is embedded within them.

smartphone an Internet-enabled cellular phone with computing ability that utilizes a mobile operating system and apps.

social informatics a field of study that centers on the social aspects of computing technology.

social media online sites or communities—such as Facebook or Twitter—where users share information, photos, video, music, and other media with other users.

softlifting the act of stealing software, usually for personal use (piracy).

software-defined networks (SDNs) the same as virtual private networks (VPNs), where the subscriber can set up and maintain a communications system using management software, on a public network.

solid-state drive (SSD) a data storage device without moving mechanical parts that utilizes an array of circuit assemblies as memory.

sonar the science and engineering of sound propagation in water.

SONET the acronym for Synchronous Optical NETwork, a published standard for networks based on fiber optic communications technology.

sound card a plug-in card for a computer that contains hardware devices for sound processing, conversion, and generation.

source code the human-readable programs that are compiled or interpreted so that they can be executed by a computing machine.

speech recognition the science and engineering of decoding and interpreting audible speech, usually using a computer system.

spider a computer program that travels the Internet to locate Web documents and FTP resources, then indexes the documents in a database, which are then searched using software the search engine provides.

spreadsheet an accounting or business tool that details numerical data in columns for tabulation purposes.

static without movement; stationary.

stellar pertaining to the stars.

streaming media audio or video that are viewable without delay or completely downloading because they are received over the Internet or other computer network by the user as a constant stream of data packets.

streaming media media such a music, videos, movies, and television shows available over the Internet.

subnet a logical section of a large network that simplifies the management of machine addresses.

supercomputer a very high performance computer, usually comprised of many processors and used for modeling and simulation of complex phenomena, like meteorology.

superconductivity the property of a material to pass an electric current with almost no losses; most metals are superconductive only at temperatures near absolute zero.

swap files files used by an operating system to support a virtual memory system, in which the user appears to have access to more memory than is physically available.

syllogistic statements the essential tenets of western philosophical thought, based on hypotheses and categories.

synchronization the time domain ordering of events; often applied when events repeatedly occur simultaneously.

synchronized events occurring at specific points in time with respect to one another.

synchronous synchronized behavior.

synergistic relating to synergism, which is the phenomenon whereby the action of a group of elements is greater than their individual actions.

syntactic analyzer a part of a compiler that scans program source code ensuring that the code meets essential language rules with regard to structure or organization.

syntax a set of rules that a computing language incorporates regarding structure, punctuation, and formatting.

T1 digital circuitry a type of digital network technology that can handle separate voice and/ or digital communications lines.

tablet (or tablet computer) is an Internet-enabled portable computing device with a touch screen user interface.

tangible of a nature that is real, as opposed to something that is imaginary or abstract.

task partitioning the act of dividing up work to be done so that it can be separated into distinct tasks, processes, or phases.

taxonomy the classification of elements or objects based on their characteristics.

TCP the acronym for Transmission Control Protocol; a fundamental protocol used in the networks that support the Internet (ARPANET).

TCP/IP networks interconnected computer networks that use Transmission Control Protocol/Internet Protocol.

TCP/IP protocol suite Transmission Control Protocol/Internet Protocol; a range of functions that can be used to facilitate applications working on the Internet.

telegraph a communication channel that uses cables to convey encoded low bandwidth electrical signals.

telemedicine the technology that permits remote diagnosis and treatment of patients by a medical practitioner; usually interactive bi-directional audio and video signals.

telemetry the science of taking measurements of something and transmitting the data to a distant receiver.

teleoperation any operation that can be carried out remotely by a communications system that enables interactive audio and video signals.

teletype a machine that sends and receives telephonic signals.

terabyte one million million (one trillion, or 10^{12}) bytes.

thermal ignition the combustion of a substance caused by heating it to the point that its particles have enough energy to commence burning without an externally applied flame.

thermodynamic relating to heat energy.

three-body problem an intractable problem in mechanics that involves the attempts to predict the behavior of three bodies under gravitational effects.

thumbnail an image which is a scaled down copy of a much larger image; used to assist in the management of a large catalog of images.

time lapse mode to show a sequence of events occurring at a higher than natural speed so it looks like it is happening rapidly rather than in real time.

title bar the top horizontal border of a rectangular region owned by a program running in a graphical user interface (GUI); it usually contains the program name and can be used to move the region around.

tomography the process of capturing and analyzing X-ray images.

topographic pertaining to the features of a terrain or surface.

topology a method of describing the structure of a system that emphasizes its logical nature rather than its physical characteristics.

touch screen an interface that allows users to control the computing device by touching its screen.

trademark rights a trademark is a name, symbol, or phrase that identifies a trading organization and is owned by that organization.

trafficking transporting and selling; especially with regard to illegal merchandise.

training data data used in the creation of a classifier.

transaction processing operations between client and server computers that are made up of many small exchanges that must all be completed for the transaction to proceed.

transducers devices that sense a physical quantity, such as temperature or pressure, and convert that measurement into an electrical signal.

transistor a contraction of TRANSfer resISTOR; a semiconductor device, invented by John Bardeen, Walter Brattain, and William

Shockley, which has three terminals; can be used for switching and amplifying electrical signals.

translational bridges special network devices that convert low-level protocols from one type to another.

Transmission Control Protocol (TCP) a stream-orientated protocol that uses Internet Protocol (IP); it is responsible for splitting data into packets, transferring it, and reassembling it at the receiver.

transmutation the act of converting one thing into another.

trigonometry a branch of mathematics founded upon the geometry of triangles.

triodes nearly obsolete electronic devices constructed of sealed glass tubes containing metal elements in a vacuum; triodes were used to control electrical signals.

Trojan horse potentially destructive computer program that masquerades as something benign; named after the wooden horse employed by the Acheans to conquer Troy.

tunneling a way of handling different communication protocols, by taking packets of a foreign protocol and changing them so that they.

Turing machine a proposed type of computing machine that takes inputs off paper tape and then moves through a sequence of states under the control of an algorithm; identified by Alan Turing (1912–1954).

twisted pair an inexpensive, medium bandwidth communication channel commonly used in local area networks.

ubiquitous to be commonly available everywhere.

ultrasonic the transmission and reception of sound waves that are at frequencies higher than those audible to humans.

Uniform Resource Locator (URL) a reference to a document or a document container using the Hypertext Transfer Protocol (HTTP); consists of a hostname and path to the document.

Universal Product Code (UPC) the first barcode standard developed in 1973 and adopted widely since.

UNIX operating system that was originally developed at Bell Laboratories in the early 1970s.

uplinks connections from a client machine to a large network; frequently when information is being sent to a communications satellite.

vacuum tube an electronic device constructed of a sealed glass tube containing metal elements in a vacuum; used to control electrical signals.

valence a measure of the reactive nature of a chemical element or compound in relation to hydrogen.

variable a symbol, such as a string of letters, which may assume any one of a set of values known as the domain.

vector graphics graphics output systems whereby pairs of coordinates are passed to the graphics controller, which are interpreted as end points of vectors to be drawn on the screen.

vector processing an approach to computing machine architecture that involves the manipulation of vectors (sequences of numbers) in single steps, rather than one number at a time.

vector supercomputer a highly optimized computing machine that provides high performance using a vector processing architecture.

velocities vector quantities that have a magnitude or speed and a direction.

Venn diagrams diagrams used to demonstrate the relationships between sets of objects, named after John Venn, a British logician.

venture capitalists persons or agencies that speculate by providing financial resources to enable product development, in the expectation of larger returns with product maturity.

video capture cards plug-in cards for a computer that accepts video input from devices like televisions and video cameras, allowing the user to record video data onto the computer.

video compression algorithms special algorithms applied to remove certain unnecessary parts of video images in an attempt to reduce their storage size.

virtual channel connection an abstraction of a physical connection between two or more elements (or computers); the complex details of the physical connection are hidden.

virtual circuit like a virtual channel connection, a virtual circuit appears to be a direct path between two elements, but is actually a managed collection of physical connections.

Virtual Private Networks (VPNs) a commercial approach to network management where privately owned voice and data networks are set up on public network infrastructure.

virtual reality (VR) the use of elaborate input/output devices to create the illusion that the user is in a different environment.

virtualization as if it were real; making something seem real, e.g., a virtual environment.

visible speech a set of symbols, comprising an alphabet, that "spell" sounds instead of words.

visualization a technique whereby complex systems are portrayed in a meaningful way using sophisticated computer graphics systems; e.g., chemical molecules.

voice over Internet protocol (VoIP) communication technology that delivers telephone calls, video calls, and voice communications via Internet Protocol.

volatile subject to rapid change; describes the character of data when current no longer flows to a device (that is, electrical power is switched off).

waveform an abstraction used in the physical sciences to model energy transmission in the form of longitudinal or transverse waves.

Web surfers people who "surf" (search) the Internet frequently.

wide area network (WAN) an interconnected network of computers that spans upward from several buildings to whole cities or entire countries and across countries.

wireless lavaliere microphones small microphones worn around the speakers' necks, which attach to their shirts.

wireless local area network (WLAN) an interconnected network of computers that uses radio and/or infrared communication channels, rather than cables.

workstations computers (usually within a network) that interact directly with human users (much the same as "client computers").

xerography a printing process that uses electrostatic elements derived from a photographic image to deposit the ink.

XML the acronym for eXtensible Markup Language; a method of applying structure to data so that documents can be represented.

Directory of Computer Sciences Organizations

A

Apple, Inc.
1 Infinite Loop
Cupertino, CA, 95014
USA
Telephone: (408) 996-1010
Email: media.help@apple.com
Web site: www.apple.com

Argonne National Laboratory: Mathematics and Computer Science Division
9700 South Cass Avenue, Building 240
Argonne, IL, 60439-4844
USA
Telephone: (630) 252-8808
Web site: http://www.mcs.anl.gov

Association for the Advancement of Artificial Intelligence
2275 East Bayshore Road, Suite 160
Palo Alto, CA, 94303
USA
Telephone: (650) 328-3123
Fax: (650) 321-4457
Web site: http://www.aaai.org

Association for Computer Machinery
2 Penn Plaza, Suite 701
New York, NY, 10121-0701
USA
Telephone: (800) 342-6626
Email: acmhelp@acm.org
Web site: http://www.acm.org

Association for Information Systems
PO Box 2712
Atlanta, GA, 30301-2712
USA
Telephone: (404) 413-7445
Email: onestop@aisnet.org
Web site: https://ais.site-ym.com

B

Bell Laboratories
600-700 Mountain Avenue
Murray Hill, NJ, 07974
USA
Telephone: (908) 508-8080
Email: execoffice@alcatel-lucent.com
Web site: http://www.alcatel-lucent.com/belllabs

Bletchley Park
The Mansion, Bletchley Park
Milton Keynes, MK3 6EB
UK
Telephone: +44 (0) 1908 640404
Fax: +44 (0) 1908 274381
Email: info@bletchleypark.org.uk
Web site: http://www.bletchleypark.org.uk

C

Cisco Systems, Inc.
170 West Tasman Drive
San Jose, CA, 95134
USA
Telephone: (408) 526 4000
Web site: www.cisco.com

Computer History Museum
1401 North Shoreline Boulevard
Mountain View, CA, 94043
USA
Telephone: (650) 810-1010
Fax: (650) 810-1055
Web site: http://www.computerhistory.org

Computing and Information Technology Interactive Digital Educational Library (CITADEL)
Web site: http://citidel.villanova.edu

Cray, Inc.
901 Fifth Avenue, Suite 1000
Seattle, WA, 98164
USA
Telephone: (206) 701-2000
Fax: (206) 701-2500
Email: crayinfo@cray.com
Web site: www.cray.com

D

Defense Advanced Research Projects Agency
675 North Randolph Street
Arlington, VA, 22203-2114
USA
Telephone: (703) 526-6630
Email: outreach@darpa.mil
Web site: http://www.darpa.mil

E

Electronic Frontier Foundation
454 Shotwell Street
San Francisco, CA, 9411-1914
USA
Telephone: (415) 436-9333
Fax: (415) 436-9993
Email: info@eff.org
Web site: https://www.eff.org

G

GE Global Research
1 Research Circle
Niskayuna, NY, 12309
USA
Telephone: (518) 387-7914
Web site: http://ge.geglobalresearch.com

Google Developers Academy
Web site: https://developers.google.com/academy/

Google, Inc.
1600 Amphitheatre Parkway
Mountain View, CA, 94043
USA

Telephone: (650) 253-0000
Fax: (650) 253-0001
Web site: www.google.com/about/
company

H

Hewlett-Packard Co.
3000 Hanover St.
Palo Alto, CA, 94304
USA
Telephone: (650) 857-1501
Fax: (650) 857-5518
Web site: www.hp.com

**Hon Hai Precision Industry Co.,
Ltd. (Foxconn)**
105 S. Puente Street
Brea, CA, 92821
USA
Telephone: (714) 626-6900
Fax: (714) 626-6901
Email: foxconn-service@foxconn.
com
Web site: www.foxconnchannel.com

I

**Institute of Electrical and
Electronics Engineers (IEEE)
Computer Society**
2001 L Street NW, Suite 700
Washington, DC, 20036-4928
USA
Telephone: (202) 371-0101
Fax: (202) 728-9614
Email: help@computer.org
Web site: http://www.computer.org

Intel Corp.
2200 Mission College Boulevard
Santa Clara, CA, 95952
USA
Telephone: (408) 765-8080
Web site: www.intel.com

**International Business Machines
Corp.**
1 New Orchard Road
Armonk, NY, 10504
USA
Telephone: (800) 426-4968
Web site: www.ibm.com

**International Standards
Organization**
1, ch. de la Voie-Creuse, CP 56
Geneva, CH-1211 Geneva 20
Switzerland
Telephone: +41 22 749 01 11
Email: central@iso.org
Web site: http://www.iso.org

Internet Society
1775 Wiehle Avenue, Suite 201
Reston, VA, 20190-5108
USA
Telephone: (703) 439-2120
Fax: (703) 326-9881
Email: isoc@isoc.org
Web site: https://www.internetsociety.
org

L

Los Alamos National Laboratory
PO Box 1663
Los Alamos, NM, 87545
USA
Telephone: (505) 667-7000
Email: community@lanl.gov
Web site: http://www.lanl.gov

M

**Massachusetts Institute of
Technology (MIT) Computer
Science and Artificial Intelligence
Laboratory (CSAIL)**
The Strata Center, Building 32,
32 Vassar Street
Cambridge, MA, 02139
USA
Telephone: (617) 253-5851
Fax: (617) 258-8682
Web site: http://www.csail.mit.edu

Microsoft Corp.
1 Microsoft Way
Redmond, WA, 98052
USA
Telephone: (425) 882-8080
Web site: www.microsoft.com

Microsoft Research (MSR)
1 Microsoft Way
Redmond, WA, 98052
USA

Telephone: (800) 642-7676
Web site: http://research.microsoft.
com

N

**NASA Advanced Supercomputing
(NAS) Division**
Ames Research Center
Moffett Field, CA, 94035
USA
Telephone: (650) 604-4377
Email: contact-nas@nas.nasa.gov
Web site: http://www.nas.nasa.gov

**National Center for
Supercomputing Applications**
1205 West Clark Street, Room 1008
Urbana, IL, 61801
USA
Telephone: (217) 244-0710
Email: help@ncsa.illinois.edu
Web site: http://ncsa.illinois.edu

**The National Museum of
Computing**
Block H, Bletchley Park
Milton Keynes, MK3 6EB
UK
Telephone: +44 (0)1908 374708
Email: lin.jones@tnmoc.org
Web site: http://www.tnmoc.org

O

**Oak Ridge Leadership Computing
Facility**
PO Box 2008
Oak Ridge, TN, 37831-6161
USA
Telephone: (865) 241-6536
Fax: (865) 241-2850
Email: help@olcf.ornl.gov
Web site: http://www.olcf.ornl.gov

Oracle Corp.
500 Oracle Parkway
Redwood Shores, CA, 94065
USA
Telephone: (650) 506-7000
Web site: www.oracle.com

P

Palo Alto Research Center (PARC)
3333 Coyote Hill Road
Palo Alto, CA, 94304
USA
Telephone: (650) 812-4000
Web site: www.parc.com

S

Samsung Electronics Co., Ltd.
85 Challenger Road
Ridgefield Park, NJ, 07660
USA
Telephone: (800) 726-7864
Fax: (864) 752-1632
Web site: www.samsung.com

SAP
3999 West Chester Pike
Newton Square, PA, 19073
USA
Telephone: (610) 661-1000
Web site: www.sap.com

SRI International
333 Ravenswood Ave.
Menlo Park, CA, 94025
USA
Telephone: (650) 859-2000
Web site: www.sri.com

T

Texas Instruments, Inc.
12500 TI Boulevard
Dallas, TX, 75243
USA
Telephone: (972) 995-2011
Web site: www.ti.com

Thomas J. Watson Research Center
1101 Kitchawan Road
Yorktown Heights, NY, 10598
USA
Telephone: (914) 945-3000
Web site: http://www.research.ibm.com/labs/watson

W

World Wide Web Consortium (W3C)
32 Vassar Street, Room 32-G515
Cambridge, MA, 02139
USA
Telephone: (617) 253-2613
Web site: http://www.w3.org

Cumulative Index

Canon, 4:75, 229

Canonic And-Or implementation, 2:77

CANs (controller area networks), 3:6

Capacitive touch screens, 2:185, 255

Capacitors, 1:160

Capek, Karel, 1:216, 3:24–25

CAPP (computer-aided process planning), 3:63–64

Carbon nanotubes, 3:49

Card readers
    ATMs, 3:30
    punched cards, 1:55, 58, 2:114

Card, Stuart, 4:221

Careers
    computer professionals, 3:54–57
    distance learning, 3:91
    multimedia development, 2:106
    system analysts, 2:248
    systems designers, 2:251

Carlson, Chester, 1:276, 278

Carnegie Institute of Technology, 3:79

Carnegie Mellon University, 3:90, 4:81, 185

Carpal tunnel syndrome, 1:66, 149–150

Carter, Thomas ("Tom"), 2:38–39

Case-based design tools, architecture, 3:22

Cash, digital, 1:69, 4:107

CAT scans, 3:65–67, 134

Catalog servers, 2:227
    See also Servers

Cataloging, electronic, 3:152

Catastrophe insurance market, 4:108–109

Catastrophe Risk Exchange (CATEX), 4:109

Cathode ray tube (CRT) displays, 1:255, 2:78–81, 254–255

Cathodes, in vacuum tubes, 1:253, 255

CATV (Community Antenna Television) systems, 1:239

Cave Automated Virtual Environments (CAVEs), 1:256, 257–258

The Caves of Steel (Asimov), 3:25, 4:127

CB radio, 3:118

CBR (constant bit rate) service, 2:14

CC (Creative Commons) licensing, 4:51–52

CCDs (charge-coupled devices), 4:231

CCTV (closed circuit television) systems, 4:141

CD drives, 3:131

CD-R (compact disk-recordable) technology, 2:244

CD-ROM (compact disk-read only memory), 1:171, 2:243–244

CD-RW (compact disk-rewritable) technology, 2:244

CDC. *See* Control Data Corporation (CDC); U.S. Centers for Disease Control and Prevention (CDC)

CDC 160/160-A minicomputers, 1:175

CDC 6600 supercomputer, 3:68

CDC 7600 supercomputer, 3:68

CDMA (Code Division Multiple Access) networks, 1:119, 3:41, 42

CDMA2000/WCDMA technologies, 3:41, 4:209

CDPD (cellular digital packet data) service, 2:281

CDS2000E Enterprise Server, 4:5

CDV (cell delay variation), 2:15

Cedeno, Judy, 4:115

Cel animation, 1:9–10

Cell Delay Variation (CDV), 2:15

Cell header generation/extraction, 4:22

Cell Loss Priority (CLP), 4:20

Cell multiplex and demultiplex function, 4:22

Cell phone towers, 2:*38*

Cell phones, 3:*40*, **40–42**
    authentication functions, 4:26
    e-mail capabilities, 4:168
    encryption needs, 4:58
    history, 2:38–41, 3:40–42
    phreaker hackers, 4:148
    social media access, 3:216, 217
    telephone system interactions, 3:246–247
    touch screens, 2:*254*

Cells (data packets), 4:19, 20

Cells, spreadsheets, 3:236–238, *237*

Cells, virtual circuits, 2:13–14

Cellular automata, 4:11, 13

Cellular digital packet data (CDPD) service, 2:281

Cellular networks
    base stations, 3:40–41
    generations of, 1:240
    increasing data transmission capabilities, 2:59
    overview, 1:238
    varying standards, 1:119

Cellular neural networks (CNNs), 4:217

Cellular technology, 2:**37–42**, *38*

Censorship: national, international, 4:**35–37**, *36*
    Arab Spring Internet blockage, 3:219–220
    Internet control and, 4:178–179
    social media protests, 3:222

Census Bureau, 1:**39–42**, *40*, 96, 100, 101, 107, 4:236

Centaur Records, 1:185

Center for Democracy and Technology, 4:37

CENTRal EXchange (CENTREX) service, 2:270

Central processing units (CPUs), 2:**42–45**, *43*
    assembly language and architecture, 2:7–9
    cache memory, 2:35–37, *36*
    mainframes, 1:155, 156, 157
    security measures, 2:217
    supercomputers, 1:232, 233
    vector processing, 1:233–234, 3:68
    See also Microprocessors; Parallel processing

Centronics connectors, 2:224

Century Optics, 4:74

CenturyLink, 4:176

Cerf, Vinton, 1:25, 4:260

CERN (European Council for Nuclear Research), 3:193, 4:32, 111

CERT (Computer Emergency Response Team), 4:87–88, 185

Certificate Authority (CA), 1:67–68, 2:270, 4:25, 99

Challenge-response password systems, 1:222

Challenger (space shuttle), 3:228, 4:125

Character-based interfaces, 3:249

Character codes. *See* Codes

Charge-coupled devices (CCDs), 4:231

Chat servers, 2:227
    See also Servers

Check out (e-commerce), 1:68

Checks, digital, 4:109

Checksums, 2:151

Chemistry, 4:**37–41**, *38*

Chemometrics, 4:40

Chen, Steve, 3:69

Chess, computer, 1:83

Database servers, 2:227
See also Servers
The Day the Earth Stood Still (film),
4:128
DB-25 connectors, 2:224
DDL (Data Definition Language),
2:238
DDoS (distributed denial of service),
1:224, 2:118, 3:213, 4:180–181
De facto standards, 1:119
De Forest, Lee, 1:86, 253
De jure standards, 1:119
De Morgan, Augustus, 1:151
Deafness, assistive technology,
4:16–17, 18
"Death Race" (video game), 1:81
Debit cards, 3:31
Debugging
origin of term, 1:60, 101, 255
project management, 3:204–205
DEC (Digital Equipment Corporation),
1:15, 44, 176
Decibel (unit), 2:24
Decideability problem, 1:251
Decimal number system. *See* Base-10
number system
Decision support systems (DSSs),
3:79–81
agriculture needs, 3:5–6
geographic information systems
and, 3:115, 116
overview, 2:109
in programming, 2:201
systems design, 2:250–251
Decision trees, 2:178, 4:68
Decrypted values, 1:67
Dede, Chris, 1:257–258
Deep Blue chess competition, 1:83,
111, 3:44–45
Deep Fritz chess program, 3:45
Defense Advanced Research Projects
Agency. *See* DARPA (Defense
Advanced Research Projects Agency)
Defense Meteorological Satellite
Program (DMSP) Operational
Linescan System, 3:*210*
Definiteness, in algorithms, 2:5
Defragmentation tools, 3:129
Delagi, Greg, 2:*262*
Delay-line storage, 1:58
Dell laptops, 2:*104*
DeMarco, Tom, 2:251

Demodulation of signals, 2:57–58
DENDRAL, 3:102–103, 144
Denial of service cybersecurity attacks,
1:224, 2:118, 3:213, 4:180–181
Denning, Peter J., 4:145
Derivatives, 1:4
DES (Data Encryption Standard), 4:57
Desargues, Girard, 1:207
Descartes, René, 1:207–208
Descendants, in object-oriented
programming, 2:159–160
Descriptive markup, 2:131, 3:85–86
See also Markup languages
Design tools, 2:28–29, **69–72,**
70, 71, 72
Desktop publishing, 3:**82–86**
journalism use, 4:200–201
office automation systems, 1:197
productivity software, 3:199–200
technology, 3:241–245
word processing *vs.*, 3:82, 262
Desktop-style windows interface, 1:270
Desktop videoconferencing, 1:198
Destroy method (Java applets), 4:192
DETC (Distance Education and
Training Council), 3:88
Deterministic models, political events,
4:237
Dethloff, Jürgen, 2:205
Deutsch Institute fur Normung (DIN),
1:120
Developer's office suite software, 3:137
Developing nations, information access,
4:161–162
Device managers, in operating systems,
2:162, 163
Devol, George C., Jr., 1:213
DFDs (data flow diagrams), 2:251
Dialects, of programming languages,
2:193
DIALOG information service, 1:114
Dialog-oriented systems, 1:133
Dick Tracy comic book series, 3:119
Dictation systems, 3:234–236, 4:16
Difference Engine, 1:20, 29–30, 95,
151, 152, 2:191, 3:191
Differential analyzers, 1:4, 53, 3:191
Differential equations, 1:4, 5
Differential GPS measurements, 4:137
Diffie, Whitfield, 4:58
Digital backs (cameras), 4:230
Digital cameras. *See* Cameras

Digital cash, 1:69, 4:107
Digital cellular systems, 2:40
Digital certificates. *See* Certificate
Authority (CA)
Digital checks, 4:109
Digital computing, 1:**49–51**
abacuses, 1:1–2, 49–50
analog computing *vs.*, 1:2–3, 4–5
mixed systems, 1:49
physics applications, 3:192, 193
speed *vs.* accuracy, 1:50, 51
Digital divide, 4:159–162
Digital Equipment Corporation (DEC),
1:15, 44, 176
Digital filmmaking, 4:*73*, 73–76
Digital images, 4:**76–78**
Digital integrated circuits, 1:126–127
Digital Landfill (art Web site), 4:8
Digital libraries, 3:152–153, 4:*79,*
79–83
Digital Library Federation (DLF), 4:79
Digital Living Network Alliance
(DLNA), 2:148
Digital logic design, 2:*73*, **73–78,** *74,*
75, 76, 78*t*
Digital Millennium Copyright Act
(DMCA), 3:225, 4:50
Digital music synthesis, 1:184
Digital photography, 4:*83*, **83–86,**
229–232
Digital rights management (DRM),
4:50
Digital signatures, 1:221, 4:58, **86–89,**
87, 88
Digital single lens reflex (DSLR)
cameras, 4:75
Digital subscriber line. *See* DSL (digital
subscriber line)
Digital telephony, 1:237–238
See also Telephone networks
Digital-to-analog conversion
chip-based, 1:51
for mixed systems, 1:49
music synthesis, 1:184, 2:142–145
time lags, 1:50–51
Digital versatile disks. *See* DVDs (digital
versatile disks)
Digital wallets, 1:69, 4:109
Digitizing tablets, 2:254
Dijkstra, Edsger W., 2:201
DIN (Deutsch Institute fur Normung),
1:120

Diode tubes, 1:253
Diodes
  optical communications, 1:202
  photo, 3:147
  in transistors, 1:245
Direct mail, political applications, 4:234
Direct manipulation systems, 1:133, 134–135
Director (multimedia authoring system), 1:14–15
Directories, search engines, 4:245
Disabilities
  assistive computer technology, 4:13–19, *14*
  educational virtual reality, 1:258
  keyboards, 1:150
  user interfaces, 3:251
  voice commands, 3:252
  whiteboard adaptations, 4:105
Disabilities Discrimination Act (United Kingdom), 4:13–14, 18
Disaster insurance market, 4:108–109
Discrete event simulation, 1:228
  See also Simulation
Discrete numbers, defined, 1:36
Discussion groups, e-mail, 1:73–74, 75
Disintermediation, 1:70
Disk defragmentation tools, 3:129
Disk management tools, 3:129
DiskOnKey flash drives, 2:243
Disney, Roy O., 1:12
Disney, Walt, 1:10, 11–12
Display devices, 2:**78–84,** *79,* 3:30, 4:156
  See also Graphic devices
Distance Education and Training Council (DETC), 3:88
Distance learning, 2:104, 126, 3:*87,* **87–92,** 4:103–106
Distant/asynchronous distance learning, 3:90
Distant/synchronous distance learning, 3:89
Distracted driving, 2:41–42, 3:42
Distributed authentication, 1:222
Distributed computing systems, 2:46–50
  See also Client/server technology
Distributed data warehousing systems, 4:71–72
Distributed denial of service (DDoS), 1:224, 2:118, 3:213, 4:180–181
Distributed processing databases, 2:239
Distributed system agents, 4:2, 3

District boundaries, data processing, 4:235
Division of Parasitic Diseases (CDC), 3:33–34
DLF (Digital Library Federation), 4:79
DLNA (Digital Living Network Alliance), 2:148
DMCA (Digital Millennium Copyright Act), 3:225, 4:50
DML (Data Manipulation Language), 2:238
DMSP (Defense Meteorological Satellite Program) Operational Linescan System, 3:*210*
DNA computing, 3:166, 4:128, 211–213, 217
DNA sequencing, 3:163–165
DNA structure, 4:39
DNS (Domain Name System), 1:222, 4:178, 185
Document cameras, 4:104
Document Object Model (DOM), 4:197
Document processing, 2:**85–87,** 3:82–86, 149–150
Document vectors, 1:115
Document viewers, 3:130
Documentation
  in object-oriented programming, 2:160
  open source applications, 3:186
  system analysis, 2:248
DoD (Department of Defense) firewall model, 4:130
Dodge, Charles, 1:185
DOM (Document Object Model), 4:197
Domain Name System (DNS), 1:222, 4:178, 185
Domain Wall Memory (DWM), 1:162, 2:139
Donor impurities, 1:243, 244
Dope sheets, 1:9
Doping, of semiconductors, 1:125, 165, 3:48
Doppler radar, 3:257
Dorsey, Jack, 3:217
Dorson, Richard M., 4:265
DOS operating system
  as command line system, 1:132, 3:249–250
  in IBM PCs, 1:18, 110
  MS-DOS, 1:84, 170, 171, 2:163, 4:267

Dot matrix printers, 2:188–189
Dotcom, Kim, 4:*48*
dot.coms, 1:69, 3:54, 4:247–248
Dots per inch (dpi), 2:188
Downlink data rates, 2:258–259
Download *vs.* upload bandwidth, 4:29–30
Dr. Strangelove: Or How I Learned to Stop Worrying and Love the Bomb (film), 4:127
Dragging, in windows interfaces, 1:270, 271
Dragon capsule, 3:230
DRAM (dynamic random access memory), 1:89, 2:137
Driverless cars, 4:44
Driving while distracted, 2:41–42, 3:42
DRM (digital right management), 4:50
Droids, 1:216
  See also Robotics
Drop-down menus, 1:271
Drugs, prescription, 3:162
Drum scanners, 4:231–232
Dry-erase boards, 2:254
DSL (digital subscriber line)
  bandwidth capacity, 4:29
  overview, 2:58–59
  service providers, 4:247, 248
DSLR (digital single lens reflex) cameras, 4:75, 84–85
DSSs. *See* Decision support systems (DSSs)
Dudley, Homer, 2:144
Duke University, 3:216
Dumb terminals, 1:158, 177–178, 4:207–208
Dummy statements, 2:2
Duplex cellular networks, 2:38
  See also Cellular networks
DuPont, 2:241
DVDs (digital versatile disks), 2:244, 3:113, 131
Dvorak, August, 1:149
Dvorak keyboard layout, 1:149
DWM (domain wall memory), 1:162, 2:139
DXplain decision support system, 3:81
Dye-based inks, 2:190
Dye sublimation, 2:190–191
Dynabook project, 1:95, 272
Dynamic data visualizations, 3:73

Education *(continued)*
    Open Source Education project,
      3:*184*
    Organick, Elliot contributions,
      3:187–188
    virtual reality use, 1:*256,* 256–260,
      257
    See also Colleges and universities
Educational software, 3:**95–98**
EDVAC (Electronic Discrete Variable
  Automatic Computer), 1:58–59, 63,
  66, 87, 2:90, 91
edX online course platform, 3:90, 4:106
EEPROM (Electronic erasable
  programmable read-only memory),
  1:161
EGP (Exterior Gateway Protocol), 4:173
Egress/ingress (radio waves), 2:257
Egypt
    Arab Spring protests, 3:219–220
    cybersecurity attacks, 4:150
EIA (Engineering Industries
  Association), 1:120
Eich, Brendan, 4:198
8-bit code
    black and white display, 1:36
    color display, 1:37
800 telephone numbers, 3:246
Einstein, Albert, 2:277, 3:141
Eisenhower, Dwight, 1:87
Electrically alterable programmable
  read-only memory (EAPROM), 2:138
Electro-acoustic music, 1:184
Electroluminescent panels, 2:83
Electromagnetic relays, 1:65
Electromagnetic spectrum, 2:279–280
Electromechanical mouse, 1:181–182,
  2:183
Electron guns, 1:255, 2:79
Electronic books. *See* E-books
Electronic calendars, 3:150
Electronic campuses, 4:**103–106**
Electronic cash (E-cash), 1:69, 222, 4:107
Electronic checks, 4:109
Electronic Data Interchange (EDI)
  protocol, 1:67
Electronic Delay Storage Automatic
  Calculator (EDSAC), 1:50, 59–60,
  65, 87
Electronic Discrete Variable Automatic
  Computer (EDVAC), 1:58–59, 63,
  66, 87, 2:90, 91

Electronic erasable programmable read-
  only memory (EEPROM), 1:161
Electronic Frontier Foundation, 4:37,
  57, 186–187
Electronic journals. *See* E-journals and
  e-publishing
Electronic libraries. *See* Digital libraries
Electronic mail. *See* E-mail
Electronic markets, 4:**106–110**
    See also E-commerce
Electronic meeting rooms, 3:59–60
Electronic Numerical Integrator and
  Computer. *See* ENIAC (Electronic
  Numerical Integrator and Computer)
Electronic Performance Support
  Systems (EPSSs), 3:52–53
Electronic purses. *See* Stored value cards
Electronic Signatures in Global and
  National Commerce (E-Signature)
  Act, 4:87
Electronic tally systems, 4:105
Electronic Visualization Laboratory
  (University of Illinois), 3:212
Electronic *vs.* digital signatures, 4:87
Electronic wallets, 1:69, 4:109
Elements (Euclid), 2:6
Ellison, Harlan, 4:127
Elographics, 2:254
Elxsi, Ltd., 4:5
Embedded computers, 3:62, 63
Embedded technology (ubiquitous
  computing), 1:136–137, 3:**98–102,**
  160–161
Embedding, objects, 3:138–139
Emirati Louvre museum, 3:*20*
Emitter terminals, of transistors,
  1:126, 245
Emoticons, 1:74, 4:187
Encapsulation, in object-oriented
  programming, 2:158–159
Encoding
    information, 4:167
    keyboards, 1:147–148
    sound data, 2:234–235
Encryption. *See* Cryptography
Encyclopedias, multimedia, 3:130–131
End-effectors, 2:208
End-to-end architecture concept, 4:259
Enemy of the State (film), 4:127
Engelbart, Douglas, 1:104–105,
  180–181, 2:186
Engelberger, Joseph, 1:213, 215

Engineering Industries Association
  (EIA), 1:120
England, Gary, 3:257
Enhanced Data rates for GSM
  Evolution (EDGE), 4:209
ENIAC (Electronic Numerical
  Integrator and Computer)
    creation, 1:87, 2:89–90, 3:71, 72
    ENIAC-on-a-chip, 1:254
    general-purpose nature, 1:6, 50
    history, 1:57–58, 63–64
    programming, 1:65–66
    security measures, 1:219
    vacuum tubes in, 1:254–255
Enigma (cryptographic machine), 1:56
Enigma (rotor machine), 4:57
Enquire software program, 4:111
Enterprise information systems, 4:3
Enterprise networks, defined, 1:195
    See also Wide area networks
    (WANs)
Entrepreneurs, 4:*110,* **110–118**
Entscheidungsproblem, 1:250, 251
Enumeration phase, hacking, 3:122
Environmental sciences, 3:35–36,
  80, 124
EPC (European Patent Convention),
  4:227–228
EPO (European Patent Office), 4:228
EPROM (erasable programmable read-
  only memory), 1:161, 2:138
EPSSs (Electronic Performance Support
  Systems), 3:52–53
Equation engines, 4:38
Erasable programmable read-only
  memory (EPROM), 1:161, 2:138
Eraserhead pointing devices, 2:186
Ergonomic keyboards, 1:149–150
Ergonomics, 1:**76–78,** 149–150,
  3:251–252, 4:155–157
Ericsson smartphones, 2:180
Error correcting codes, 2:55–56, 55*t,*
  56*t,* 150
Erwise (browser), 4:33
ESA (European Space Agency), 1:168
ESNET (Energy Sciences Network),
  4:174, 176
Estridge, Phil, 1:110
Ethernet networks, 1:195, 278, 4:184
Ethics, 1:23, 27, 4:**118–121**
Euclid, 2:5, 6
Euclid's algorithm, 2:5

Gross, Alfred J., 3:**117–119**

Gross Electronics, 3:118, 119

Grötrupp, Helmut, 2:205

Groupware
computer supported cooperative
work and, 3:58–60
for electronic collaboration, 1:198
productivity software, 3:200–201

Groupware servers, 2:227
See also Servers

Grove, Andy, 1:128, 130, 131

Groves, Leslie, 2:277, 4:125

Groves, Robert Martin, 1:41

GSM (Global System for Mobile)
networks, 1:119, 3:41

Guardbands, 4:27

GUIs. *See* Graphical user interfaces
(GUIs)

Gulliver's Travels (Swift), 4:125–126

"Gunfight" (video game), 1:80

Guns, analog-computer controlled, 1:4

Gunter, Edmund, 1:230, 231

Gurus, 4:**144–146**

Gyros (gyroscopes), 3:9

H

H. L. Hunley (submarine), 3:39

Hackers, 4:**147–151**, *148*

Hacking, 3:**121–125**
ATMs, 3:31–32
cookiejacking, 4:47
Palin, Sarah e-mail, 1:75
timeline of cybersecurity attacks,
1:220–225
See also Internet control and
cyberwarfare

Haddock, Jon, 4:9

HAL (fictional computer), 4:127

Half-duplex radio systems, 2:38

Haloid Company, 1:276

Hamilton, Edmond, 4:126

Hamming code, 2:55–56, 56t

Hamming, Richard ("Dick"), 1:34, 2:55

Hand-drawn animation, 1:9–10

Hand-held video game units, 1:82

Handheld scanners, 2:168
See also Scanners

Handoff, in cellular communications,
2:39, 3:41

Handshakes, Telnet use, 4:264

Handwriting recognition, 2:167, 186

Hanging chads, 4:237

Hankey, Rosalie, 4:265

Hanna, William, 1:13

Hard copies, defined, 2:86

Hard-disk loading, 3:224

Hard drives, 2:106, 241–242, 243

Hardware authentication tokens,
2:217–218

Hardware engineering, careers, 3:54, 55

Hardware representation, in
programming languages, 2:1

Hart, Michael, 3:151

Harvard Cyclotron, 3:66

Harvard Mark I/II/III/IV computers,
1:54–55, 60, 62, 101, 102, 108, 268,
3:253–254

Harvard University
edX online course platform, 3:90,
4:106
Facebook launch, 3:216, 263–264,
4:117
Zuckerberg, Mark affiliation, 3:263

Hashtags, 3:217

Hazen, Harold Locke, 1:53

HDLC (High-level Data Link Control),
2:12

Head crashes, 2:243

Head-mounted displays (HMDs)
early developments, 2:272–273
educational use, 1:257, 259
wearable computing, 3:100

Header data, in virtual circuits, 2:13–14

Header Error Control (HEC), 4:20,
21–22

Headers, of packets, 2:151

Heal, Laird, 1:258

Health care. *See* Medical systems

Hearing impairments, assistive
technology, 4:16–17, 18

Heath Robinson (cryptographic
machine), 1:56–57

Hebb, Donald O., 3:180

HEC (Header Error Control), 4:20,
21–22

HECC (High-End Computing
Capability Project), 1:191

Heilig, Mort, 2:272

Hellman, Martin, 4:58

Help systems, application wizards,
1:271–272

Henry, Joseph, 2:141

HEPNET, 4:174

Hertz, Heinrich, 2:279, 4:205

Heuristics
artificial intelligence development,
1:22
defined, 1:22
inference engines, 3:104
knowledge-based systems, 3:143,
144

Hewlett-Packard Company, 2:62,
3:125–126, 4:115, *216*

Hewlett, William, 3:*125*, **125–127,**
4:113–114

Hexadecimal number system, 1:35,
36, 91

HIARCS (higher intelligence auto-
response chess system), 3:46

Hidden Markov Models (HMMs),
3:233–234

Hidden surface removal, 2:100–101

Higgs boson, 3:193

High definition television (HDTV),
2:82, 4:153–154

High-definition video, 3:111, 114,
4:74–75

High-End Computing Capability
Project (HECC), 1:191

High-level Data Link Control (HDLC),
2:12

High and low pressure areas (weather),
3:258

High Order Language Working Group
(HOLWG), 2:199

High order languages, 2:157–158, 199

High Performance Computing and
Communications (HPCC) program,
2:171

High precision/high recall search results,
4:244

High precision/low recall search results,
4:244

High-speed trains, 3:208

Higher intelligence auto-response chess
system (HIARCS), 3:46

Hilbert, David, 1:251

Hiller, Lejaren, 1:185, 3:168

Hillis, W. Daniel, 2:200

Histograms, 3:75

History of computers. *See* Early
computers; Early pioneers;
Generations, computers

Hitachi, 1:109, 155

HMDs. *See* Head-mounted displays
(HMDs)

HMMs (Hidden Markov Models), 3:233–234

Hodges, Larry, 2:274–275

Hoff, Marcian ("Ted"), 1:129

Hoffman, E. T. A., 4:126

Holberton, Frances Snyder, 1:66

Holey Optochip, 1:165–166

Holler, F. James, 4:40

Hollerith codes, 2:114

Hollerith, Herman, 1:39, 96, *99,* **99–101,** 107, 2:114

Hollerith tabulating machines, 1:99–101, *100,* 3:71

Holograms, 3:147

HOLWG (High Order Language Working Group), 2:199

Home entertainment, 4:*152,* **152–155**

Home location registers, 3:246–247

Home servers, 2:227
    See also Servers

Home system software, 3:**128–132,** 137

Home theater systems, 4:*152*

HomePlug Powerline Alliance, 2:147–148

Honeywell, 2:90–91

Hopfield, John J., 3:180

Hopkins Beast, 1:213

Hopper, Grace, 1:60, **101–103,** *102*

Horty, John, 3:149

Host-based databases, 2:238

Host-based intrusion detection systems, 3:213–214

Host blocking, 4:36

Hounsfield, Godfrey Newbold, 3:*65,* **65–67**

HPCC (High Performance Computing and Communications) program, 2:171

HTC smartphones, 1:240, 2:181

HTML editors, 3:129

HTML (Hypertext Markup Language)
    Berners-Lee, Tim contributions, 4:111, 145
    browser use, 1:274, 4:31, 32
    defined, 1:73
    e-banking applications, 4:92
    e-journal format, 4:102
    e-mail use, 1:72
    Java applets and, 4:191–192
    JavaScript embedded programs, 4:194–199
    overview, 2:*133,* 133–134

source code documentation, 2:160
    XHTML development, 2:134–135

HTTP (Hypertext Transport Protocol)
    Berners-Lee, Tim contributions, 4:32–33, 111, 145
    browser use, 4:30–32
    cookies, 4:45–47
    defined, 1:67

HTTPS (Hypertext Transport Protocol with Security extension)
    defined, 1:67
    e-banking use, 4:93
    e-commerce use, 1:67–68

Hughes, Chris, 4:117

Human brain research, 4:63

Human-computer interaction. *See* User interfaces

Human factors, user interfaces, 4:**155–157,** 256

Human Rights Watch, 4:36

Human *vs.* computer strengths, 1:76–77

Hurst, George Samuel, 2:254

Hybrid digital-analog music production, 2:142

Hydra chess computer, 3:45

HyperCard, 1:105

Hyperlinks
    dynamic links, 4:100
    hypertext and, 4:34
    integrated software, 3:139
    search engine results, 4:242, 243
    sponsored links, 4:243

Hypermedia and multimedia, 1:*104,* 2:**103–107,** *104*
    documents, 2:86
    encyclopedias, 3:130–131
    history, 1:104–105, 2:105
    indexing speech recognition applications, 3:235, 236
    office automation systems, 1:199
    realism, 4:157
    user interfaces, 3:250–251

Hypertext, 1:**103–105,** 4:32–33, 34, 111

Hypertext Markup Language. *See* HTML (Hypertext Markup Language)

Hypertext Transport Protocol. *See* HTTP (Hypertext Transport Protocol)

Hypertext Transport Protocol with Security extension (HTTPS). *See* HTTPS (Hypertext Transport Protocol with Security extension)

I

I Have No Mouth, and I Must Scream (Ellison), 4:127

I Love You virus (2000), 1:223

i-Minitel, 1:179

I/O controllers, 2:66

I/O (input/output) devices. *See* Input/output (I/O) devices

I, Robot (Asimov), 1:216, 4:127

I, Robot (film), 4:127

I, Robot (game), 1:15

IBM Corporation, 1:**107–112,** *108*
    701 computer, 1:88, 108, 4:4
    704 computer, 4:4
    7090 computer, 1:33, 88
    Amdahl, Gene Myron involvement, 4:4
    Blue Gene P supercomputer, 3:46
    C-T-R origins, 1:101, 107, 268
    carbon nanotube development, 3:49
    character code developments, 2:52
    CHRISTMAS.EXE worm, 1:263
    collaboration in industry, 1:170, 171, 2:62, 4:113
    computer assisted instruction development, 3:50
    Deep Blue chess competition, 1:83, 111, 3:44–45
    flash drives, 2:243
    FORTRAN association, 2:193, 194
    Harvard Mark I involvement, 1:54–55, 108
    Internet backbone connections, 4:175
    intranet, 4:189
    Lotus acquisition, 3:240
    Magnetic Tape Selectric Typewriter, 3:259, 262
    microcomputer development, 1:168
    optical microchip development, 1:165–166
    patents, 4:229
    PDA introduction, 2:180
    RAMAC 305 computer, 1:108
    RS/4000 computer, 4:173
    SGML development, 2:132
    space program computers, 3:227–228
    supercomputer development, 1:235, 2:175

Laser technology, 3:**145–148,** *146*

Laserwriter printers, 3:82, 85, 243

Lasseter, John, 1:14

LastPass, 4:114

Lathrop, George Parsons, 4:126

Latitude lines, 3:173

Lawrence Livermore National Laboratory, 4:149

LCD. *See* Liquid crystal display (LCD)

LDP (Linux Documentation Project), 3:186

Learning Company, 3:97

Learning disabilities, assistive technology, 4:17

Learning, machine, 3:180–181

Learning Management Systems (LMSs), 3:51–52, 53, 95–97

Least significant numbers, 1:3

Lebanon, cybersecurity attacks, 4:150

Lederberg, Joshua, 3:144

LEDs. *See* Light emitting diodes (LEDs)

Legal cases
    malicious software, 2:118
      software patent protection, 4:228, 229
      Sperry-Rand lawsuit, 2:90–91
    See also Antitrust litigation

Legal systems, 3:**148–151**

Legislation
    computer fraud, 1:42–46
    disabilities, 4:13–14, 18
    driverless cars, 4:44
    hacking, 3:124
    Internet regulation, 3:222, 4:178, 179
    piracy, 3:225, 226
    privacy concerns, 1:210, 211
    telecommunications, 4:186, 246

LEGO-Logo, 2:128

Lego Mindstorms system, 2:128

Leibniz, Gottfried Wilhem von, 1:20, 4:62, 254

Leibowitz, Joe, 4:*225*

Leica (dog), 2:214

Lenses, video cameras, 4:74, 75

LEO (low earth orbit), 2:211, 258–259, 4:139–140

Level 3 Communications, 4:176

Levin, Ira, 4:126

Lex (lexical analyzer), 2:2

Lexical analyzers, 2:2, 63

LEXIS-NEXIS information service, 1:114, 3:149

Libraries, digital, 4:*79,* 79–83

Library applications, 3:**151–153,** 4:233–234

Library of Congress, 4:81

Libya, Arab Spring effects, 3:221

Licensing agreements, software, 3:223–224

Licklider, Joseph, 4:183–184

LIDAR (LIght Detection And Ranging), 4:44

Life cycle methods (Java applets), 4:192

Light emitting diodes (LEDs)
    fiber optics development, 1:202, 2:91
      infrared radiation communications, 2:259
    joysticks, 2:97
    optical mice, 1:182, 2:184

Light pens, 2:113, 186

"Like" feature, 3:264

Line printers, mainframes, 1:158

Linear encoding, 2:234

Linear integrated circuits, 1:126

Linear interpolation, 1:11

Linear Pulse Coding Modulation (LPCM), 2:234

Linear regression, data mining, 4:67

Link, Edwin, 1:226–227

Link layer, OSI Reference Model, 2:151

Linking, objects, 3:138–139

Links, hypertext, 1:105

Links, in networks, 1:193–194, 2:154

Linux Documentation Project (LDP), 3:186

Linux operating system
    development, 2:164–165
    documentation project, 3:186
    mobile applications, 4:209
    open source concept and, 3:185
    scalability, 2:216, 4:145

Lipstick Enigma (artwork), 4:8

Liquid crystal display (LCD)
    CRTs *vs.,* 1:255, 2:84
    overview, 2:81–82
    projection technology, 4:104
    touch screens, 2:254–255

LISP (LISt Processing), 2:**123–125**

List servers, 2:227
    See also Servers

Live Free or Die Hard (film), 4:128

Live Messenger, 4:169

Live streaming technology, 2:237

LivePerson, Inc., 4:189

LiveScript. *See* JavaScript

LMDS (local multipoint distribution service), 2:281

LMSs (Learning Management Systems), 3:51–52, 53, 95–97

Local area networks (LANs)
    bandwidth measurement, 2:17
    bridging devices, 2:*31,* 31–34
    computer supported cooperative work and, 3:57–60
    Internet backbone connections, 4:173
    mainframe connection, 1:158
    network design considerations, 2:147–149
    in office automation systems, 1:197
    origins, 1:239, 4:184
    overview, 1:195
    peer to peer networking and, 1:138–139
    twisted pairs, 1:194, 2:257
    wireless, 2:281

Local/asynchronous distance learning, 3:90

Local direct connection, mainframes, 1:158

Local loops, 4:28

Local multipoint distribution service (LMDS), 2:281

Local/synchronous distance learning, 3:89

Location aware mobile computing, 4:209

LOCI (calculator), 3:254

LOCK (Logical Coprocessing Kernel), 2:217

Locking, for concurrency control, 2:239

Lodge, Oliver Joseph, 4:205

Logarithms
    analog computer calculations, 1:4
    defined, 1:3
    Napier, John development, 1:230, 231
    slide rule calculations, 1:3, 230, 231

Logic
    artificial intelligence development, 1:21
    Boolean, 1:114–115, 116, 2:25–30, 4:245
    digital computing use of, 1:49
    query languages, 1:94
    Turing, Alan work, 1:251

Logic gates, 1:126–127, 2:73

Logic Theorem Machine, 4:220, 253

Logical Coprocessing Kernel (LOCK), 2:217

Logical diagrams. *See* Flowcharts

Logicon, Inc., 2:203

Logo (programming language), 2:*125–126*, **125–130**, *129*

London Grand Prix simulator, 1:*227*

Long, Edward, 1:211

Long term evolution (LTE) technology, 1:240, 2:59, 4:209

Long-term memory, 1:133–134

Longitude determination, 3:173, 174

Looping, in programming, 2:201

Loosely typed languages, 4:197

LORAN (long range navigation), 3:10–11, 175

Lorraine Motel (artwork), 4:9

Los Alamos National Laboratory, 1:235, 2:175

Lossy compression, 2:120, 235, 4:77

Lost update problem, 2:239

Lotus 1-2-3, 3:137, 239, 4:114

Lotus Corporation, 4:114

Lotus Freelance Graphics, 3:200

Lotus Notes, 3:201

Lotus Smartsuite 97, 3:138

Lovebug virus (2000), 1:223

Lovelace, Ada King (countess). *See* King, Ada Byron

LoveLetter worm, 2:118

Low earth orbit (LEO), 2:211, 258–259, 4:139–140

Low precision/high recall search results, 4:243

LPCM (Linear Pulse Coding Modulation), 2:234

LSI. *See* Large-scale integrated (LSI) circuits

LTE (Long Term Evolution) technology, 1:240, 2:59, 4:209

Lucas, George, 1:18, 4:74

Lucent Technologies, 1:33, 34

Lynx (browser), 4:33

M

MacBook laptop series, 1:19, 146, 2:*79*

Machine language, 1:91, 2:9, 64

Machine Readable Cataloging (MARC), 3:152

The Machine Stops (Forster), 4:126

Macintosh operating systems, 1:18, 19, 171, 2:265–266

Macintosh personal computers
  desktop publishing development, 3:82, 85
  innovations, 1:144–145
  introduction, 1:18, 144
  Microsoft Excel, 3:239–240
  virus attacks, 1:263
  as WIMP system, 1:133, 272

Macro viruses, 1:262–263
  See also Viruses

Macromedia, 1:14–15

MAD (Michigan Algorithm Decoder), 3:188

MAE (Metropolitan Area Exchange), 4:175

Magic mouse, 1:183

Magnavox, 1:80

Magnetic cores, 1:60, 2:136

Magnetic disks
  information retrieval systems, 1:113
  optical storage *vs.*, 1:204
  second generation computer use, 1:88
  as storage device, 1:160, 2:241–243
  virtual memory, 1:161

Magnetic drums, 2:241

Magnetic ink character recognition (MICR), 2:114, 167–168

Magnetic resonance imaging (MRI), 3:135

Magnetic stripe cards, 2:113, 3:**155–157**, *156, 157*

Magnetic tape
  information retrieval systems, 1:113
  as input device, 2:113
  optical storage *vs.*, 1:204
  second generation computer use, 1:88
  as storage device, 1:160, 2:241
  UNIVAC use, 1:88
  videotape technology, 3:110–111

Magnetic Tape Selectric Typewriter, 3:259, 262

Magnetospirilllum magneticum, 4:212

Magnification programs, 4:15

Mail trap doors, 1:221

Main memory. *See* Memory; Random access memory (RAM)

Mainframes, 1:**155–159**, *156*
  Amdahl corporation, 4:4
  Andor Systems, 4:5
  communication devices, 2:56
  defined, 1:18, 79
  early networks, 1:239
  first video games, 1:79
  IBM, 1:88, 108–109, 155–156, 2:45, 52, 4:4, 5, 6
  journalism use, 4:200
  minicomputers *vs.*, 1:173, 174

Major search engines, 4:244–245

Malaria, computer modeling, 3:36

Malaysia, cybercafes, 4:61

Malware. *See* Invasive programs; Trojan horses; Viruses; Worms

Management information systems (MISs), 2:109, 110, 3:79–81

Manchester Mark I, 1:59, 64–65

Mandelbrot, Benoit B., 3:159

Mandelbrot sets, 3:159

Manhattan Project
  Feynman, Richard involvement, 4:123–124, 125
  Kemeny, John G. involvement, 3:141
  Organick, Elliot involvement, 3:187
  von Neumann, John involvement, 2:276, 277

Manipulators (robot arms), 1:215, 2:208, 3:63

MANs (metropolitan area networks), 1:195, 2:147–149

Manufacturing
  automation, 3:*194*, 194–197
  chips, 3:*47*, 47–50
  computer-aided, 3:38–39, 60–65, 4:255
  computer-integrated, 3:64
  decision support systems, 3:80
  expert systems, 3:103
  nanoscale technology, 4:217
  process control, 3:*194*, 194–197
  robotics use, 1:213, 214, 215, 2:207–208

Map overlay operations, 3:116

Map reclassification operations, 3:116

Maps
  computer generated, 3:*174*
  data visualization, 3:73
  weather, 3:257
  See also Geographic information systems (GISs)

SATAN (Security Administrator Tool for Analyzing Networks), 3:214

Satellite technology, 2:**211–215**
>   data links, 2:258–259
>   European Space Agency programs, 3:229
>   flight management systems, 3:11, 15
>   global surveillance, 4:139–142
>   railroad use, 3:207
>   *See also* Global Positioning Systems (GPSs)

Satellite-to-satellite communications, 2:212

Satisficing concept, 4:253

Saudi Arabia, cybersecurity attacks, 4:150

Saverin, Eduardo, 4:117

Sayre, David, 2:193

Scaling, 2:**215–217**

Scanners
>   digital photography and, 4:231–232
>   as input device, 2:114
>   optical character recognition, 2:168

Scanning codes, keyboards, 1:148

Scanning phase, hacking, 3:122

Scheduling, decision support systems, 3:80

Schlumberger Excellence in Educational Development (SEED), 4:40

Scholarly Publishing and Academic Resources Coalition (SPARC), 4:101, 102

Schreyer, Helmut, 2:282

Scientific Computing and Imaging Institute (University of Utah), 3:211

Scientific visualization, 3:**209–212**, *210*

SCORM (Sharable Content Object Reference Model), 3:52, 98

Screen readers, 4:15

Script Kiddies (hackers), 4:148

SCRIPT tags, 4:194–195

Script viruses, 1:263
>   *See also* Viruses

Scripting
>   JavaScript, 4:194–199
>   Visual Basic Scripting Edition, 4:269

Scriptoria (copying rooms), 3:86

Scroll bars, in windows interfaces, 1:271

SCSI (small computer systems interface) standard, 2:66

Sculley, John, 1:144

Scullin, Frederick J., Jr., 1:45

SDNs (software-defined networks), 2:270

SEACOM undersea cable, 4:162

Seals, privacy, 4:224

Search concept, in problem-solving, 1:21–22

Search engine optimization (SEO), 4:243

Search engines, 4:*242*, **242–245**
>   Boolean algebra in, 2:29–30
>   digital libraries, 4:80–81
>   information overload concerns, 4:163–164
>   information retrieval, 1:113–116
>   overview, 1:275
>   Web-based, 1:116
>   *See also specific sites*

Search expressions, 4:243

Search for ExtraTerrestial Intelligence (SETI@home) project, 3:27

Search spaces, 1:21–22

Search strategies, 1:113

Search.com, 4:245

Seaton, Charles W., 1:39

Second generation computers, 1:88

Second generation programming languages, 1:91–92

Secondary Action (animation), 1:14

Secondary storage. *See* Storage devices

Sectors, of floppy disks, 2:242

Secure Computing Corporation, 2:217

Secure Electronic Transactions (SET) protocol, 1:68

Secure Sockets Layer (SSL) protocol, 1:67–68, 4:54, 93, 225

Security, 1:**219–226**, *220*
>   applications, 3:213–215
>   Certificate Authority, 1:67–68, 2:270, 4:25, 99
>   cookies, 4:45–47
>   credit online, 4:52–55
>   data mining concerns, 4:69
>   database management systems, 3:77–78
>   digital signatures, 1:221, 4:58, 86–89, *87, 88*
>   e-banking, 4:92–93
>   e-commerce, 1:67–68, 4:98–99
>   e-mail, 1:75
>   hardware, 2:217–219

intranets, 4:188–189
>   legislation, 1:42–46
>   software, 2:219–222, *220*
>   Telnet concerns, 4:263
>   *See also* Hackers; Hacking; Internet control and cyberwarfare

Security Administrator Tool for Analyzing Networks (SATAN), 3:214

Security applications, 3:**213–215**

Security hardware, 2:**217–219**

Security software, 2:**219–222**, *220*

SEED (Schlumberger Excellence in Educational Development), 4:40

Sega video games, 1:82, 4:154

Segmentation and Reassembly (SAR) sublayer, 4:22

Segmentation, image, 4:43

Selectric typewriter, 3:259, 262

Selegue, John P., 4:40

Self-replicating systems, 2:276–277

Selfridge, Oliver, 4:220

Semi-Automated Business Research Environment (Sabre) System, 3:16–17, 18

Semiconductor lasers, 3:147

Semiconductors, 1:125–126, 128, 164–165, 242–243

Semtech, 1:165

Sendmail, 3:186

Senses, virtual reality and, 2:273

SEO (search engine optimization), 4:243

September 11, 2001 terrorist attacks, 3:18, 4:157, 266

Sequencing, in programming, 2:201

Sequoia supercomputer, 1:235, 2:175

Serial and parallel transmission, 2:**222–225**

Serial communications, 2:150–153

Series circuits, 2:29, *30*

Server file systems, 2:228

Servers, 2:**225–228**, *226*
>   mainframes, 1:155–156, 158
>   minicomputers, 1:173–174
>   proxy, 2:227, 4:101–102
>   Web servers, 2:225, 227, 4:30–31, 188
>   *See also* Client/server technology

Service providers, 4:**246–249**
>   *See also* Internet service providers (ISPs)

Snail mail, 1:73

Sniffing (networks), 1:223

Snort network security program, 3:214

Snow White and the Seven Dwarfs (animated film), 1:12

SNRs (signal-to-noise ratios), 2:93

Snyder, Richard, 1:87

SOAP (Simple Object Access Protocol), 4:170

SOAR project, 4:220, 221

SoC (system-on-a-chip), 1:127

Social impact, 4:**254–257**

Social informatics, 4:254, 257

Social media, 3:**216–223**
 journalism use, 4:202
 political applications, 4:234
 social impact, 4:256–257
 See also specific sites

The Social Network (film), 3:263–264, 4:75

Soft copies, defined, 2:86

Softlifting, 3:224

Software
 Bell Labs research, 1:33
 computer science research, 1:46–48
 copyright concerns, 4:50
 data warehousing systems, 4:72
 early developments, 1:33
 ergonomic considerations, 1:78
 ethics concerns, 4:119
 home system, 3:128–132
 human factors, 4:156–157
 information technology standards, 1:120
 integrated, 3:136–139
 patent protections, 4:228, 229
 See also specific types

Software-defined networks (SDNs), 2:270

Software engineering, careers, 3:57

Software and Information Industry Association (SIIA), 3:225

Software piracy, 3:**223–226,** *224*

Sojourner rover, 2:209

Solar Sunrise incident (1998), 4:181

Solar time, 3:174

Solid ink printers, 2:190

Solid Logic Technology (SLT), 1:109

Solid-state drives (SSDs), 2:*240*

Solitons, 2:95

SONET (Synchronous Optical NETwork), 4:173

Sony
 Betamax VCR, 2:262
 digital cameras, 4:230
 e-reader, 4:*95*
 video cameras, 4:73–74
 video game development, 1:82, 4:154

SOPA (Stop Online Piracy Act), 3:222, 4:179

Soul Catcher project, 4:64

Sound Blaster sound cards, 2:236

Sound cards, 1:15, 2:235–236

Sound devices, 2:*232,* **232–237,** *233*

Sound editors, 3:170–171

Sound files, 2:121, 3:113–114

Sound-oriented music models, 3:169

Sound servers, 2:227
 See also Servers

Soundings (weather measurements), 3:256

Source code, open source concept and, 3:183

Source documents, defined, 2:86

South Park (television show), 1:10

Soviet Union. *See* Russia

Soyuz space capsules, 3:229

Space debris, 2:214

Space Exploration Technologies (SpaceX), 3:229, 230

"Space Invaders" (video game), 1:81

Space Launch System (SLS) rockets, 3:231

Space travel and exploration, 3:**226–233**
 Apollo missions, 1:189–190, 191, 3:227–228
 global surveillance, 4:139–142
 space shuttle program, 1:*188,* 190, 191, 3:228–229
 virtual reality training, 2:*272*

SpaceScience World, 1:257–258

"SpaceWar" (video game), 1:15, 79

Spamming, 1:75, 4:266

SPAN (NASA Space Scientists network), 4:175

SPARC (Scholarly Publishing and Academic Resources Coalition), 4:101, 102

Spatial query processing, 3:116, 117

Speakers, 2:233–234

Speaking impairments, assistive technology, 4:16

Special Interest Group on Design Automation Award, 4:5–6

Special needs. *See* Disabilities

Special purpose registers, 2:8
 See also Registers

Specialty search engines, 4:244

Speech-generation devices, 3:251

Speech recognition, 3:**233–236,** *234*
 assistive computer technology, 4:16
 browsers and, 4:34
 for input, 2:114
 user interfaces, 3:250–251
 voice commands, 3:252

Speedup (parallel processing), 2:174–175

Spense, Bill, 4:218

Sperry-Rand, 2:89, 90–91

Spiders, 4:242–243, 244, 245

Spielberg, Steven, 1:23

Spintronics, 1:162, 2:139

Spiral systems design, 2:250

Spirit (rover), 3:232–233

SPMD (Single Program, Multiple Data), 2:173

Sponsored links, 4:243

Spoofing, 1:223

Sports
 data mining applications, 4:69
 GPS applications, 4:138
 video games, 1:15

Spotify, 2:237

Spreadsheets, 3:**236–240,** *237, 238, 239*
 integrated software, 3:137
 invention, 1:168
 productivity software, 3:198–199, 201
 what-if analysis capabilities, 3:201, 238

Springer e-journals, 4:102

Sprint network, 4:175, 176

SPSS software, 3:94

Sputnik missions, 2:211, 214

SQL, 1:94, 2:**238–240,** *239,* 3:76–77

Squash and Stretch (animation), 1:14

SRAM (static random access memory), 2:137

SRI (Stanford Research Institute), 1:213–214

SSDs (solid-state drives), 2:*240*

SSL (Secure Sockets Layer) protocol, 1:67–68, 4:54, 93, 225

Thermal wax transfer, 2:190–191

Thiel, Peter, 4:*110*

Thin client/server technology (TCST), 2:49

Thin film transistor active matrix LCDs, 2:83

"THINK" slogan, 1:111, 267, *267*

Third generation computers, 1:88

Third generation programming languages, 1:92–93

Third-party endorsements, 4:53–54

Third-person 3-D video games, 1:15

Thompson, John W., 4:116

Thompson, Ken, 1:25, 33–34, 2:197–198

Three-body problem, 3:27

Three-dimensional animation, 1:9, 10

3D HDTV, 4:153–154

3D-ICs (three-dimensional integrated circuits), 1:128

Three-dimensional image projection, 4:*7*

Three-dimensional integrated circuits (3D-ICs), 1:128

3D interfaces, 4:156

3D mouse, 1:182, 2:184

3D printers, 3:62

Three Laws of Robotics (Asimov), 3:25, 4:127

Three-tier client server systems, 2:49

3-CCD technology, 4:73, 74

3G cellular technology, 1:240, 4:209

Throughputs, for system analysis models, 2:247–248

ThumbDrive flash drives, 2:243

Thumbnail images, 1:271

Tier 1 service providers, 4:247

TIGER (Topologically Integrated Geographic Encoding and Referencing) system, 1:41

Tik-Tok (fictional robot), 4:126

Tik-Tok of Oz (Baum), 4:126

Tiling windows interface, 1:270

Time-division multiplexing, 2:93, 3:41–42

Time-sharing jobs, 1:156

Time zones, 1:118, 3:174

Timing (animation), 1:14

Titanic (film), 4:8

Titchmarsh, E. C., 1:249

Title bars, 1:270

Tito, Dennis, 3:232

Tokens, for authentication, 2:217–218, 4:25, 107

Toll-free telephone numbers, 3:246

Top Grossing Film of All Time, 1 € 1 (artwork), 4:8

Top hats (joysticks), 2:96

Top-tier backbones, 4:176

Topalov, Veselin Aleksandrov, 3:46

Torricelli, Evangelista, 1:208

Torvalds, Linus, 2:164–165, 3:185, 4:145

Total internal reflection, 1:202

Touch mouse, 1:183

Touch screens, 2:**253–256,** *254*

    multi-touch interfaces, 1:19, 147, 183, 2:181, 3:252

    PDAs, 2:179, 181

    as pointing device, 2:185

Touchpads, 2:184–185

Toy Story (film series), 1:10, 18

Trackballs, 1:181, 182, 2:186

Trade secrets, 4:229

Trailers, of packets, 2:151

Training data, in pattern recognition, 2:177–178

Trains. *See* Railroad applications

Transac S-2000, 1:88

Transaction processing systems, 1:156, 3:16–17

Transactional speech recognition applications, 3:235, 236

Transactions, in databases, 2:239

Transatlantic transmission, 4:206

Transceivers, optical, 1:165–166

Transducers, ultrasound, 3:133

Transistors, 1:**241–247,** *242*

    defined, 1:32

    first uses, 2:22

    in integrated circuits, 1:125, 126

    invention, 1:32, 34, 66, 88, 125, 126, 2:20

    in second generation computers, 1:88

Transit exchange agreements, 4:175–176

Transit networks, 4:174

Transmedia Glide Write, 3:*260*

Transmission Control Protocol/Internet Protocol. *See* TCP/IP (Transmission Control Protocol/Internet Protocol)

Transmission Control Protocol (TCP) dominance, 2:47

FTP and, 4:133–134

history, 4:184–185

overview, 1:139

Telnet and, 4:134

Transmission convergence sublayer (ATM transmission), 4:21–22

Transmission lines, 2:256

Transmission media, 2:**256–259**

Transmissive liquid crystal displays, 2:83

Transponders, railroad use, 3:206

Transport layer

    firewall implementation, 4:130–131

    OSI Reference Model, 2:151–152, 153

    TCP protocol, 4:259–262

Transportation Security Administration (TSA), 3:18

Transposition (cryptography), 4:57

Transreflective liquid crystal displays, 2:83

Traveling salesperson problem, 3:180

Travelocity.com, 3:18, 4:99

Travelport, 3:17

Treatment (animation), 1:9

TREC (Text Retrieval Evaluation Conference), 1:116

Tree topology networks, 1:193, 2:155, 156

Trek Technology, 2:243

TRI-X film, 4:84–85

Trigonometric functions, 1:3, 4

Trilogy Systems Corporation, 4:4–5

Triodes, 1:164, 253

TRIPS (Agreement on Trade Related Aspects of Intellectual Property Rights), 4:228–229

Tripwire, 3:213

Trojan horses, 1:44, 223, 261, 262, 2:117–118

Tron (film), 4:128

Trusted Computer Systems Evaluation Criteria (TCSEC), 2:219

Truth tables, 2:27–29, 27*t*–29*t*

TSA (Transportation Security Administration), 3:18

TTYs (text telephones), 4:17, 18

Tunisia, Arab Spring beginnings, 3:219, 220

Tunneling, VPNs, 2:270

TurboTax, 3:*2*

Voice-driven applications, 4:169

Voice mail, 1:74, 198

Voice-over-Internet-protocol (VoIP), 3:247, 4:248

Voice recognition. *See* Speech recognition

Volatility of RAM, 1:160

Volume software licenses, 3:223–224

von Neumann, John, 2:**275–277,** *276*
  artificial life model, 4:11
  EDVAC development, 1:58–59, 66, 2:90, 91
  Kemeny, John G. collaboration, 3:141
  stored-program concept development, 1:87
  Turing, Alan collaboration, 1:248

von Neumann machines, 1:58–59, 87

Voting, data processing, 4:236, 237

Voting districts, data processing, 4:235

Voyager (space probe), 3:231, 232

VPCs (virtual path connections), 4:21

VPI (Virtual Path Identifier), 4:20–21, 22, 23

VPNs (virtual private networks), 2:268–271

VR. *See* Virtual reality (VR)

VRML (Virtual Reality Modeling Language), 1:10, 11

Vulnerabilities, security software and, 2:220, 3:124

W

W3C. *See* World Wide Web Consortium (W3C)

WAAS (Wide Area Augmentation System), 4:137–138

Wafer-scale integration (WSI), 1:128

Wafers, 3:48

Wal-Mart, 4:69

Walkie-talkies, 3:117, 118

WALL-E (film), 4:128

Wallace and Gromit (animated characters), 1:10

Walt Disney Studios, 1:12–13, 14, 3:126

Walters, Grey, 1:213

Wang, An, 3:**253–255,** 262

Wang, Charles, 4:115

Wang Computer System, 3:262

Wang Laboratories, 3:253, 254

Wang Word Processing System, 3:254, 259, 262

Wannabes (hackers), 4:148

WANs. *See* Wide area networks (WANs)

"Warcraft" (simulation game), 1:83

Warez Dudez (hackers), 4:149

WarGames (film), 4:128

Warnock, John, 3:243–244

Waterfall paradigm, 2:249, 251

Watson (IBM computer), 1:23

Watson, James, 4:39

Watson, Thomas A., 1:240, 2:23

Watson, Thomas J., Jr., 1:108, 109–110, 268

Watson, Thomas J., Sr., 1:107–108, *267,* **267–269**

Wave interruption touch screens, 2:255

Wave table synthesis, 2:235

Wavelength division multiplexing (WDM), 1:202, 2:93

Wearable computing, 2:101, 3:100, 101

Weather forecasting, 3:210, *255,* **255–259**

Weather monitoring, 2:212, 3:119

Web. *See* World Wide Web

Web animation, 1:14–15

Web browsers. *See* Browsers

Web servers, 2:225, 227, 4:30–31, 188

Webb, Jim, 4:234

Webphone, 1:179

Web sites
  as art, 4:8
  intranets, 1:67, 195, 4:188–190
  journalism, 4:202
  political applications, 4:233, 234, 235

WebStar server program, 2:225

Wei, Pei, 4:33

Weighted information retrieval, 1:115, 116

Weiser, Mark, 3:101

Wells, H.G., 3:24, 25

Werbos, Paul J., 3:180

Wergo Records, 1:185

West Publishing Company, 3:149

Western Electric Company (WECo), 1:31–32, 33

Western Music Notation, 3:168

Westlaw, 3:149

Westworld (film), 4:128

What-if analysis, 3:201, 238

Wheatstone, Charles, 1:152, 2:113, 114

While Rome Burns (Woollcott), 4:265

Whirlpool project, 3:20

Whirlwind computer, 1:60

White Hat hackers, 4:148

Whiteboards, interactive, 4:104, 105

Wi-Fi (Wireless Fidelity), 4:209

Wide Area Augmentation System (WAAS), 4:137–138

Wide area networks (WANs)
  Internet backbone connections, 4:172–173
  mainframe connection, 1:158
  network design considerations, 2:147–149
  origins, 1:239
  overview, 1:195
  VPNs *vs.,* 2:268

Wiener, Norbert, 4:62–63

Wii, 1:*80,* 2:*96,* 98

Wilkes, Maurice V., 1:50, 59, 64, 65, 87, 249

Williams, Evan, 3:217

Williams, John, 4:69

Williams, R. Stanley, 4:*210*

Williams, Sir Frederic, 1:59, 64–65

Wily Hacker attack (1986), 1:223

WIMP (windows, icon, menu, and pointer) systems, 1:133, 3:241
  See also Graphical user interfaces (GUIs)

Window interfaces, 1:*269,* **269–273,** 2:86

Window manager functionality, 1:134

Windows Media Player, 2:237

Windows operating system
  accessibility utilities, 4:18
  creation, 1:84
  encryption abilities, 4:58
  GUIs, 2:163–164
  Internet Explorer bundle, 1:85, 274, 4:172
  introduction, 1:171
  Microsoft Excel performance, 3:240
  multitasking capabilities, 1:171
  Visual Basic programming, 4:268
  windows interfaces, 1:272

Windows Phone mobile operating system, 4:208

Windows technology, 1:95

Winklevoss, Cameron, 3:263

Winklevoss, Tyler, 3:263

WIPO (World Intellectual Property Organization) Copyright Treaty, 3:225

Wire frames, 2:100

Wired control switching offices, 3:245

Wireless communications

AirPort technology, 1:144

Apple TV, 1:145

Gross, Alfred J. contributions, 3:117–119

mobile computing devices, 4:207–210

mobile virtual private networks, 2:271

portable devices, 1:240

See also Broadcast telecommunications; Cell phones; Smartphones

Wireless lavaliere microphones, 4:103

Wireless local area networks (WLANs), 2:281, 4:209

Wireless local loops (WLLs), 2:281

Wireless modems, 2:258

Wireless mouse, 1:183

Wireless technology, 2:**279–281,** *280*

Wireless Telegraph and Signal Company Limited, 4:206

Wireless telegraph systems, 2:257, 279, 4:205–206

Wireless transmission, 2:258–259

Wireshark network security program, 3:214

Wirth, Niklaus, 2:1, 195, 197

Wisconsin Integrally Synchronized Computer (WISC), 4:4

Wizards, application, 1:271–272

Wizards, gurus *vs.,* 4:146

WLANs (wireless local area networks), 2:281, 4:209

WLLs (wireless local loops), 2:281

Wolfram Mathematica, 3:94

Women

Association for Computing Machinery chapters, 1:26

early programming, 1:65–66

See also specific women

Wong, Ray, 2:218

Woodland, Joseph, 2:203

Woollcott, Alexander, 4:265

Word processors, 3:**259–262,** *260*

desktop publishing *vs.,* 3:82, 262

integrated software, 3:136–139

office automation systems, 1:197

productivity software, 3:197–198

Wang systems, 3:254, 259, 262

WordPerfect software, 3:128, 262

WordStar software, 3:139

Work prints (animation), 1:9

Workplace impact, 4:255

Worksheets, in spreadsheets, 3:236

World Intellectual Property Organization (WIPO) Copyright Treaty, 3:225

World Trade Center, 4:157

World Trade Organization (WTO), 4:51, 228–229

World War II (1939-1945)

computer development, 1:53–58, 61–62

cryptography use, 4:57, 59

radio communications development, 3:118

World Wide Web, 1:**273–276**

Berners-Lee, Tim contributions, 2:226, 4:32–33, 111, 145, 186

hypermedia model, 2:105

Internet flexibility and, 1:239

invisible Web, 4:245

servers, 2:225, 227, 4:30–31, 188

standards, 1:121, 2:47

See also Browsers; Internet; Search engines; *specific sites*

World Wide Web Consortium (W3C)

Berners-Lee, Tim contributions, 4:111, 169–170

browser development, 4:34, 169–170

information technology standards, 1:120

XML coordination, 2:134

Worldspan LP, 3:17

WORM (write once/read many), 2:244

Worms

first cases, 1:222

Morris worm, 1:45

overview, 1:44, 263–264, 2:117

payloads, 1:262

via e-mail attachment, 1:75

viruses *vs.,* 1:261, 263

Wozniak, Stephen

Apple founding, 1:17, 18, 143

Atari involvement, 1:82

biographical overview, 1:19

departure from Apple, 1:18

Jobs, Steve collaboration, 1:142, 4:113

Wright, S. Fowler, 4:126–127

Write once/read many (WORM), 2:244

Writing, history, 3:82–83

WSI (wafer-scale integration), 1:128

WTO (World Trade Organization), 4:51, 228–229

WYSIWYG

desktop publishing development, 3:82, 84–85, 241–242

word processors, 3:198, 261

X

X rays, 3:134

X-Windows system, 1:272

X3D (modeling language), 1:10–11

Xbox console series, 1:82, 4:154

Xenakis, Iannis, 1:185

Xerography, 1:276, 278, 2:189

Xerox 800 word processor, 3:262

Xerox 8010 Star computer, 1:137

Xerox 9700 printer, 3:242–243

Xerox Corporation, 1:133, 137, **276–279,** *277*

Xerox Palo Alto Research Center (PARC)

Alto computer, 1:251, 272, 278, 4:184

CoLab project, 3:59–60

computer research, 1:278

desktop publishing development, 3:82, 244

inadvertent worm creation, 1:263, 2:117

Interpress page description language, 3:243–244

mouse development, 2:186

windows interfaces, 1:272

Xerox Star computer, 1:133, 278

XHTML (eXtensible hypertext markup language), 2:134–135

Xmarks, 4:114

XML (eXtensible markup language), 2:*132*

browser development, 4:34

desktop publishing use, 3:86, 244

music applications, 3:169

overview, 2:134–135

Web browsing and, 4:170